Alexand
The Lond
& Politi

September 2012

Behavioural Economics and Finance

Standard models in economics and finance usually assume that people are rational, self-interested maximizers, effectively coordinated via the invisible hand of the price mechanism. Whilst these approaches produce tractable, simple models, they cannot fully capture the uncertainties and instabilities that affect everyday choices in today's complex world. Insights from the other social and behavioural sciences can help to fill the gap, and behavioural economics is the subject that brings economics and finance together with psychology, neuroscience and sociology. *Behavioural Economics and Finance* introduces the reader to some of the key concepts and insights from this rich, interdisciplinary approach to real-world decision-making.

The book covers a range of themes, including learning, social influence, inequity aversion and other models of social preference, bounded rationality, heuristics and biases, prospect theory, regret theory, moods and emotions, happiness, time inconsistency, present bias and bad habits. Each theme is explored theoretically and illustrated with findings from the latest experimental/neuroeconomic research. Concepts are explained intuitively, complemented by mathematical boxes where relevant, and illustrated with real-world case studies. To inform those readers without much knowledge of the behavioural sciences, the book begins with introductory chapters on psychology and neuroscience. Chapters showing how behavioural microeconomic principles can be applied to the analysis of aggregate phenomena, including financial instability and macroeconomic outcomes such as wellbeing, are also included.

Behavioural Economics and Finance offers a unique interdisciplinary perspective on the socio-psychological factors underlying human decision-making. Real-world case studies illuminate the key issues, and new concepts are introduced step by step to show how behavioural approaches can evolve from standard models. By bringing together a wide range of ideas and evidence, the book shows why and how a more interdisciplinary approach can provide economists with a much fuller understanding of human behaviour in the real world.

Michelle Baddeley is Fellow and Director of Studies (Economics) at Gonville & Caius College, Cambridge University, UK.

Routledge Advanced Texts in Economics and Finance

Behavioural Economics and Finance

Michelle Baddeley

Routledge
Taylor & Francis Group

LONDON AND NEW YORK

First published 2013
by Routledge
2 Park Square, Milton Park, Abingdon, Oxon OX14 4RN

Simultaneously published in the USA and Canada
by Routledge
711 Third Avenue, New York, NY 10017

Routledge is an imprint of the Taylor & Francis Group, an informa business

British Library Cataloguing in Publication Data
A catalogue record for this book is available from the British Library

Library of Congress Cataloging in Publication Data
Baddeley, Michelle, 1965-
 Behavioural economics and finance/Michelle Baddeley.
  p. cm.
 1. Economics – Psychological aspects.   2. Finance – Psychological
aspects.   I. Title.
 HB74.P8B33 2012
 330.01'9 – dc23

                                               2012004329

ISBN: 978-0-415-61477-1 (hbk)
ISBN: 978-0-415-61478-8 (pbk)
ISBN: 978-0-203-10451-4 (ebk)

Typeset in Times New Roman
by Keystroke, Station Road, Codsall, Wolverhampton

Printed and bound in Great Britain by
TJ International Ltd, Padstow, Cornwall

To Chris

Table of contents

List of illustrations

Figures

Table

Boxes

Acknowledgements

Writing books is not always an easy task, particularly for an economist, and I embarked on the process of writing this book somewhat reluctantly. But I have been pleased to discover that exploring behavioural economics and its many dimensions is an interesting and rewarding task, so I would like gratefully to acknowledge the support of my commissioning team at Routledge, including Thomas Sutton, Robert Langham and Simon Holt. They encouraged me to put together a proposal in the first place and guided my writing through its initial stages. Thank you also to my production editor, Lindsey Hall, and copy editor, Anne Sweetmore, for their patient help and enthusiasm. I would also like to thank the six anonymous reviewers for their many constructive comments and suggestions. All errors, omissions and imprecisions remain my own.

My father – Kiram Baddeley – has always enthusiastically encouraged my research and on this occasion I am especially grateful: he drew the template for the neuronal network diagram in chapter 3, and without his advice my analyses of neuroscience would be less than third-rate. My thanks also go to my PhD supervisor – Geoff Harcourt – who, many years ago when I was still dabbling in applied macroeconomics, suggested that specializing in behavioural economics might suit me well. I'm sorry that I took so very long to listen to his advice. I would also like to thank my collaborators Christopher Harris and Wolfram Schultz: from them I have learnt about many interesting dimensions of behavioural economics and neuroeconomics which I might not otherwise have discovered. In addition, I thank Christopher Burke and Philippe Tobler, who have generously agreed for me to use some of our research material in the illustrations. Thanks also to my fellow Fellows at Gonville and Caius College – early, stimulating discussions with them incubated my knowledge and interests in neuroscience and experimental psychology. Finally, I am grateful to my family and friends for their patient and unstinting support and encouragement whilst writing this book.

Part 1
Background

1   Introduction

What is behavioural economics?

Behavioural economics is a fascinating and rapidly growing field, of increasing interest to policy-makers and business, as well as to academic economists. It brings together a range of techniques and concepts and, because it is such a broad field, it can be difficult to define it precisely. Some could argue that all economics is behavioural economics because economics is about behaviour, albeit in a restricted context. Others would define behavioural economics very narrowly as the study of observed behaviour under controlled conditions, without inferring too much about the underlying, unobservable psychological processes that generate behaviour.

Whilst this book takes a broad view of the psychological insights that will be interesting, nonetheless it is important to recognize that behavioural economics, economic psychology and psychological economics are not necessarily the same thing; there are many parallels between them, but subtle differences too. Strictly speaking, behavioural economics takes insights specifically from one branch of psychology – behavioural psychology (discussed in more detail in chapter 2), which involves the experimental study of observed choices and decisions. Similarly, many behavioural economists are interested only in observable and measurable impacts on behaviour and preferences, and so would be less interested in the underlying psychological processes; they would argue that these underlying variables are not easily measurable and so cannot form the basis of an objective science.

For the purposes of this book, behavioural economics will be defined broadly as the subject that attempts to enlarge our understanding of behaviour by blending economic approaches with insights from psychology – in particular from specific fields within psychology, including behavioural psychology, cognitive science, personality theory, developmental psychology, social psychology and evolutionary psychology. The related field of neuroeconomics brings together behavioural economics and neuroscience.

Why behavioural finance?

This book is about theories that can be applied to a wide range of economic and financial decision-making. Whilst behavioural economics and behavioural finance are often treated as separate, albeit related, disciplines, the distinction between them is artificial. Many of the fundamental insights of behavioural economics, such as prospect theory, are applied widely in behavioural finance. Similarly, financial factors have profound impacts on economic decision-making; for example, in planning for the future, households will need access to financial institutions to enable borrowing or saving: financial instability has consequences for the broader macroeconomy. Also, a lot of interesting new research covered in this book explores financial decisions as well as economic decisions. Many of the neuroeconomic studies included in this book are neurofinance studies.

The origins of this separation of behavioural economics and behavioural finance reflects developments in mainstream neoclassical economics and Jean-Baptiste Say's conception of money as a 'veil' over real activity. These approaches include assumptions such as the neutrality of money – that monetary and financial factors do not have long-term impacts on the real side; and the Modigliani–Miller theorem of financing neutrality – given perfect capital markets, firms' valuations are unaffected by financial structure because the financing costs associated with different financial instruments (loans, equity, bonds) are equalized. Given these assumptions, some economists concluded that finance is not a crucial variable in understanding investment and capital accumulation.

More recently, especially with the arrival of a series of serious financial crises, there is increasing recognition that real decisions are intertwined with financial decisions. One lesson that the fallout from financial crises has taught us is that it is misleading to treat economics and finance as separate subjects – economic decisions affect financial decisions and *vice versa* – and it is important to understand how the two interact. Therefore, as far as is feasible in one book, key developments in behavioural finance will be analysed alongside behavioural economics concepts. For readers who are interested specifically in behavioural finance, some more dedicated readings are listed in 'Further reading'.

A quick history of behavioural economics

Historically, economics had many links with psychology, but as mathematical tools were used to simplify and structure economic theory, the subject moved away from psychological analysis. Also, with the increasing focus amongst economists on quantitative styles of decision-making, psychology's focus on subjective motivations did not rest easily with a focus on objective, analytical, mathematical methods of capturing economic decision-making. Economics, until the major resurgence of behavioural and psychological economics in the 1980s and 1990s, was removed from other psychological approaches. In understanding why, it is useful to explore the historical development of behavioural economics and some of the behavioural approaches that preceded economics as we see it today.

David Hume (1711–76)

Early analyses of economic psychology focused on the moral dimensions of decision-making. David Hume wrote with optimism of a society in which all people were benevolent:

> If every man had a tender regard for another . . . the jealousy of interest . . . could no longer have place; nor would there be any occasion for . . . distinctions and limits of property and possession . . . Encrease to a sufficient degree the benevolence of men . . . and you render justice useless . . . 'tis only from selfishness and the confin'd generosity of men . . . that justice derives its origin.
>
> (Hume 1739, pp. 547–48)

The role of the market in solving economic problems might be more complex than Hume suggests, but the psychological forces of benevolence and philanthropy can be justified if there are market failures such as externalities and free-rider problems. Benevolence does imply some sort of interdependence amongst people's utility: this is something that standard analyses of independent, atomistic agents cannot capture, but it is a strong focus in modern behavioural economics.

Adam Smith (1723–90)

Adam Smith was also interested in these questions. Whilst his name is popularly associated with his rhetorical justification of free markets, and the accompanying metaphor of the invisible hand of the price mechanism coordinating individual behaviour in socially beneficial directions, as described in *An Inquiry into the Nature and Causes of the Wealth of Nations* (1776), Adam Smith also thought carefully about socio-psychological motivations, especially the role played by emotion and sentiment – foreshadowing a number of areas in modern behavioural economics, particularly models of social influence. In *The Theory of Moral Sentiments* he emphasizes the importance of imaginative sympathy in human nature:

> How selfish soever man may be supposed, there are evidently some principles in his nature, which interest him in the fortune of others, and render their happiness necessary to him.
>
> (Smith 1759, p. 9)

He also foreshadows the importance of emotions, with his emphasis on social, unsocial and selfish passions – focusing on the importance of vividness in events in determining how strongly we respond to them. Linking with modern analyses of bad habits and inconsistent plans, he analyses self-deceit and the impact of customs and fashions – which are also the focus of modern behavioural economics analyses of social influences and group bias. Vernon L Smith (1998) notes that, whilst on first inspection there may seem to be a contradiction between Adam Smith's *The Wealth of Nations*, emphasizing self interest, and *The Theory of Moral Sentiments*, emphasizing sympathy, in fact these concepts can be reconciled if cooperation and noncooperation can both be understood in terms of a 'self-interested propensity for exchange' in friendships as well as markets.

Jeremy Bentham (1748–1832)

Jeremy Bentham analysed a number of behavioural/psychological motivations of human action, especially the impacts of pleasures and pains. He was the founder of utilitarianism. His conceptions of utility were focused on the balance of pain and pleasure, and formed the basis for the emphasis on utility in modern economic theory. If welfare, utility and happiness are quantifiable, then right and wrong can be measured by reference to the greatest happiness principle: the greatest happiness for the greatest number. This principle has flaws in that it assumes happiness to be objectively quantifiable and easily aggregated, implying that people's utilities are separable.

A second principle – of psychological hedonism – can be used to guide legislators, and focuses on the fact that people will maximize self-interest; for Bentham, pain and pleasure are the 'sovereign masters' motivating what we do (Harrison 1997). Something is good if the pleasure outweighs the pain; it is evil if the pain outweighs the pleasures. Legislators can formulate rewards and punishments to exploit this psychological hedonism principle and thereby promote the greatest happiness principle (Harrison 1997). Bentham emphasized the quantification of happiness and developed a hedonic calculus – a detailed taxonomy ranking key features of pleasures and pains. Bentham's emphasis on happiness has its parallels in today's happiness and wellbeing literatures.

Vilfredo Pareto (1848–1923)

Vilfredo Pareto is probably best known by economists for his mathematical rigour, his concept of Pareto efficiency and his influence in general equilibrium theory. Less well known is that he developed an interest in social psychology later in his career. He spent time specifying the nature of social relationships, foreshadowing modern behavioural analyses of social influence. In *Trattato di sociologia generale* (1916) – translated as *The Mind and Society* (1935) – Pareto explored a range of behavioural/psychological influences and divergences between logical and nonlogical conduct, focusing on feeling residues (instincts) divided up into classes to explain individual differences and derivations (logical justifications) – paralleling the dual-processing models seen in modern behavioural economics. He also recognized the importance of diversity in skills and in describing cyclical sociological forces, conceived these as a struggle between foxes and lions, adopting Machiavelli's distinction between cunning foxes and courageous lions.

Irving Fisher (1867–1947)

Irving Fisher is renowned for his early analyses of investment and interest rates, and the balance between impatience to spend and opportunities for investment. He sets out the impatience principle, in which the rate of pure time preference (the discount rate) captures interest as the reward for postponing consumption; this forms the bedrock of modern analyses of intertemporal decision-making (Fisher 1930; Baddeley 2003). However, Fisher's analysis of this principle suggests a rule for subjective, psychological motivations – it is the 'inner impatience' of consumers that is balanced against 'outer opportunities' for rewards from interest. Thaler (1997) emphasizes Fisher's focus on 'personal factors' as determinants of time preference. In recognizing that time preference is affected by individual differences in foresight as the outcome of 'thinking', self-control as the outcome of 'willing', and factors affecting susceptibility to fashions and fads, Fisher's ideas connect with modern behavioural economics. Thaler also argues that Fisher's analysis of money illusion is another illustration of how Fisher foreshadowed modern behavioural economics, as it is a form of bias consistent in the analyses of Kahneman, Tversky and others; and Fisher's analysis of the failure of nominal interest rates to adjust quickly to changing price levels is the outcome of people's confusion about the difference between real and nominal values. This also links with Akerlof and Shiller's (2009) identification of money illusion as one of the animal spirits constraining rational decision-making.

John Maynard Keynes (1883–1946)

It is more widely known that John Maynard Keynes had a keen interest in the psychological drivers of behaviour. In *The General Theory of Employment, Interest and Money*, Keynes (1936) argues that economic and financial decision-making is driven by a series of funda-mental psychological laws: the propensity to consume, attitudes to liquidity, and expectations of returns from investment. Keynes applies his psychological analysis most clearly when analysing the interactions between the players in financial markets and the macroeconomy.

Short-termist speculators, preoccupied by a thirst for liquidity, are driven by social influences and conventions to 'beat the gun' and 'outwit the crowd'; thus speculation becomes like 'a game of Snap, of Old Maid, of Musical Chairs – a pastime in which he is the victor who says Snap neither too soon nor too late . . .' (Keynes 1936).

In Keynes's analysis, psychological factors also propel business entrepreneurs facing uncertainty. Entrepreneurs have 'sanguine temperament and constructive impulses' embarking on 'business as a way of life'. It is impossible to predict the long-term future prospects of a new enterprise, so those who do start up new businesses are not preoccupied with quantifying profit expectations. The psychological force of 'animal spirits' takes over, 'so that the thought of ultimate loss which often overtakes pioneers . . . is put aside as a healthy man puts aside the expectations of death'. The problem comes because entrepreneurs are easily discouraged by crises of confidence, and adverse economic, political and social changes will slow entrepreneurial investment, thus slumps and depressions are exacerbated. Keynes also strongly emphasized the role of emotion and sentiment in economic decision-making. In a world of fundamental uncertainty, judgments will rest on flimsy foundations and this introduces fragility into the system. Keynes argues that whilst a social view of economic progress requires a long-term view, longer-term outlooks cannot rest on strictly rational grounds because in a world of uncertainty it is rational for profit-seekers to focus on the short term. Paradoxically, it is the emotionally based animal spirits of entrepreneurs that propel the far-sighted behaviours necessary to justify sufficient capital accumulation for sustained economic growth (Keynes 1936, pp. 161–62).

For Keynes, economic behaviour is the outcome of a complex mixture of the rational and psychological/emotional. This fits with modern neuroeconomic models in which behaviour is the outcome of a complex interaction of emotion and cognition. There are further parallels: Keynes's ideas about herding, reputation and beauty contests are resurfacing in modern models of behavioural economics, including literatures on herding, social learning, reputation, beauty contests and animal spirits; for examples see Bhatt and Camerer (2005), Camerer (1997, 2003a, 2003b) and Ho *et al.* (1998). Keynes's dual focus on reason and emotion also foreshadows the focus in neuroeconomics on interacting systems in the brain; for example, Loewenstein and O'Donoghue (2004) assert that animal spirits are a reflection of the interaction of deliberative and affective systems.

Friedrich von Hayek (1899–1992)

One of Keynes's intellectual adversaries was Hayek, but Hayek too had a keen interest in the psychological and behavioural motivations underlying decision-making. In *The Sensory Order*, Hayek (1952) analyses the nature of mind and distinguishes two 'orders' via which we classify objects into the phenomenal and physical: the subjective, sensory, perceptual order versus the objective, scientific, 'geographical' order. This division mirrors the focus in modern behavioural economics and neuroeconomics on interacting neural systems, e.g. Kahneman's (2003) separation of an intuitive system 1 from a reasoning system 2 in maps of bounded rationality. Hayek (1952) also analyses in detail the processing of stimuli and the biological aspects and characteristics of the nervous system, constructing a theory of mind in which the mental order mirrors the physical order of events seen in the world around us. His assessment of modern behavioural economics would probably be damning, however, because he concludes that 'human decisions must always appear as the result of the whole of human personality – that means the whole of a person's mind – which, as we have seen, we cannot reduce to something else' (Hayek 1952, p. 193).

George Katona (1901–81)

George Katona's early work on economic psychology inspired some economists to return to psychological analysis. Katona (1951, 1975) uses ideas from cognitive psychology to analyse how individuals learn from groups; he distinguishes between different forms of learning, for example the mechanical forms of learning such as the 'stamping-in' of simple rules of thumb and heuristics versus learning via problem-solving and understanding (Katona 1975, p. 47). Behaviour is not about understanding deeper processes and direct experience of problems, but is about relying on simple observation of others to acquire information. Developing socio-psychological themes, Katona argues that group forces and group motives are important, reflecting not only imitation and conscious identification with the group, but also group-centred goals and behaviour. Imitation and suggestion reinforce group situations and group coherence, but are not necessary conditions for being part of a group. Reference groups provide standards for behaviour, and group-centred belonging and motivation are more likely to be important in small groups. Katona (1975) argued that people prefer short cuts and follow simplifying rules of thumb and routines, foreshadowing the 'fast and frugal heuristics' analysed by Gigerenzer and Goldstein (1996) and others, as explored in chapter 6. Individual differences of opinion are ignored, and similarities in small parts of information are transmitted to large numbers of people. Socio-cultural norms, attitudes, habits and membership of groups will influence decisions. Discussion of beliefs with friends and associates will mean that the groups to which a listener belongs determine the information selected. Social learning will continue until the majority has a uniform belief system (Katona 1975).

Modern behavioural economics versus standard approaches

Many would envisage behavioural economics and neuroeconomics as providing conceptual alternatives to standard neoclassical models, which focus on a conception of people as *Homo economicus* – people are assumed to be clever and well informed, decision-making is rational and systematic, and economic actions are described as the outcome of mechanical data processing. A lot has been done to soften the standard approach, especially in microeconomic analysis, for example by recognizing the nature and implications of asymmetric information and other forms of market failure, and by introducing Bayesian models to replace standard models of optimizing behaviour. These extensions can explain nonmaximizing behaviour by allowing it to be constrained by uncertainty and/or affected by strategic interactions between people and firms. Behavioural economics is another way to illuminate some of the deeper foundations of suboptimal behaviour.

One way or another, neoclassical economics is often at the core of methodological debates in behavioural economics. So, whether or not you think that standard neoclassical economics has merit, it is important to understand its fundamental assumptions in order to see when, why, and by how much its assumptions are modified or abandoned in behavioural economic models.

What are the standard assumptions of neoclassical economics?

Models of *Homo economicus* involve a number of assumptions about information and behaviour. Most standard approaches assume that people fit the following descriptions. They are:

- Well informed in an ergodic (stable) world, using information efficiently.
- Independent in two senses –
  atomistic: they do not look to others when deciding what to do
  selfish: their utility is determined only by their own comforts.
- Maximizers, using information efficiently by applying mathematical algorithms (e.g. constrained optimization, Bayesian updating) to generate behaviour that is systematic and objectively determined. Rationality in standard models implies 'well behaved' preferences, that is, preferences are consistent and transitive. They are also convex and monotonic: averages are preferred to extremes, and more is preferred to less. Utility and profits are generally translated into monetary terms on the assumption that money is an objective measure of value.
- Rational agents, forward looking in a systematic way, and discounting the future using exponential discount functions in which preferences over time are consistent.
- Homogeneous, that is, identical (on average at least) so that one model can capture everyone (on average at least).

These standard assumptions imply that, at the extreme, people are conceived as mathematical machines and therefore understanding and controlling behaviour is in many ways more similar to an engineering problem than a socio-psychological problem.

The microeconomic assumptions above are also used as micro-foundations to construct aggregate models of the macroeconomy and financial markets so that the whole becomes a sum of constituent parts. In order to enable this aggregation, further assumptions are made to enable aggregation, including the following:

- The representative agents hypothesis that the average behaviour of all agents within a group can be described by the behaviour of one representative agent. For example, if the representative household is a utility maximizer, then this describes the behaviour of all households enabling aggregation from microeconomic foundations. Aggregate consumption is the consumption of the representative household multiplied by the number of households.
- The efficient markets hypothesis that current asset prices fully reflect all currently available information and so asset prices follow a random walk, that is, are not predictable because any predictable changes in asset prices would be arbitraged away.
- Consumption smoothing – people aim for a steady stream of consumption over their lifetime and are enabled in this by an ability to save or borrow via perfect financial markets.
- Ricardian equivalence – rational agents view different forms of government finance as equivalent. If governments finance spending via borrowing to keep taxes low today, then rational agents will realize that today's relatively large disposable incomes are ephemeral, and government borrowings will have to be repaid via higher taxes in the future. A rational consumption smoother will plan for these future tax rises by cutting consumption today and saving more for tomorrow.

In macroeconomics and finance, aggregation does introduce additional problems for standard models and, in developing a good behavioural theory, we confront the same dilemma. Whilst behavioural economics almost by definition abandons the representative agents hypothesis, this still generates questions about how we can understand the macroeconomy and financial markets if there is heterogeneity amongst people, although this problem can be addressed to some extent via agent-based modelling, in which subpopulations of agents are characterized using different behavioural assumptions.

The degree of divergence of behavioural models versus standard models varies across behavioural economics. Some would see behavioural economics as basically consistent with standard neoclassical approaches, with some extra psychological variables embedded, for example into utility functions, to increase realism, though at some cost in terms of tractability. For example, Camerer and co-writers argue that behavioural economics

> increases the explanatory power of economics by providing it with more realistic psychological foundations . . . [This] does not imply a wholesale rejection of the neoclassical approach . . . [which] provides economists with a theoretical framework that can be applied to almost any form of economic (and even noneconomic) behavior.
>
> (Camerer *et al.* 2004b, p. 3)

Other behavioural economists take a more radical approach and would argue that the foundations of neoclassical economics are badly flawed and need to be replaced with a more fundamentally psychological approach to analysing economic decision-making. Earl (2005) sets out some axiomatic foundations for psychological economics, but emphasizes that these can be expressed 'permissively' as tendencies describing what people often do, rather than as 'non-negotiable axioms'. Choices will be fickle, susceptible to random influences and context, for example with fashions and fads. Consumer and workplace behaviours may be pathological to some degree, including dysfunctional strategic decision-making, and extreme behaviour including impulsive spending or obsessive-compulsive behaviour. Some may exhibit these behaviours to a large degree; others in a minor way, but it will mean that our economic decisions will be affected by irrational obsessions and aversions.

Earl's axiomatic foundations of psychological economics emphasize the importance of perception and context; the social nature of behaviour; the impacts of noneconomic variables; the importance of bounded rationality – specifically when information is too complex for human cognition; satisficing (versus maximizing) choices; attention biases occurring when attention is not allocated optimally, leading to inconsistencies; heuristics and biases shaping perceptions and judgments; temporal biases, for example as seen in models of hyperbolic and quasi-hyperbolic discounting. Other influencers include emotions; impacts of context on decision rules; limited learning constrained by people's preconceptions about the world; pathological behaviours, for example impulsive spending; impacts on choices of personalities and attitudes as well as simple preferences; and altruistic choices (Earl 2005).

Axiomatic foundations unify economics and psychology in psychological economics, but Earl argues that economic psychology and psychological economics are different too: the former involves economists taking subjects traditionally in the psychologists' preserve, such as addiction and altruism, and analysing them using economic models and concepts. Psychological economics comes from the other direction, and involves challenging standard economic models by embedding insights from psychology to enhance understanding of economic decision-making, as in Frey's (1997) broad study of motivation (Earl 2005).

Methodological tools

Behavioural economics adopts a number of methodological tools and approaches from other areas of economics, including game theory and experimental economics. These subjects already have their own large and rich literature, and there is not the space to explore them in detail in this book alongside the enormous behavioural economics literature. A quick summary is given below, alongside some reading recommendations in 'Further reading'.

Game theory

Many areas of behavioural economics focus on strategic interactions between people, and standard game theoretical tools are used as a starting point in these analyses. Putting game theory together with behavioural insights produces the large, diverse field known as behavioural game theory, surveyed comprehensively by Camerer (2003b) and partly covered here in the chapters on learning (chapter 4) and sociality (chapter 5). In explaining behavioural game theory, Camerer makes a distinction between games, which are strategic situations; and game theory, which gives explanations for choices. In standard game theory, there is a divorce of theory and evidence and limited empirical evidence. Camerer (2003b) cites von Neumann and Morgenstern (1944): 'the empirical background of economic science is definitely inadequate. Our knowledge of the relevant facts of economics is incomparably smaller than that commanded in physics at the time when mathematicisation of that subject was achieved' (p. 4). Camerer suggests that this gap between theory and evidence, seen in standard game theoretic approaches, can be remedied to an extent by the inclusion of experimental techniques. This can be achieved by starting with classical game theory and games incorporating private information and probabilistic information about others' preferences and/or types.

Behavioural game theory is often based on classical game theory, which assumes that people are self-interested strategic maximizers, but adapted to allow for additional behavioural constraints including limits to strategic thinking, attitudes towards others' payoffs and learning. Evidence from behavioural game theory can be interpreted in a number of ways, particularly as much of it is based on experimental evidence: violations could reflect irrationality or weaker versions of rationality (e.g. as explored by Herbert Simon, see chapter 6 on definitions of bounded and procedural rationality); 'other-regarding' preferences (e.g. for reciprocity, equity); strategic thinking; and/or reputation-building.

For the purposes of this book, the reader is assumed to have a basic working knowledge of game theory and its key concepts, including Nash equilibrium, mixed strategy equilibrium, reaction functions, backward induction and subgame perfect equilibrium. For the learning chapter in particular, it would be useful to know some classic games such as the Prisoner's dilemma, battle of the sexes, buyer–seller, and stag-hunt games. For those who would like to learn more about game theory to enhance their understanding of related areas of behavioural economics, some good introductions are listed in the 'Further reading' section.

Experimental economics

Empirical testing of behavioural economics models uses a range of data, and some data are similar to those used in standard economic analysis. In terms of the methodological tools used by behavioural economists, there have been some innovations, and data-based statistical and econometric analyses are increasingly being supplemented by experimental evidence. In fact, some areas of behavioural economics have emerged from experimental economics. Behavioural models can explain experimental results that, for one reason or another (and there is plenty of controversy about the reasons), do not fit with simple predictions from standard theory.

Vernon L Smith pioneered the use of experiments in economics, and initially used market experiments as pedagogical devices in his principles of economics lectures (as described in his 2002 Nobel prize speech: www.nobelprize.org/nobel_prizes/economics/laureates/2002/smith-autobio.html). Experimental methods can be integral to behavioural economics because they enable close observation of actual choices under carefully controlled conditions, thus allowing the experimenter to abstract from ordinary complicating factors. If properly constructed, experiments can allow us properly to control conditions so as to capture the real drivers of behaviour.

The main advantage of an experimental approach is that it gives us new types of data to illuminate economic decision-making that will, in some circumstances, be better than the 'happenstance' data of conventional economics/econometrics. Experimental methods are also used in neuroeconomic studies, particularly when the tight analytical structure of game theoretic methods can be used to complement a wide range of neuroscientific techniques (as explored in more detail in chapter 3). This enables the construction of neuroeconomic experiments that can be conducted quickly, efficiently and neatly to test neuroeconomic hypotheses clearly.

Experimental investigations can, however, be fraught with problems, as explored by Smith (1994), Binmore (1999) and others. Experimental designs must be 'clean', with proper controls, clear and simple instructions and clear, salient incentives. Results in experimental context can be conflated with impacts from methodological variables (repetition, anonymity); demographic factors (gender, age, socioeconomic group); cultural factors; game structure, and/or labelling and context. Designing a clean, uncomplicated experiment is not easy to achieve and needs a lot of careful thought.

One aspect of experimental design that attracts strong views from economists is the issue of deception. Is it a methodological problem? In principle, incorporating deception into experiments conflicts with the focus in experimental economics on truthfulness as an essential element in 'clean' experiments. On the other hand, particularly in neuroeconomic experiments, where the experimental environment necessarily is highly constrained, it is often impossible to avoid some limited deception. Sanfey *et al.*'s (2003) fMRI study of social emotions (explored in chapter 8) used a contrived offer algorithm, in which the experimental subjects were told that they were responding to decisions from real people when in fact they were responding to offers generated by the experimenters. Sanfey *et al.* argued that their deception was necessary given the 'heavy logistic demands' of fMRI studies, and did not affect/confound the interpretation of results. The use of limited deception, and only where essential, is sometimes unavoidable in neuroeconomic studies, especially imaging studies, because the experimental context is so restricted by technical, logistical and financial considerations.

In addition to the challenge of designing a clean experiment, it is also important to recognize the limitations of experimental evidence. Aside from some natural/field experiments, results from experiments may suffer from hypothetical bias – experimental subjects may behave in a very different way when they know that they are not making a real-world decision. Results may have limited external validity and may not be generalizable to the world outside the lab. This may reflect the selection of experimental subjects, especially as they are often university students whose behaviour may not represent the behaviour of people outside an academic environment. Results from behavioural experiments have been generalized mainly by increasing the size of payoffs. Richer, more sophisticated experiments need to be designed if insights from behavioural experiments are to be applied more widely. Some experiments do have inherent external validity, including natural experiments where people's ordinary behaviour is already controlled by the situation in which they find themselves. In natural experiments, the experimenter is not interfering and distorting decisions. For example, DellaVigna and Malmendier's (2004) study of gym membership, explored in chapter 10, is an example of a natural experiment.

Field experiments are used frequently in behavioural development economics – often via the adoption of randomized controlled trials incorporating techniques developed for medical/pharmaceutical testing. Randomized controlled trials are used to capture the impact of different 'treatments' or policy interventions. They are constructed by randomly selecting some groups for an intervention. Other groups are used as a control groups. Comparing the behaviour of treatment groups and control groups enables quantification of treatment effects. There are potential ethical problems with randomized controlled trials, because some groups are given access to potential beneficial interventions whilst others are not. This issue is addressed in medical trials by abandoning the random allocation of people into treatment groups versus control groups as soon as strongly significant impacts from interventions are identified.

Experimental economics is also limited by problems with experimental incentive structures. In real-world situations, people face complex but often very salient incentives, and it can be hard for an experimenter to identify meaningful incentive structures, particularly if subjects initially motivated by intellectual curiosity, for example, are then distracted and demotivated by (perhaps insultingly) small experimental payments. Gneezy and Rustichini (2000a, 2000b) have explored this problem in arguing that extrinsic motivations such as money and other concrete rewards crowd out intrinsic motivations, including intellectual curiosity and a desire to be helpful. Demotivated experimental subjects can distort experimental results.

The behavioural economics literature on its own is vast, and there is not the space here for a detailed account of experimental economics too. There are a few comprehensive accounts of experimental economics, and for those interested to find out more, some sources are suggested in 'Further reading'.

Behavioural policy implications

Behavioural economics has many insights to offer policy-makers across a range of areas, and there is currently great interest in behavioural techniques and in designing policies to facilitate behaviour change, for example, energy and environment policies, and development policy, as outlined in chapters 4–5 on social norms, peer effects and learning. Policies must be sustainable and scalable to lead to significant behavioural change.

Recently, policy-makers have been focusing in particular on Thaler and Sunstein's (2008) libertarian paternalistic 'nudge' approach – based on the insight that policy-makers should apply an understanding of the 'architecture of choice' by simplifying choices and eliminating or exploiting behavioural biases. Nudging tools are popular with governments. Richard Thaler advises Prime Minister David Cameron's behavioural insight team, and Cass Sunstein advises Barack Obama.

Whilst behavioural nudging seems seductively simple, there are problems with the nudging approaches. Some nudges are just superficial quick fixes that may not lead to deep and lasting behaviour change. For example, some behavioural biases lead some consumers to use too much electricity, but in controlling energy use it is not enough just to switch off some lights when heating is the major energy drain. Similarly, sometimes policies will change just a single behaviour when whole sets of behaviours need to adapt. Studies of sanitation in India show that people will be encouraged by social pressures to install more latrines, but awareness of the need for good sanitation does not necessarily generalize to other behaviours to improve sanitation, such as hand-washing (Pattanayak *et al.* 2009).

More generally, given the growing influence of behavioural economics in policy-making, it is important for policy-makers to recognize not only behavioural economics' insights, but also its limitations. Sometimes more traditional policies will be more effective in dealing with particular types of policy problem, for example, traditional policy tools such as regulation and taxation might be better ways to encourage households and businesses to use energy more efficiently and/or to dissuade large retailers and manufacturers from exploiting impulsive, visceral reactions to food advertising and cigarette packaging. The key is a good balance between innovative but effective policy tools based on insights from behavioural economics alongside more traditional styles of policy-making.

To capture some of the policy dilemmas that may (or may not) be resolved using insights from behavioural economics, key concepts in the microfoundations chapters (chapters 4–10) are illustrated with case studies to illuminate how principles from behavioural economics connect with real-world problems.

The structure of *Behavioural Economics and Finance*

In standard models, the focus on mathematical algorithms in decision-making leads to an impression of decision-making as a strictly cognitive process of calculation and deliberation. Behavioural economics allows that decisions are more complex, being the outcome of interactions between preferences (selfish and social), strategy, beliefs, cognition, emotions, personality, identity, etc. In this, behavioural economics relaxes standard assumptions to give models in which people learn from their mistakes; look to others when making decisions and/or when seeking happiness; make systematic mistakes; and use quick decision-making rules, including rules of thumb and heuristics, rather than efficiently balancing the benefits and costs of searching for more information. Decisions are affected by skills and personalities, and also by moods and emotions. People aren't necessarily good at planning systematically for future events and, particularly when immediate pleasures tap into emotional and visceral influences, this means that people will be susceptible to impulsive decision-making that may be detrimental to their long-run welfare (such as smoking or eating unhealthy foods).

Behavioural Economics and Finance provides a broad introduction to key debates, and a range of behavioural principles are explored. The literature is already enormous and is growing rapidly, so it would be impossible to cover in one book all the interesting things that behavioural economists are doing. So the chapters here focus on the aspects of behavioural economics that are relatively well established and/or have received a lot of attention – including learning, sociality, heuristics and biases, prospect theory, personality and cognition, reason and emotion, time discounting and planning, bad habits, financial instability and behavioural macroeconomics, including wellbeing and happiness.

The book begins with brief surveys of psychology and neuroscience to give the reader a basic working knowledge of the behavioural science principles less familiar to economists. The order of the remaining chapters is aimed gradually to relax various behavioural assumptions characterizing standard economic models. In behavioural economics, people are not necessarily well informed, though they can learn to make better choices over times; sometimes they learn from others' actions, and they may be affected by social influences in a broader way too. Learning and social influence are explored in chapter 4. Sociality, social preferences and identity will also affect decision-making. These factors can be incorporated as extensions to standard models, for example, some models of inequity aversion embed social preferences into otherwise standard utility functions. Sociality and identity are explored in chapter 5.

More radical behavioural economics models take on some of the more fundamental assumptions and foundations of standard economic analysis. Famously, Kahneman and Tversky criticized the rationality assumptions underlying standard conceptions of expected utility theory (EUT), arguing that experimental evidence reveals a range of behavioural paradoxes and anomalies that are inconsistent with the stable, consistent preferences assumed within the EUT approach. Behaviour is often not strictly rational. People use heuristics and are prone to behavioural biases, and these phenomena are analysed in chapter 6. Prospect theory is Kahneman and Tversky's behavioural alternative to EUT. The foundations of prospect theory and related models, including Thaler's mental accounting model and Loomes and Sugden's regret theory, are analysed in chapter 7.

Standard economic models often assume that people are homogeneous, exhibiting similar responses, and this enables economists to simplify from the complications of human diversity to give mathematically tractable models. By contrast, for a long time psychology has acknowledged the importance of mood, emotions and individual differences, including differences in cognitive ability, noncognitive skills and personality. Elster and others have emphasized the role of emotions in economic decision-making, and there is a large literature on emotions in behavioural economics, including social emotions in inequity-aversion models, fear and greed in financial markets, and impulsivity in intertemporal decision-making. Heckman has found that individual differences in cognitive and noncognitive skills have profound effects on people's future prospects, and key aspects of personality become fixed very early in life, with consequences for people's future prospects. Moods, emotions and personality are explored in chapter 8.

Another fundamental assumption of standard models is that people are forward looking in a systematic way. These approaches assume that people's exponential discount functions are stable throughout their lifetime (and sometimes beyond). Yet experimental and other evidence again reveals that people do not necessarily plan their lives so effectively. Behavioural models of time inconsistency can capture anomalies at both micro- and macro-levels, for example, to explain why people simultaneously hold revolving credit/credit card debt at high interest rates alongside illiquid assets on which they earn little interest. Why don't they sell some of their illiquid assets to pay off their credit card debts? As explored in chapter 9, this conundrum can be resolved by constructing behavioural discount functions either to supplement or replace the standard exponential discount functions. Unstable time preference can lead people into temptation, procrastination and destructive habits, reflecting not only misguided attempts to plan for the future, but also the influence of emotions and visceral factors. Bringing together some insights about emotions from chapter 8 and about present bias from chapter 9, chapter 10 analyses bad habits, including addiction, using some principles from behavioural economics.

Chapters 11 and 12 focus on aggregate behaviour in financial markets and in the macroeconomy more widely. Financial decision-making is affected by behavioural biases, moods and emotions, and time inconsistency, and in chapter 11 these phenomena are used to analyse the behavioural foundations of financial instability. Whilst behavioural economics has made much progress in illuminating our understanding of real-world microeconomic behaviour, the field has yet to construct a convincing model of behavioural macroeconomics, a problem explored in chapter 12. As observed above, the problem of aggregation complicates the construction of plausible theories of the macroeconomy, but some broad trends can be captured by applying behavioural economics to an analysis of the real-world behaviour of households and businesses. Behavioural economics also focuses on broader measures of welfare, and these are addressed in the literature on wellbeing and happiness, also described in chapter 12.

A note on mathematics

Mathematical exposition characterizes modern economics, and this is not necessarily a bad thing if mathematical and intuitive explanations complement each other. Sometimes it is easier to explain things using simple equations, and a number of behavioural economists have set out their models using some (usually straightforward) mathematics.

Other times, it is more meaningful to express things in words – especially as the human brain is not always well built to process mathematical arguments. But there is a lot of heterogeneity in people's preferences for mathematics, and for this reason the main text is written to suit people who prefer to avoid the mathematical language. For those who can follow a mathematical argument more quickly, mathematical presentations of the essential principles and models are separated into boxes. Readers can ignore the mathematical translations if they prefer because all the principles and models are explained in the main text using words and/or diagrams.

Further reading

Some introductions to behavioural economics

Ariely D (2008) *Predictably Irrational – The Hidden Forces that Shape Our Decisions*, New York: Harper Collins.

Camerer CF, Loewenstein G and Rabin M (2004) 'Behavioral economics: past, present and future', in Camerer CF, Loewenstein G and Rabin M (eds), *Advances in Behavioral Economics*, Princeton, NJ/ Oxford: Oxford University Press.

DellaVigna S (2009) 'Psychology and economics: evidence from the field', *Journal of Economic Literature*, 47(2), 315–72.

Earl P (1990) 'Economics and psychology: a survey', *Economic Journal*, 100, 718–55.

Fisher I (1930) *The Theory of Interest*, New York: Macmillan.

Forbes W (2009) *Behavioral Finance*, Chichester, UK: John Wiley.

Fudenberg D (2006) 'Advancing beyond advances in behavioral economics', *Journal of Economic Literature*, 44(3), 694–711.

Hume D (1739) *A Treatise of Human Nature*, Harmondsworth, UK: Penguin.

Kahneman D (2011) *Thinking, Fast and Slow*, London: Allen Lane.

Pesendorfer W (2006) 'Behavioral economics comes of age: a review essay on advances in behavioral economics', *Journal of Economic Literature*, 44(3), 694–711.

Shleifer A (2000) *Inefficient Markets – An Introduction to Behavioral Finance*, Oxford: Clarendon Press/Oxford University Press.

Simon HA (1998) 'Behavioural economics', in Eatwell J, Milgate M and Newman P (eds) *The New Palgrave Dictionary of Economics, Vol. 1*, London: Macmillan, pp. 221–25.

Thaler R (ed.) (2005) *Advances in Behavioral Finance*, New York: Russell Sage Foundation.

Thaler R and Sunstein C (2008) *Nudge – Improving Decisions about Health, Wealth and Happiness*, New Haven, CT: Yale University Press.

Behavioural game theory/classical game theory

Binmore K (1992) *Fun and Games – A Text on Game Theory*, Lexington, MA: Heath & Co.

— (2007) *Game Theory – A Very Short Introduction*, Oxford: Oxford University Press.

Camerer C (2003) *Behavioral Game Theory: Experiments in Strategic Interaction*, New York: Russell Sage Foundation.

Dixit A and Skeath S (2004) *Games of Strategy* (2nd edn), New York: WW Norton.

Kreps DM (1990) *Game Theory and Economic Modelling*, New York: Oxford University Press.
Osborne MJ (2004) *An Introduction to Game Theory*, New York: Oxford University Press.

Experimental economics

Bardsley N, Cubitt R, Loomes G, Moffatt P, Starmer C and Sugden R (2009) *Experimental Economics – Rethinking the Rules*, Princeton/Oxford: Princeton University Press.
Binmore K (1999) 'Why experiment in economics?' *Economic Journal*, 109(453), F16–F24.
Friedman D and Sunder S (1994) *Experimental Methods: A Primer for Economists*, Cambridge: Cambridge University Press.
Holt CA (2007) *Markets, Games and Strategic Behavior*, Boston, MA: Pearson/Addison-Wesley.
Kagel JH and Roth AE (eds) (1995) *The Handbook of Experimental Economics*, Princeton, NJ: Princeton University Press.
Samuelson L (2005) 'Economic theory and experimental economics', *Journal of Economic Literature*, 43(1), 65–107.
Selten R (2007) *Economics Lab: An Introduction to Experimental Economics*, Routledge Advances in Experimental and Computable Economics, Abingdon, UK: Routledge.
Smith VL (1994) 'Economics in the laboratory', *Journal of Economic Perspectives*, 8(1), 113–31.

Experimental software

This book is about behavioural economics models rather than experimental techniques, but there is now a wide range of software available that will be useful for some behavioural economic studies, both for constructing and implementing experiments, and for management of experiments, including recruiting and registering subjects. Much of it is free, and here are some links to experimental software and advice:

Caltech Social Science Experimental Lab   www.ssel.caltech.edu
http://software.ssel.caltech.edu/wiki

Mechanical Turk (mturk)   www.mturk.com/mturk/welcome
universitat pompeu fabra   www.upf.edu/leex/links/
z-tree (Universität Zürich)   www.iew.uzh.ch/ztree/index.php

2 Foundations: psychology

Introduction

Behavioural economists have turned to psychologists and neuroscientists to gain a deeper understanding of the psychological and biological processes driving human action. For this reason, a full understanding of behavioural economics requires a good working knowledge of some basic concepts and approaches from psychology and neuroscience. The aim of this chapter and the next is to introduce and explain some fundamental concepts and techniques from psychology and neuroscience, focusing specifically on their implications for behavioural economics and neuroeconomics. Psychology and neuroscience are themselves enormous fields, and it would take a library full of books and journals to cover them properly. A single chapter cannot cover all that is interesting and relevant, and we will be forced to take a 'pick-and-mix' approach – focusing on just some of the psychological and neuroscientific concepts that have inspired and informed behavioural economists, or that could do so. For those who would like to learn more, some introductory psychology and neuroscience texts are set out in the 'Further reading' sections.

Psychology is about individual minds and action. The dictionary definition of psychology is: 'the scientific study of the mind and its functions especially those affecting behaviour in a given context' (*Concise Oxford Dictionary of Current English*). Behavioural economics often draws heavily on approaches from psychology, particularly from behavioural psychology, which focuses on observed behaviour and lends itself to the task-driven, goal-oriented nature of economic experimental contexts. However, other branches of psychology also offer important insights for economists, especially about what underlies people's decisions.

The incorporation of psychology into economics is controversial. For some economists, embedding a deeper understanding of what motivates choices and decisions is anathema because, for example in positivist, neoclassical approaches, the focus is on objectively measurable data such as observed choices. Earl (2005) observes that such criticisms may reflect the fact that psychology as a discipline lacks a grand unifying theory. There are many different psychological approaches, but fragmentation within psychology not only discourages economists from making an investment in understanding psychological theories, it also encourages a piecemeal, *ad hoc* approach to embedding psychological insights into economics (Earl 2005). This selective use of psychological insights in behavioural economics may undermine its credibility for some.

This chapter explores some basic insights from psychology that may be useful to economists, focusing in particular on personality theory, behaviourism and social psychology because, in different ways, these approaches have been developed in the behavioural economics literatures.

Personality theory

Personality theories analyse characteristics of individuals that lead to consistent patterns of behaviour and, as economists are generally interested in trying to explain consistent (or inconsistent) choices, personality theory has a number of insights to offer. As explained below, experimental approaches to behavioural economics incorporate insights from behaviourism by focusing only on objective information such as observed choice, rather than on less easily measurable variables including personality. More recently, however, the importance of personality is being recognized because individual differences in levels of generosity can explain differing degrees of sociality; impulsiveness can explain impatience and time inconsistency.

Freud's psychoanalytic theory

One of the pioneering approaches to analysing personality and traits was Sigmund Freud's psychoanalytic theory. In Freud's approach, behaviour is the outcome of interplays between basic drives, needs and conflicts (Pervin 1984). Freud analysed a very wide range of forces affecting personality, focusing on different levels of consciousness: conscious, preconscious and unconscious thought (Freud 1899). In modern behavioural economics there is a focus on automatic versus deliberative processing, and this mirrors the Freudian distinctions of conscious, preconscious and unconscious thought.

Freud also, perhaps most famously, emphasized the role played by erogenous zones at various stages of childhood development, including oral, anal and phallic stages during which instincts develop. He developed his analysis of instincts to focus on the life instinct, *eros* and the death instinct, *thanatos* (Freud 1921). Obstacles to healthy development during childhood mean that people can develop fixations if they become stuck in a particular development stage. These fixations lead to the emergence of pathological oral, anal or phallic personalities. For Freud, early sexual conflicts impeded development through these stages with consequences for adult behaviour (Freud 1940). Freud thought that psychiatric disorders, for example hysteria, could be explained via reference to these early conflicts, and attempted to untangle these conflicts in a clinical setting via the use of cathartic hypnotic techniques, as pioneered by the neurologist Jean-Marie Charcot.

Freud also identified roles for different elements of personality, arguing that personality is driven by interactions between the pleasure principle and the reality principle. The id is driven by the pleasure principle impulsively to seek gratification of basic instincts. The ego is driven by the reality principle to delay gratification in a rational, practical way. The superego is the rigid, sometimes judgmental moral compass that guides ethical attitudes. According to Freud, childhood development proceeds as the child's ego learns to delay gratification (Freud 1921, 1949). Nonetheless, the ego plays a subordinate role in the sense that it is victim not only of the competing pressures from the id and superego, but also of reality. As economists are interested in consistent choices, the personality traits that propel those choices can illuminate our understanding of economic behaviour. Freud analysed identification – the process via which we integrate the characteristics of others into our personality. He thought that identification with the same-sex parent develops during the phallic phase; other forms of identification include narcissistic identification – identifying with people similar to oneself; goal-oriented identification – identifying with successful people; object-loss identification – identifying with lost objects and people; and aggressor identification – identifying with authority figures (Pervin 1984).

Although, for some, Freud's theories are discredited as scientific theories because there is no objective evidence to support them, Freudian themes can still be found in modern behavioural economics. Akerlof (see chapter 10) explores a number of Freudian themes in his analyses of cognitive dissonance, illusion and identity: Freud's emphasis on basic instincts and drives is mirrored in some analyses of addiction. Tuckett (chapter 11) applies modern psychoanalytic tools to the analysis of emotional finance. Freudian insights about the development of personality have resurfaced in analyses of Keynes, for example in Winslow's analysis of Freudian themes in Keynes's conceptions of money (see chapter 12).

Jung's archetypes

Carl Jung developed a psychoanalytic approach grounded in the analysis of individual psyches. Whilst he split with Freud, his approach was grounded in tools and approaches from psychoanalysis, focusing on unconscious, sometimes irrational drives as well as conscious, rational thoughts, with layers of personality comprising the conscious, the personal unconscious and the collective unconscious. He developed Plato's concept of archetypes – universal symbols resting in the collective unconscious – and envisaged these as elements of our personalities, for example, 'mother' – the nurturing part; 'anima' – the feminine part; 'animus' – the masculine part. Jung's archetypes rest in the collective unconscious and are universal, and so are seen throughout history in culture, folk tales and literature (Jung 1991). Jung also identified different psychological types, reflecting attitudes (extraversion versus introversion), perceptions (intuition versus sensing), and judgments (thinking versus feeling), and his analysis of personality types was the foundation of the Myers–Briggs Type Indicator (MBTI) developed by Katharine Cook Briggs and Isabel Briggs Myers, as explained below (Jung 1923; Grigorenko and Sternberg 1995).

Modern personality theory

More recently, theories of personality have concentrated on the analysis of personality traits. George Kelly (1955) developed the construct theory of personality, which is built upon the analysis of the bipolar constructs (for example, good versus bad) that enable us to categorize people and events to interpret and make sense of the world around us. By understanding similarities and differences we generate a structure into which we fit our experiences. Kelly identified a range of constructs, from essential core constructs through to peripheral, inessential constructs. This interpretation of the world is inherently subjective, and Kelly identified the problem that our understanding of the world is shaped by the way in which we construct our understanding of it. This foreshadows more recent literature on personality in economics, including Borghans *et al.* (2008). It also links to the framing effects and context dependence identified by Kahneman and Tversky, and others.

Gordon Allport's trait theory analysed the impact of traits on habitual thought patterns, both cognitive and emotional. Allport observed that traits are relatively stable for the individual, but variable across individuals. He saw personality traits as unifying features and divided traits into various categories: central traits essential to an individual versus secondary traits, seen only in certain circumstances and contexts; cardinal traits, the traits that define individuals and make them distinctive; and common traits, which are specific to particular social and cultural contexts (Allport 1937). He believed that traits are interconnected and important to the formation of identity (Allport 1955).

Measuring cognitive skills

Individual differences can be measured in a wide range of ways. Cognitive functioning and intelligence can be defined in terms of ability to solve problems, and this gives some objectivity to the concept. Nonetheless, difficulties in measurement will emerge because intelligence is not a monolithic characteristic. Early tests of cognitive skills were developed by Alfred Binet, Théodore Simon and William Stern, who devised the intelligence quotient (IQ) test. Early IQ tests tended to focus on intelligence as one overarching characteristic. More recently, general intelligence has been characterized as reflecting a hierarchy of cognitive skills. Two of the major factors underlying general intelligence include fluid intelligence, the ability to think laterally and problem-solve; and crystallized intelligence, gained from learning and experience (Cattell 1971). Someone with high levels of crystallized intelligence may perform less well in certain tasks than someone with high levels of fluid intelligence, and *vice versa*.

It is important to note that measuring cognitive skills cannot be completely objective. Performance can be determined by factors not related to cognitive functioning, for example, performance in IQ tests is dependent not only on cultural factors and linguistic difference, but also on incentives and noncognitive skills such as conscientiousness and motivation (Borghans *et al.* 2008). Intelligence can also be difficult to define because it has many facets.

Personality tests

Capturing noncognitive skills and personality traits is even more complicated than measuring cognitive skills. It is difficult to establish an objective basis for individual differences in personality. Kelly developed an early personality test in the form of the role construct repertory test (rep test). This test drew on some features from Jung's insights. Subjects were asked to list key figures (for example, mother, father, teacher) and make connections between them on the basis of similarities and contrasts. The rep test is no longer widely used, but a number of personality theories and tests have evolved since.

More recently, tests have evolved that focus on a single trait or small number of traits, for example Barratt's impulsivity scale, the Baron-Cohen–Wheelwright empathy quotient, and Hans Eysenck's multi-factor personality tests of impulsiveness, empathy, conformity and psychoticism (Eysenck 1967, 1975, 1991; Eysenck and Eysenck 1975, 1976, 1978). Some tests are used by economists today, including the MBTI, mentioned above, and the Big Five personality test.

Myers–Briggs Type Indicator

In order to capture the insights of the personality theorists in real, clinical contexts, a number of personality-testing methods developed. Jung's structure, as described above, inspired the Myers–Briggs approach to capturing personality styles, where the styles reflect a person's interaction with their environment. The MBTI captures aspects of conscious mental activity according to the following features: introversion versus extroversion; intuition versus sensing; thinking versus feeling; and judging versus perceiving, giving sixteen types of personality styles. The MBTI taxonomy is similar to Jung's structure, although Myers is more tightly organized (Myers 1981; Grigorenko and Sternberg 1995)

Big Five theory

Another method of personality testing often used in economic analyses, for example in Heckman's analysis of personality and the life cycle, is the Big Five personality test. These tests were developed originally by Tupes and Christal (1961) and subsequently by McCrae and Costa (1987; Costa and McCrae 1992, 2005). The Big Five captures aspects of personality along five dimensions: openness, conscientiousness (versus undirectedness), extraversion (versus introversion), agreeableness (versus antagonism) and neuroticism (OCEAN). This taxonomy is used either in self-report questionnaires or in peer ratings of a person's personality. The five dimensions are assessed according to polar adjectives reflecting Kelly's bipolar constructs as described by McCrae and Costa (1987). For example, openness is captured by dimensions such as simple–complex, conforming–independent, unanalytical–analytical. Similarly, conscientiousness is captured by adjectives including lazy–hardworking, stupid–intelligent, unfair–fair; extraversion by timid–bold, retiring–sociable, inhibited–spontaneous; agreeableness by ruthless–softhearted, critical–lenient, callous–sympathetic; and neuroticism by unemotional–emotional, patient–impatient, objective–subjective (McCrae and Costa 1987).

The Minnesota Multiphasic Personality Inventory and the Rorschach test

Some personality tests have been designed specifically to capture psychopathologies. The one that is commonly used by mental health professionals is the Minnesota Multiphasic Personality Inventory (MMPI) originally devised by Hathaway and Kinley (1943). Modern versions of the test incorporate a wide range of test items, which capture the thoughts, feelings and behaviours of the subjects. Interpreting the answers can be problematic because it is not possible to establish whether respondents are being truthful, or reading the questions properly, so additional items are included to capture the validity of answers, for example, a 'lie' scale designed to judge how honest the respondent is. Also, the focus is not on the individual scores on specific test items, but instead on the whole personality profile constructed when collections of items are interpreted as a whole.

Overall, the tests used specifically by mental health professionals are designed to enable assessment of psychopathologies, so might be less relevant to economists who are interested in the behaviour of 'normal' subjects. Nonetheless, insights from tests traditionally used by mental health practitioners may have some value, for example, *The Economist* has reported a revival of interest in the Rorschach ink-blot test – which assesses subjects' responses to random ink-blot patterns – because some aspects of this test correlate with intellect and cognitive functioning (Meyer *et al.* 2011; *The Economist* 2011a).

Cognitive functioning

Behavioural economics focuses not only on personality traits, but also on cognitive skills and functioning, particularly as cognition links clearly into standard economics' focus on assumptions of rationality. Cognition and emotion will be affected by individual differences, and behavioural economists have started to explore the links between cognitive functioning and emotional processing. These interactions are explored in more detail in the sections on neuroeconomics in chapter 3 and in chapter 8, which explores the role of emotions and personality in economic and financial decision-making.

Some psychological analyses have explored the role of cognitive functioning over the life cycle. Walter Mischel and colleagues rejected the view that personality traits were always stable and consistent, and found that behaviour was dependent on situational cues. In a series of studies, they demonstrated that self-control correlates with individual differences, and better cognitive functioning leads to better life chances in adulthood. Children's behaviour in a residential camp setting was observed in one study, and the situation–behaviour profiles of the children were analysed. The stability of these profiles varied across individuals, for example, levels of aggression varied depending on whether a child was approached by a peer versus an adult: one child would be more aggressive in response to an approach from a peer, whereas another might be more aggressive in response to an approach from an adult. Behavioural differences were attributed to differences in cognitive-affective processing reflecting competences, beliefs, goals; over time, experience leads to the development of situation–behaviour relations reflecting dispositions and cognitive-affective processing, so cognition and emotion affect social information processing in different ways in different people (Mischel and Shoda 1995).

Mischel and his colleagues are famous for the 'marshmallow experiment' to test self-imposed delay of gratification in children: nursery-school children were shown sets of two treats (for example, marshmallows); they waited with one treat and were told that if they managed to resist the temptation to eat that one treat, then they would get both at the end of some predetermined period (Mischel and Ebbesen 1970; Mischel *et al.* 1972). There was considerable stability in these traits from childhood into adulthood, and they correlated with future wellbeing. The same children were studied at fourteen years old; those who had shown more evidence of self-control in early childhood had better emotional and cognitive functioning and, later in life, were more socially and academically competent than those who had exerted less self-control in the early tests (Mischel *et al.* 1989). The results from Mischel and colleagues' studies link to the behavioural economics literature on present bias and self-control, including implications for future wellbeing, reflecting Mischel's finding that behaviour in early childhood correlates with future performance (see chapters 9 and 10).

Cognitive functioning can be linked with assumptions about cognition in economics, for example, in analyses of heuristics and biases. It can also capture some individual differences beyond personality traits – in terms of cognitive and noncognitive skills and their impact on a person's daily functioning.

Aspects of cognition that affect economic and financial decision-making include motivation, memory and perception – for example, motivation will determine effort levels by workers. Also, memory and perception will affect expectations; memory will play an important role when we are judging the likelihood of future events – our judgments and perceptions will be affected by how easily we can remember similar events, as explored in the discussion in chapter 6 of Kahneman and Tversky's analysis of heuristics and biases.

Behavioural psychology

Economic models of learning emerged from early work by behavioural psychologists. The personality theories of Sigmund Freud and the psychoanalysts were controversial, and the behavioural psychologists rejected Freudian approaches to understanding what underlies behaviour as subjective and speculative. Instead, they focused on analysing objective facts: observed choices, and the direct and indirect impacts of stimuli upon these choices. This focus on observed behaviour fits neatly with the focus in experimental economics on revealed preference and observed choices and game theory. Behavioural psychology developed from Nobel prize-winning physiologist Ivan Pavlov (1849–1946). Pavlov pioneered the analysis of classical conditioning. He was studying the digestive systems of dogs and noticed that they often started salivating before they tasted food; salivation was an unconditioned response to the unconditioned stimulus of receiving food. Pavlov hypothesized that a conditioned stimulus could induce a conditioned response, and so set metronomes running a few seconds before feeding meat powder to his dogs. He found that once the dogs had learned the connection between the metronome and the food, they would start salivating on hearing the metronome and before receiving the meat powder. Salivation was a learned, conditioned response, and Pavlov found that the salivation response could be conditioned on a range of stimuli, including rotating disks and lights (Pavlov 1927).

Watson and Rayner (1920) generalized Pavlov's findings about conditioned responses and conducted the famously unethical study of Albert B to establish that phobias were the outcome of conditioning, not of early sexual conflicts as asserted by the Freudians. Albert B was approximately nine months old when the study commenced: 'the infant was confronted suddenly and for the first time successively with a white rat, a rabbit, a dog, a monkey, with masks – with and without hair, cotton wool, burning newspapers, etc. . . . . No one had ever seen him in a state of fear and rage. The infant practically never cried.'

When Albert B reached eleven months, Watson and Rayner decided to see if they could condition a fear response by banging a bar behind Albert's head to make an unexpectedly loud and frightening sound. Their lab notes read: 'White rat suddenly taken from the basket and presented to Albert. He began to reach for rat with left hand. Just as his hand touched the animal the bar was struck immediately behind his head. The infant jumped violently and fell forward, burying his face in the mattress. He did not cry, however. Just as the right hand touched the rat the bar was again struck . . . Again the infant jumped violently, fell forward and began to whimper.'

After an interval they again struck the bar whilst presenting the rat to Albert. 'The instant the rat was shown the baby began to cry. Almost instantly he turned sharply to the left, fell over on left side, raised himself on all fours and began to crawl away so rapidly that he was caught with difficulty before reaching the edge of the table.' In this way Albert was conditioned to fear the white rat. They also found that the conditioned fear response endured over time and was generalized to other similar objects: to a greater or lesser extent the fear response could also be elicited when a toy rabbit, toy dog, Santa Claus mask and cotton wool were produced.

Edward L Thorndike's theory of learning developed these concepts of conditioning to focus on operant conditioning and the laws of effect, exercise and recency (Thorndike 1911). Thorndike's laws underlie models of learning in economics, and are based on studies of animal behaviour. Thorndike's experiments included a study of thirteen young cats, aged between four and nineteen months. The cats were confined in small boxes secured via various combinations of loops, levers, bars, boards and bolts. The cats initially followed their instincts and impulses in trying to escape – Thorndike carefully distinguishes instinct as 'any reaction an animal makes to a situation without experience', and impulse as 'the consciousness accompanying a muscular innervation . . . the direct feeling of doing. [For example] hunger is the impulse which makes the cat claw . . . by impulse I never mean the motive to the act' (Thorndike 1911, pp. 21–22). Thorndike found that eleven of thirteen cats soon learned to escape the boxes via a process of trial and error until: 'all the other non-successful impulses will be stamped out and the particular impulse leading to the successful act will be stamped in by the resulting pleasure, until, after many trials, the cat will, when put in the box, immediately claw the button or loop in a definite way'.

From this, Thorndike constructed laws about how learning progresses by making associations between stimuli, actions and rewards: the law of effect is that the actions which produce pleasure give positive reinforcement and will be repeated – learning will build on pleasure and reward; the law of exercise is that more often a positive (negative) association is made, the more (less) likely it is to be used and *vice versa*; and the law of recency is that recent events will be more salient and so recent responses are more likely to be repeated, but impacts of prior rewards and punishments will decay over time. Insights from Thorndike's analyses are adopted in economic models of reinforcement learning and neuroeconomic theories of reward learning, both explored in chapter 4. The law of exercise also has implications for models of habits, as seen in chapter 10.

BF Skinner used Thorndike's analysis of operant conditioning/instrumental learning to inform extensive experimental studies of animal learning, and focused his analysis purely on observable choices and, via rewards and punishments, used the experimental environment to manipulate choices. He fostered an extreme version of behavioural psychology – radical behaviourism, which confines itself to studying inputs and behavioural outcomes. Whilst experimenters might manipulate the conditions under which choices are made to see how behaviour is affected, the focus is on observables: the inputs and outcomes in terms of behaviour, not the unseen underlying processes driving it (Skinner 1974). In extreme behaviourism, personality traits and individual differences are not the focus of analysis and, much as early neoclassical theorists treated the firm as a black box focusing on observable inputs and outputs to production, similarly in radical behaviourism choices are made in a black box – information and stimuli go in, choices come out, and the experimenter concentrates just on observed behaviour rather than the processes underlying it.

Behavioural psychology has had a profound influence on modern behavioural economics and helps to explain the distinction between it and economic psychology. In contrast to economic psychology, the areas of behavioural economics that are closest to mainstream economic theory adopt the methodology of behavioural psychology by focusing on choices using experimental methods and abstracting from the cognitive and emotional processes underlying economic decision-making. It could be argued that the behavioural approach has in some ways been made obsolete by technology: as the sophistication and precision of neuroscientific tools and techniques has increased, the objective information available to a scientist is no longer confined to studying what people actually do (or don't do), because it is now possible objectively to measure the physiological responses underlying observed action. As for psychology more generally, the development of new neuroscientific tools has led to the evolution of neuroeconomic analyses – observable data are no longer confined to what people do, we can also measure what is going on in their brains and nervous systems whilst they do it, as the neuroeconomic studies explored in this book demonstrate.

Social psychology

Social psychology blends psychology and sociology by reconciling psychological insights about the role of personality and individual differences with the sociologist's emphasis on group influence and context dependence. In exploring the impacts of social groups and contexts on individual behaviour, sociologists distinguish between informational influences – which can sometimes be analysed in an objective way (as in the Bayesian social learning models analysed in chapter 4) and normative influences – norms and influences from peers and social groups that affect our perceptions of how we *should* behave.

It is often difficult empirically to distinguish between informational and normative influences, though psychological surveys and neuroeconomic analyses may provide some clues. Sociological forces create interdependence and encourage imitation and herding. Sociological forces interact with psychological forces and will affect individual behaviour if groups act in concert without any clear coordinating mechanism – explained by Carl Jung as the outcome of a collective unconscious, an inherited understanding that is universal in all of us. Early studies of social psychology also focused on the influences from crowds and group pressure on individual actions, drawing on themes from Le Bon's analysis of mob psychology and the hypnotic influence of crowds (Le Bon 1896). Some themes in social psychology also develop from the psychoanalysts who followed some of Freud's insights. Alfred Adler focused on conscious social factors and the connections between people and the world around them, including the inferiority and superiority complexes (Adler 1979). Herding that is the outcome of social pressure rather than rational calculation is seen in a wide range of human behaviours, for example in formation of mob processes (flash mobs), political choice, consumer preferences (fashion trends, dietary choices) and financial speculation.

Festinger (1957) describes strong urges to overcome cognitive dissonance, that is, to establish noncontradictory belief systems (as discussed in more detail below), and group influence can be important in reconciling dissonance. We may persuade ourselves to buy something at an excessively high price if we see others doing the same. In this way, individual differences of opinion are ignored and similarities in small parts of information are transmitted to large numbers of people. Socio-cultural norms, attitudes, habits, and/or membership of groups will influence decisions. Discussion of beliefs with friends and associates will mean that information selected as most relevant is determined by the groups to which the listener belongs. Social learning will continue until the majority has a uniform belief system (Katona 1975).

Social learning theory

Social context is the focus of social learning theories developed by Julian Rotter, Albert Bandura and Walter Mischel. These social psychologists rejected the strict determinism of the trait theorists by allowing that learning takes place within social contexts via observational learning and influences from role models. Rotter developed elements from personality theory and behaviourism to explain that behaviour is affected by subjective expectations that are influenced by personality, and external reinforcements that are influenced by external events including social context. Loci of control have internal (individual) and external (social) dimensions. Personalities with a strong internal locus of control take responsibility for their own actions. Those with a strong external locus of control attribute events to context, including social context (Rotter *et al.* 1972).

Albert Bandura analysed the impact of social learning and imitation, particularly of aggression in children. Imitation of aggression was tested on a sample of thirty-six boys and thirty-six girls with an average age of fifty-two months. The children were divided into three treatment conditions: the control group, aggressive condition, and nonaggressive condition. For the aggressive and nonaggressive conditions, the children were given prior exposure to the behaviour of an adult role model. For this prior exposure, the children and their role models played in separate corners of a room. An inflatable 'Bobo' doll was placed in the adult's corner, and the adult role model behaved in two ways: in the nonaggressive condition, the adult role model ignored the doll; in the aggressive condition, the adult performed a choreographed sequence of different, violent acts towards the Bobo doll (striking with a mallet, kicking, punching the nose, verbal aggression). In the next stage, the behaviour of the children in the presence of the Bobo dolls (with no adult role model present) was analysed. Children in the aggressive condition were significantly more likely to engage in aggressive physical and verbal behaviours than children in the nonaggressive and control conditions; they were imitating the range of violent behaviours exhibited by their adult role models (Bandura *et al.*1961).

Social influences and social pressure

There is considerable evidence in social psychology that social contexts and social pressures have a significant impact on individual decisions. A famous case is that of Kitty Genovese, a New York woman who was stabbed repeatedly whilst, according to some accounts, many neighbours looked on without helping or calling the police. This case is often used to illustrate constraints on social responsibility, including bystander effects, diffusion of responsibility, social passivity and obedience to authority.

Many social psychologists and sociologists focus their analysis on understanding when and why we fail to cooperate with others in such stark ways. Stanley Milgram is famous for a number of experiments assessing social factors including social influences and social interactions. One of these is Milgram's 'six degrees of separation' study of social networks, in which a randomly selected 'starting person' had to find a way to get a letter, via friends and acquaintances they knew personally, to a randomly selected 'target person' whom they did not already know; the degree of separation was the number of people the starting person had to go through to get to the target person; the median was five intermediate persons amongst the (then) US population of approximately 200 million people (Milgram 1967). The experimental design was somewhat questionable, but this study nonetheless established the close connectedness of people and inspired the growth of social network theory in mathematics and economics (see e.g. Watts and Strogatz 1998; Watts 2003).

Another of Milgram's studies analysed social influences, specifically, obedience to authority. Experimental subjects were instructed to punish other subjects' mistakes with electric shocks. In reality, there were no shocks and the punished subjects were actors pretending to feel pain; the punishers were not aware of this, but were nonetheless willing to inflict close-to-fatal shocks on others when instructed to do so by experimenters. Their behaviour was interpreted as reflecting obedience to authority, which the subjects rationalized by putting responsibility on the authority figure as the one really making the decisions (Milgram 1963).

Milgram's shock experiment showed that people are affected by influence of others, particularly authority figures. Haney *et al.* (1973) extended the analysis into a study of roles and situational influences. They constructed a mock prison, with students allocated into roles of prisoner and guard. Haney *et al.* found that the students fell into their fake roles very quickly, with both sets of students exhibiting aggressive behaviour. The student prisoners showed signs of feeling increasingly depersonalized, for example, they began voluntarily identifying themselves by their prisoner number, not their name. The student guards inflicted real humiliations on the student prisoners. The study had to be stopped after just five days for ethical reasons: the students' behaviour was becoming increasingly sadistic and pathological. The inference drawn was that people in harsh environments will react in increasingly antisocial ways because of the context in which they find themselves, not necessarily because of their personal characteristics. Zimbardo later applied this insight in his witness testimony in the Abu Ghraib trials (Haney *et al.* 1973; Zimbardo 2007). Tajfel (1970) also established that identity affects social interactions and contributes to discrimination, an insight that is developed in chapter 5 on sociality and identity.

Solomon Asch (1955, 1956) studied social influence in a more benign context. He devised controlled experiments in which people were asked to make simple judgments about the lengths of lines. The subjects made their decisions in a group context without knowing that all the other experimental participants were collaborating with the experimenter. These collaborators were instructed by the experimenter to make deliberately false statements about the length of the lines. A large minority of the experimental subjects were susceptible to intra-group pressure. They made mistakes in 37 per cent of cases because they were persuaded by deliberately misleading decisions from the experimenter's collaborators, and the effects increased with group size and consensus within the group. It is plausible that situational pressures operate in an economic and financial context too, though perhaps for information reasons as much as social reasons, for example in financial markets, as explored by Robert Shiller (Asch 1955, 1956; Shiller 1995; Bond and Smith 1996).

Social psychological principles can also be seen in psychological analyses of marketing and persuasion. Robert Cialdini (2007) analyses some of the principles of influence and persuasion, including reciprocation, commitment and consistency, social proof, liking, authority, and scarcity. Reciprocation is a strong tendency in human behaviour, reflecting a sense of obligation to others; Cialdini cites a study in which a researcher sent Christmas cards to strangers and received many cards in return without people asking who he was and/or why he had sent them a card. Commitment and consistency reflect the fact that we are committed and consistent in our plans and actions, which can create problems when we are automatically consistent in a way that does not suit our own best interests. Similarly, we may force ourselves into thinking that we are being consistent, even when we are not – which links into issues of cognitive consistency and dissonance, discussed above. Social proof is about doing what others do and believing what others believe. Liking reflects the fact that when we are complimented by someone who is personable and attractive, then we will be inclined to like them, and so inclined to do what they want us to do. We also like people more if they are similar to us. People are more likely to do what we want them to do if we have authority, as shown by the experiments of Milgram. Finally, scarcity affects our perceptions, according to Cialdini. When opportunities are limited and scarce, they seem more enticing. This can explain people's susceptibility to scams and swindles, for example the Bernard Madoff Ponzi scheme scam exposed in 2008 exploited the fact that people were willing to invest in a scheme when they were told it was a rare opportunity available only to a few select, worthy investors.

Conclusion

Behavioural economics is increasingly turning to psychology for insights into economic and financial behaviour, and this chapter has outlined some of the parallels. Psychology encompasses a large number of techniques and approaches, and in this chapter we have focused on the areas of psychology that have touched economics most closely. These commonalities are explored in more detail in the following chapters. Cognitive psychology also provides the background for cognitive neuroscience and neuroeconomics, and these approaches are explored in chapter 3.

This has necessarily been a superficial survey of an enormous literature, and for those who are interested to learn more detail specifically about the psychological approaches set out in this chapter, some suggestions for further reading follow.

Further reading

Bandura A (1976) *Social Learning Theory*, Harlow, UK: Pearson.

Breedlove SM, Rosenzweig MR and Watson NV (2007) *Biological Psychology – An Introduction to Behavioral Cognitive and Clinical Neuroscience* (5th edn), Sunderland, MA: Sinauer Associates.

Butler G and McManus F (2000) *Psychology – A Very Short Introduction*, Oxford: Oxford University Press.

Cialdini RB (2007) *Influence – The Psychology of Persuasion*, New York: Harper Collins.

Myers D, Abell J, Kolstad A and Sani F (2010) *Social Psychology*, New York: McGraw Hill Higher Education.

Pervin LA and Cervone D (2010) *Personality: Theory and Research* (11th edn), New York: John Wiley & Sons.

Saklofske DH and Zeidner M (1995) *Perspectives on Individual Differences: International Handbook of Personality and Intelligence*, New York: Plenum Press.

Stevens A (2001) *Jung – A Very Short Introduction*, Oxford: Oxford University Press.

Storr A (2001) *Freud – A Very Short Introduction*, Oxford: Oxford University Press.

3 Foundations: neuroscience and neuroeconomics

It ought to be generally known that the source of our pleasure, merriment, laughter and amusement, as well as of our grief, pain, anxiety and tears is none other than the brain. It is the organ which enables us to think, see and hear; to distinguish the ugly and the beautiful, the bad and the good, pleasant and unpleasant. Sometimes we judge according to convention and at other times according to expediency. The brain is the source of fears and frights which assail us, often by night, but sometimes even by day, of thoughts that will not come, forgotten duties and eccentricities.

(Hippocratic Corpus, Ancient Library of Alexandria)

Introduction

Neuroscience is the scientific study of the nervous system, its anatomical structure and physiology, and in the past was regarded as just a branch of biology. However, in the past fifty years it has become an interdisciplinary science that includes neurochemistry, medical neurology and surgery, psychology, linguistics, logic, electronics, computer science and neuroimaging. Neuroscientific methods are used in the analysis of cognitive psychology, including studies of perception, memory, comprehension, judgment and action, and neuroeconomics is emerging as a new member of the family of neurosciences.

What are nerves and how do they work?

The human nervous system comprises the central nervous system: the brain and spinal cord within the cranium and vertebral spinal canal, and the peripheral nervous system of nerves that extend throughout the body. Peripheral nerves carry signals from sense receptors in skin, ears and other tissues to the cord and brain. They also deliver motor signals from the brain to muscles and glands throughout the body.

The basic unit of the nervous system is the neuron, or nerve cell, which transmits electrochemical signals as nerve impulses. The human brain is an astonishing neural network comprising billions of neurons. Neurons are discrete cells, but they are linked to one another by synapses, or neural junctions. Nerve impulses travel down neuron fibres as waves of electrical depolarization known as action potentials, but are not able to cross synapses between neurons. Instead, the nerve impulse stimulates release of neurotransmitter into the synapse, which evokes an impulse in an adjacent neuron.

Neurons have four structural features: dendrites, cell bodies, axons and axon terminals. Dendrites are multiple slender fibres that transmit impulses toward the cell body. The cell body is an integration zone, where signals in the form of action potentials from many different

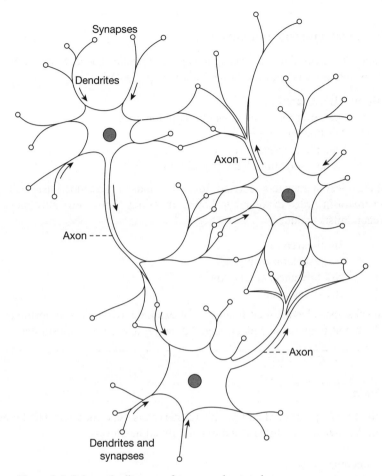

Figure 3.1 Schematic diagram of a neuronal network

dendrites are integrated. Axons are fibres that conduct signals from the cell body to axon terminals adjacent to synapses. When a nerve impulse from one neuron arrives at a terminal, it triggers the release of chemical neurotransmitter into the synapse. This attaches to the receptors in the dendrites of the next neuron and initiates a nerve impulse (action potential) in the postsynaptic neuron. Synapses link axonal fibres to dendrites within a neuronal network, as shown in Figure 3.1.

The neurotransmitters released into synapses can be either an excitatory or inhibitory. If excitatory, they will promote the ongoing nerve impulse; if inhibitory, they will stop it. Different neurotransmitters are associated with different functions, as outlined in Box 3.1. Most synapses in the nervous system release acetylcholine but specific parts of the brain use other neurotransmitters, such as serotonin, dopamine or noradrenaline, which affect emotional behaviours.

To summarize: signals pass through the neural networks of the brain and spinal cord, mediated by a combination of electrochemical impulses modulated by each neuron and by the release of synaptic neurotransmitters.

Box 3.1   Neurotransmitters and hormones

Neurotransmitters are released into the synaptic gap, as explained above. Some of the neurotransmitters and impacts relevant for decision-making include:

Neurotransmitter	Implicated in
dopamine	reward processing, reward prediction error
serotonin	wellbeing, happiness
acetylcholine	attention, arousal, reward
noradrenaline	stress, attention, fight-or-flight impulse

Hormones are chemical messengers secreted from the glands of the endocrine system into the bloodstream in order to modulate bodily functions. Those probably most interesting to economists include:

Hormone	Implicated in
oxytocin	trust, social bonding
testosterone	risk tolerance, aggression
cortisol	stress, fear, pain

Some of these substances have a dual function, for example, oxytocin is a hormone released into the bloodstream from endocrine glands and is also a neurotransmitter.

Anatomy of the brain

The anatomy of the brain, spinal cord and peripheral nerves is very complex. The human nervous system can be divided into three structural and functional levels:

- higher brain or cerebral cortex
- lower brain and brain stem
- spinal cord and peripheral nerves.

The brain is also divided into lobes, including frontal, parietal, occipital and temporal lobes and cerebellum – as illustrated in Figure 3.2.

The cerebral cortex and the subcortical nuclei are of greatest interest for cognitive studies and psychological investigations, including those used by neuroeconomists. It has been estimated that there are approximately 100 billion neurons in a healthy human brain. The brain shows regions mainly of two kinds, comprised of either grey matter or white matter.

Grey matter is composed of numerous nerve cell bodies, interconnecting dendrites, short axons and supporting cells called neuroglia. It is rich in synapses and very active metabolically, requiring a constant supply of glucose and oxygen, so it is well supplied by blood vessels and is highly vascular. The most striking grey matter region of the human brain is the folded outer covering of the cerebral hemispheres, called the cerebral cortex, containing six layers of cells and measuring 2–5 mm in thickness.

A prominent cerebral cortex is evolutionarily a feature of mammal brains. If a human cortex were unfolded, it would cover an area of a quarter of a metre. Packing this into the

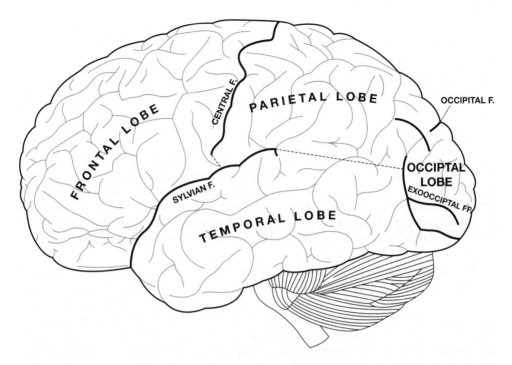

Figure 3.2 Lobes of the brain (Source: *Gray's Anatomy of the Human Body,* 20th US edn, originally published in 1918)

cranium produces folds, known as convolutions or gyri, with fissures or sulci between them. The two largest cortical fissures on each side are between the temporal and parietal lobes of the cerebrum – the Sylvian fissures; and between the frontal and parietal lobes – the fissures of Rolando. These are important because the motor areas lie in front and sensory areas behind these fissures. The prefrontal lobes are those portions of the frontal lobes that lie in front of the motor areas.

Grey matter is also present in subcortical areas of the brain, including the basal ganglia, nuclei in the brain stem, hind brain, and it extends into the spinal cord. The limbic system of nerve tracts and nuclei lies closely adjacent to the cortex, and includes basal nuclei and tracts connecting with the hypothalamus and the amygdala.

White matter is composed mainly of myelinated long axons that connect different regions of the brain and spinal cord. These long axons are coated with a whitish myelin sheath, which insulates the axon from surrounding neurons and improves transmission of nerve impulses (electrical action potentials). White matter is much less metabolically active than grey matter and so is less vascular.

Given the complex anatomical structures in the human brain, some conventions have emerged to enable identification of specific areas. Korbinian Brodmann devised maps of the cerebral cortex, and key neural structures are now often categorized using Brodmann's areas, some of which are noted below. Often a neuroscientist will be interested in identifying specific regions of interest, for example in functional magnetic resonance imaging (fMRI) studies as explained below.

Brain areas and functions

Evolutionary biologists focus on the division of brain regions according to evolutionary development. In these approaches, the brain is roughly divided into three main areas – the triune division into reptilian, mammalian and hominid parts. The triune anatomical division can be loosely associated with some broad functions: the reptilian parts of the brain are often associated with basic instincts and impulses; the mammalian parts with basic perception and social interaction; and the hominid part with higher cognitive function (Camerer *et al.* 2005).

As noted above, a prominent cerebral cortex is a feature of mammalian brains: the significant enlargement of the cerebral cortex is most developed in hominid brains, and the prefrontal cortex is often associated with deliberative thinking in neuroeconomic studies. Reflecting the triune division, some neuroeconomic insights about brain structure reflect evolutionary themes, for example, some neuroeconomists postulate that violations of standard utility theory have been replicated with animals, perhaps because behaviour is propelled by older, less evolved circuitry rather than more highly evolved cognitive structures.

A list of some key brain areas and functions is set out in Box 3.2.

The prefrontal cortex is associated with planning and cognition; the parietal lobe with motor action; the occipital lobe with visual processing; and the temporal lobe with memory/recognition/emotion. There is also evidence that areas in the prefrontal cortex are associated with social cognition, for example, Brodmann area 10 in the prefrontal cortex is associated with 'mind-reading' and empathy. Limbic structures are associated with emotional behaviour, subconscious motivations and sensations of punishment or pleasure. A number of neuroeconomic studies, particularly studies exploring interactions between cognition and emotion, have identified a role for limbic and connecting structures, including the amygdala, insula, nucleus accumbens (which forms the main part of the ventral striatum) and the

---

Box 3.2   Brain areas and functions

Area	Function
amygdala	negative emotions, e.g. fear
anterior cingulate cortex	executive function, conflict resolution
caudate nucleus/putamen, in the striatum	reward processing
cerebellum	attention and timing, pleasure, fear
insula	hunger, disgust, social snubs
hippocampus	memory and learning
nucleus accumbens	pleasure and reward, addiction
occipital cortex	visual processing
parietal cortex	motor action, mathematical reasoning
prefrontal cortex	planning, cognition
prefrontal cortex – Brodmann area 10	theory of mind, mind-reading
temporal cortex	memory, recognition, emotion

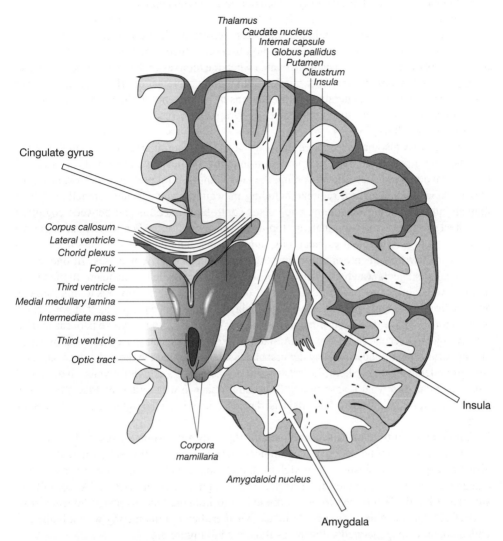

Thalamus
Caudate nucleus
Internal capsule
Globus pallidus
Putamen
Claustrum
Insula

Cingulate gyrus

Corpus callosum
Lateral ventricle
Chorid plexus
Fornix
Third ventricle
Medial medullary lamina
Intermediate mass
Third ventricle
Optic tract

Insula

Corpora
mamillaria

Amygdaloid nucleus

Amygdala

Figure 3.3 Neuroanatomical structures (Source: *Gray's Anatomy of the Human Body*, 20th US edn, originally published in 1918)

anterior cingulate cortex. The amygdala is implicated in the processing of fear and the insula with pain, disgust, and also social snubs, inequality and unfairness; the anterior cingulate performs executive functions and resolves conflicts. Some of these neuroanatomical structures are identified in Figure 3.3.

Modularity

Some neuroscientists focus on modularity in the brain – certain functions are associated with specific anatomical areas, though many of these functions will interact and overlap. The visual system is, perhaps surprisingly, particularly important in decision-making because it is integral to accumulating and processing information and stimulating the motor system to make 'winner-takes-all' binary choices. Areas associated with language, religion and humour have been identified (Camerer *et al.* 2005). Another area of potential interest to economists is the mirror system and 'mentalizing' modules, activated when observing other persons, which recreates similar internal states in the observer. Mirror neuron systems in the pre-motor cortex of monkeys are usually activated when the monkey makes a movement, but also when the monkey observes another monkey making the same action. If mirror neurons are responding to internally generated representations of actions, not to the actions themselves, then potentially they are also implicated in sympathetic responses to social situations (Rizzolatti *et al.* 2002).

Functions may also be coordinated. In many cases a number of areas will be implicated in specific neural processes, for example, brain-imaging studies have identified a distributed network involved in arithmetic reasoning: the lateral and ventral prefrontal cortex, posterior parietal lobe and subcortical regions including the caudate nucleus and cerebellum. There may be interactions between automatic versus controlled functions and between cognition and affect. Cognition may dominate in 'top-down sense-making', when we use our cognitive powers to fit the world to our expectations, impose order, imagine patterns, miss unexpected changes, overwrite old information, and this can explain hindsight biases. In one study, experimental subjects watched a video of basketball passes made by one team. In the video, a gorilla walks on for forty seconds. One half of the subjects were oblivious to this (Simons and Chabris 1999, cited in Camerer *et al.* 2004a). O'Shea (2005) explains that we engage unconsciously in top-down sense-making using our experience to recognize patterns that, in strictly objective terms, should be unfamiliar. For example, we can see a paragraph in which all the words are jumbled, with only the first and last letter retained in the right place, and still we can understand it. O'Shea illustrates with an example: 'I cdnulot blveiee that I cluod aulaclty uesdnatnrd what I was rdgnieg. It deosn't mttaer in what order the ltteers in a word aer, the only iprmoatnt thing is that ethe frist dan lasat ltteer be in the righit pclae . . .' (O'Shea 2005, p. 7).

This human ability to make sense of patterns that only approximately resemble a familiar item is used in computer security – computers recognize words precisely, whereas human visual perception is sophisticated enough to smooth out irregularities, so we are able to rec-ognize patterns even when they are distorted. This insight is used in CAPTCHA (completely automated public Turing test to tell computers and humans apart) security mechanisms. CAPTCHA tools enable computers to detect whether they are interacting with a human or with automatically generated software, as illustrated in Figure 3.4.

Neuroscientific data and techniques

Economic decisions and choices can be analysed using a range of neuroscientific techniques including psychopathology, neuroimaging and brain stimulation, physiological measurement and genetic studies, as explored below.

Figure 3.4 CAPTCHA images

Psychopathology studies

Psychopathology, the study of psychiatric disorders and conditions, can be used to make inferences about how the absence of normal function is related to particular neural systems and responses. The sort of abnormalities studied include brain lesion patient studies; mania, which leads to more unconventional behaviour if people are ignoring social signals; eating disorders; Parkinson's disease and damage of dopamine neurons and reward structures; Alzheimer's, associated with loss of memory function; autism, associated with constraints on empathy, amongst others. Insights about depressive illness have also been linked by economists to stock market performance, for example Kamstra *et al.*'s (2003) study of the links between stock market performance, seasonal affective disorder and weather patterns.

Lesion patient studies analyse the behaviour of patients with lesions on particular specific brain structures in order to make some inferences about the functions of those areas. If a lesion in a specific area impairs decision-making in particular contexts, then it is inferred that this area is implicated.

The most famous lesion patient study was of Phineas Gage, a railroad manager who suffered a nonfatal accident in 1848, when an iron rod was pushed through his brain. Dr John M Harlow's (1868) drawing of the injury, depicted in Figure 3.5, shows an iron rod passing above the left eye and up through the top of the head, probably damaging the frontal lobe on both sides.

Whilst Phineas Gage initially seemed to be largely unaffected by his accident and recovered relatively quickly, people soon noticed significant changes in his behaviour. Previously he had been responsible, hard-working and sensible. After the accident he became impulsive and unreliable, and he soon lost his job. His changed behaviour has been attributed to the damage

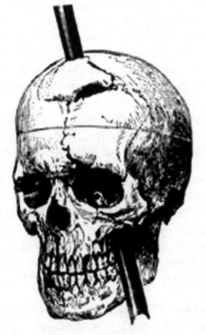

Figure 3.5 Phineas Gage's injury (Source: Harlow 1868)

caused to his frontal lobes, areas associated with cognitive processing (Harlow 1868; Ratiu *et al.* 2004).

Lesion patient studies are particularly important to neuroeconomics because early studies by neuroscientists including Antonio Damasio established a link between brain damage and impaired financial decision-making function. He used these insights to develop the somatic marker hypothesis, asserting that bodily signals guide action – explored in more detail in chapter 8. Somatic markers are links between stimuli and somatic (in the body) emotional responses. Emotions become associated with past events, and in new situations these learned emotional responses will guide behaviour. Antonio Damasio and colleagues have studied a range of lesions, including lesions similar to Phineas Gage's (Damasio *et al.* 1996). For example, Adolphs *et al* 's (1995) study of lesion patients revealed that amygdala lesions were associated with impairments of emotional processing, particularly fear processing. More recently, the amygdala is an area studied by neuroeconomists interested in negative emotional processing in risky situations, for example fear in financial markets, as explored in chapter 11.

Neurometrics

Many neuroeconomic studies use neuroscientific techniques to map and measure brain function. Shibasaki (2008) analyses a range of neuroscientific tools used to capture brain activity in conscious subjects, either at rest or when undertaking cognitive tasks. Some, for example electroencephalography, are more than sixty years old. In the past ten years, highly sensitive electronic, computer and imaging techniques have improved in accuracy, making noninvasive functional assessments of conscious brains an exciting and expanding area of neuroscience. These techniques can be divided into two groups, reflecting different physical aspects of the functioning brain – electrophysiological and haemodynamic.

Electrophysiological methods draw on the fact that neurons transmit nerve impulses as electrochemical action potentials. Modern electroencephalography (EEG) can detect cerebral electrical activity (action potentials) as impulses pass to different brain regions. It can do so with great accuracy and with a temporal resolution of milliseconds. Sets of EEG scalp electrodes are easy to apply, subjects are comfortable and the equipment is relatively cheap. However, spatial resolution is poor so it can be difficult to map electrical activity to brain regions precisely.

Magnetoencephalography (MEG) is not dissimilar to EEG but requires a magnetically neutral environment, which can be difficult in an electronics laboratory. More recently it has become possible to stimulate brain areas noninvasively using transcranial magnetic stimulation (TMS).

Haemodynamic techniques capture blood flows. The brain takes 15 per cent of the blood supplied from the heart to the whole body in basal conditions. It uses a disproportionately large amount of energy, compared with other organs, to support neuronal and synaptic activity, especially in grey matter areas such as the cortex and basal ganglia. Therefore brain activity requires a constant supply of glucose and oxygen to maintain its metabolism. This requires an efficient system of arteries, capillaries and veins to provide blood at constant pressure and temperature. Reduced cerebral blood flow, low blood oxygen or glucose, and hypothermia quickly lead to loss of consciousness.

Functional brain-imaging techniques map either blood flow, glucose and/or oxygen usage in different brain regions as experimental subjects are performing specific tasks. The maps can be superimposed on anatomical brain scans to give spatial resolution of active areas.

For example, positron emission tomography (PET) depends on the emission of characteristic positron gamma rays from radioactive tracers within the brain. Special gamma cameras are needed to detect these gamma rays and radioactive material has to be injected intravenously during the scan. Positron-emitting water (15-oxygen H_2O) can be used to map cerebral blood flow, and a positron-emitting glucose analogue (18-fluorine deoxyglucose) can map areas of markedly increased brain metabolism. PET has the advantage that it can enable quantitative measurements of activity in specific regions; however, whilst it has good spatial resolution, its temporal resolution is poor because of the rapid decay of radioactivity.

Newer PET compounds, which bind to neurotransmitter receptors, can demonstrate the distribution of serotonin or dopamine in the brain. Though valuable for specific uses, PET is time-consuming, expensive, and requires close access to a cyclotron to produce the short-lived positron-radioactive tracers. Its use for cognitive studies is therefore limited (Shibasaki 2008).

Functional magnetic resonance imaging (fMRI) is another technique designed to capture brain activity whilst subjects are engaged in specific tasks. It has developed dramatically over the past ten years. It depends upon the physical principle that oxygenated haemoglobin in red blood coming from the lungs is magnetically different from deoxyhaemoglobin in blue blood, the oxygen from which has been used up. The change in signal from red to blue blood demonstrates the parts of the brain that are metabolically active and receiving larger amounts of blood oxygen. Functional MR images of the brain are therefore blood oxygen level-dependent (BOLD). Functional images can be mapped easily onto standard anatomical images of the brain, which can be made in any plane, so that it is easy to identify activity in small brain regions such as the amygdala and hypothalamus, as well as localized cortical areas. Functional MRI scans need high-field magnets, which are expensive, claustrophobic and noisy, so it is initially difficult for the subject to perform cognitive tasks. Also, it can be difficult to interpret the data because a BOLD signal response may be capturing an inhibitory response not an excitatory response. However, fMRI is safe and does not use X-rays or radioactive tracers, so scans can be repeated.

In brain-imaging studies, information is usually communicated visually in the form of a brain 'map' identifying significant areas based on an average structural image from all subjects in a sample. An example of an fMRI scan is shown in Figure 3.6. This scan captures

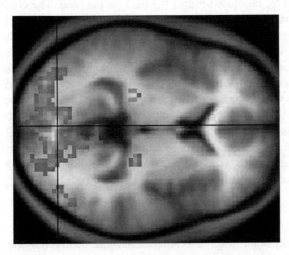

Figure 3.6 An fMRI scan (source: Washington Irving on *Wikipedia*, copyright disclaimed, http://en.wikipedia.org/wiki/File:FMRI.jpg)

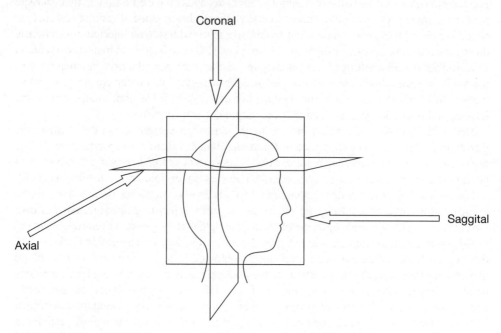

Figure 3.7 Planes of the brain

fMRI differential activation in the visual cortex in response to complex moving visual stimulus versus a rest condition (viewing a black screen).

Brain images are often described in terms of the specific plane or perspective of the scan, as illustrated in Figure 3.7.

The planes are named using visual associations. The sagittal plane captures the direction of an arrow flying into the face (from *sagitta*, the Latin for arrow) and is the vertical plane through, or approximately parallel to, the nose towards the back of the head. The coronal (= crown) plane slices vertically through the crown of the head from the top of the skull towards the spine and perpendicular to the tip of the nose. The horizontal or axial (= axe) plane is from the front to the back of the head, as if the top of the head has been cut off with an axe.

Overall, despite their sophistication, brain-imaging techniques are not infallible. Some critics observe that just because an area of the brain is picked up within a scanner, that does not mean it is the primary area responsible for functioning. There may be other areas, systems and processes involved, and it can be difficult to attribute causality precisely using some neuroscientiic techniques. Choosing which neurometric techniques to use will depend on the questions to be answered and the availability of equipment. It seems likely that for cognitive psychological studies, such as those used in neuroeconomics, a combination of EEG or MEG studies mapped onto fMRI scans will become the protocol of choice.

Brain stimulation

It is difficult to establish causality with brain-imaging techniques, but other neurophysiological techniques, including brain stimulation, are less susceptible to this limitation. Brain areas can also be stimulated directly in a number of ways. Transcranial magnetic stimulation (TMS) uses electromagnetic induction temporarily to activate specific areas of the brain, and has been used in neuroeconomics to study empathy and trust (e.g. Baumgartner *et al.* 2011). The brain can also be studied directly using electrical brain stimulation (EBS) – the direct stimulation of neurons using electrodes. EBS studies show that rats and drug addicts will work hard for EBS and will trade other rewards for EBS (Camerer *et al.* 2005).

Physiological techniques

Psychophysiological measurement includes measurements of involuntary bodily responses including eye movements or 'saccades', heart rate, blood pressure, galvanic skin response, sweating response, pupil dilation and facial musculature. Neurophysiology can also be used to inform the use of drugs: for example, alcohol affects specific neurotransmitter systems associated with stress and reward. Impacts of administering or measuring hormones can also reveal some of the neural correlates of decision-making, as identified by Zak and colleagues in their studies of oxytocin (chapters 5 and 8) and by Coates and Herbert in their studies of testosterone and financial risk-taking (chapter 11).

Genetic analysis

Economists are increasingly interested in the genetic correlates of behaviour. With the human genome project, our knowledge of genes and their make-up has grown rapidly. Before then, the main method for testing genetic influences was twin studies, which exploited the fact that some twins are identical or monozygotic (twins from the same egg and sharing the same DNA) and others are nonidentical or dizygotic (from different eggs). When identical twins are separated at birth, it is possible to make inferences about the influence of genes versus environment according to differences later in life. There are limitations with twin studies, however, and the perennial question of whether to attribute these differences to nature or nuture remains unresolved.

With the human genome project, it became possible to investigate the genetic correlates of behaviour in much more depth, and to link phenotypes and polymorphisms, including individual characteristics such as personality traits and risk preferences, with a person's genotype or genetic make-up. Another way to correlate behaviour with genetic information is via gene 'heat maps', which capture the level of gene expression. Genotypes determine the level of gene expression and give rise to phenotypes depending on the level of gene expression; gene heat maps pick up the level of expression of genes, for example by linking features of DNA with observed behaviour such as risk-taking. Studies have also been done linking genotypes to neural activations. Haynes (2011) found that variability in risk preferences was associated with particular genotypes, which in turn are associated with differences in amygdala activation.

Neuroeconomics

What is neuroeconomics?

Neuroeconomics is about applying tools and approaches from cognitive neuroscience to analyse economic decision-making. As a discipline, it has emerged from recognition by behavioural economists, from Kahneman and Tversky onwards, that cognition and perception amongst real people do not fit the strict model of rational behaviour, especially when perception does not match an objective reality. The problem can be to establish an objective scientific basis for cognition and perception, and neuroeconomics offers a solution. Whilst behavioural economics is distinct and perhaps less controversial than the growing field of neuroeconomics, neuroeconomics is in essence a development of behavioural economics, but one that focuses (largely) on insights and techniques from positivist, objective analyses of neuroanatomy and neurophysiology. Some would argue that the approach is too reductionist – human behaviour is more complex than can be captured just by studying brain function; others argue that neuroeconomics isn't really economics, as explored in the controversies section below.

Camerer *et al.* (2004a, 2005) give some good early surveys of the essential ideas, tools and techniques. Neuroeconomics applies the tools, insights and findings from neuroscience and biological psychology to the analysis of economic decision-making. It is an eclectic approach combining and extending methods from behavioural and experimental economics with those from neuroscience and psychology, including experimental, evolutionary, cognitive, ecological and social psychology.

Neuroeconomic data

Camerer, Loewenstein and Prelec have observed that standard economics limits a deep understanding of behaviour and treats the brain as a 'black box'. One reason for this is the problems with objective measurement of thoughts and feelings: neuroeconomics offers an answer to the economist William Stanley Jevons' scepticism about capturing feelings. Neuroeconomics offers methods of measurement – blunt ones, admittedly, at this stage, but as techniques increase in sophistication, finer measurement will become easier (Camerer *et al.* 2005; Camerer 2007). Rustichini (2005b) agrees that neuroeconomics provides new data and methods to test useful predictions about various aspects of economic behaviour, including incentives, preferences and feasibility constraints, and to explain deviations from the axiomatic theory of subjective expected utility.

Neuroscience offers alternative *objective* methods of measurement. Money as a measure has limitations: it has its own utility, and various neuroscientific studies have shown that it is directly rewarding itself, which raises the question of how to separate the utility of money from the utility of the things that money buys. Studying neural responses can illuminate questions of value that may be less prone to some of the contradictions implicit in using monetary measures of value. Neuroscientific measurement is also more direct and therefore more reliable than self-report (Camerer *et al.* 2005). Neuroeconomics can identify empirical links between games and choices, and can provide more insight than revealed preference theory provides.

Neuroscientific techniques can add precision because knowing the neural mechanisms helps to explain the behaviour. The fact that raising oxytocin 'exogenously' increases trustworthy behaviour enhances our understanding of how hormones affect moods and behaviour. The recognition in neuroscience that choices are not predetermined, and that biological states affect choices, deepens our understanding of choices, especially as choices do not necessarily reflect preference; for example, we would not usually choose to fall asleep at the wheel whilst driving.

Neuroscience can also deepen our understanding by identifying when the same brain circuitry is involved in apparently distinct decisions. If there is a common neural correlate, then this may reflect that similar systems are engaged. For example, the insula is activated when people feel they have been treated unfairly in experimental games. It is also activated with ambiguous gambles and with poor strategic thinking. Some common mechanism may be unifying apparently distinct behaviours.

Whilst the prospects for neuroeconomics and its tools may look promising, it is nonetheless important to recognize the limitations. The field is young. Tools are new, relatively crude and expensive. Just because we can measure neural activations, that does not necessarily imply we can measure thoughts and feelings directly (Huang 2005).

Neuroeconomic models and theories

Whilst neuroscientific tools offer neuroeconomists new measurement methods, neuroeconomics offers more than a toolkit. It also offers theoretical insights to understand the links between brain and economic behaviour. Neuroeconomists emphasize in particular the importance of consilience and of multiple interacting systems.

Consilience

Consilience represents the fact that neuroeconomics is an eclectic approach, bringing together economics, evolutionary psychology, cognitive psychology, behavioural psychology/ecology and social psychology to form a general theory of human behaviour, possibly allowing the development of a unified approach. Glimcher and Rustichini (2004) and Glimcher (2011) envisage neuroeconomics as a unifying mathematical theory. Economics brings the analytical structure of decision theory, psychology brings the deeper understanding of cognition and emotion, and neurobiology the study of mechanism. Similarly, Camerer *et al.* (2004a, 2005) suggest that neuroeconomics has the power to unite apparently disparate subjects: 'Anthropologists emphasise acculturation. Psychologists emphasise cognition and contexts. Sociologists emphasise social norms and constraints. [Most] Economists emphasise rationality. Neuroscience has the power to unify them all . . .' (Camerer *et al.* 2004b, pp. 572–3).

Glimcher *et al.* (2005) focus on understanding how the neural architecture generates decisions. Just as neuroscience can illuminate economic questions, economics gives ideas and theories for neuroscience: for example, the insights from microeconomics and game theory about models of strategic thinking, mixed strategy equilibrium and subjective expected utility theory. Glimcher *et al.* (2005) conclude that there is a two-way exchange filling important gaps: economists have overly simplistic views of brain function; neuroscientists have underestimated the complexity of human decision-making. Unifying economics and neuroscience may provide better answers if the disciplines can engage in effective dialogue.

Multiple systems approaches

Neuroscience also offers alternative ways of modelling behaviour that are less dependent on the strict, monolithic versions of rationality seen in standard mainstream approaches. Glimcher uses a metaphor of a clockwork digesting duck, constructed by eighteenth-century French inventor Jacques de Vaucanson. Glimcher (2003) observes that mainstream economics often assumes that we process information as if we are mathematical machines, as if we were Vaucanson's clockwork duck. In reality, human cognition is more complex and reflects an interaction of various systems.

Cognitive neuroscientists often take a multiple-systems approach, focusing on the insight that the brain is composed of different interacting systems, for example, automatic and controlled systems interact. Neuroscience is not dependent on a simple distinction between rational and irrational. Some neuroeconomic analyses take Plato's metaphor from classical philosophy: behaviour is like a chariot pulled by two horses of appetite and spirit, guided by the 'charioteer' of reason (Glimcher 2003). Neuroeconomics abandons the strict dichotomy between the rational and the irrational: for example, neuroscientists recognize the important role played by emotions in guiding decisions, an issue explored in the context of Damasio's somatic marker hypothesis in chapter 8 (Damasio 1994/2006). Overall, neuroeconomics presents a model of the interconnected mind in which choices are not strictly dichotomous and the world is not understood in terms of black and white. Rather there are shades of grey as different functions and areas interact and interconnect. The brain is not just the sum of its parts.

Concepts from neuroscience can be used to capture these interacting neural systems and to reconcile emotional versus cognitive and controlled versus automatic processes (Camerer 2007; Camerer *et al.* 2004a, 2005; Cohen 2005):

> The neuroeconomic theory of individual replaces the (perennially useful) fiction of a utility maximizing individual which has a single goal, with a more detailed account of how components of the individual – brain regions, cognitive control, and neural circuits – interact and communicate to determine individual behaviour.
>
> (Camerer 2007, p. 28)

Evolutionary themes emerge when analysing how the instinctive affective system interacts with the deliberative cognitive system. Human behaviour is often a compromise between highly evolved animal emotions and instincts, and more recently evolved human deliberation and foresight (Loewenstein 1996). The distinctions in economics between cognitive versus emotional, and automatic versus controlled systems, reflect Kahneman's distinction of intuitive system 1 processes and reasoning system 2 processes (Kahneman 2003, 2011), as explained in more detail in chapter 8. Automatic functions are quicker and therefore more neurologically efficient. Controlled functions are slower, but more deliberative and careful. On a basic level, there will be primacy of affect 'affect gets there first' because affective systems are designed to ensure survival and therefore evolve in response to selection pressures. However, in the battle between affect and cognition, the winner takes all – and will depend on the context.

This insight can be important to understanding choices, because emotions and visceral factors will play varying roles depending on the level of emotional intensity. At low levels of emotional intensity, affect is advisory. At medium levels, conscious conflict is resolved via effort (e.g. self-control). At high levels, affect is overpowering. Dual-systems approaches have been developed to reflect emotional intensity in economic decision-making, for example, Bernheim and Rangel's models of 'hot' versus 'cold' systems in addiction, and Brocas and Carillo's (2008) conception of the brain as a dual system prone to conflicts in the face of asymmetric information, impatience and misaligned incentives, explored in more detail in chapters 9 and 10.

Cognition dominates effortful cognition, and studies show that emotional reactions can be blocked by deliberative thinking. Students will appreciate the posters on their walls less if they've had to think too carefully about why they like them; emotions will affect memory and dominate cognitive processes in wishful thinking (Wilson and Schooler, 1991; Camerer *et al.* 2004a, 2005; Urry *et al.* 2006). Also, cognition often dominates perception in top-down sense-making. We fit the world into our expectations of it, sometimes imagining order where there is none and missing unexpected changes (Camerer *et al.* 2005).

There will also be coordination of affect and cognition reflecting the interaction of different neural areas in economic decision-making. Lesions to the anterior cingulate cortex are associated with dampened emotional responses, for example in card gambles, perhaps because the coordination of affective and cognitive processes has been disconnected (Bechara *et al.* 1997). Other evidence that emotional and cognitive systems interact is seen in social decision-making. When people feel they have been treated unfairly, this creates conflicts between cognition and emotion, as explored in chapter 8. Neural tussles have also been observed in brain-imaging studies of intertemporal decision-making, as explored in chapter 9.

Controversies in behavioural economics and neuroeconomics

Interdisciplinary approaches bringing together psychology, neuroscience and economics are controversial, and whilst neuroeconomics as a discipline is growing rapidly, it has confronted significant scepticism, particularly initially. Perhaps this reflects the fact that economists used to working with abstract, parsimonious mathematical models regard neuroeconomics as rather too alien and quirky in its approach. Some economists working within a standard approach argue that embedding a deeper understanding of what underlies observable choices and decisions is an anathema. For them, the focus should be on objectively measurable data, and for many mainstream economists this is observed choice.

This point is debatable, however, especially as the increasing sophistication of neuroscientific techniques means that simple choices are no longer the only phenomena that can be measured objectively. There is an enormous, highly regarded neuroscientific literature on decision-making. Neuroeconomists are just drawing parallels between the neural responses seen whilst people are making *economic* choices and established neuroscientific evidence about what people are doing when making other sorts of choices. Neuroscientists have established that rewards such as food, addictive substances, etc. activate dopamine pathways, and so it is not such a leap to infer that money, as a reward, is activating similar pathways, which allows us (carefully) to consider similar inferences about making money to those a neuroscientist might make about eating food. At their best, models and data-collection techniques from neuroscience allow us rigorously and scientifically to test hypotheses about the cognitive and/or emotional decision-making systems implicated in economic decision-making.

Gul and Pesendorfer (2008) make a case for 'mindless economics', justifying approaches that treat the brain as a black box and concentrate just on observed choices. They criticize (their perception of) neuroeconomics' focus on physiology and psychology, and neglect of utility and choice. Ironically, this seems essentially to be a *normative* critique from a *positivist* perspective. There *are* neuroeconomists, and an increasing number of them. Are Gul and Pesendorfer saying that there *shouldn't* be? Camerer (2008) responds by making a case for 'mindful economics', justifying the role of nonchoice data in developing analytical models of choice. He illustrates with a range of examples and argues that boundaries between disciplines do not need to be as sharp as Gul and Pesendorfer suggest.

Glimcher (2011) observes that neuroscience and economics appear to have little in common because they focus on different 'primitives': the primitives in neuroscience are brain activations, neurons and synapses; primitives in economics include choice, preference and utility. Links between them can be forged, however, because (potentially at least) there are common elements, for example, neural activations in the medial prefrontal cortex can link choice to expected utility. Neuroeconomists are starting to make some inroads with approaches that combine the primitives from the difference disciplines, for example, Fehr and Rangel's (2011) analyses of the links between choice, experienced utility and neural responses. There is significant added value to be found in combining theoretical and empirical insights from neuroscience, psychology and economics.

Caplin and Dean (2008b) also defend neureconomics against Gul and Pesendorfer's critique, which they interpret as having two elements: first, the assertion that economic models are designed only to illuminate choice, and so data that are not about choices are not a good test of economic models; second, the assertion that economists are interested in choice, and so won't be interested in models that cannot be differentiated on the basis of choice data.

Caplin and Dean argue against this conception of neuroeconomics via a couple of illustrations. First, in models of information search, any set of choice data can be reconciled using a simple model of information search. Standard models cannot differentially capture observed choices. On the other hand, a behavioural model incorporating inconsistencies and biases from behavioural economics can discriminate between different choices. Second, Schultz *et al.*'s (1997) analysis of reward-prediction error can be used to construct an objective neuroeconomic model of choice. Dopamine neurons encode reward, which can be linked to utility and thus to a model of choice. Also, models of reward-prediction error link to ideas about adaptive expectations in economics and can be used as a building block in learning theory, as explored in more detail in chapter 4.

Neuroeconomic models of reward-prediction error from Schultz onwards provide the basis for testable predictions about choice. Also, many economists from a range of perspectives would probably agree that an economist should not be forced to focus exclusively on observed choices, especially as neuroscientific techniques are developing to enable objective measurement of the physiological processes propelling decision-making. If economics is to be useful, understanding that the same choices may be propelled by different factors is important. Adjusting an example from Romer (2000) and Camerer *et al.* (2005) – if I offer someone a peanut and they choose not to take one, it is important that I know whether their choice merely reflects a dislike of peanuts, versus the knowledge that it will induce a life-threatening allergic reaction. The difference is important.

Unifying scientific disciplines does have a better historical pedigree than Gul and Pesendorfer admit. Other disciplines also have more in common than their separation into silos might imply. Glimcher (2011) notes the development of consilience between chemistry and biology in the early twentieth century. Also, whilst there has always been an objective link between our physiology and the physics of the material world around us, historically physicists and medical physicians operated independently until the development of medical technologies, particularly imaging technologies, enabled the integration of physics and medicine (Baddeley 2008). Similarly, as the techniques for monitoring our neural responses improve, we will be able to link economic decision-making with brain function, and that will allow us properly to break down the barriers between economics and neuroscience.

What's next?

In understanding the systems affecting economic and financial decision-making, an interdisciplinary approach is needed that incorporates ideas from a range of disciplines, including psychology, sociology, neuroscience and neuroeconomics. In this and the preceding chapter, we have briefly introduced some of the key ideas from the enormous literature on psychology, neuroscience and neuroeconomics to form a basic foundation for the exploration of the behavioural topics covered in the subsequent chapters.

This chapter and the last cover just a small portion of some of the major themes in psychology and neuroscience, focusing in particular on insights that are relevant to later chapters. There is a lot more to be explored, and some suggestions for further reading are outlined below.

The main lessons to be taken from these chapters is that economic decisions reflect an interaction of cognitive and emotional factors. Psychology and neuroscience have a lot to offer in extending economists' understanding of these influences. For the subsequent chapters, analysis of cognitive factors rests relatively easy with standard mainstream approaches to learning and (some analyses of) social decision-making. So we will abstract from cognitive limitations and emotional factors in the first couple of chapters that follow, and focus on developing the standard models to incorporate behavioural factors in a relatively standard way, for example by allowing learning and introducing extra elements into standard utility functions. Then we will move on to explore when and how decisions are affected by cognitive limits/distortions and/or emotional and affective influences.

Further reading

Breedlove SM, Rosenzweig MR and Watson NV (2007) *Biological Psychology – An Introduction to Behavioral Cognitive and Clinical Neuroscience* (5th edn), Sunderland, MA: Sinauer Associates.

Camerer CF, Loewenstein G and Prelec D (2004) 'Neuroeconomics: why economics needs brains', *Scandinavian Journal of Economics*, 106(3), 555–79.

Camerer CF, Loewenstein G and Prelec D (2005) 'Neuroeconomics: how neuroscience can inform economics', *Journal of Economic Literature*, 43(1), 9–64.

Frank L (2011) *The Neurotourist – Postcards from the Edge of Brain Science*, Oxford: One World.

Glimcher PW (2011) *Foundations of Neuroeconomic Analysis*, New York: Oxford University Press.

Glimcher PW, Fehr E, Camerer C, Rangel A and Poldrack RA (eds) (2008) *Neuroeconomics – Decision Making and the Brain*, San Diego, CA: Academic Press.

Hanaway J and Gado MH (2003) *The Brain Atlas – A Visual Guide to the Human Central Nervous System* (2nd edn), Hoboken, NJ: John Wiley & Sons.

Huettel SA (2009) *Functional Magnetic Resonance Imaging* (2nd edn), Sunderland, MA: Sinauer Associates.

O'Shea M (2005) *The Brain – A Very Short Introduction*, New York: Oxford University Press.

Poltiser P (2008) *Neuroeconomics – A Guide to the New Science of Making Choices*, Oxford: Oxford University Press.

Ward J (2006) *The Student's Guide to Cognitive Neuroscience*, Hove/New York: Taylor & Francis.

Part 2

Behavioural microeconomic principles

4　Learning

Introduction

This chapter explores models of learning from behavioural economics. 'To learn' is defined in the *Concise Oxford English Dictionary* as 'to gain knowledge of or skill in by study, experience or being taught'. So learning is about updating knowledge but, as Camerer (2003b) observes, economic theory sometimes neglects questions of learning. If knowledge is perfect and people are strictly rational, then the correct choice can be identified from the start, and people will jump from one equilibrium to the next only when information changes.

More recently, economic models have analysed equilibrium in the presence of imperfect or asymmetric information, but Camerer (2003b) argues that these models tend to focus on limit properties; if it takes a long time to reach the limiting behaviour, predicting the *path* of equilibration is potentially a lot more useful and interesting. In understanding how equilibrium is reached, experimental evidence is often more practically useful than theory, but collecting reliable experimental evidence can also be problematic.

Camerer and Weigelt (1988) emphasize the importance of learning in experimental games, for example in trust games, public goods games and beauty contests. Camerer (2003b) also outlines some characteristics of a good learning theory: it should be parsimonious, it should have predictive power and coherence, but at the same time it should reveal new insights. Camerer (2003b) describes learning models in the context of quantitative time-dependent functions of strategies known as *attractions*, which are like a stock of learning that builds up over time as new information comes along. Different learning models are characterized according to the learning rules that update these attractions, as illustrated below in the context of some learning theories.

Learning theories can be grouped into a few broad categories: evolutionary approaches, reinforcement versus belief learning (BL) models, including hybrids of these, for example, Camerer and Ho's (1999) experience-weighted attraction (EWA) model. Other learning models include anticipatory learning models, which assume sophistication, imitative learning, learning direction theory and rule-based learning. The most influential of these approaches are outlined below. In addition, there are social learning models, which have some parallels in sociology and social psychology. These models are also explored in the context of the literature from psychology and sociology in chapter 5.

Belief learning

In BL models, the attractions are built by attaching probabilities to each strategy combination from other players, giving a time-dependent belief function in which beliefs about others' actions are updated as history unfolds. Players track the relative frequency of other players' strategies, and these relative frequencies generate beliefs about other players' actions in the next period. This information is used to calculate expected payoffs given these beliefs.

Variants of BL models emerge depending on the weights attached to past actions. Brown (1951) develops a fictitious play (FP) model incorporating a more 'appealing' assumption that players respond to average of the observed history with previous observations counted and weighted equally. In Cournot models, following Cournot (1838), players choose the best response to their opponent's most recently observed action; only the opponent's last action is counted.

Boylan and El-Gamal (1993) found in lab sessions that sometimes the Cournot model outperforms the FP model, but at other times FP outperforms Cournot. To provide further comparative tests of BL models, Cheung and Friedman (1997) put together experimental evidence to show that equilibrium predictions lack predictive power, and for most studies one of the players moved away from equilibrium initially.

A belief learning model

Assuming that beliefs are not directly observable, Cheung and Friedman construct their empirical learning rules based on a schema in which players and institutions/mechanisms generate interactions and feedback between actions, outcomes and beliefs. Actions interact with payoff functions to generate outcomes; outcomes interact with learning rules to generate beliefs. Beliefs interact with decision rules to generate actions; and then the process starts again. They construct a three-parameter learning model to capture these different BL approaches by postulating a set of beliefs and jointly estimating the decision rule and learning rule. They use the Cournot rule to capture current beliefs based on most recently observed actions, and an FP rule in which current beliefs are based on simple averages of all previously observed states of the world. Past states are discounted with declining weights, depending on how far back in time these states were, with the impact of past states captured by a learning parameter, as explained in Box 4.1.

Box 4.1   Mathematics of belief learning models

Cheung and Friedman (1997) construct a BL model with revised beliefs about states of the world and the following learning rule:

$$\hat{s}_i(t+1) = \frac{s_i(t) + \sum_{u=1}^{t-1} \gamma_i^u s_i(t-u)}{1 + \sum_{u=1}^{t-1} \gamma_i^u}$$

where $s_i(t)$ captures past states of the world for player i at time t, $\hat{s}_i(t)$ captures beliefs about the next period, and u captures the lag relative to the current period. Past states of the world are discounted by γ – a factor that can be interpreted as the learning parameter capturing the learning rate and/or memory length. It weights impact of historical observations with weights summing to 1.

When $\gamma = 0$, the past is irrelevant and the rule reduces to a Cournot rule; and $\gamma = 1$ gives a fictitious play rule, that is, all past observations are weighted equally and beliefs become a simple average of past states. Weighted fictitious play (WFP) is described by $0 < \gamma < 1$.

Decision rules can be constructed from this learning rule, and Cheung and Friedman construct the following decision rule for $a_i(t)$ – person i's action in period t. For a given set of beliefs, probability of a first action, a, is given by:

$$P(a_i(t) = 1 \mid \hat{r}_i(t); \alpha_i, \beta_i) = F(\alpha_i + \beta_i \hat{r}_i(t))$$

where $\hat{r}_i(t)$ is the expected payoff difference from the first action, β_i is the evidence weight capturing each player's subjective responsiveness to the expected payoff difference; and α_i is her idiosyncratic tendency to favour the first action.

A behavioural explanation can be assigned to the relative magnitude of the weights: when past observations are assigned no weight, as in the Cournot rule, then this captures recency effects that occur when recent and easily remembered information has a disproportionate impact on beliefs – possibly the outcome of applying the availability heuristic, as discussed in chapter 6. If older observations are given a greater weight than more recent observations, this suggests that first impressions have a disproportionate impact, and this might reflect the application of anchoring and adjustment heuristics, also discussed in chapter 6. It seems unlikely that past states would be assigned negative weights, but if they are, then the rule would be unstable.

The BL rule gives a decision rule based on the probability that a player will choose a given action; this will be determined by three elements. Firstly, a player's responsiveness to the relative payoff from an action – the evidence weight; secondly, a player's idiosyncratic preference for that action; and thirdly, the learning parameter. Cheung and Friedman apply their learning rules to the study of choices in experimental games.

Cheung and Friedman's experiments

In their controlled laboratory experiments, Cheung and Friedman used computerized experiments based on five groups of games: hawk–dove, coordination (stag hunt), prisoner's dilemma, buyer–seller, and battle of the sexes. (For those unfamiliar with the structure of these games, refer to an introductory game theory text such as Dixit and Skeath 2004.) Players were matched in two ways: mean matching, in which each player was matched once against each possible opponent; and random matching. Cheung and Friedman also incorporate two variants of historical data conditions: the 'history' condition, in which players are given information about states in previous periods; and the 'no history' condition, in which no historical information is given.

Using probit techniques, they estimate the probability of a given action using relative payoffs, idiosyncratic preferences and past states of the world as explanatory variables. In some experiments, they found that play was consistent with mixed strategy Nash equilibrium and rational play. For coordination games, they found that parameters on all three explanatory variables are significantly different from zero, with a learning parameter estimated between

0 and 1, supporting adaptive BL over Cournot or FP. Overall, the findings from coordination games are broadly similar to findings from the analysis of buyer–seller and battle of the sexes games.

The implication that Cheung and Friedman draw from their analysis is that players are heterogeneous. Estimates of the parameters enable classification of players into types: Cournot players with short memories; intermediate players with adaptive BL; and long-memory players using FP rules. They find that the distribution of player type is invariant to payoff, but the learning parameter decreases in more informative environments and the evidence weight parameter is positive for most players. Most data are also consistent with the more sophisticated model of *anticipatory learning*, in which players use information about others' payoffs, not just the frequency of their choices.

Overall, Cheung and Friedman conclude that, together, their findings support BL models over reinforcement learning (RL) models. The support for this assertion is mixed, however, and some economists have found similarly robust support for RL models, as discussed in the following section.

Reinforcement learning

Reinforcement learning (RL) models in economics draw on insights from behavioural psychology about stimuli and reinforcement in conditioning, consistent with Skinner's radical behaviourism (introduced in chapter 2). A lot of the work on conditioning in experimental psychology, including Skinner's experiments, concentrated on experimental testing of animal models. Harper (1982) studied mallard ducks foraging for food. Mallards live in small groups and obtain food by foraging. They have extremely small brains, but still were able to exhibit rational behaviour consistent with predictions from game theory. The experiments were conducted in Cambridge University botanical gardens in 1979 with a flock of thirty-three mallards. Two experimenters threw bread balls: one throwing two-gram bread balls every five seconds, the other every ten seconds. The mallards quickly learned to identify the mixed strategy equilibrium (of $^2/_3$ ducks in front of experimenter 1; $^1/_3$ in front of experimenter 2), though some argue that this equilibrium is also consistent with less objective factors such as pecking order, conflict, etc.

Reinforcement learning models also take from behavioural psychology the focus on observed behaviours in an experimental context, rather than on underlying drivers of those behaviours. It links to the behavioural psychology concept of Pavlovian learning, as explained in chapter 2. The focus is on the *law of effect*: all behaviour is a learned response to previous reinforcement, so RL is about conditioning. We learn to do something because of the rewards it delivers, or not to do it because of the costs it imposes. In RL models, the time-dependent value function is a weighted average of past payoffs and past attractions. Our RL attractions build up either via cumulative processes or as weighted averages, with probabilities of choosing a given strategy determined by past reinforcements. This impact from past reinforcement generates anchoring on previous strategies because choices are reinforced by previous payoffs, but there may also be spillovers to similar strategies. Nonetheless, an RL model will imply that behaviour exhibits some inertia, changing slowly, similarly to adaptive expectations in macroeconomic theory. This insight is also incorporated into neuroeconomics in Schultz's (2002) and Schultz *et al.*'s (1997) models of reward prediction error, as discussed below.

A reinforcement learning model

One advantage of RL models is that they imply a relatively simple form of learning that is easy to understand and model. It captures reasoning when players have no knowledge about payoffs from strategies they have not chosen, and so strategies not chosen will be hard to quantify. Erev and Roth (1998) have conducted some influential analyses of RL applied to ultimatum games (UGs) and public good games (PGGs). These games are explored in more detail in chapter 5, but essentially the ultimatum game is a game in which player A offers player B some share of a sum of money; if player B refuses the offer, then both players get nothing. The public good game involves players making individual contributions to financing a hypothetical public good; if the combined contributions are insufficient, then the public good is not provided.

Erev and Roth's experimental evidence shows that people converge onto uneven divisions in market games and PGGs, but converge to nearly equal offers in UGs, and whilst this result might seem anomalous if explained in a nonlearning context, Erev and Roth claim that RL can explain this apparent anomaly.

Erev and Roth (1998) examine learning in experiments with 100 periods or more of games, with unique equilibrium in mixed strategies. They assess *ex ante* and *ex post* predictive power by simulating each experiment using parameters from the other experiments. They develop their model from the insight that traditional game theory assumes perfect rationality and equilibrium, but construct a more general model that captures learning in different types of games. They link this general model into a cognitive version of game theory, which blends economics and psychology with 'forgetting' and 'experimentation' incorporated to improve predictive power.

Erev and Roth start by assuming that initially players have equal propensities to play all strategies. However, over time, particular strategies are differentially reinforced, and so players update their learning attractions accordingly, as captured by an updating function. People are assumed to follow probabilistic choice rule: probabilities that strategies are played reflect the relative propensity to play the strategy. The updating function can be generalized to capture reinforcement from similar strategies, and can also be adapted to incorporate adjustable reference points to address the insight from Kahneman and Tversky's (1979) prospect theory that choices reflect changes not levels of utility, explored in more detail in chapter 7. The construction of Erev and Roth's RL model is explained mathematically in Box 4.2.

Box 4.2 The mathematics of Erev and Roth's reinforcement learning model

In their RL model, Erev and Roth (1998) first specify initial propensities, and these are initially equal for all strategies, where q_{nk} is player n's propensity to play strategy k.

When $j = k$ the strategy is reinforced and the process of reinforcement is captured by a *reinforcement function*:

$$R(x) = x - x_{min}$$

where x is the payoff from playing that strategy.

Erev and Roth vary the number of parameters in their model, and the *updating function* for the one-parameter model is given by:

$$q_{nj}(t+1) = \begin{array}{ll} q_{nj}(t) + R(x) & if \quad j = k \\ q_{nj}(t) & otherwise \end{array}$$

This shows that propensity to play strategy j in the next period will increase if $j = k$ and the strategy has been reinforced in period t, but if $j \neq k$ there will be no reinforcement and the propensity to play j will be unchanged.

The probability p_{nk} that the player will play strategy k is given by the *probabilistic choice rule* reflecting the relative propensity to play k:

$$p_{nk}(t) = \frac{q_{nk}(t)}{\sum q_{nj}(t)}$$

For the three-parameter model, the updating function is modified to incorporate forgetting and reinforcement spillovers from similar strategies:

$$q_{nj}(t+1) = (1 - \varphi)q_{nj}(t) + E_k[j, R(x)]$$

where φ is the forgetting parameter and $E_k[\ldots]$ is a spillover effect capturing the generalized experience of playing strategies k which are similar to the selected strategy j. This partly resolves a problem with RL models, as noted above, that they cannot capture reinforcement from strategies not played. With this adjustment, even if a strategy has not been played before, its updating function can be modified if *similar* strategies are played instead.

The generalized experience captured in the updating function is simplified by Erev and Roth into a 'three-step' function capturing the spillover effects given various degrees of similarity between j and k:

$$E_k(j, R(s)) = \begin{array}{ll} R(x)(1 - \varepsilon) & if \quad j = k \\ R(x) \times \varepsilon / 2 & if \quad j = k + 1 \\ 0 & otherwise \end{array}$$

where ε captures experimentation/generalization and s is the payoff from playing strategy k. As noted above, E_k captures experience and includes learning spillover effects from similar strategies, moderated by forgetting (the recency effect) reducing the impact of past experience.

The impact of experience varies. It can lead to quick convergence, have little impact, or lead to initial divergences away from equilibrium. In essence, RL models have a strong link with behavioural psychology, and they capture Thorndike's law of effect, explained in chapter 2 – outcomes in the past are more likely to be repeated in the future. Choice behaviour is probabilistic and learning follows a *power law* of practice: learning curves are steep initially, but they flatten as experience accumulates.

Erev and Roth's empirical evidence

Erev and Roth use an innovative approach to the data and empirical methodology. They study repeated matrix games with unique mixed strategy equilibria, each of which involves at least 100 rounds of play, but their analysis is not focused entirely on their own data. They use data from eleven other studies (including nine studies of zero-sum games) conducted by other experimenters from the 1960s to the 1990s. This methodology is used to escape the 'tooth-brush' approach: experimenters use their methods like toothbrushes – they favour their own. This creates a problem because if they use only their own experiments, they may unconsciously adapt their experimental designs to fit the model that they have constructed. Using others' data sets forces them to 'tie their hands' to escape this trap.

Their hypotheses are constructed around three main types of model: a one-parameter 'basic reinforcement' model, a three-parameter model incorporating additional parameters for 'experimentation' and 'forgetting' and a four-parameter FP-like model that adds initial beliefs, assumed to be frequency of others' actions. These models are used in computer simulations of each experiment, predicting the probability of each action at each period and the predictions of one-parameter, three-parameter and four-parameter models are compared using a mean-squared deviation (MSD) criterion. For the three-parameter RE model, they add two psychological assumptions: an experimentation effect and a recency effect/forgetting, as explained in Box 4.2.

In the FP-like model, responsiveness to others' actions is incorporated explicitly in the form of excepted value calculations to capture beliefs. The model also incorporates a 'habit' parameter. The number of times a strategy was played in the past influences the probability that it will be played in the future. This is captured using an average return variable incorporating the expected value of a strategy.

Erev and Roth's (1998) empirical findings are that the one-parameter basic reinforcement model outperforms equilibrium predictions, but fails to account for late movements towards equilibrium. Their analysis suggests less responsiveness to opponents than is observed in most experiments. For the three-parameter RE model, it outperforms the basic models, improves on the one-parameter reinforcement model, and has the lowest MSD of all models tested. For the four-parameter FP-like model, there is no significant decrease in MSD relative to the RE model, though the habit parameter contributes to the model's descriptive power.

Erev and Roth (1998) conclude that learning is an important omission from standard models. There are three relevant learning processes: encoding past events, converting knowledge into production rules (strategies such as minimax and tit-for-tat are production rules); and strengthening production rules. Agents pick optimal strategies and stick to them, reflecting Thorndike's law of effect as seen in cats, pigeons and other animal experiments. Thorndike's laws (explained in chapter 2) incorporate reinforcement, but deeper processes are relevant too. Capturing these different influences can enable the consilience of game theory and cognitive psychology to give a low-rationality version of game theory. This could better explain real-world phenomena, for example, academic job markets in which employers gradually learn to advertise earlier in response to early deadlines amongst competing institutions.

Overall, Erev and Roth advocate the development of a 'cognitive game theory' which combines the insights about learning from economics and psychology. They suggest developing John Anderson's ACT* (adaptive character of thought) theory, which distinguishes production rules from learning. A cognitive game theory would retain a strategic approach whilst allowing bounds to rationality. These could include games in which players fail to consider all possible strategies, do not maximize and/or do not allow an explicit role for preferences.

Experience-weighted attraction

Theoretically, RL incorporates an assumption that information about foregone payoffs is ignored, and BL assumes that players ignore information about past strategies. Empirically, Cheung and Friedman's (1997) evidence supports BL, and Erev and Roth's (1998) evidence supports RL. A hybrid model that reconciles the two should have superior explanatory power. Camerer and Ho (1999) provide a solution in the form of the hybrid EWA model, which captures updating of values in belief-based model to generate a time-dependent value function that 'nests' RL and BL, filling the gaps and limitations of both approaches. EWA is a backward-looking model of adaptive learning based on past experience, either in the form of direct reinforcement or as evidence about the history of other players' strategies. EWA combines RL and weighted ficticious play (WFP) models, in which past actions of other players are assigned declining weight over time, and thereby provides an encompassing model with RL and BL as boundary cases.

Thorndike's law of effect asserts that successful strategies will be repeated because past experiences are reinforced. EWA models allow for this, and also incorporate a 'law of simulated effect', capturing the fact that strategies that would have been successful are also repeated more often (Camerer 2003b, p. 305). The weighting from applying the law of simulated effect also has psychological interpretations. It may represent opportunity costs, counterfactuals and regret. It may be affected by imagination and/or reliability of information. By combining the traditional law of effect with the law of simulated effect, EWA models nest BL and RL models in the form of WFP.

Experimental evidence about EWA models

Camerer (2003b) sets out some empirical evidence in support of EWA, stating that in studies of about thirty-one data sets, EWA fits/predicts out of sample more accurately than RL or WFP, except in games with mixed strategy equilibria. He examines specifically the evidence from two types of games: continental divide games and beauty contests.

Continental divide games

The continental divide game captures conformity to others' strategies. For example, new media firms will locate where there are strong linkages with other local industries. A choice between Silicon Valley and Hollywood will generate an economic tug-of-war, won by doing what most other firms are doing. This hypothesis is captured empirically using a simple experiment in which seven players each choose an integer from 1 to 14. The best response is to choose a low number when others choose low, and a high number when others choose high. If unsure, it is best to pick a number with largest range of payoffs. Camerer (2003b) concludes that the experimental data from continental divide games fits better with EWA models than alternatives, because EWA captures the interaction of beliefs about what other firms are doing and reinforcement from the payoff externalities, which emerge when a large number of firms do the same thing, for example, all firms will benefit from other firms' investments in local infrastructure.

Beauty contests

In addition to the evidence from continental divide games, Camerer (2003b) also relies on evidence from beauty contests to support EWA models. Beauty contest games are inspired by Keynes's (1936) insights. Foreshadowing the beauty contests developed by modern behavioural economists, Keynes uses a metaphor of a newspaper beauty contest. Competitors are asked to pick not the 'prettiest faces', but 'those which he thinks likeliest to catch the fancy of the other competitors'. In beauty contests, speculators in financial markets reach a 'third degree' of reasoning. They do not form beliefs about fundamental, true values or payoffs, but instead are trying to guess what others think, and they are trying to second-guess average opinion of average opinion: 'It is not the case of choosing those which, to the best of one's judgment, are really the prettiest, nor even those which average opinion genuinely thinks the prettiest. We have reached the third degree where we devote our intelligences to anticipating what average opinion expects average opinion to be. And there are some, I believe, who practise the fourth, fifth and higher degrees' (Keynes 1936, p. 156). Keynes postulates that financial speculators are engaged in this form of strategic thinking: they are preoccupied with forecasting average opinion of average opinion, rather than with their own objective judgments about the value of an asset, and this contributes to financial instability, as explained in chapter 11.

Using Keynes's beauty contest metaphor as a starting point, Nagel (1995) designed a form of beauty contest game – the 'p beauty contest' – to capture levels of reasoning, with a prize going to player(s) who select a strategy closest to some product p of the average strategy. For a set of strategy choices including 1 to 100 in a game played a finite number of times, if play is random, then a naïve player might expect an average guess of 50 from the others, and so will guess $p \times 50$; but more sophisticated players will realize that they cannot assume other players' actions will be random. Sophisticated players will adopt strategic reasoning to make inferences about the strategic choices of other players, because they realize that other players also know the rules of the game. Assuming complete rationality, the game is dominance-solvable with inferior strategies eliminated via a process of backward induction. For example, with $p = {}^2/_3$, in round 1 players will realize that choices greater than ${}^2/_3 \times 100$ are bound to lose, because they are strictly dominated, so 68 to 100 will be eliminated, leaving 1 to 67, and players will take the average of this, that is, an average of ${}^1/_2 \times {}^2/_3 \times 100 = 33.5$. In round 2, players will predict that others make the same judgment, and so guess that others would not pick in the range 1 to 67, selecting an average of ${}^1/_2 \times ({}^2/_3 \times {}^2/_3) \times 100 = 22$, and so on.

A player is strategic of degree n if he/she selects a number $50p^n$, which approaches zero as n approaches infinity, assuming $p < 1$. With 'deep' reasoning, this process will continue a large number of times until a Nash equilibrium strategy of 0 is reached. Real-life evidence from experimental beauty contests suggests, however, that people do not think the problem through thoroughly. In lab experiments, most people use only two to four levels of iterated reasoning, and the iterative process is driven by naïve best replies, rather than by elimination of dominated strategies. This is a robust finding, and studies by Nagel, Thaler and others show that a range of players, from *Financial Times* readers to business CEOs, show limited depths of reasoning (Camerer 2003b). For Keynes's speculators, in modern language: if traders don't backward induct (and this may be for strategic reasons), they will not immediately sell, perhaps because they don't expect others to sell. This reluctance to sell on the basis of predicting others' actions will generate persistent speculative bubbles.

The length of the game in terms of the number of iterations can be explained in a range of ways. It may reflect limits on cognitive ability and working memory. It may also reflect strategic motivations and assumptions about others' rationality: if you are a strategic thinker, then you will not choose zero because you might anticipate that others would not reason that far. Selecting zero assumes too much about others' reasoning capacity/motivation.

In the context of learning, beauty contests are interesting because simple learning does takes place. Ho *et al.* (1998) conducted the first replication of Nagel's study using different values of p to assess the impact of learning. In initial rounds, players showed one to three steps of iterated reasoning, but there was transfer of learning from one game to the other, as players learned to learn: players converged more rapidly and showed greater depth of reasoning in subsequent games.

Camerer (2003b) also describes p-beauty contests designed specifically to test EWA learning models. In these experiments, each player picks a number from the interval [0, 100]. The player closest to the target number wins where the target is p multiplied by the average guess. By iterated deletion, if $p = 2/3$, then numbers in the range [67, 100] cannot win and so are deleted. Then $2/3 \times 67 = 44$, so numbers in the range [45, 67] are deleted. Iterated reasoning proceeds deleting $2/3 \times 44 = 29$ and then $2/3 \times 29 = 20$, and so on until, assuming strong rationality, the Nash equilibrium of zero is reached, as in the Nagel experiments.

Camerer (2003b) shows that both BL and EWA perform well in explaining beauty contest play. RL neither fits nor predicts because six of seven players each period are not earning or learning anything because the opportunities for reinforcement in the beauty contest game are very limited. If players are learning about others' beliefs, they must be forming beliefs about those beliefs, and so it follows that RL models cannot explain the findings.

The results can also capture the phenomenon of sophisticated players realizing that others are learning, and these ideas are captured in models of anticipatory/sophisticated learning models too. In these models, players use information about others' payoffs to reason thoughtfully about what the other player might do. They form beliefs based on best response functions where these functions include some information about others' payoffs.

Comparative econometric evidence on EWA versus RL and BL models

There has been some econometric testing of learning theory, for example, Salmon (2001) assesses the empirical evidence on learning models and concludes that it is disappointing, partly because early econometric analyses were conducted when our knowledge of the statistical properties of estimators were not so well understood. Salmon's econometric evaluation of learning models involves simulating RL, BL and EWA models. Whilst model identification is generally poor, the EWA models perform relatively well, allowing a sharp distinction of RL and BL models.

Overall, both RL and BL have empirical support in hybrid/encompassing models, and EWA models capture elements of both. It is difficult to separate the explanations econometrically, partly because data on observed actions do not reveal the underlying cognitive processes that enable learning. Neuroeconomic analyses may be able to capture something of what's going on behind revealed preferences and open the 'black box' that underlies decision-making (Camerer *et al.* 2005).

In comparing the various models of learning, Camerer argues that they can also be compared according to the legitimacy of the underlying informational assumptions, that is, judging the plausibility of learning theories rests on the sort of information that is required. If people use information that is not captured in the theory, then the theory is incomplete; if the theory demands more information than people are feasibly able to use, for example as seen in rational expectations assumptions, then the theory is too complex (Camerer 2003b). Information use depends not only on information available, but also on cognitive capacities.

Camerer (2006) explains the different levels of information needed in the different theories: the information needed ranges from the player's choice, their opponent's choice, received and foregone payoffs for players and opponents, and best response.

The different learning theories vary considerably in terms of their assumptions about minimal information needed, with evolutionary theory having the minimum information requirement because if everything is instinctive then no information is needed. Some of the informational implications can be used to compare and contrast learning theories. That people learn faster when they have full payoff information contradicts RL; the fact that people look up information about their own previous payoffs is inconsistent with BL theory. That people behave differently when they have information about others' payoffs supports theories based on more sophisticated learning processes and theories incorporating imitative learning.

Social learning and information cascades

Social learning models are based around the insight that people will imitate other players' strategies. Many social learning models are based on principles of Bayesian reasoning, in which people's probabilistic judgments are updated in response to others' actions (see Chamley 2003 for a survey). For example, if a person is facing a choice between two restaurants – restaurant A and restaurant B – their estimate of the likelihood that restaurant B is better increases if they see a lot of people eating in restaurant B.

Social learning generates herding – a general category of behaviours in which people follow groups of others, and may do so for all sorts of reasons. It is the phenomenon of individuals deciding to follow others and imitating group behaviours, rather than deciding independently and atomistically on the basis of their own, private information. Herding theory has its roots in Keynes, who focused on motivations to imitate and follow the crowd in a world of uncertainty, and this may happen for a range of reasons.

Social learning theories

Bikhchandani *et al.* (1992) focus on social learning in the context of uniform social behaviour. They identify four primary herding mechanisms encouraging people to do what others do: sanctions on deviants, positive payoff externalities, conformity preference and communication. Bikhchandani *et al.* observe, however, that these social influences cannot fully explain the fragility of mass behaviour and changes in attitudes, seen for example in changing attitudes towards common phenomena such as cohabitation, sexuality, communism and addiction.

Bikhchandani *et al.* propose that social learning in the form of 'information cascades' also generates uniform social behaviour. An information cascade occurs 'when it is optimal for an individual, having observed the actions of those ahead of him, to follow the behaviour of the preceding individual without regard to his own information' (Bikhchandani *et al.* 1992, p. 994). Bikhchandani *et al.* enumerate many examples of phenomena explicable as information cascades, including political campaigning – for example US presidential nomination campaigns; foraging and mating behaviour (see also Danchin *et al.* 2004); medical practice, including surgical fads and 'iatroepidemics' – epidemics of treatment-caused diseases; competing bids during corporate takeovers; and peer influence/social stigma in labour markets when the long-term unemployed are discriminated against in hiring decisions.

Banerjee (1992) develops a similar model of herding and social learning. People are heavily influenced by what others are doing, for example in fertility choices, technology adoption and voting patterns, and this is because we learn from the herd: it is rational to pay heed to what others are doing because they may have better information. This generates inefficient outcomes because when information cascades are generated, private information becomes uninformative and a herding externality is created. Banerjee uses again the example of restaurant choice. There are two restaurants, A and B: restaurant A is favoured *a priori* by 51 per cent; restaurant B is favoured *a priori* by 49 per cent. Then 100 people make sequential decisions about which restaurant to choose. If 99 out of 100 people have private signals indicating that restaurant B is better, then aggregate evidence suggests that restaurant B should be preferred on average. This does not mean that it will be preferred in practice.

Imagine that Alice is the first person to choose, but she has a misleading private signal, for example, a newspaper review written by a biased restaurant critic, favouring restaurant A. If Bob chooses next, then he must balance three pieces of information: the *a priori* probability which favours restaurant A; his correct private signal which favours restaurant B; and the social information – Alice's observed choice. If he uses Bayesian reasoning, then he will weight the second and third pieces of information equally, these conflicting signals will cancel out and he will rationally choose restaurant A even though, all things considered, it is not the best restaurant.

An information cascade is generated because the third person to choose – Chris – will choose restaurant A because the misleading information conveyed by Alice and Bob's choices has overwhelmed Chris's private information, generating herding towards a restaurant that, all information considered, is less preferable. From that point onwards, assuming that all subsequent decision-makers apply Bayes's rule, all private information becomes uninformative. Information is used inefficiently because all subsequent private signals are ignored, even though they contain information that would be useful and relevant for decision-makers as a whole.

The implication is that private information may have no influence on choices of the herd. Banerjee refers to this negative consequence, in which relevant private information is ignored as a herding externality. Bikhanchandi *et al.* (1992) develop a similar model of informational cascades as an explanation for localized conformity emerging when it is optimal for an individual to follow the actions of his/her predecessor and to disregard his own private information. Just as is seen in Banerjee's model, each sequential decision conveys no real new evidence to subsequent members of the herd, and so private information becomes uninformative. To summarize: according to Bayesian theories, herding and informational cascades emerge because members of the herd are ignoring their own private signals and favouring herd information about the actions of their predecessors. This means they will potentially ignore a large volume of important private information.

If the herd path fosters increasing noise within the system, then the process of opinion formation will become unstable. Further research is needed to assess the extent to which expert herds move in either stable or unstable directions. This can be done by assessing the extent to which herd leaders (experts) are selected on objective versus subjective grounds, and by assessing the extent to which herd leaders turn out to be right in the end. This would be another direction for fruitful future research.

Herding phenomena are consistent with different statistical hypotheses, for example, Kirman (1993), using a Markov chain approach, develops the 'ants' model in which ants 'convert' by copying another ant. For example, ants faced with two symmetrical food sources will tend to concentrate on one or the other source, rather than distributing themselves evenly across both. This behaviour pattern may be interpreted as recruitment activity by ants. With positive externalities from foraging behaviour, the joint exploitation of one source will give more benefit to the group than an even distribution of effort over two different sources (Kirman 1993).

Overall, models of herding and social learning based on Bayesian updating models assume that agents are using sophisticated logical methods, but the outcome can be good or bad depending on whether the decision-makers are sent down a correct or incorrect track by the actions of their predecessors.

Experimental tests of Bayesian herding

Anderson and Holt (1996, 1997) construct an illustration of how this reasoning process works, and test the hypotheses experimentally using an urn experiment. Imagine that you, along with a group of other experimental subjects, are asked to participate in an experiment. You are told that there are two urns: urn A and urn B. Urn A contains two red balls and one black ball; urn B contains one red ball and two black balls, as shown in Figure 4.1.

Then you are asked to draw a ball from an unmarked urn and guess which urn is being used. The experimenter has concealed the urn's label so it could be urn A or urn B. All things being equal, you are more likely to draw a red ball if urn A is being used, and less likely if urn B is being used. But your choice is complicated by the fact that you see other people making guesses too. Other subjects are taking a ball from the unmarked urn, concealing its colour from the group, replacing it in the urn and announcing their guess. According to Anderson and Holt, people judge the probability that urn A is being used according to the choices of their predecessors, with choice made sequentially by each subject in turn based on the application of Bayes's rule. In the first round, for example, if the first person to choose guesses urn A, that is a signal that it was a red ball, because red balls are more likely in urn A.

Anderson and Holt explain how a rational person would judge the probability that urn A is being used if the choices are made sequentially, with each experimental subject observing the others' decisions one by one, inferring the colour of the ball from their choices, and applying Bayes's rule accordingly. In this way, probabilities are updated as new social information comes along. If a person sees their predecessor picking urn B, then they will update their probabilities to make the probability of urn B more likely. An arithmetical analysis of Bayes's rule is summarized in Box 4.3.

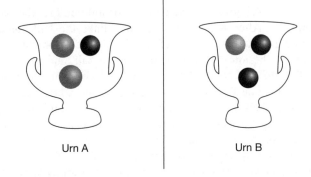

Urn A   Urn B

Figure 4.1 Urn of balls

Box 4.3   Bayesian updating and information cascades

Anderson and Holt show that people judge the probability that urn A is being used according to the choices of their predecessors, with choice made sequentially by each subject in turn, and applying Bayes's rule – an amalgamation of prior probabilities, conditional probabilities and posterior probabilities.

Prior probabilities

$Pr(A)$ and $Pr(B)$ are the prior probabilities that the urn is, respectively, urn A or urn B, and given that this is determined by the toss of a coin, $Pr(A) = Pr(B) = 1/2$.

Conditional probabilities

Each player infers from their predecessors' choice the colours of balls that they have chosen. From the social signals (n, m) they infer some combination of balls, where n is number of signals favouring urn A in which red balls are more likely and m is number of signals favouring urn B in which black balls are more likely. $Pr(n, m \mid A)$ is the conditional probability of signals (n, m) if the urn is urn A, and $Pr(n, m \mid B)$ is the probability of seeing the combination (n, m) if urn B was used. The posterior probability that it is urn A is given by Bayes's rule:

$$Pr(A \mid n, m) = \frac{Pr(n, m \mid A) Pr(A)}{Pr(n, m \mid A) Pr(A) + Pr(n, m \mid B) Pr(B)} = \frac{2^n}{2^n + 2^m}$$

An example

If, after three rounds, a player has signals that two red balls and one black ball have been drawn, then $Pr(n, m \mid A) = 2/3 \times 2/3 \times 1/3 = 4/27$ and $Pr(n, m \mid B) = 1/3 \times 1/3 \times 2/3 = 2/27$.

Applying Bayes's rule gives the posterior probability of urn A:

$$Pr(A \mid n = 1, m = 2) = 2/3 = 67 \text{ per cent}$$

If Bayes's rule is applied then Table 4.1 gives the posterior probabilities that the ball comes from urn A. For example: if Alice announces that she thinks the ball comes from urn A, then the others would assume that she picked a red ball. Then Bob chooses. Perhaps he chooses a black ball, but he infers that Alice drew a red ball, and from this concludes that the probability that the ball comes from urn A is 50 per cent. He could rationally choose either urn, but imagine that he guesses urn A. Then Chris chooses, and perhaps he also chooses a black ball, but he assumes that both Alice and Bob had picked red balls and so, if he is using Bayes's rule, then he infers that urn A has been chosen because red balls have been picked twice, against his single draw of a black ball. Overall, he judges that the probability of urn A is 67 per cent (Table 4.2), so he will also choose urn A even though he picked a black ball. From that point onwards, if people are using Bayes's rule then the posterior probabilities of urn A lead the herd down the route

Table 4.1 Applying Bayes's rule to judge the probability of urn A

	Urn B chosen			
Urn A chosen	*Never*	*Once*	*Twice*	*Three times*
Never	50%	33%	20%	11%
Once	67%	50%	33%	20%
Twice	80%	67%	50%	33%
Three times	89%	80%	67%	50%

of choosing urn A. Each individual will effectively ignore their private signal, and private information is lost.

Anderson and Holt (1996, 1997) use this urn experiment to test the Bayesian herding as social learning hypothesis. In one set of experiments, seventy-two undergraduate economics students were paid fixed cash payments for correct decisions. One was selected as monitor to choose an urn and pour contents into an unmarked urn. Then the subjects were chosen in random order to draw a ball one by one and announce their prediction to the group. Each drew a ball, which represented their private signal; the others weren't allowed to see which ball they drew. The subjects announced their decision, and this gave a signal to the others about whether urn A or urn B had been used. Anderson and Holt observed information cascades in forty-one of fifty-six periods in which there was an imbalance between private signal and previous inferred signal. They calculated the 'efficiency' of decisions as the percentage of decisions consistent with the optimal expected payoff if Bayes's rule had been used, and found that two-thirds of subjects made decisions with 100 per cent efficiency, that is, in perfect conformity with Bayes's rule. Similar results have been found in a large number of studies of Bayesian social learning hypotheses. More recently, Fishman and Gneezy (2011) have tested the hypothesis using Banerjee's example of restaurant choice, and found that in situations of limited information/experience, restaurant queues were longer, which would be consistent with people deciding that longer queues signalled quality.

The outcome predicted by the Bayesian social learning hypothesis is not infallible, for a number of reasons. Bob's decision was on a knife's edge – he could have, legitimately and correctly, applied Bayes's law to choose urn B and send the herd in the right direction. Alternatively, people may apply a form of iterative thinking. They realize that they could make a choice that matches what their predecessors have done, but that it conflicts with their own private signal, so they will also realize that others may be doing the same. They will realize that the others are choosing an urn just on the basis of predecessors' choices, not because they have actually picked a red ball. For example, Chris may not infer that Bob picked a red ball just because he chose urn A, and so Chris may apply a corrective factor to allow for his degree of uncertainty about why Bob chose urn A.

Anderson and Holt's laboratory experiments generally focus on discrete signal/action models. More recently, Çelen and Kariv (2004), amongst others, have used experimental evidence to distinguish between herding as a broad descriptive category of copying behaviours, and informational cascades as a specific form of learning that arises in uncertain situations.

Empirically, herding as a Bayesian learning process is consistent with evidence from a large number of economic experiments, including Anderson and Holt (1996, 1997) and many others. However, this evidence does not establish that a Bayesian explanation is superior to other explanations, including those drawing upon ideas from other social sciences. Nonetheless, even in the Bayesian models, the basic premise is that economic decisions are, in essence, the outcome of a cognitive process employing a mathematical algorithm to process information and form expectations. In addition, the focus tends to be on a dichotomous division of behaviour into rational or irrational; a person is assumed to be rational if their behaviour is consistent with Bayesian updating. Sociological influences are confined to learning from others' actions, and psychological and emotional factors are accorded very little role at all.

Other behavioural approaches to social learning

Katona (1951, 1975) uses a cognitive psychology approach to analyse group learning. Herding reflects 'stamping in' of simple rules of thumb and heuristics, rather than problem solving and understanding. According to Katona, learning is about relying on simple observation of others to acquire information. On the interactions between individuals and groups in a social learning context, group forces and group motives are important, reflecting not only imitation and conscious identification with the group, but also group-centred goals and behaviour. Imitation and suggestion reinforce group situations and group coherence, but are not necessary conditions for being part of a group. Reference groups give standards for behaviour, and group-centred belonging and motivation are more likely to be important in small groups. Social learning is more selective and simple than individual learning, because people adopt short cuts and follow simplifying rules of thumb and routines. Imitation qualifies as a 'fast and frugal heuristic' in social situations (Gigerenzer and Goldstein 1996; chapter 6 in this volume).

Learning themes emerge in the macroeconomic literature too. Topol (1991) analyses herding as the outcome of rational trading, in which traders weight information about prices paid by other traders against private judgments of fundamental value. Acemoglu (1993) analyses rational learning about others' decisions via signal extraction from aggregate data. Ideas about imitative learning are also developed in analyses from Austrian economics, which explore Hayek's insights about knowledge as a path-dependent process (Hayek, 1952; Rizzello 2004). Paralleling the sequential herding theories of Bayesian theorists, social learning in Austrian economics differs from ordinary problem-solving in that serial processing of information is important, generating path dependency and propelling the acquisition of knowledge along a path determined by past beliefs.

A significant behavioural constraint occurs if people do not have the numeracy to be able to think in the sophisticated way assumed in models of Bayesian learning. Anderson (1998) argues that this is a consequence of the nature of memes, the cultural analogy of genes. The problem originates in the input format of data, and in algorithms used, but if prompted by clear signals the human brain is able to deal with probabilities effectively. For example, if students are asked to judge the probability of two coincident events within the context of a statistics class, then they will know what to do. However, if outside their classes they are confronted with a problem requiring probability judgments in a situation in which it is not obvious that this is what is required, then they may make an instinctive, intuitive judgment which may generate statistical mistakes (Kyburg 1997). Anderson suggests that Bayesian approaches could be refined using the advantages of a frequentist approach by using mental, visual imagery and graphic display. In this way, some frequentist methods could be incorporated effectively into a Bayesian framework, allowing human cognition to process subjective probabilities more effectively.

Social influence

One question so far unanswered is how to distinguish social learning from social influences more broadly. The social learning models above focus on a rational process of updating, in which the individual uses information about predecessors' decisions to update their probabilistic judgments by applying Bayes's rule. This is what generates information cascades, a rationally based form of sequential social learning.

In Keynes's (1936, 1937) analysis of financial markets, he explored three main motivators of copying others and following conventions, and these are mirrored in the modern literatures on social influence: learning, 'beauty contests' and reputation. The first two can be reconciled with the economic theories of learning and iterated reasoning discussed above. Beauty contests also link into payoff externalities and reflexivity. You may spend time second-guessing other players in a market and, if you believe that they will buy, then you will buy too, because the increases in demand will lead to rising prices from which you will benefit. So beauty contests combine learning and strategic aspects.

In Keynes's analysis, herding behaviours are linked back into an analysis of probabilistic judgment in a Bayesian setting (Keynes 1921, 1936, 1937). Differences in posterior judgments of probable outcomes may not reflect irrationality, but instead may emerge as a result of differences in prior information. Rational economic agents may have an incentive to follow the crowd, and herding will result as a response to individuals' perceptions of their own ignorance. This herding will be rational if an individual has reason to believe that other agents' judgments are based upon better information than their own: other people's judgments become a data set in themselves. In this way, people will incorporate others' opinions into their prior information set, and their posterior judgments may exhibit herding tendencies. Shiller (2000, 2003) analyses these ideas in the context of feedback theories of endogenous opinion formation, in which beliefs about the system determine the path of that system, for example as seen in stock markets. These ideas are also developed by Topol (1991), Shleifer (2000), Brunnermeier (2001) and Sornette (2003), amongst others.

The word 'herding' can also be used to describe more general classes of behaviour in which people follow others for less precise reasons. Social influences may be broader and more diffuse, and may reflect an interaction of simple learning and other social incentives and pressures. Groups can have a broader, more diffuse influence on individual behaviour for reasons other than learning, and this can explain the more general types of herding and social influence. This is not necessarily irrational. Crowds may be wise if the aggregation of everyone's individual knowledge allows a crowd collectively to identify sensible courses of action (Surowiecki 2004).

Another explanation for imitation is reputation. Reputation is not about learning from others; it has a broader interpretation. Keynes observed that following others may help individuals to maintain good reputations; it makes sense to follow the crowd because there is safety in numbers. Scharfstein and Stein (1990) incorporate this insight about social influence into their analysis of herding in fund managers' decisions. Fund managers have to convince people that they are investing wisely and, as short-term performance is not a good indicator of skill, they rely for their reputations on comparisons with peers, building upon Keynes's (1936) insight that it is better to be conventionally wrong than unconventionally right. This will provide incentives to follow others and disregard private information in order to build their reputations. Managers will have an incentive to disregard private information in a world in which reputation matters.

Empirically, it can be difficult to untangle group influences on individual behaviour (though neuroeconomic analyses can offer some insights, as explored below). The problem is that, as Manski (1993, 2000) observes in his analyses of reflection effects and social interactions, empirically it can be difficult to identify and separate group influences from contextual influences.

Overall, social influences can come via learning, social rewards and/or social pressure. Above we have analysed some of the models of social learning that emerge from Bayesian updating, but how do other social influences affect people's behaviour?

Important insights about the impact of social psychology on herding behaviour have come from Le Bon's (1896) assertions that mob psychology is the outcome of the hypnotic influence of crowd behaviour on individual decisions. In distinguishing social learning from social pressure, elements of Bayesian and socio-psychological theories may coincide. Herding may occur through beliefs in, first, the higher competence of the persons being observed; and second, simple group or peer pressure without necessarily higher competence. To herd for the former reason would be rational and sensible; to herd for the latter reason may not.

Purely Bayesian accounts are difficult to reconcile with experimental evidence showing that people follow majority opinion even if it contradicts more accurate private information (Asch 1955, 1956). Asch's experiments, explained in chapter 2, demonstrated that experimental subjects have a tendency, even with very unambiguous tasks, to make the wrong choice when they see a group making a wrong choice. This finding has been replicated in a large number of sociological studies (for a meta-analysis see Bond and Smith 1996). Shiller argues that this evidence about the impact of social influence is not necessarily inconsistent with the Bayesian hypotheses outlined above – it is just rational social learning taken to its extremes. Asch's experimental subjects were making rational judgments about the probabilities of different scenarios, and concluding that a large group of other individuals was very unlikely to be wrong about a simple decision; the individuals judged that it was more likely that their own judgment was wrong. This led to a tendency to discount personal perceptions in favour of the information communicated by the group (Shiller 1995). Shiller observes that herding operates even without face-to-face interactions, and is therefore not an outcome of social pressure. Instead, he argues that the response of large groups of people is taken as valid information because it is rationally assumed that large groups are unlikely to be wrong (Shiller, 1995). Also, social pressure may emerge from imagined responses as well as real and direct responses – for example, there is evidence that real and imagined events are associated with similar cognitive responses. Tendencies to herd may reflect individual differences, including personality traits such as empathy and conformity, because these might generate predispositions to follow others, as explored in more detail in chapters 7 and 12.

Overall, decisions to follow others reflect sociological and psychological factors and this leads us away from a dichotomous conception of herding as either rational or not rational, reflecting the fact that economics incorporates a binary, dichotomous criterion for rationality according to whether behaviour does or does not conform to strict definitions of rationality. Enlarging the analysis of herding away from conceiving of it as a purely objective phenomenon also allows the possibility that herding reflects interactions between different cognitive and emotional decision-making systems, which – as noted in chapter 2 – is something that neuroscientists and neuroeconomists explore. Some neuroeconomic studies of interacting neural systems are explored in the neuroeconomics section below.

Evolutionary approaches

Evolutionary approaches to herding build on the insight that we are born with a strategy and play it instinctively; for example, strategies to provide food, escape predators and find mates, enabling the survival of the fittest. This idea is paralleled in evolutionary biology and neuroscience too. But, as noted by Camerer (2003b), the word 'learning' in this context may be misleading because it is not about individual learning and instead links to inherited strategies (for example, in animals) and/or cultural evolution over long periods.

Herding behaviour is widely observed throughout the animal kingdom, in species as diverse as honey bees, ants, antelope, sheep and cows. Herding animals monitor the actions of others, thus providing social information about resource availability and mating potential (Danchin *et al.* 2004). Evolutionary biology can help explain why herding instincts are endemic. In other animals, especially our close relatives, herding may have (had) an evolutionary value in a social context; it is not just about individuals maximizing their own outcomes. For example, animals will monitor the actions of other individuals, as this gives social information about resource availability and mating potential (Danchin *et al.* 2004). Amongst monkeys, imitation has been selected for as a successful strategy enabling the rapid transmission of good ideas throughout a species (Surowiecki 2004). Emotional contagion is observed in children, for example when they cry. Emotional contagion is imitative and is, initially, a state of vicarious distress, which precedes mind-reading abilities but may contribute to the development of empathetic capacities (Prinz 2005).

Cohen (2005) argues that the human brain has evolved into a confederation of mechanisms that usually cooperate, but sometimes compete. Proximate mechanisms, defined as current behaviours which have evolved in response to natural selection pressures when motivated by emotional responses that appear irrational and motivated by emotions, in fact are engaging evolutionarily old but highly conserved brain mechanisms, which may be locally optimal but are not necessarily universally optimal. Also, instincts that have evolved to increase chances of survival may be just that – instinctual, and therefore not manifested as a deliberative Bayesian-style thought process.

Herding may have evolutionary advantages for humans too, not just because of informational influences, but because the presence of more conformist individuals susceptible to intra-group pressure generates evolutionary advantages. Simon (1990) argues that, amongst social animals, the evolutionary fitness of altruists will exceed that of the selfish: 'docility' (receptivity to social influence) is an evolved instinct that has survived and permeated the human population to serve important evolutionary purposes. Docile people have the intelligence and motivation to learn quickly from social information, and do not screen social information for contribution to personal fitness. Docility allows people to believe large numbers of propositions without any direct proof. Docile individuals are also more adept at social learning, making them more able to acquire knowledge, skills and 'proper behaviours' – the values, goals and attitudes that are useful in overcoming environmental obstacles – thus contributing to the evolutionary fitness of human populations. According to Simon, a genetic predisposition to imitate others has evolved, serving a social purpose in encouraging socially constructive empathy and altruism, helpful in overcoming dissent and conflict. However, such conformism might also allow tyranny and oppression, illustrating the fact that the trait of docility may not necessarily suit a complex modern world.

These evolutionary theories can show how instincts such as herding have evolved in a social context, if not in an individual context. The way that humans make choices in risky situations (for example, the overweighting of low probabilities, the dependence of probability judgments on context) are seen in animals too – for example, in monkeys and honey bees, suggesting that human neural circuitry is 'old' and adapted to basic survival instincts (Camerer *et al.* 2004a). On the other hand, in evolutionary terms, instinctive tendencies may be more appropriate only in primitive settings: sociability and aversion to aggression may have evolved to allow the development of the stable social structures essential to the competitive success of small communities.

Herding instincts will be counter-productive if the survival purpose of evolved instincts has been perverted by situational factors in modern 'artificial' contexts. An instinct to follow others may have been important to survival in a primitive setting, but that does not mean it is an effective strategy in the heavily interconnected, globalized, computerized world in which assets, information and expectations can move very quickly. If large-scale herding in financial markets reflects the overriding influence of normative influence and/or emotional factors, then maybe herding is an inappropriate proximate mechanism and is not well suited to the modern context because it can generate instability on a very large scale. This raises the question of whether the basic instincts manifested in proximate mechanisms such as herding are well adapted to a modern, technological age.

An evolutionary approach is not inconsistent with ideas about Bayesian reasoning, if Bayesian reasoning is a skill that has evolved to serve social purposes. For example, with heterogeneity in personality types, rule-based decision-making (such as Bayesian updating) helps to ensure consensus amongst divergent personalities, fostering effective societal decision-making processes despite natural heterogeneity. However, human instincts are hard-wired processes that have not evolved recently enough to be necessarily useful in a modern context. An ingrained instinct to herd may be a maladaptation in modern contexts, especially fast, liquid financial markets, unlike evolved motor and perceptual abilities that enable us to read and write.

Neuroeconomic analyses of learning and social influence

In debates about what happens when people learn, neuroeconomics can help illuminate some issues. Tools such as fMRI can be used to establish links between learning and differential brain activation, exploiting parallels with research in economics, experimental psychology and neuroscience. In addition to providing new research tools, neuroeconomics may offer new theoretical approaches that blend insights from different economic models and escape the binary classification of herding into rational versus nonrational.

Belief learning and reinforcement learning

Neuroeconomic testing of BL models is more difficult because of the problem of empirically capturing the BL function. Nonetheless, Lohrenz *et al.* (2007) have associated fictive learning with activations in the caudate nucleus, an area implicated in neural processing of reward. In working–shirking games, Hampton *et al.* (2008) identified neural correlates of sophisticated learning/strategic reasoning in the superior temporal sulcus, an area implicated in perception and emotion. Bhatt and Camerer (2005) found that poor strategic thinking in the second stages of beauty contest games was associated with differential activations in the insula, an area implicated in self-awareness as well as negative emotional processing, perhaps reflecting the fact that self-focus harms strategizing.

Reward learning and reward prediction error

RL models from economics are broadly associated with rewards, and link to insights about reinforcement from psychology, including Thorndike's laws of effect, recency and exercise (see chapter 2). Schultz *et al.*'s (1997) study of reward prediction error is developed from the same psychological insights about RL, and captures the adaptive nature of learning (see also Schultz 2002, 2006, 2008; Schultz *et al.* 2008): neuroeconomic insights about learning develop from an application of neuroscientific models of reward learning and reward prediction error to economic scenarios.

Reward prediction error is similar to adaptive expectations in macroeconomics: neural activations correlate not with a stimulus, but with the difference between prediction and actual occurrence of an event. This enables reward learning when events are unexpected. Learning from 'mistakes' – the divergence between the predicted and actual outcome – triggers reward mechanisms. Single-neuron experiments on monkeys have shown that dopaminergic neurons in the ventral striatum, a neural area associated with reward processing, also encode reward prediction error. There is also evidence of cue-conditioning. Initially, neurons fire when rewards are received, but over time responses become cue-conditioned so that neurons fire with the cue, not with the reward. The inference is that the dopamine neurons are not simply encoding the rewards, but are also capturing predictions about the likely time and magnitude of the reward. Caplin and Dean (2007, 2008a, 2008b, 2009) have applied these insights from neuroscience in developing a neuroeconomic theory of learning based on rigorous analytical foundations.

Observational learning

Insights from the neuroeconomic analysis of reward learning have also been applied to observational learning, following models of reward prediction error in which prediction errors are used to increase the accuracy of predictions in the future via a process of learning (Schultz 2006). Burke *et al.* (2010a) conducted an imaging analysis of social learning to identify subjects' neurological responses to observed actions and outcomes from others, versus their individual actions and outcomes. Burke *et al.* postulate that, in social learning, individual prediction errors are supplemented by observational prediction errors. This approach has elements of RL in its focus on individual action and outcome prediction errors, and also captures social learning from observing the actions and outcomes of others in its analysis of observational action and outcome prediction errors, linking into BL models and neuroscientific models of fictive, vicarious learning, as explained below.

In this experiment, there is a two-stage learning process: observing others' actions biases the player to imitate that action; and observing others' outcomes allows the player to refine the values associated with each stimulus. These hypotheses were analysed using fMRI and a simple 'two-armed-bandit' game, with one 'good' stimulus generating a reward and one 'bad' stimulus giving no reward. If, for example, stimulus A is associated with an 80 per cent probability of reward and stimulus B is associated with a 20 per cent probability of reward, then the subjects' task is to learn to choose the best stimulus. Behavioural findings showed that more observable information about others' outcomes as well as actions (versus actions alone) led to more correct choices and higher earnings. Imitation was observed in 66 per cent of trials even when only others' actions (not outcomes) were observed. Imitation was observed in 41 per cent of trials when both outcomes and actions were observed, because players were able to observe when others were getting it wrong.

The individual outcome prediction error was correlated with activity in the ventral striatum, associated with processing reward (as mentioned above); the dorsolateral prefrontal cortex (DLPFC), which is associated with cognition and attention; and the ventromedial prefrontal cortex (VMPFC), implicated in risky decision-making. This links with other studies identifying DLPFC activations with prediction error, conflict and uncertainty over which

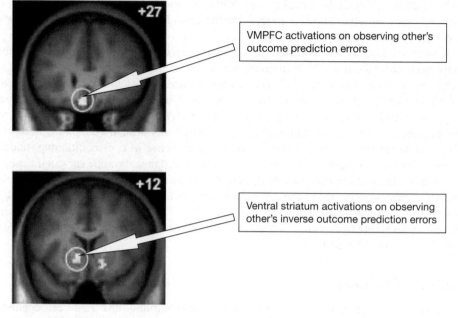

Figure 4.2 fMRI activations during observational learning

action to select. For the action prediction error, there was no response in ventral striatum. The findings from observational learning connect with social learning models; the fMRI activations are shown in Figure 4.2.

Observational action prediction error correlated with activity in the DLPFC. Observational outcome activations came from observing others' outcomes, and may reflect vicarious or fictive learning about rewards that have not been experienced, but could have been experienced. Observational outcome prediction error correlated with positive activations in the VMPFC and in other studies, the VMPFC has been implicated in processing of reward expectations derived from diverse sources of information, and the VMPFC may be one of the areas involved in the mirror system that allows us to understand others' intentions. A particularly interesting finding was identified for observational outcome prediction error when negative activations in the ventral striatum were identified: when the subjects observed 'inverse outcomes' i.e. others' actions delivering losses, the ventral striatum was activated. Whilst this finding may suggest that observing others' losses drives a process of prediction error learning, it is also possible that watching another person lose is rewarding in itself. This would be consistent with other studies suggesting that the ventral striatum is implicated in social competition and punishment of others, and in situations of advantageous inequality when a person sees someone else receiving less money. Behavioural models of inequity aversion can capture some of these phenomena, as explained in chapter 5.

A similar methodology was applied in the analysis of group influence in a financial trading game. Burke *et al.* (2010b) analysed neural activations when players were balancing social information about a group's opinion, and private information about the recent performance of a financial stock. Related analyses also suggested that amygdala and ventral striatum activation might correlate with conformist decisions (buying a stock when a group is buying it) versus contrarian decisions (buying a stock when the group *is not* buying it), depending on an individual's characteristics and personality traits. As explained above, the ventral striatum is implicated in reward processing. Other studies have shown that the amygdala is implicated in aversive learning, that is, when people are feeling fearful. This fMRI analysis of emotions and social learning in financial trading tasks is explored in more detail in the context of financial instability in chapter 11.

More broadly, neuroscientific insights may illuminate some of the processes operating and enable us to assess the importance of mirror neurons and theory of mind to herding behaviour. Social pressure may emerge from imagined and empathetic responses as well as real and direct responses. Singer *et al.* (2004) and Singer and Fehr (2005) analyse the motivations for responding to others, and suggest that imagining experiences of others is associated with similar neurocognitive responses to direct experience itself. This suggests that unravelling some of the neurocognitive foundations of herding behaviour may illuminate some of its key aspects.

Case study: social influences in real-world networks

Social influences are particularly important in networks. In online social networks such as Facebook, for example, people are propelled by an awareness of their interactions with other people, not only via learning, but also via social pressure. A Facebook page becomes the image that someone wants to present to the world. In online social networks, information spreads very rapidly, speeding up learning, and enabling rapid communication and coordination. Social learning and other social influences also have profound impacts in other networks, too, for example in propelling changes in attitudes towards energy conservation and health behaviours, as explained below.

Social influences on household energy decisions

In terms of informational influence, social learning about energy efficiency can take place effectively within group settings. Nye and Burgess (2008) and Nye and Hargreaves (2010) outlined evidence from two UK experiments conducted by Global Action Plan, in which environmental information was communicated in a social setting. One (the Environmental Champions programme) was office-based and focused on 280 people, with a team of energy champions drawn from different departments. These champions engaged in a three-month communication campaign, providing practical information about environmentally friendly behaviour leading to a 38 per cent reduction in waste production and a 12 per cent reduction in energy consumption. The second programme – the EcoTeams programme, focused on household habits and involved neighbourhood meetings to inform communities about energy use. There were a number of positive impacts: 16 per cent adopted green energy tariffs, 37 per cent installed energy-efficient light bulbs, and 17 per cent reduced domestic heating. Participants observed that the scheme worked because, whilst participants were environmentally aware before participating, the EcoTeams programme imparted the practical knowledge to the participants.

Firms' reputation-building and corporate social responsibility

Social influences will affect firms as well as households. Corporate attitudes towards fairness are important, and firms are not invariably engaged in an unquestioning pursuit of profit; they will act according to environmental principles in some circumstances. For example, a US Chamber of Commerce decision to oppose policies to address climate change led to resignations by Apple, Nike, Pacific Gas and Electric, Exelon and PNM Resources (Brown and Hagen 2010; Johansson-Stenman and Konow 2010).

A significant social influence on firms' behaviour is reputation, and firms' corporate social responsibility (CSR) programmes invariably incorporate a commitment to environmental responsibility. To some extent this is a response to consumer pressure, and firms do worry about consumers' perceptions of what is fair, especially in terms of pricing (Kahneman *et al.* 1986). Reputations with competitors and investors will also affect firms' CSR programmes.

Firms will also have an impact via innovation, and this can play a role in changing environmental attitudes and behaviour. Firms are driving the adoption of carbon labelling even though it is expensive and there are no international standards. This might partly reflect reputation-building and/or informing consumers to encourage them to buy more. Profit motivations may also play a role, and there may be direct informational value to the firm as well as to consumers in determining the carbon footprints of products. Walkers, by calculating carbon footprints for the production of their crisps, were able to learn from their carbon labelling, enabling them to save energy and cut costs at the same time. They were buying potatoes by gross weight and so farmers were keeping potatoes in humidified sheds to add extra water – and weight. Walkers had to fry this water off in the production of crisps. The process of assessing the carbon footprint of the crisps revealed useful information about additional costs of production, and Walkers changed its purchasing strategy to buying by dry weight. Energy was saved both from the humidification and also from the reduced frying time (*The Economist* 2011, p.14).

Regulators can also have an impact on firms' decision-making. When firms' social motivations interact with strategic considerations, this can introduce additional complexities, for example Shogren *et al.* (2010) assert that a regulator's subsidy can interact negatively with social motives of a firm concerned about reputation. Selfish firms will make an optimal effort and socially oriented firms will be subsidized less than is optimal.

Firms' concerns about reputation can also encourage them into more environmentally sustainable production methods. There may also be reputational competition amongst firms, and this can be encouraged via information disclosure. Environmental blacklists such as the Toxics Release Inventory can generate social nudges that enable consumers to learn which firms to avoid. Bad publicity affects relationships with investors and competitors as well as customers (Thaler and Sunstein 2008). Thaler and Sunstein suggest that a Greenhouse Gas Inventory requiring most significant emitters to disclose their emissions could have similar beneficial effects to the Toxics Release Inventory, particularly in light of the current salience of climate change problems in the public consciousness.

A study of social influences in Indian villages

In behavioural development economics, social learning and peer effects from observing the actions of others can have a profound impact, particularly because social capital and social networks can be vital when market institutions are not well developed. One area in which social pressures and social learning in networks can improve living standards is health and sanitation, a particular problem in rural underdeveloped regions with high levels of infant mortality. Pattanayak *et al.* (2009) explore the 'shame or subsidy' debate: experts disagree about the relative impacts of monetary incentives/public goods provision versus shaming and social pressure as emotional motivators to encourage the development of healthy social norms. They hypothesized that social pressure and peer monitoring could be as effective as subsidies in encouraging people to develop healthier habits. Learning will also play a role, and Pattanayak *et al.* explored the effectiveness of sanitation campaigns focusing on information, education and communication about good sanitary practices.

They tested their hypotheses using a randomized experimental design to explore the effectiveness of sanitation campaigns in the Indian state of Orissa. They selected twenty villages for a treatment trial and another twenty villages as a control group, with 1050 households in total. The villages in the treatment group were exposed to an information, education and communication campaign to educate people about sanitation, safe water and hygiene. In addition, all forty villages (the control group plus the treatment group) were given access to subsidies to enable villagers to buy latrines. Pattanayak *et al.* postulated, though, that knowledge was not enough, and that behaviour would not change without emotionally salient triggering events. They incorporated community-led sanitation into their experimental design, including three tools: a walk of shame – a community walk during which examples of poor hygiene were identified to the group; defecation mapping – in which villages participated in identifying the spatial distribution of defecation and its effects; and fecal calculations – in which the volume of fecal matter and its likely impacts were discussed.

They found that the information, education and communication campaign had a strongly significant impact in increasing the adoption and use of latrines in the villages: latrine ownership increased from 6 to 32 per cent in the treatment villages. They also found that shame and subsidies together were more effective than subsidies alone. There was significant heterogeneity across villages: in some villages many people participated; in others very few, perhaps reflecting social complementarities. The more people in your network are choosing an action, the more likely you are to choose it too. They found that learning did not generalize, however, and there were no other significant sanitation behaviour changes. Having more latrines did not lead to hand-washing, for example. They concluded that sanitation worldwide can be improved via the implementation of 'social marketing' tools such as social pressure and peer monitoring in policy design.

Conclusions and policy implications

Models of learning from behavioural economics capture the fact that rational individuals do not move immediately towards equilibrium outcomes. It may take them a long time to reach equilibrium – if they ever reach it at all. Learning processes are varied: we learn from our beliefs about others, based on how they have behaved in the past – an approach that is closely related to standard game-theory analyses of evolutionary learning. However, psychological motivations are important too, and these are developed into economic models of RL by embedding insights from psychology about conditioning and reward learning.

Developments in neuroscience have also deepened our understanding of learning, for example, the model of reward prediction error captures the fact that we learn from our mistakes, an insight that links to models of expectations conventionally seen in economics, including the adaptive expectations hypothesis. Another important device for learning is social learning: this can be understood axiomatically in terms of Bayes's rule, but there are broader explanations, too, about the impact of others on our choices.

In terms of policy implications, the evidence about the effectiveness of markets as equilibrating devices is mixed: learning, by definition, cannot easily be understood in terms of static market models. In some learning experiments players do play a rational mixed strategy equilibrium, but at other times psychological factors, such as memory and forgetting, determine the path of learning. Also, as shown in the literature on beauty contests, there may be limits to the depth of reasoning preventing people from reaching Nash equilibria. These insights are particularly relevant for financial markets, in which social learning can have a large impact, especially when speculators' rewards are divorced from long-term performance. This will mean that incentives are constructed to encourage speculators to engage in iterated reasoning and participate in beauty contests, rather than trying accurately to capture the true long-term value of assets. Overall, in devising policies to promote learning, insights about the constraints and influences on learning by households and firms should be addressed.

5 Sociality and identity

Introduction

Learning models, explored in chapter 4, relax the assumption – often seen in standard models – that people act independently of others. With social learning we treat others' actions as a source of information, and many social learning models incorporate this insight into a Bayesian analysis. Broader social influences, also explored in chapter 4, will lead us to imitate others, not only because of positive, informational influences from others, but also because we are susceptible to normative influences such as social pressure and social norms.

Impacts from the social groups around us will, however, be more pervasive if they affect our preferences, utility and identity. In these cases, sociality will lead to further violations of standard assumptions about independent homogeneous agents. We have preferences not only for our own utility and welfare, but also for that of those around us, as explored in behavioural economic models incorporating other-regarding preferences. Behavioural economists have investigated the impact of social preferences to explain departures from the standard assumption of self-interest. Some models incorporate sociality by incor-porating social preferences as extra elements in people's utility functions. This does not involve a radical departure from standard models and from the central assumption of rationality, though it can help to explain evidence that seems anomalous in terms of standard approaches. Other models are more radical, for example, analyses of social identity. In this chapter we explore sociality more broadly, moving from the focus in social learning theories on others' actions as information into analyses of social preferences, rewards and interactions.

Some experimental evidence

Sociality is central to many models from behavioural game theories – which are behavioural versions of standard game theory incorporating noneconomic factors, for example learning and other-regarding preferences including altruism and empathy. Some versions of behavioural game theory were developed in response to robust experimental studies of a wide range of games showing that people do not always play games selfishly, and so behaviour does not converge onto the Nash equilibria predicted by standard game theory – see Camerer (2003b) for a thorough survey. Some of the games commonly used in these experimental analyses are summarized in Box 5.1

Box 5.1   A box of games

Ultimatum game

Player A (the proposer) is given a sum to divide between herself and player B (the responder). If B rejects A's offer, both players get zero. If B accepts A's offer, players get the share proposed by A. Standard game theory predicts that A will offer the minimum possible amount and B will accept it because anything is better than nothing.

Dictator game

Player A – the dictator, is given a sum of money and offers a share to player B; player B cannot veto the offer and must take what he's given by A. Standard game theory predicts that player A will maximize by offering B the minimum possible amount.

Envy games

These games are variants of dictator or ultimatum games designed to disentangle preferences about relative advantage. Player A has a choice between dividing a small amount equally between themselves and player B, versus a larger amount but with proportionately more offered to player B. For example, player A is told to choose between:

1.   £10 divided equally so that A keeps £5 and gives £5 to player B; and
2.   £15 divided unequally with player A keeping a lesser share of £6 and giving £9 to player B.

Standard game theory predicts that A will prefer option 2 because they will prefer more to less, and will ignore how it is distributed.

Public good games

In these games, each player must make a contribution to a public good. Their benefit may exceed their contribution but because, by definition, access to public goods is free and nonrivalrous, there is no economic incentive to contribute. Standard game theory predicts scenarios in which players free-ride on others' contributions.

Trust games

Trust games are two-stage games:

In stage 1, player A – the trustor – offers a sum of money to player B – the trustee. A's contribution is multiplied by some factor by the experimenter and then given to player B.

In stage 2, B decides how much to return to A.

If A is generous/trusting and B reciprocates, then there is a Pareto improvement because both players will be better off. However, standard game theory predicts backward induction: A figures that B will not send anything back because he has no monetary incentive to do so, and so A doesn't send anything in the first place. (Sometimes known as investment games or gift-exchange games.)

Centipede games

Centipede games are multistage versions of trust games; sums of money are sent back and forth between A (the trustor) and B (the trustee) until one or other player 'takes' by deciding how much to keep for themselves and then ends the game. If the player decides to continue playing, then they 'pass' at each stage. Standard game theory predicts backward induction as for the trust game, but in real-life experiments people backward induct only a couple of steps (Camerer 2003b).

Solidarity games

In a solidarity game, three players roll a die to determine a win. Before rolling the die, each player announces how they will allocate 'gifts' to the losers.

This game can be used to separate some of the explanations for generosity in simpler games such as the ultimatum game; for example, some studies find that the same total amount is given regardless of the size of the group, and therefore apparent generosity is not about inequity aversion; gifts for each loser are positively correlated with expectations of gifts from them (Bolton and Ockenfels 2000).

Ultimatum games and dictator games

Possibly the most widely known game in behavioural economics is the ultimatum game. The experimenter gives Alice (the proposer) a fixed sum – say £100; Alice is instructed to offer Bob (the responder) some proportion of that sum – a minimum of £1 to a maximum of £100; if Bob agrees, then they both get the shares proposed by Alice, but if Bob refuses, both get nothing. Standard game theory assumes monotonicity, that is, that more is preferred to less, and so Alice will want to keep as much for herself as possible. She will offer Bob £1 and keep £99 for herself. Via backward induction, she figures that Bob will prefer £1 to nothing and so will accept. Thus standard game theory predicts offers and acceptances close to zero. Accepting zero is still a Nash equilibrium – players are maximizing payoffs given the choices of other players.

Experimental evidence shows, however, that people do not play in this way in the real world – Güth *et al.* (1982) conducted the first comprehensive testing of the original ultimatum game and found that players were often guided by what they thought was a fair or just outcome. Assuming that 50 per cent was perceived as a 'fair' offer, proposers usually offered responders a lot more than zero and relatively close to 50 per cent; and proposers rejected offers around 20 per cent. These findings were replicated across many studies (including animal studies, for example with monkeys playing for juice). In a meta-analysis of results from the ultimatum game, Camerer found that the mean offer was around 30–40 per cent and offers below about 20 per cent were rejected. The findings were also scalable with similar results for small versus large sums of money, though there were some cultural differences (Camerer 2003b; Henrich *et al.* 2004). Andersen *et al.* (2011) analysed strategies played by people in poor villages of north-east India, for whom increases in monetary stakes had a far larger impact. They found that if the stakes are sufficiently high, then responders will accept low offers.

Experiments with trust games

Berg *et al.* (1995) explore trust, reciprocity and social history and try to answer questions about why we trust, and whether or not trust is a primitive response. They construct a repeated game, but one that abstracts from reputation and contractual pre-commitments by using a trust game designed to test trust and trustworthiness. This game tests the extent to which people trust others and in turn reciprocate trust by being trustworthy themselves. Trusting and being trustworthy represent two challenges to narrow self-interest: trusting is a risky strategy and may not be reciprocated; trustworthiness yields no direct, immediate return.

Berg *et al.* note that a problem with trust games (and similar games, including ultimatum and dictator games) is that experimental subjects may want to impress experimenters with their generosity, so they incorporate some experimental design features to reduce the likelihood of experimental bias, introducing a double-blind procedure in which the subjects make contributions anonymously using envelopes and boxes. The experimenter cannot know (and the subjects know that the experimenter cannot know) who has been generous, and so there are neither sanctions nor rewards for altruistic choices. In this way, Berg *et al.* hope that their experimental design will allow them to abstract from relationships, social influences, communication, etc.

Berg *et al.* use two groups of subjects in two rooms: subject As in room A and subject Bs in room B. All subjects are given $10 to either keep or share. The game then proceeds in two stages. In stage 1, subject A decides how much of her $10 to send to an anonymous counterpart in room B (the trustee). This amount is tripled and sent to a player B in room B. Stage 1 tests the trust of players A; if they do not trust the people in room B then they will send no money. In stage 2, A's contribution is tripled and given to player B. Player B must then decide by how much to reciprocate. Essentially, stage 2 is a dictator game; player B has complete control over the outcome and player A cannot veto his or her choice.

Standard game theory predicts the following set of subgame perfect equilibria: player B's dominant strategy will be to keep everything – if B is purely self-interested then he has no incentive to reciprocate by being trustworthy and returning something to A. Via backward induction, player A reasons therefore that their best strategy is to send nothing because anything that they do send is kept by B. Assuming that A is purely self-interested, then she has no incentive to send anything to B in the first place.

The problem for both players is that they get stuck in something like a prisoner's dilemma: both players could have done better by being generous. With no trust and no reciprocity, A keeps $10, B does nothing, and both suffer as a result because neither of them gets any more than their initial payment. On the other hand, if A had been maximally generous and offered $10, then this would have been tripled to $30. If B had sent half back to A, $15, then there would have been a Pareto improvement. Both players would have been unequivocally better off. Both are made better off by trusting and reciprocating, and this links into evolutionary analyses in which making and returning kindnesses have evolutionary advantages in social environments, as discussed below.

Contributing nothing and not reciprocating is the standard game theory prediction, but the experimental results resemble those seen in ultimatum games. In Berg *et al.*'s study, almost all room A subjects were trusting; thirty out of thirty-two subjects (94 per cent) sent something to room B, though there was a large degree of variability in the amounts sent. There is less evidence of reciprocity from the players in room B, though 57 per cent did reciprocate by sending back more than A sent and, on average, players in room A did at least get their money back. Apart from that, the extent of trust and reciprocity was not correlated. To assess the impact of social norms, Berg *et al.* also analysed the impact of social history – that is, information about average responses in previous rounds. They found that these social norms did have some impact, especially for players in room B.

The selection of experimental evidence outlined above suggests that people do not generally make choices consistent with the standard assumptions of game theory. There are a number of potential explanations: it could just be that people are inherently generous. Social norms may dictate that people play in a generous way. As explained in the context of learning models in chapter 4, it may take time to learn the best strategies; if people have learnt social norms of generosity outside the lab, then it takes time and experience to unlearn them. Responses may reflect strategic reasoning, for example if people believe that stinginess will at some point be punished by the other player. Overall, there is an empirical problem in separating these hypotheses about motivation, and a number of theoretical models have been devised to explain the results, as explored in the following section.

Social preference models

Sen (1977, 1991) argues that the focus on a single assumption of self-interest in standard models suggests that people are 'rational fools', considering only a single preference ordering given by their own self-interest, without recognizing that they have preferences over a range of alternatives. Conversely, in his comparative analysis of Adam Smith's (1776) *An Inquiry into the Nature and Causes of the Wealth of Nations* and his (1759) *Theory of Moral Sentiments*, Vernon L Smith (1998) hypothesizes that Adam Smith's two sets of ideas, whilst apparently contradictory, are actually consistent. The self-interest in *The Wealth of Nations* and the sympathy in *The Theory of Moral Sentiments* are different facets of the same thing – a 'self-interested propensity to exchange'. In *The Wealth of Nations* it is exchange of money and goods; in *The Theory of Moral Sentiments* it is exchange of friendship. In this way, Vernon L Smith asserts that self-interest and other-regarding sympathy are connected.

Behavioural models have to some extent addressed these debates by building models incorporating other-regarding preferences. In attempting to reconcile the experimental results and varying interpretations, behavioural economists have come up with a range of theoretical explanations for the range of social preferences revealed in the experiments outlined above. These models focus on the different reasons for cooperation and altruism, including traits of kindness and fairness, warm-glow giving, inequity aversion, preferences for relative as well as absolute payoffs, and strategic thinking. A selection of the models is outlined below.

Social utility models

Social utility models are, to a greater or lesser extent, encompassing in the sense that they attempt to reconcile the range of experimental evidence – from the market games evidence in which people exhibit self-interest, through to the games that reveal generous behaviour in other contexts, for example the ultimatum, dictator and trust games.

Bolton and Ockenfels's equity, reciprocity and competition model

Bolton and Ockenfels's (1998, 2000) equity, reciprocity and competition (ERC) model is a general model devised to capture other-regarding preferences. They argue that models with altruistic preferences cannot fully explain play in ultimatum games, dictator games and solidarity games, because needs of others and reducing inequality are not necessarily primary goals.

Bolton and Ockenfels suggest that a good model should explain a number of statements about empirical regularities from experimental analyses:

*   Statement 1: in dictator games, on average dictators keep at least half but give less than the whole pie;
*   Statement 2: in ultimatum games, responders accept all offers of the whole pie and reject all offers of nothing;
*   Statement 3: in ultimatum games, the proposer will propose a payoff to themselves of at least half but less than the whole pie, that is, offering some proportion less than half to the responder;
*   Statement 4: average offers in ultimatum games exceed average offers in dictator games.

Developing a comparative model from Bolton (1991) and Bolton and Ockenfels (1998), the ERC model assumes narrow self-interest, but with people balancing trade-offs between their absolute pecuniary payoffs and relative payoffs. Relative payoffs are judged against a social reference point, assumed to be an equal share to each player: for a game with two players, a share of 1/2. The model is designed to capture play in one-shot games and, unlike Fehr and Schmidt's (1999) model (discussed below), it allows for incomplete information. Given imperfect information, experimental 'observables' are used to construct two thresholds at which behaviour deviates from monotonicity – the proposer's offer threshold in the dictator game, and the responder's rejection threshold in the ultimatum game.

From this, Bolton and Ockenfels construct a general *motivation function*, which incorporates monetary payoffs and relative shares. They illustrate their hypotheses using an example motivation function for a two-player game, incorporating a social reference point of equal shares. This function is also constructed so that larger deviations from equal share have a proportionately larger impact in lowering utility. Each player's type is given by the ratio of weights they assign to pecuniary versus relative payoffs, with the weights determined by context, for example, age, education, politics, religion. Narrow self-interest increases as the weight on pecuniary payoffs increases. Their model is as described mathematically in Box 5.2.

Bolton and Ockenfels argue that their model is consistent with experimental evidence from a range of experimental contexts, including dictator and ultimatum games when generosity is observed, and auction games, which reveal competitive play as predicted by standard game-theory models. They argue that their model can reconcile apparently anomalous findings. This develops findings from Roth *et al.* (1991), who identified differences in outcomes from market games versus bargaining games, including the ultimatum game. Roth *et al.* describe evidence from experiments in Israel, Japan, the USA and Yugoslavia. Market games converged on the equilibria predicted by standard models, but there was a wide variety of standard and nonstandard outcomes for ultimatum games, suggesting that cultural differences may play a role in the formation of other-regarding preferences. Other studies also find that other-regarding behaviour is not necessarily replicated in our close primate

Box 5.2   Mathematics of Bolton and Ockenfels's ERC model

Bolton and Ockenfels construct two thresholds at which behaviour deviates from monotonicity, which, given incomplete information, are based on experimental observables:

$r_i(c)$: proposer's offer thresholds in dictator games

$s_i(c)$: responder's rejection thresholds in ultimatum games.

General motivation function

From these thresholds, Bolton and Ockenfels construct a general motivation function:

$$v_i = v_i(y_i, \sigma_i)$$

where y_i is i's monetary payoff and σ_i is i's relative share of the total payoff – the proportion of the total kept by player i. Each player's relative share is determined by y, c and n, giving:

$$\sigma_i = \sigma_i(y_i, c, n)$$

The total payout is:

$$c = \sum_{j=1}^{n} y_j$$

It follows that $y_i = c\sigma_i$

For example, in a two-player dictator game, the share kept by the dictator is given by σ_D and so the dictator's payoff is $c\sigma_D$ and the recipient's payoff is $(1 - \sigma_D)c$.

An example motivation function

Bolton and Ockenfels's example motivation function for a two-player game incorporating a social reference point = 1/2 is given by:

$$v_i(c\sigma_i, \sigma_i) = a_i c\sigma_i - \frac{b_i}{2}\left(\sigma_i - \frac{1}{2}\right)^2$$

where $a_i \geq 0$, $b_i > 0$.

Each player's type is given by the ratio of weights to pecuniary (the first term on the right-hand side) versus relative payoffs (the second term on the right-hand side): a/b. Strict narrow self-interest increases as $a/b \to \infty$.

The quadratic form allows that larger deviations from equal share have proportionately larger impact in lowering utility. Weights can be assigned to different objectives depending on context and individual differences.

relatives. Jensen *et al.* (2007) for example use experimental techniques to identify rational maximizing behaviour amongst chimpanzees playing the ultimatum game.

Bolton and Ockenfels's emphasis on narrow self-interest means that their model fits more neatly with mainstream assumptions of rationality, but they assert that their motivation function can also connect different social preferences seen in different contexts, for example, sometimes people exhibit social preferences for fairness; other times they want to reciprocate; and other times they want to compete. The ERC model can reconcile evidence about equity, reciprocity and generosity with evidence about competitive self-interested behaviour, allowing heterogeneous preferences to reflect differing motivations. The ERC model is also consistent with interplays of equity and strategy. For example, generous offers in ultimatum games may not reflect pure altruism, but instead may reflect proposers strategically anticipating how responders might react.

Inequity aversion in Fehr and Schmidt's fairness, competition and cooperation model

Fehr and Schmidt's model develops Loewenstein *et al.*'s (1989) analysis of inequality aversion within an experimental context, using subjects' responses to hypothetical dispute scenarios in which the experimental subject is either acknowledged or snubbed by a hypothetical partner in a range of scenarios, including nonbusiness interactions with a peer, and business interactions between a customer and salesperson. Subjects were asked to grade their satisfaction with the hypothetical solution. Loewenstein *et al.* used the fit of reported satisfactions to a range of social utility functions, and found that a utility function which incorporated discrepancies in the payoffs between the members of each pair correlated well with reported satisfaction.

Fehr and Schmidt developed Loewenstein *et al.*'s (1989) model to construct their own model of fairness, competition and cooperation (FCC) capturing the impacts of inequity aversion on utility. In this model, utility is affected by payoff differentials between players. If a person has a smaller payoff than other players, this will lower their utility; if they have a larger payoff, that will raise their utility, as described mathematically in Box 5.3.

Fehr and Schmidt describe two forms of inequity aversion: advantageous inequity aversion – inequity aversion experienced by people in a position of relative advantage; and disadvantageous inequity aversion – inequity aversion experienced by people in a position of relative disadvantage. To illustrate with examples, a banker who is unhappy about poverty is experiencing advantageous inequity aversion; a poor person who is unhappy about bankers being rich is experiencing disadvantageous inequity aversion.

Overall, Fehr and Schmidt's (1999) insights are somewhat similar to Bolton and Ockenfels (1998, 2000), though Fehr and Schmidt are less reliant on an assumption of narrow self-interest and assert that seemingly irrational behaviour in ultimatum games and dictator games reflects inequity aversion. Like Bolton and Ockenfels, Fehr and Schmidt claim that their FCC model can reconcile a range of experimental results showing that people are sometimes cooperative and sometimes selfish – in contrast to standard approaches predicting self-interested and uncooperative behaviour in all contexts. The FCC model can capture the range of responses including the fairness and cooperation seen in ultimatum games, public good games with punishments and gift exchange games, and also the uncooperative competitive behaviour observed in market games and public good games without punishment.

Fehr and Schmidt's assertion about the generality of their model has created some controversy. Binmore and Shaked (2010a, 2010b) assert that the empirical support for the

---

Box 5.3   Mathematics of Fehr and Schmidt's FCC model

Fehr and Schmidt (1999) develop Loewenstein *et al.*

For *n* players $i \in \{1, \ldots, n\}$ with monetary payoffs given by $x = x_1, \ldots, x_n$ the utility function for player *i* is given by:

$$U_i(x) = x_i - \alpha_i \frac{1}{n-1} \sum_{j \neq i} \max\{x_j - x_i, 0\} - \beta_i \frac{1}{n-1} \sum_{j \neq i} \max\{x_i - x_j, 0\}$$

In the two-player case, this simplifies to:

$$U_i(x) = x_i - \alpha_i \sum_{j \neq i} \max\{x_j - x_i, 0\} - \beta_i \sum_{j \neq i} \max\{x_i - x_j, 0\}$$

They assume that $\beta_i \leq a_i$ and $0 \leq \beta_i < 1$.

Utility is maximized where $x_i = x_j$ and the utility loss from disadvantageous inequity aversion, $x_i < x_j$, is larger than the utility loss from advantageous inequity aversion, $x_i > x_j$.

---

inequity aversion model is not as robust as Fehr and Schmidt claim; Fehr and Schmidt (2010) respond that Binmore and Shaked have not posed a fundamental challenge to their approach. The dispute remains unresolved. More nuanced empirical testing of the various theories of inequity aversion will be helpful in resolving the debate.

Other models

The models presented above are an introduction to other-regarding preferences. There are many other models designed to capture other-regarding preferences, some of which are similar to the Fehr and Schmidt model – including models of fairness, kindness and reciprocity, for example, Rabin (1993); Kahneman *et al.* (1986); Falk and Fischbacher (2006). Fehr and Gintis (2007) assert that formal models of inequity aversion (Fehr and Schmidt 1999) and reciprocal fairness (Falk and Fischbacher 2006) are indispensable tools in analysing social phenomena, but there are a large number of other theoretical explanations for generous behaviour.

Other models have focused on the emotional satisfaction derived from giving, for example, Andreoni's (1990) model of warm-glow giving, capturing the fact that utility increases with the act of giving, for example, in donations to public goods. Theories of altruism and warm-glow giving have been applied to ordinary daily activities, including the trade-offs between volunteering and work. Sauer (2011) analyses volunteering and finds that it is optimal when warm glow and expected future economic returns sufficiently outweigh disutility of extra work effort and childcare costs. Highly educated women receive more warm glow, and there are substantial economic and noneconomic returns to volunteering, with returns to effort particularly high for those in part-time work.

Another set of theories revolves around the insight that generosity and altruism may represent investments in our interpersonal relationships and connections, as seen in social capital and social network theories – enormous literatures in themselves and beyond the scope of this book, but for those interested to learn more, see Dasgupta (2007); Goyal (2009) on social networks; Putnam (2001) and Halpern (2005) on social capital.

Cooperation and punishment

The models outlined above present theoretical explanations for other-regarding behaviour, but what sort of actions encourage people to cooperate and/or to punish people who don't? In understanding why people sometimes cooperate and at other times do not, it is helpful to think about what deters people from violating social norms of reciprocity, and what people can do to encourage others to cooperate.

Altruistic punishment (AP)

Studies in behavioural economics and neuroeconomics have shown that people are willing to pay to punish norm violators. They also find that people who are initially cooperative will start to defect if they are not punished. Fehr and Gächter (2000) study AP of social norm violations. They begin by defining social norms as behavioural regularities based on socially shared beliefs about how to behave. Social norms are enforced via informal social sanctions, and these sanctions determine work effort, consumption choices and common pool resources, as well as provision of public goods. Social history is important, and people do punish inappropriate behaviour even when this is costly to themselves. Fehr and Gächter (2000) explore these insights in an experimental study of AP based on an adaptation of Fehr and Schmidt's (1999) FCC model to a public good game. Their experimental game was conducted in two stages: a contribution stage and a punishment stage. In the punishment stage, the players were given the opportunity to use monetized punishment points to punish defectors. They found that without punishment there was almost complete defection from social norms, but with punishment a large proportion cooperated.

There were further differences, dependent on the level of anonymity in the interactions. They divided the treatments into partner and stranger treatments. When subjects were playing with strangers, they were less likely to cooperate; when they were playing with known partners and violations were punished, 82.5 per cent of subjects cooperated fully. At the other extreme, in the no-punishment stranger treatments, over time contributions converged onto full free-riding. A similar experimental design has been adapted for neuroeconomic analysis by de Quervain *et al.* (2004), who found that AP stimulated neural responses usually associated with reward processing, as explored in more detail in the neuroeconomics section below.

Extrinsic versus intrinsic motivations

Interactions between individual and cooperative goals also affect choices. Constructing markets for things that have traditionally been sustained on the basis of social values can threaten the existence of socially beneficial actions. Titmuss (1970) described the negative impact of introducing payments for blood donation: payments undermined social values and therefore dampened people's willingness to donate. Frey and Jegen (2001) examined this phenomenon in the context of motivation crowding theory, drawing on insights from psychology about the 'hidden costs of rewards': monetary incentives drive extrinsic motivation (motivation driven by external rewards) and undermine intrinsic motivations, which are internally driven motivations such as curiosity, helpfulness and self-realization. Crowding out of intrinsic effects undermines the focus in standard economic theory on the importance of monetary rewards and incentives.

Bénabou and Tirole (2003) adapt these insights and incorporate them within an economic analysis of principal–agent problems. External rewards offered by a principal (for example, a teacher) affect the intrinsic motivations of an agent (for example, a student) so that external incentives are weakly reinforcing in the short run and negatively reinforcing in the long run because they crowd out intrinsic motivations. There are many examples from experimental economics. In one study, university students were asked to solve a puzzle. Those who were not paid, and so were presumably doing the puzzle for the intellectual challenge, put more effort into the task than the students who were paid (Deci 1975).

Gneezy and Rustichini (2000a) report results from a field study of parents collecting children from school. Parents would often arrive late, forcing the school to make sure a teacher was available to look after the children until their parents arrived. The school decided to introduce a fine as a deterrent, but the plan backfired and more parents arrived late with a late fine than without one. This phenomenon may reflect the fact that, once a fine was introduced, arriving late was then interpreted as costly service, and any guilt that parents may formerly have felt about arriving late was eliminated if they were given the chance to pay for arriving late. The extrinsic disincentive (the fine) crowded out the intrinsic motivation – to cooperate by trying to arrive on time as often as possible.

Gneezy and Rustichini (2000b) found similar results in an analysis of the performance of experimental subjects (students from the University of Haifa, Israel) completing a series of quizzes, and offered a range of different incentives – with payments made in New Israeli Shekels (NIS). One group was given no payment; the second, third and fourth groups were paid 10 cents, 1 NIS and 3 NIS, respectively. Performance was lowest in the second group. Those who were not paid at all performed better than those with a small 10-cent payment. Gneezy and Rustichini found similar results for a study of volunteer work by high-school children, and concluded that excessively small payments can be demotivating, leading to worse performance than no payment at all, because small payments crowd out intrinsic motivation without offering external incentives sufficient to bite into extrinsic motivation.

Bénabou and Tirole (2006) used concepts of intrinsic and extrinsic motivation to explain pro-social behaviour. In many contexts, people exhibit pro-social behaviour involving altruism or reciprocity. This reflects not only intrinsic motivations, but also social pressures and social norms, which link into reputations and self-respect. Taking into account this mix of motivations and heterogeneity in propensities towards altruism and self-interest, Bénabou and Tirole constructed a model in which choices were the outcome of three motivators: intrinsic motivation, extrinsic motivation and reputation-building. Extrinsic rewards not only crowd out intrinsic motivations, but they also 'spoil' the reputational and/or self-image value of pro-social choices.

Ariely *et al.* (2009a) explore intrinsic motivation, specifically personal preferences for giving, extrinsic motivation and also image motivation. They formulate an 'effectiveness hypothesis': extrinsic rewards are less effective for visible pro-social actions; they deter pro-social behaviour because they dilute its signalling value. They explore these hypotheses using experimental evidence from subjects randomly assigned to one of two US charities, either the American Red Cross or the National Rifle Association. Charities were labelled as 'good' or 'bad' according to participants' perceptions of the majority's view, and the subjects were asked to engage in a simple but effortful task (pressing X and Z on a computer keyboard). Performance in this task was rewarded with donations by the experimenters to the subject's charity. Public and private conditions without monetary incentives led to greater effort by the subjects in the public condition, that is, when their efforts were revealed. Monetary incentives did not increase effort in the public condition; in the private condition there were significant increases in effort. Ariely *et al.* interpret these results as support for their effectiveness hypothesis: monetary incentives work better for anonymous giving; for public giving they impact negatively, perhaps because of the negative impact on the social signalling value of philanthropy when efforts and payments are public knowledge.

Evolution and social cues

Seabright (2004) analyses the importance of cooperation in social groups, and explores some of the evolutionary origins of cooperation, reciprocity and trustworthiness even amongst strangers. There is evidence that cognitive control has evolved within a social context; human children and chimpanzees use similar cognitive skills when dealing with physical tasks, but human children have more sophisticated cognitive skills when engaged in social tasks, including social learning and empathy or theory of mind (Herrmann *et al.* 2007). There is also anthropological evidence about the role of cultural factors: some cultures have no sharing norm, suggesting that sharing is a cultural construct (Henrich *et al.* 2001).

Cooperation can also be sustained by social cues such as smiling. Centorrino *et al.* (2011) explored the role of smiling in cooperation, and tested the hypothesis that a convincing smile is costly but has evolved to sustain cooperation and trust. Using the trust game, they conducted experiments in which people watched video clips of potential trustees who were otherwise strangers before deciding whether not to send them money. The trustors were also asked to rate how genuine they found the trustees' smiles. Smiles from trustees playing for higher stakes were rated as significantly more convincing. The convincing smiles also were significantly correlated with the trustworthiness of the trustees as measured by their willingness to reciprocate by sending money back. Smiling was also found to be an honest signal: those smiling convincingly returned more money on average, and this may reflect the fact that convincing smiles are costly and rewards from encouraging cooperation appear to induce effort.

Ostracism in social networks

Punishment can be effective in social networks. Fowler and Christakis (2010) and Randa *et al.* (2011) examined punishment within social networks. They conducted online experiments using *Mechanical Turk* (*MTurk*) to investigate large-scale cooperation in social networks. The experimental subjects played public good games either with or without punishment, and were assigned partners either randomly or by choosing their own. When partners were randomly allocated, cooperation was equally beneficial to all partners and there was no incentive to cooperation and so it decayed over time, confirming Fehr and Gächter's (2000) study. Also, it may be true that social factors are as much a carrot as they are a stick: people are inclined to cooperate because they benefit in terms of their own social connectedness. Questions of depersonalization and identification (as explored in more detail in the identity section below) may also be relevant: if people feel they have built a positive cooperative relationship with someone they know and/or have interacted with before, that will encourage them to partner with that person again.

Fowler and Christakis (2010) found that voluntary costly punishment can help sustain cooperation. Subjects were influenced by the contributions of others, including those with whom they did not interact initially. These social influences persist over time and spread through the social network to up to three degrees of separation and cooperation cascaded through the social network. Randa *et al.* (2011) developed this study to show experimentally that people make and break social networks in response to cooperation versus defection by others. Cooperation decays over time if social links are outside the control of individuals (because they are fixed or determined randomly) or if links are updated infrequently. However, if subjects have short-term control of their social connections, they can decide to break links with defectors and form links with cooperators. When people can choose who they do (and don't) interact with, it creates an incentive to cooperate because defectors will be excluded from social networks if they behave uncooperatively.

Identity

Another way in which social context can affect behaviour is via its impact on identity. Identity can be incorporated into economic analyses of social interactions using insights from sociology, and specifically from social identity theory.

Social identity theory

Sociologists have established that identities are easy to create and have a significant impact on social behaviour. Tajfel (1970) conducted a study in which he randomly assigned boys to groups using a minimal group paradigm that involved grouping people on a minimal, largely arbitrary basis. In this case, the boys were assigned to groups on the basis of whether they had under- or over-estimated the number of dots in a visual image, and whether they preferred one artist or another. Thus identity was formed on the basis of very limited input. The boys were assessed as they played a penny game: they were asked to decide how many pennies they would give their group – the in-group; and how many pennies they would give to the other group – the out-group. The boys made offers that strongly favoured their own in-group. Tajfel (1970) and Tajfel and Turner (1979) developed social identity theory by applying these insights about the role played by social identity to analyses of intergroup conflict and discrimination.

In behavioural development economics, similar ideas are applied to the analysis of post-conflict behaviours. For example, Bauer *et al.* (2011) explored egalitarian motives in children exposed to armed conflict, and found that intergroup conflicts had significant impacts on children's cooperative behaviour. They studied children soon after the 2008 war between Georgia and Russia for control of South Ossetia. They asked them to play variants of dictator games and envy games, with sweet treats as rewards. Envy games disentangle advantageous and disadvantageous inequity aversion by exploring what happens when players are facing higher total payoffs, both to themselves and to the other player, but at a relative disadvantage to themselves. For example, children choose between offering two sweets to another child and keeping two for themselves, versus offering four sweets to another child and keeping three sweets for themselves. Bauer *et al.* found that the children's experience of conflict during the Ossetia war had impacts on their other-regarding preferences, and was associated with increased egalitarianism and decreased competition when playing games with their in-group, but parochialism and increased competition when playing games with the out-group. Similar results were found for adults in Sierra Leone.

Alexander and Christia (2011) also analyse sociality in a postwar setting using evidence from public good experiments. These were conducted on religiously diverse Catholic Croat and Muslim Bosniak communities in postwar Mostar, Bosnia-Herzegovina. Alexander and Christia found that cooperation could be achieved using sanctions, but that the effectiveness of these sanctions depended on whether the communities were segregated or integrated. In mixed but segregated communities, participants contributed low amounts whether or not there were sanctions, but in integrated mixed communities contributions were more than doubled even without sanctions, and with sanctions contributions were more than tripled. This evidence suggests that institutional environments play an important role in reintegrating postwar communities, perhaps indicating that postwar reconstruction should focus on building institutions designed to moderate ethno-religious differences in identity.

Chen and Li (2009) found that induced group identity had a significant impact in increasing altruistic behaviour towards in-group versus out-group members. Subjects in their experiments were more generous towards in-group versus out-group members; they were also more likely to reward in-group members and less likely to punish in-group members, and showed a substantial decrease in envy and increase in cooperativeness towards in-group versus out-group members.

Akerlof and Kranton's identity theory

Economists have taken insights from sociology to develop economic models of identity. Akerlof and Kranton (2000, 2011) construct a model of identity based on social categories, and argue that people's identities are moulded by sociological factors. In their identity model, utility depends on identity or self-image, an individual's own actions and the actions of others. They state that since the actions of self and others determine an individual's own consumption, the elements of their utility function are sufficient to capture standard economic variables.

Within this approach, identity is endogenous because it is determined by individuals' actions and the actions of others. Identity is also affected by social categories: this is a categorical model of identity. Finally, identity is affected by an individual's characteristics and the extent to which those characteristics match the prescribed behaviour for a particular group. People have some limited choice over their identity, but the pressures to remain within a particular category are strong, and ostracism often makes it difficult for people to redefine their own identities. Akerlof and Kranton (2000) use their model to analyse identity in a number of different contexts. Actions that seem irrational in a standard model make more sense in an identity model: for example, self-mutilating actions such as tattooing, plastic surgery, body piercing, starvation and steroid abuse are irrational, costly acts from a standard economic perspective; but in a model of identity they generate utility by reinforcing a person's identity and sense of belonging to a group. The actions of others can also affect utility via identity. If a man is insulted and baited by his fellow workers, thereby undermining his masculine identity, then he will experience disutility for that reason. Violating prescriptions for a particular identity will also have impacts on utility: if a person violates the prescriptive norms of their group, for example, if a man wears a dress, then this may have negative impact on others' utility by undermining their sense of identity. Identity has wider impacts too: with herding, for example, when a person identifies strongly with a group, their perceptions of social pressure from that group can lead them more easily to lose faith in their own judgments and copy the actions of others in their group. It might be rational to submit to group pressure, to empathize and to obey rules of etiquette in a world where social context is important and where social factors enhancing status and reputation are important.

Akerlof and Kranton's approach has been criticized for its focus on the individual within social categories. Davis (2006, 2010) argues that identity is more complex than Akerlof and Kranton allow. Akerlof and Kranton embed identity into a standard framework around utility function; in essence it is about self-image, broadly defined. Identity goes beyond self-image: the Akerlof and Kranton approach does not allow for multiple identities, and does not distinguish personal identity from social identity.

Davis (2006) observes that there are two main alternatives to Akerlof and Kranton's approach: Sen's (1999, 2004) commitment approach, and the complexity approach. In Sen's approach, individuals recognize that commitments to social groups reflect a recognition that groups, and the behavioural rules that define those groups, have an intrinsic value, so the value of the individual to the group is as important as the value of the group to the individual. Davis (2006) identifies another alternative to Akerlof and Kranton's identity theory: the complexity models (for example, Kirman and Teschl 2004) which focus on individuals interacting within social groups – not market institutions. People's identities form via interactions with social groups and their social identifications with others, creating feedback effects between self-image and social context – a complexity not fully captured in Akerlof and Kranton's individualistic approach.

Neuroeconomic analyses

There have been a relatively large number of neuroeconomic studies of social decision-making. This reflects the growth of social neuroscience, the increasingly successful collaborations between neuroscientists and social economists, and also the fact that behavioural game theory can give a clean, tight experimental context in which relevant social factors can be controlled to study their neural correlates. For example, Sanfey (2007) observes that the study of social decision-making can be enhanced by using formal mathematical approaches from economics constrained by known neural mechanisms.

Cohen (2005) also argues that the evolution of the brain has been formed by social influences; with smaller groups the chances of repeated interaction were greater. As sociality evolved, strong emotional responses to selfish and exploitative behaviour increased fitness; worrying about reputation was a necessary adaptation to a world in which individuals had a high chance of repeated interaction with a small group of people. Evidence for the operation of ancient emotional structures in the context of social influence includes evidence from ultimatum games, in which altruistic behaviours are associated with activations in areas associated with emotional processing such as the insula (Sanfey *et al.* 2003). Evidence from neuroscientific analysis of economic games suggests that social rewards are associated with activations in areas associated with processing of rewards, for example, the ventral striatum, and these activations are in addition to activations from financial rewards. Also, activations are particularly pronounced when cooperation is reciprocated (Rilling *et al.* 2002; Sanfey 2007).

De Quervain et al.*'s analysis of altruistic punishment in the trust game*

As explored above, players who violate social norms and defect in trust games inspire in their opponents a desire to punish altruistically. In exploring the neural basis of altruistic punishment (AP), de Quervain *et al.* (2004) focus on the social brain and associated moral emotions, noting that human cooperation has evolved without modern law enforcement institutions, and occurs even between unrelated individuals who will never meet again, reflecting mechanisms encouraging strong reciprocity.

de Quervain *et al.* identify a role for AP and reward. 'Altruistic' punishment occurs when people voluntarily incur costs when they punish defectors for violating social norms, and models incorporating AP give better predictions than models assuming self-interested preferences. AP can help explain evolutionarily unprecedented levels of cooperation in human societies, but where does it come from? de Quervain *et al.* focus on its evolutionary roots. They define biological altruism as costly acts for the individual in the present that confer economic benefits on others in the future. This enables the survival of the species. But why would someone be biologically altruistic if there is no direct personal gain? The answer is that we have evolved to feel pleasure from AP, and here de Quervain *et al.* make a distinction between biological and psychological altruism: if we derive real psychological satisfaction from AP, then it is not psychological altruism, but it does mimic the effects of biological altruism. In this way, de Quervain *et al.* argue that AP has deep evolutionary roots, and has evolved as a proximate mechanism. Proximate mechanisms are the present, immediate factors responsible for a given behaviour, and reflect the evolution of internal physiology in response to natural selection. AP bestows social benefits and so is a proximate mechanism that has been selected to ensure people receive hedonic/psychological rewards from AP. If punishment gives relief/satisfaction to the punisher, then that is a beneficial action for the species in evolutionary terms.

In structuring their neuroeconomic study, de Quervain *et al.* outline a series of hypotheses. Norms evolve to encourage cooperation, reciprocity and fairness even between unrelated individuals. In trust games, norms encourage A to trust B by sending money to B. B reciprocates, demonstrating trustworthiness when he/she sends money back. Social norms between genetically unrelated individuals are enforced through altruistic sanctions, and these have a neural basis. Satisfaction from AP will be associated with activation of brain areas associated with goal-directed reward processing, including the striatum.

de Quervain *et al.* incorporate punishment into an experimental design based around a trust game similar to Berg *et al.*'s trust game (described above). Two human players, a trustor (A) and a trustee (B), interact anonymously in a trust game. They are rewarded with real monetary payoffs converted into monetary units (MU). Each player starts with 10 MU, and if A gives 10 MU to B, the experimenter quadruples the amount so that B receives 40 MU. Then B can either keep all 50 MU, or can send 25 MU back to A.

Extending the Berg *et al.* experimental design, de Quervain *et al.* also incorporate a third stage into the game, in which if A perceives B to be an untrustworthy defector, then A is given the opportunity to punish the violation of the reciprocity norm using up to 20 punishment points (PP). Two types of punishment affected the punished defectors: symbolic punishment, in which the PP had no monetary equivalent and so did not reduce defector's payoffs; and effective punishment, which led to a real reduction in defectors' payoffs of 2 MU per PP. For the punishers, there were two scenarios: costly punishment, for which the punishers had to pay 1 MU per PP; and free punishment, in which the PP incurred no monetary cost on the punisher.

There were four different treatment conditions used in randomized sequence, covering scenarios in which B's choice to defect was made freely versus determined by a random device; and punishment was/was not costly for A and B. These treatment conditions were as follows.

- Intentional, costly (IC): B is intentionally untrustworthy, then A can pay for PPs to punish B with effective punishment – in this case punishment is costly for both A and B. Twelve of fourteen A subjects punished B subjects.

- Intentional, free (IF): A does not have to pay to punish defectors. All fourteen A subjects punished B if he/she kept all the money.
- Intentional, symbolic (IS): For intentional defections by B, punishment was symbolic and was free for both A and B.
- Nonintentional, costly (NC): B's decision was determined randomly and punishment was costly. Only three of fourteen A subjects punished B in the NC scenario.

The experiment was run with fifteen healthy, right-handed male subjects. Each player A played the game seven times with different player Bs, and fourteen out of fifteen times A trusted B, so these findings broadly confirm Berg *et al.*'s finding that people generally exhibit trust. However, for all players A, B was trustworthy in three of seven trials and untrustworthy in the remaining four, so there is less evidence of trustworthiness and reciprocity than there is of trust. Questionnaires were completed during the ten-minute interval between brain scans: player A indicated on a seven-point Likert scale (from −3 to +3) whether he perceived B's action in the previous trials to be fair or unfair.

As explained in chapter 2, positron emission tomography (PET) brain scans monitor blood flow following injections of substances (usually glucose) containing radioactive isotopes, which emit gamma rays as they decay. Brain scanning was used only to analyse the trials in which player A trusted but player B did not reciprocate, leading A to punish untrustworthy behaviour; de Quervain *et al.* were interested specifically in subject A's neural responses whilst deciding whether or not to punish B for being untrustworthy, so scans were done of subject A for the one-minute deliberation period when he/she decided whether or not to punish B. In brain-imaging studies, contrast conditions are used to allow quantitative comparisons of brain activation under different scenarios; if the differential activation in a particular area is large enough, then it is inferred that that area of the brain is implicated.

The main hypotheses were that there would be differential activation in reward-related areas in the brain for five contrast conditions, as follows.

- IF–IS contrast: between free versus symbolic punishment when B has defected intentionally captures A's desire to punish. Effective punishment is likely to be more satisfying than symbolic punishment because it is perceived to be fairer and more just than symbolic punishment. Those with the strongest activation in reward-related areas for the IF–IS condition should also be those who incur the largest punishment costs.
- IC–IS contrast: between costly and symbolic punishment when B has defected intentionally capture's A's willingness to pay to punish. If punishment is satisfying, then subjects should be willing to incur punishment costs, leading to great differential activation for the IC–IS contrast.
- IF–NC contrast: the nonintentional, costly condition should not stimulate any desire to punish because B's behaviour is determined randomly by factors outside their control, so B has not defected intentionally and in that sense is not at fault.
- IC–NC contrast: again, B's behaviour is unintentional and so would not be perceived as unfair.
- Combined contrast [IC+IF]–[IS+NC]; this captures the coincidence of the desire and opportunity to punish captured by [IC+IF] versus no opportunity to punish in IS and no desire to punish in NC. [IS+NC] will not be satisfying and so will not activate reward processing structures.

The PET imaging results revealed that the caudate nucleus played a prominent role, with a lesser role for the thalamus and prefrontal/orbitofrontal cortex.

Caudate activations

For all five contrast conditions, there was increased blood flow to the caudate nucleus of the dorsal striatum (an area of the basal ganglia system associated with goal-directed reward processing). There were below-average activations in IS and NC conditions in which there was neither opportunity nor desire to punish, and a positive correlation between brain activation and actual punishment in IC condition.

The caudate nucleus is known to play a prominent role in processing rewards, in particular reward expectation. One pathway for dopaminergic cells is through basal ganglia, including the caudate nucleus. This is connected by dopamine pathways to the orbital cortex and areas associated with higher order planning of action. Caudate activations have been identified in lesion experiments with rats (Martin-Soelch *et al.* 2003); single-neuron recordings in nonhuman primates (Hikosaka *et al.* 1989; Apicella *et al.* 1991); neuroimaging studies (e.g. Koepp *et al.* 1998); and studies of cocaine consumption (Breiter *et al.* 1997) and nicotine (Stein *et al.* 1998).

To capture expected satisfaction from punishment, de Quervain *et al.* compared caudate activations for the IF versus IC condition for eleven of the subjects who all punished at the same level. In the IF condition, because these eleven subjects punished at the same level (the maximum punishment), it follows that differences in caudate activations must reflect expected satisfaction from punishment; it cannot reflect differences in punishment because punishment levels were the same. If higher activation in the IF condition predicts larger investment in punishment in the IC condition, this is consistent with the hypothesis that activations in the dorsal striatum reflect expected satisfaction. If so, these subjects will be willing to invest more in punishment. Results confirm this hypothesis: higher caudate activation in the IF condition correlates with higher activation in the IC condition. Other neuroimaging studies with positive correlations between caudate activations and increases in monetary rewards suggest that the positive correlation between caudate activation and size of punishment in this study is explained by expectations of greater satisfaction from punishment. This is consistent with the caudate's role in integrating reward and behavioural information in goal-directed behaviour.

Other neural activations

Other significant activations were found, including higher activations in the thalamus in the IC and IF conditions relative to the IS condition, but no significant differential thalamus activation when IC and IF are compared with NC, when the desire to punish should be absent. There were also significant differential activations in the prefrontal and orbitofrontal cortex. In the IC condition, punishers face a trade-off between the emotional satisfaction versus the monetary cost of AP. Reconciling this conflict requires integration of separate cognitive operations in the prefrontal and orbitofrontal cortex. Significant activations were found in Brodmann's area 10, associated with integration of different cognitive operations in achieving higher behavioural goals and difficult choices requiring reward value coding. The role of the orbitofrontal cortex indirectly supports the idea that punishment is satisfying. If it were not, no benefits and costs would have to be weighed against each other in the IC condition, and so the orbitofrontal cortex would not be activated.

Overall, de Quervain *et al.* conclude that their findings are consistent with the ideas about proximate mechanisms: evolution has ensured that we feel pleasure from AP and so respond in biologically altruistic ways even though we experience no objective benefits ourselves.

Overall, de Quervain *et al.* conclude that results support social preference models, for example those of Rabin (1993), Fehr and Schmidt (1999) and Camerer (2003b).

Neuroeconomic studies of empathy and trust

Sociality in decision-making is propelled by empathy and trust. Economic action is often about 'mentalizing', that is, guessing what others will do. Theory of mind involves making inferences about the beliefs, feelings and actions of others (Frith and Frith 2003; Camerer *et al.* 2005). It is possible that behaviours such as herding emerge from such empathetic behaviour if people make decisions on the basis of mentalizing responses. Empathy and theory of mind are also connected with emotional processing: explored in chapter 8.

Some experimental studies are surveyed by Singer and Fehr (2005), who argue that mentalizing and empathizing can explain how people respond to situations involving incomplete information. Singer *et al.* (2004) uncover evidence revealing that empathizing with the pain of others activates areas associated with the affective processing of pain. They also found heterogeneity in empathetic abilities across people. Avenanti *et al.* (2005) use transcranial magnetic stimulation (TMS) techniques which, as explained in chapter 3, involve stimulating specific neural areas to find out how this affects behaviour. Using TMS, Avenanti *et al.* identified motor responses associated with empathetic inferences about others' pain. Previous research shows that children with autism or Asperger's syndrome have trouble understanding emotions and social cues. This inability to empathize has been linked into relatively low levels of activation in the medial prefrontal regions and higher levels of activation in the ventral prefrontal cortex (PFC) of Asperger's patients, with higher activation in the ventral PFC suggesting perhaps that some sort of compensation is being made in patients who realize that their ability to empathize is constrained (Camerer 2003b; Camerer *et al.* 2005).

To investigate the hormonal dimensions of trust in social settings, a number of researchers have studied the impact of oxytocin, a hormone associated with social bonding. For example, Zak *et al.* (2005) analysed a trust game with 212 individuals, males and females. Blood levels of dihydrotestosterone (DHT) were measured and significant sex differences were found: men responded to distrust with increased levels of DHT, women did not. In other studies, higher oxytocin levels were found during online social networking; the 5 per cent of people who do not release oxytocin on stimulus are likely to be less trustworthy. Testosterone may also play a role in AP by inhibiting oxytocin release. Zak came to identify oxytocin as the 'morality' hormone, and the role of oxytocin was established either by measuring its levels or by administering it using nasal sprays.

Kosfeld *et al.* (2005) analysed the trust game and risk experiments with 194 healthy males who were given intranasal doses of oxytocin in spray form. The experimenters also measured demographic and psychological characteristics. They found that administering oxytocin significantly increased the average transfer levels in the trust game, inferring that oxytocin is involved in prosocial behaviour. Conlisk (2011), whilst sympathizing with the overall approach of these studies, does however identify a number of empirical shortcomings in the analyses and, similar to Binmore and Shaked's (2010a, 2010b) critique of Fehr and Schmidt's analyses, described above, concludes that Zak and colleagues are forming strong conclusions on the basis of limited evidence.

King-Casas *et al.* (2005) conducted a hyperscanning experiment to capture the neural correlates of trust for repeated games. They found significant differential activations in the caudate nucleus which, as explained in chapter 4, is implicated in the processing of reward expectation. King-Casas *et al.* postulate that trust and expectations of future reward are connected because the caudate nucleus modulates both.

Interactions between fairness and self-interest can also be captured using neuroeconomic techniques. For example, Baumgartner *et al.* (2011) explored social norms about decisions relating to fairness using TMS, a noninvasive brain stimulation technique (explained in chapter 3). They used TMS to generate a 'deviant' case, and found that the deviant subjects were less likely to reject unfair offers in an ultimatum game. They compared the deviant subjects' neural activations with those from normal subjects. When there was a conflict between fairness and self-interest, normal subjects had significantly greater activations in the dorsolateral and the ventromedial PFC.

Neuroscience can provide a quantitative analysis that is useful in constraining social utility functions, but more research is needed on characterizing emotional responses, their neural substrates and social context. As noted in chapter 2, it is important to be cautious when interpreting imaging results, especially as there may be many systems and processes involved, not just the region of interest selected by the experimenters, and for this reason it may be difficult to attribute causality precisely.

Case study: social norms and environmental decision-making

As explored in this chapter and chapter 4, sociality can affect decision-making in a number of ways, reflecting the impacts of social preferences and values, and of normative influence/ peer pressure. These insights can be applied to the analysis of real-world environmental decision-making by households and firms.

Fairness and inequity aversion

Gowdy (2008) applies insights from behavioural economics and experimental psychology to the issue of climate change, specifically to the question of reducing CO_2 emissions. He argues that resolving the current crisis of sustainability needs more emphasis on broader facets of human behaviour, for example, greed, egoism, cooperation and altruism. Models of extreme rationality will be of limited value in encouraging people to consider more carefully their energy and environmental decisions; financial incentives may in fact crowd out intrinsic motivations and feelings of collective responsibility, and so environmental policy should draw on cooperative, nonmaterialistic aspects of human nature. Frey (1997) argues that monetary incentives can crowd out civic motives, but money can also 'crowd in' civic motivations when it is used to acknowledge the social worth of individual contributions (Frey and Oberholtzer-Gee 1997).

Individual preferences and attitudes will be affected by differences in age, gender, education, socio-economic status and political affiliation. Costa and Kahn (2010) postulate that political opinions play a role reflected in rising polarization in environmental attitudes across political groups in the USA: they report that liberals and environmentalists are more responsive to environmental nudges than average, and their econometric estimates indicate a 3–6 per cent reduction in energy consumption in Democrat households, against a 1 per cent *increase* in consumption in Republican households, which may reflect the fact that nudges encourage Republican households to use more energy either because they are 'defiers' or because of a boomerang effect. Fairness can be incorporated into individual utility functions (e.g. see Fehr and Schmidt 1999 on inequity aversion), but subjectivity is still problematic, as the question remains of how to assign weights to inequity aversion.

Distributive preferences cover accountability, efficiency, need and equality (Gowdy 2008). Equality raises moral questions, and accountability implies that polluters should pay proportionally for emissions.

Concerns about fairness will also affect the global management of environmental decision-making, especially with respect to the developing world. Dealing with climate change will need cooperation, trust and reciprocity, and even when cooperative frameworks are imperfect, participation can establish credibility and good will (Gowdy 2008). Given that the North got rich by burning fossil fuels, is it fair to tell the developing world to stop using them? Stiglitz (2006) argues that a fair solution could be to implement a common global carbon tax and allow each country to keep the tax revenues, so that if less developed countries are polluting more, they will also have more taxation revenue to spend on reducing capital and labour taxes.

Social norms

There is also a large literature from behavioural economics on the impact of social pressure and social norms on environmental decision-making. Social norms will drive public-spirited behaviour and conditional contributions to public goods, and these norms and pressures will be affected by the values and attitudes outlined above.

Schultz (1999) notes that descriptive norms can be communicated in written information; conformity does not require the direct observation of others. He investigated participants' awareness of causal relationships between descriptive social norms and behaviour, and found that normative information about average recycling by neighbourhood families increased the amount and frequency of recycling. Similarly, Goldstein *et al.* (2008) analysed hotel towel reuse and tested the impact of different types of information; hotel guests were given cards asking them to reuse towels either to help the hotel or, for the normative appeal, to do what their fellow guests were doing. In the third control condition, the card did not include any specific reasons for towel reuse. Goldstein *et al.* found that the card appealing to the norm led to significant increases in towel recycling.

Schultz *et al.* (2007) analysed the impact of norms, including descriptive norms (which provide points of comparison for example, to others' consumption) and injunctive norms (which incorporate instructions). Norms can also be categorized according to their impacts: norms can be constructive, for example, descriptive norms can encourage people who are consuming too much relative to others to consume less in the future; but descriptive norms can also be destructive if they generate a 'boomerang effect' – if they encourage people who are consuming less than others to move their consumption towards the average by consuming more. Norms can also be reconstructive: for example, injunctive norms such as a pictogram of a smiley faces versus a frowny face can reinforce normative signals, overcoming boomerang effects.

Schultz *et al.* studied these norms by analysing the energy consumption behaviour of 290 households in San Marcos, California. All households had visible energy meters which were read before, during and after the interventions. The households were left written messages on door-hangers. Half were just given descriptive information about consumption in other households; the other half were given the descriptive information plus an injunctive visual signal indicating social approval/disapproval in their energy consumption. Below-average consumption was rewarded with a happy emoticon (smiley face) and above-average consumption was punished with a sad emoticon (frowny face). Schultz *et al.* found that the descriptive norm message about average neighbourhood use did lead to energy savings, but there was a boomerang effect dependent on whether the household's consumption was relatively high or relatively low. When the injunctive message was combined with the injunctive emoticons to indicate social approval/disapproval, the boomerang effect was eliminated.

Nolan *et al.* (2008) extend these finding using two studies aimed at assessing the weight that people ascribe to social norms as factors affecting their energy conservation decisions. The first study surveyed 810 Californians to explore stated reasons for engaging in energy conservation and testing actual factors influencing conservation behaviour; respondents were asked a series of questions about their energy conservation beliefs, motivations and actual behaviour. Self-reported beliefs were assessed according to answers to questions: How much will saving energy benefit society/the environment? How much money can you save? How often do your neighbours try to conserve energy?

Behaviour/intentions were judged by the answer to the question 'How often do you try to conserve energy?' Motivations were assessed by questions about reasons for trying to save energy, for example, using less energy saves money, protects the environment, benefits society, other people are doing it. Responses were rated on a four-point scale from 'not at all important' to 'extremely important'. The findings revealed an inconsistency between the stated motivations and actual behaviour: 'because others are doing it' was judged to be the least important reason at the self-reported motivation stage, but the highest correlation with actual conservation behaviour was a person's beliefs about whether their neighbours were doing it.

Nolan *et al.*'s second study was a field experiment involving 981 Californian households in San Marcos, assessing participants' awareness of the extent to which their behaviour was affected by different messages. The experimental design was similar to Schultz *et al.*'s (2007) study. Normative information was circulated in the forms of messages on door-hangers; each message was illustrated with a graphic icon. The messages urged the householders to conserve energy via specific conservation behaviours (for example, taking shorter showers, turning off lights/air-conditioning). There were four appeal treatments, each appealing to different motivations: three appeals used non-normative messages: protecting the environment (environmental responsibility); benefiting society (social responsibility); and saving money (self-interest). The fourth appeal was based on a descriptive norm with factual information about the energy conservation behaviour of recipients' neighbours. There was also an information-only control treatment – people were just told that they could save energy by taking the various actions without appealing to any specific motivation.

Actual energy use in-home was the dependent variable, and electricity meter readings were taken before and after the intervention. This reliance on objective information from meter readings prevented inaccuracies due to self-reporting and/or imperfect memory bias. The data showed that normative social influence had a direct impact on conservation behaviour, and the social norm condition led to the biggest reduction in energy consumption; people conserved more energy under the social norm condition than under the control condition or the other informational conditions; however, the householders did not detect the influence of these messages; they did not appear to realize that they were affected by the descriptive norm. Nolan *et al.* concluded that these findings suggest that naïve psychology-based beliefs about energy conservation are inaccurate. Trying to encourage people to be socially responsible/ protect the environment rarely succeeds in increasing pro-environmental behaviours – perhaps because people have already adjusted their behaviour to these factors. In changing recalcitrant behaviour, new motivations and messages are needed so that normative messages can reach new populations who might not otherwise want to conserve energy.

Allcott (2011), drawing on research by Schultz *et al.* (2007), Goldstein *et al.* (2008) and Nolan *et al.* (2008), focused on the role played by social norms in guiding energy conservation strategies, and identified three pathways via which social norms play a role: a tournament pathway via which people gain utility from outperforming their neighbours' frugality; a conditional cooperation pathway via which people contribute to a public good if others do so too; and a social learning pathway. Allcott notes that boomerang effects can be explained most easily in terms of the second and third pathways, though he also emphasizes the role of feedback.

Allcott analysed data from a randomized natural field experiment using home energy reports in collaboration with the OPOWER electricity utility in Minnesota. The electricity consumption of 80,000 treatment and control households was analysed. Each household was sent a home energy report with two features: an action steps module, giving energy-saving tips; and a social comparison module, comparing the household's energy consumption with that of its 100 geographically closest neighbours. The monthly programme led to decreases in energy consumption of 1.9–2.0 per cent, but with decay effects; impacts decreased in the period between receiving one monthly report and the next, but then increased again once the next report was received.

Allcott infers that this reflects an interaction of social norms and bounded rationality/heuristics, in particular the availability heuristic (discussed in chapter 6). There is an 'attention channel': people do know about energy conservation strategies, but they need reminders because attention is malleable and nondurable. Receiving a home energy report reminded people about the strategies that they should be following. Given bounded attention to social norms, social norms will only affect behaviour when norms are at the top of the mind.

Familial influence and identity

Attitudes will also be moulded by family upbringing. Developmental psychology focuses on the role of education in embedding habits from a young age, and these habits can be transferred within the family structure. Families will be influenced (via either learning or social pressure) by the recycling habits of other family members. Grønhøj and Thøgersen (2012) analysed the impact of parental attitudes and behaviour on adolescents' recycling behaviour. They focused on the fact that parents play a key role in teaching pro-environmental practices, and on the role of parental influence on values. Family norms take two forms: descriptive norms – normative information is conveyed via parents' actions; and injunctive norms – parents' instructions to their children about pro-environmental behaviours. Nonetheless, there may be differences across families, reflecting generation gaps and differences in parenting style. Also, issues of identity will be important – the extent to which the child identifies with the parents will affect the transmission of environmental values across generations.

Grønhøj and Thøgersen (2012) analysed evidence from a stratified sample of 601 Danish households representative of the Danish population in terms of socio-economic characteristics. Families were interviewed via internet-based surveys using questions to capture the influence of individual pro-environmental attitudes versus the social influence of family norms on adolescents' pro-environmental behaviour. Families were asked about their attitudes and actions with respect to specific pro-environmental practices, including buying eco-friendly products; reducing electricity use; and separation of waste for recycling. Adolescents were also asked about the parents' attitudes and actions. The impacts of generation gaps – the difference in age between parents and child – were also analysed alongside the relative weight of personal attitudes versus social influences.

Grønhøj and Thøgersen tested three hypotheses: adolescents' behaviour depends on family norms; their behaviour is more influenced by descriptive norms than injunctive norms; and the larger the generation gap, the weaker the influence of norms. They found that adolescents' pro-environmental behaviour was heavily influenced by their own attitudes, but also by the existence and strength of parental pro-environmental attitudes and actions. Parents' actions – the descriptive norms – dominated the injunctive norms, and the impact of the descriptive norms was also dependent on the child's perception of their parents' behaviour – the extent to which their parents' actions were visible and unambiguous. Grønhøj and Thøgersen conclude that parents are important role models and can play a key role in moulding the pro-environmental behaviour of adolescents

Conclusions and policy implications

There is a large behavioural economic literature on sociality, which explores experimental evidence showing that people often behave in altruistic and cooperative ways, and this is broadly inconsistent with a standard economic assumption of self-interest. A range of approaches can be constructed to capture other-regarding preferences and other forces generating cooperation, reciprocity and trust, and these models focus on a range of assumptions about self-interest: from Vernon L Smith's hypothesis that sociality is just another form of self-interest, to models that focus on the idea that helping others is genuinely rewarding and is an end in itself.

Policy can be designed to harness our social nature, as explored in the context of environmental decision-making in the case study section. Policy 'nudges' that incorporate social information and cues can be very effective, not only in the context of environmental problems, but also in encouraging people to cooperate in other ways, for example via organ donation, by charity and philanthropy and/or by volunteering. Also, social networks, particularly mobile and online networks, have become powerful tools for social cooperation, as witnessed by public demonstrations during the Arab Spring and the 2011 English riots.

The increasing focus on social preferences and attitudes in economic behaviour has paralleled a revival of interest in social themes in politics. In the UK, Prime Minister David Cameron's conception of a 'Big Society' – a 'third sector' based in small social communities – draws on themes of sociality. The hope is that the social connections that characterize the Big Society can enable communities to overcome economic, social and political problems, obviating the need for top-down governance. Ironically, in some ways this Big Society concept develops insights from Keynesian economist Ernst Schumacher's left-leaning analysis of the benefits of small communities and decentralization, as elucidated in *Small is Beautiful* (1973). In a similarly ironic way, left-leaning Maurice Glasman has recently developed conservative themes in his conception of 'Blue Labour', a model that rejects the focus on centralization traditionally associated with left-wing thought.

The modern concept of a Big Society has reshuffled the political cards in a number of ways. Traditional conservative ideology focuses on the importance of free markets in allowing the invisible hand of the price mechanism to allocate resources efficiently. The economic analysis underlying this ideology is based on an assumption of self-interest. Market failure justifies government intervention, and left-wing ideology has tended to focus on the importance of governments as a reflection of the failure of self-interest in efficiently allocating resources when markets fail. The Big Society concept turns all of that inside out: a Big

Society will not work unless people are altruistic, cooperative and helpful. If people are selfish, then the Big Society will not go far in resolving economic and social problems, and governments will be needed to intervene. Whether or not the Big Society third sector has a useful role to play will depend on our social natures. The origins of cooperation and self-interest are often very deep-seated, and so policy initiatives to harness our instincts for cooperation must reflect a deep understanding of the behavioural and evolutionary roots of cooperation.

In terms of future research, there is a lot still to be done. Models need to be formulated that fully capture the experimental evidence on self-interest and altruism, for example to resolve debates between Fehr and Schmidt versus Binmore and Shaked. More neuroeconomic research is needed to unravel the neural and evolutionary roots of cooperation and self-interest. More experimental work would help to capture social interactions and preferences in societies that are increasingly characterized by a complex mix of online and offline social interactions.

6 Heuristics and biases

Introduction

In chapters 4 and 5 we explained how behavioural economists have broadened the foundations of standard economic models by allowing interactions with others. Behavioural learning theories allow that people do not know the best strategy immediately and so they acquire knowledge via some process of learning, including social learning from others' actions (chapter 4). Other behavioural economists focus on extending standard utility functions by allowing for sociality – people are affected by social preferences, rewards and interactions (chapter 5). These models of learning and sociality embed an implicit or explicit rationality assumption generally involving the application of mathematical algorithms to enable good decision-making.

Other behavioural economists have focused on limits to rationality and/or different conceptions of rationality. This allows us to understand why learning is sometimes limited or nonexistent, and why people repeat mistakes, raising questions about the existence and nature of rationality: are people rational? For some behavioural economists (not all) the answer is 'not always' – rather than an unequivocal 'no'. Whether or not we are able to act in a rational way depends on the context in which we find ourselves. This chapter explores some approaches to softening economists' assumptions about rationality, focusing in particular on Herbert Simon's insights about bounded rationality under conditions when rationality may not be about mathematical maximization and statistical reasoning, but will nonetheless involve systematic processes of reasoning. In the context of bounded rationality, this chapter focuses on a range of biases and heuristics that affect decision-making under uncertainty. In understanding the influence of biases and heuristics, it is useful to outline some different conceptions of rationality as seen in economic analyses. Then some key elements of Kahneman and Tversky's, Thaler's and others' models of quasi-rational decision-making – including biases, heuristics, cognitive dissonance and choice overload – will be explored.

Defining rationality

In economics, standard decision-making models focus on behaviour as the outcome of a mathematical process. This assumes 'hyper-rationality' – that people are using a high level of rationality to guide their choices. Keynes (1921, 1936) analysed constraints on rationality, but his analyses pre-dated the development of strict axioms of rationality by von Neumann and Morgenstern (1944) and Savage (1954), and in this section we focus on analyses of rationality that have emerged since the widespread adoption of rationality axioms in economic theory. Keynes's more general thoughts about limits on rationality and statistical reasoning are explored in the context of prospect theory in chapter 7.

Procedural versus substantive rationality

Herbert Simon (1955, 1972, 1979) replaces the global rationality of economic man with a model of bounded rationality. An uncertain future, bounds to rationality, including cognitive and information processing constraints as well as imperfect information, will mean that people, at best, are able to act in a broadly reasonable rather than a strictly rational way. They will be 'satisficers' rather than maximizers (Simon 1979). Simon also analyses rational behaviour as 'behaviour appropriate to the achievement of given goals, within the limits imposed by given conditions and constraints' (Simon 1972, p. 161). It follows that a wide range of definitions of rationality can be constructed, depending on how broadly the given conditions and constraints are defined. Simon's concept of bounded rationality focuses on decision-making when there are constraints on information and cognitive capacity. Whilst much analysis of bounded rationality has focused on data inputs, rationality may also be bounded because humans are not always good at processing numerical and probabilistic information. Simon (1972) notes that rationality will also be bounded when situations are particularly complex and so it is not easy to identify the best course of action.

Simon analyses the strong assumptions about information and information processing associated with the standard economic model, in which rational agents use tools of differential calculus to maximize their utility or profits. Simon describes this as substantive rationality – rationality based on an underlying mathematical process reflecting the application of a mathematical algorithm. Subjective probabilities can be consistent with substantive rationality assuming Bayesian rationality, that is, the application of Bayes's rule (described in chapter 4 in the context of Bayesian learning). This is still substantive rationality because it is grounded on an algorithmic approach: a mathematical/statistical rule is known and applied.

Procedural rationality is a broader concept, is not dependent on the use of mathematical algorithms, and reflects a response to constraints on computational capacity with an emphasis on problem-solving rather than optimizing. That means that it is harder to define precisely. Intuition guides behaviour, and judgments are the outcome of 'appropriate deliberation' rather than algorithmic, substantive decision-making (Simon 1955; Baddeley *et al.* 2004; Baddeley 2006a). Nonmaximizing behaviour may be justified as reasonable in an uncertain world if people are using heuristics, quick decision-making devices, in a systematic way. Limits on human cognition and the misapplication of heuristics will mean that judgments and decisions are prone to behavioural biases. Procedural rationality is something like Thaler's (2000b) concept of quasi-rationality, in which people make their decisions in a purposeful, regular way, but whilst their decisions are reasonable the reasoning process is not consistent with the axioms seen in standard economic analyses

Ecological rationality

Vernon L Smith (2003a) analyses the different versions of rationality that are seen in different contexts, especially to explain contrasting behaviour in experimental markets. In a vision of rationality drawing on the Austrian economists, particularly von Hayek, Smith observes 'we have examples where people don't do as well as rational models predict. We have examples where they do better. And we are trying to understand why.' Asset markets do not converge quickly and, in the lab, may exhibit instabilities such as bubbles and crashes even though, according to Smith, they do usually converge in the end. Experimental consumer markets, on the other hand, often converge quickly.

Developing concepts of constructivist rationality seen for example in Hayek – that effective social institutions are the product of conscious deductive reason – Smith develops the alternative but complementary concept of ecological rationality. Ecological rationality focuses on the ecology of the environment in which decisions take place. It is less about different types of agent and their levels of rationality, and more about agents responding to different incentives in different institutional environments and contexts. There is an evolutionary aspect to learning and rationality, and 'social-grown' norms such as trust and reciprocity lead to social, cooperative outcomes that are better than the market equilibria, including suboptimal Nash equilibria from rational defection, seen in standard economic analysis.

This approach can reconcile the apparent anomalies in experimental evidence. Experimental economics reveals outcomes that are unknown and unintended, and this generates 'ecological rationality', which may or may not correspond to the rational model of constructivism. In his vision of ecological rationality, information is asymmetric and dispersed and unknowable by a single person or group. Incentives must be in place to encourage people to reveal knowledge and make the system efficient. Overall, individual irrationality leads to social rationality, which benefits society at large: for example, risky, speculative behaviour can benefit society – an insight with which Keynes might agree because Keynes emphasized the dilemma that whilst liquid financial markets are unstable, they also have an important role to play in supporting investment.

Kahneman's maps of bounded rationality

Kahneman (2003, 2011) develops Simon's approach to bounded rationality by blending it with an analysis of the architecture of cognition. He postulates that two systems are implicated in decision-making: thinking via reasoning, and deciding via intuition. Reflecting this division, he divides cognition into two systems. System 1 includes cognitive operations that are spontaneous, effortless and fast. They operate automatically and are often affected by emotions and habit. System 1 processing is not deliberative in nature and this, together with the impact of emotions and visceral influences, means that system 1 operations are difficult to control. System 2 processes are effortful and rule-governed. They reflect deliberation and control and, whilst they operate more slowly than system 1 processes, because they are the outcome of careful, conscious thought, they are more flexible and adaptable.

Kahneman's cognitive maps are a development of his collaborations with Tversky on heuristics and biases (e.g. Tversky and Kahneman 1974, see below) and prospect theory (e.g. Kahneman and Tversky 1979, see chapter 7 of this volume). If behaviour is strictly rational in a standard economic sense, then fast thinking in the form of heuristics has no place and biases are ruled out. Similarly, as explained in chapter 7, prospect theory focuses on reference points and changes. These are consistent with limits to reasoning and ambiguities in decision-making, and are more consistent with models of bounded rationality than the standard rationality assumptions. Distinguishing between automatic emotional systems and deliberative cognitive systems is also an essential theme in neuroeconomics, particularly in neuroeconomic analyses of emotional processing.

Heuristics and decision-making

The various conceptions of rationality outlined above allow that individual behaviour may or may not be fully rational depending on the circumstances and contexts. How do these views of rationality and behaviour translate into an understanding of everyday decision-making? In real life, people use decision-making shortcuts known as heuristics. Gigerenzer *et al.* (1999) and Todd and Gigerenzer (2000) explain that the mind has an 'adaptive toolbox' for decision-making involving heuristics, which are simple rules enabling smart choices to be made using minimal information and exploiting the structure of information given the environment context.

Heuristics are often associated with Kahneman's concept of intuitive system 1 thinking. They do not involve careful deliberation, but neither are they irrational. Heuristics are common-sense rules of thumb derived from experience, and they may be procedurally rational because they are used by people to make relatively quick decisions in uncertain situations when a full assessment of available information is difficult and/or time-consuming. Imitation, for example, qualifies as a 'fast and frugal heuristic', saving time and effort in social situations (Gigerenzer and Goldstein 1996). It is also used in liquid, fast-moving financial markets. When thinking about buying/selling shares from their portfolio, a potential investor may have little real knowledge about what is going to happen to share prices in the future and, given this limited information, they will adopt the heuristic of following the crowd. They will buy when the market is rising and others are buying, and they will sell when the market is falling and other are selling.

Different classes of heuristics are characterized by 'simple building blocks' capturing how the search for information is conducted. Heuristics can outperform complex algorithmic methods of decision-making, an insight also confirmed in the analysis of investment decision-making: simple rules of thumb in investment project management approximate more complex algorithmic tools incorporating discounting methods and so, given the ease of the simpler methods, they are preferable in terms of economizing on information search and decision-making effort (Baddeley 2006a, 2006b).

Heuristics generally can be distinguished according to how reasonable they are, although without a clear algorithm to draw the line between rational and stupid, judging whether something is a sensible heuristic can be subjective. Generally, heuristics can be justified as procedurally rational, and biases involve misjudgments of information and/or events. There may be some overlaps. Whilst heuristics are generally reasonable decision-making tools given uncertainty, if they are misapplied then they may generate systematic behavioural biases, as discussed below. By definition, a bias is a deviation in judgment and may be the outcome of bounded rationality.

Most ordinary people make common mistakes in their probability judgments. This reflects bounded rationality: information is mishandled, reflecting limits on the cognitive processing ability of the human mind (Gould 1970; Tversky and Kahneman 1974; Anderson 1998). Anderson (1998) asserts that the problem identified by Kahneman and Tversky originates in the input format of data and in algorithms used: if prompted by clear signals, the human brain is able to deal with probabilities more effectively. For example, if students are asked to judge the probability of two coincident events within the context of a statistics class, then they will know what to do. However, if they are confronted with a problem requiring probability judgments in a situation outside their classes, in which it is not obvious that this is what is required, then they may make a judgment using instincts and intuition rather than statistical reasoning (Kyburg 1997).

Cognitive biases can be categorized into individual and group biases, and individuals will be affected by motivational biases and cognitive biases (Skinner 1999; Baddeley *et al.* 2004). Motivational biases reflect interests and circumstances, and may link into principal–agent problems. They can often be significantly reduced with clearly defined tasks and incentive structures. Overall, motivational biases are less of a problem because they are under rational control and can be manipulated using incentives. Cognitive biases are more problematic because they emerge from incorrect processing of the information; in this sense they are not under conscious control.

Tversky and Kahneman on heuristics and biases

Tversky and Kahneman (1974) analyse heuristic principles used as devices to reduce the complexity of tasks and to form intuitive judgments of probability – often useful devices, but sometimes leading to systematic mistakes. They draw an analogy with visual perception: we judge the distance of an object by our visual perception of its sharpness and clarity, which is often a useful guide, but in specific circumstances it will be misleading: in fog we overestimate distances; in sunny weather we underestimate them. Similarly, whilst heuristics can be useful devices to enable quick and efficient decision-making, their use does lead to decision-making biases.

Tversky and Kahneman (1972, 1974) explore the connections between heuristics and biases for a range of heuristics commonly employed, including representativeness, anchoring/ adjustment and availability. For Tversky and Kahneman, heuristics are intuitive decision-making tools, but the problem is that a range of biases can emerge from the mis-application of these quick decision-making tools. Tversky and Kahneman illustrate with some experimental examples of systematic mistakes from misapplication of heuristics. In describing their experimental evidence, they note that they encouraged their experimental subjects to be accurate and rewarded them for correct answers to deter wishful thinking and other irrational influences not associated with the application of heuristics.

Overall, a large number of heuristics and biases have been identified, and we cover only a selection here; a comprehensive range of the various studies can be found in Kahneman and Tversky's (1982, 2000) edited volumes. See also Ariely (2008) for a simple introduction.

Representativeness

The representativeness heuristic is a principle of analogical reasoning in which people judge the similarity between events and processes to judge probability; probabilities are judged by the degree to which A resembles B. Tversky and Kahneman (1974) use the example of Steve – if we are given information about him, information which is not objectively informative, such as that he is 'very shy and withdrawn' and has 'a passion for detail', then we judge the probability that he is a librarian by how much he represents our stereotypes about librarians. Attribution errors and belief bias are generated when we decide according to stereotypes because personality-based explanations are over-emphasized and situational influences are under-emphasized.

Kahneman and Tversky (1979) identify six types of bias that emerge from this heuristic: insensitivity to prior probabilities (base-rate neglect); insensitivity to sample size; misconceptions of chance, including gamblers' fallacy; insensitivity to predictability; the illusion of validity; and misconceptions of regression reflecting a behavioural version of Galton's fallacy (see below).

Base-rate neglect and probability matching

Tversky and Kahneman (1974) observe that judgments are often insensitive to prior probabilities: 'when worthless evidence is given, prior probabilities are ignored'. This is the problem of base-rate neglect. If people are given narrative information about an event, even if this information is essentially worthless, then it will lead people to disregard statistical rules. For example, Tversky and Kahneman describe an experiment studying the probabilistic judgments for two experimental conditions: in the first condition, the experimental subjects were told that they were given a sample of biographical/personality descriptions drawn from populations mixed of engineers and lawyers. There were two treatment conditions with different mixes of lawyers and engineers: in one condition there were seventy engineers and thirty lawyers; in the other there were thirty engineers and seventy lawyers. If the subjects were given no personal information about the sample, they correctly judged the probabilities – applying Bayes's rule the ratio of the odds should be 5.44 – it is 5.44 times more likely that an engineer will be drawn from population 1 than from population 2. When the subjects were given a biographical sketch of each person in the sample, then they ignored the base rate frequency.

In one experimental treatment, the subjects were told about a person in the sample called Dick. Dick was thirty years old, married, highly able and motivated, successful and well liked. In this case the subjects judged the likelihood that Dick was a lawyer to be 50 per cent regardless of whether he was sampled from population 1 or population 2. Subjects ignored the base rate and judged the description as equally representative of an engineer and a lawyer. It seemed that the subjects were being distracted by narrative information, comparing their sample of subjects via judgments of representativeness and ignoring the prior probabilities.

A related bias is probability matching. Probability matching occurs when choices vary with the probability of different events. Bliss *et al.* (1995) make a distinction between base-rate neglect and probability matching. Base-rate neglect involves discounting the relative frequency with which events occur. Probability matching occurs when reactions reflect the probabilities of the various consequences rather than the probability of the event itself. For example, bomber pilots in the Second World War were allowed either a flak jacket or a parachute, but the two together were too heavy to carry so they could not have both. Strafing from enemy guns was three times more likely than being shot down. The flak jacket was better protection against enemy guns; the parachute was better protection against being shot down. Objectively, enemy gunfire was always more likely and so it was always better always to take the flak jacket. Yet, on average, the pilots were observed taking flak jackets three times out of every four and parachutes on the fourth occasion (Lo 2001).

Insensitivity to sample size

Insensitivity to sample size reflects an application of the representativeness heuristics in the sense that, regardless of sample size, people judge the likelihood that a particular sample result will be seen by reference to the equivalent population parameter; for example, in a sample of men, the average height will be six feet and the probability that the sample would have average height greater than six feet was judged to be the same whether the sample size was ten men or 1000, yet the likelihood of extreme values is higher in small samples because outliers are more likely to be diluted. Tversky and Kahneman illustrate this with an urn experiment: one draw of five balls reveals four red and one white; a second draw of twenty balls reveals twelve red and eight white. Experimental subjects were asked which of those two draws was more likely to be from an urn containing two-thirds red balls and one-third white balls. People focused their judgments on the simple proportions: the draw of four red balls out of five (80 per cent red) was judged to be more representative than the draw of twelve red and eight white (60 per cent red).

Objectively, however, if probability rules are applied, then the draw of twelve balls is more likely to come from an urn with two-thirds red balls, but the experimental subjects were ignoring the fact that the draw of five was a smaller sample. Tversky and Kahneman (1974) also observe that judgments of posterior odds are usually less extreme than correct values, reflecting an underestimation of the impact of evidence. Tversky and Kahneman (1974) do not explain this specific example in terms of representativeness, nor do they address the question that a simple comparison of proportions should have led them to the second answer (60 per cent is closer to 67 per cent than 80 per cent), but presumably they are asserting that a sample draw of 80 per cent red balls is judged to be more representative of an urn with mainly red balls than an sample draw of 60 per cent red balls.

Gambler's fallacy and the illusion of control

Tversky and Kahneman (1974) also identify a number of biases reflecting 'misconceptions of chance' and they link these to the representativeness heuristic because these biases emerge from making spurious comparisons between events. With misconceptions of chance, people judge that even very small segments of larger sequences are representative of the whole sequence. They expect the short sequence to represent the essential characteristics of a process, and so will also expect to see those characteristics of the process locally – in each part of the sequence. Individuals were asked to judge the relative likelihood of a series of coin tosses (heads or tails): for example, H-T-H-T-T-H versus H-H-H-T-T-T. In reality, small sequences that are locally representative, for example, H-T-H-T-T-H, will contain too many alternatives and fewer runs than would be expected from a random process.

The representativeness heuristic also leads to a misconception of chance known as gambler's fallacy. The gambler's fallacy is the belief that when a series of trials have all had the same outcome, then the opposite outcome is more likely to occur next time, since random fluctuations seem more representative of the sample space. If there has been a long run of reds on a roulette wheel, then a gambler will often predict a black ball without reflecting that the roulette wheel has no memory and is not self-correcting, so will not know that it's time to have a black ball win after a lot of red ball wins. Gamblers are ignoring the fact that each trial is independent of the next. This bias is seen even amongst scientists in what Tversky and Kahneman (1974) call the 'law of small numbers'. Small samples are falsely assumed to be as representative of a population as large samples and so results from small samples will be over-valued and over-interpreted.

The gambler's fallacy also links to another form of bias: the illusion of control. This occurs when people act as though they can influence a situation over which they have no control. If lottery ticket holders have chosen their own numbers rather than using random number selection then they will value their lottery tickets more highly, even though the probability of a win is identical in both cases.

Insensitivity to predictability

This form of bias involves people discounting the reliability of evidence. For example, Tversky and Kahneman (1974) describe an experiment in which experimental subjects were provided with descriptions of the performance of a student teacher during a practice lesson. The subjects were then divided into two groups. One group was asked to evaluate the student's performance; the other group was asked to predict the student's career performance in five years' time. The percentile scores for the evaluations and predictions were 'identical': scores on career success were the same as scores on teaching performance in one lesson. Tversky and Kahneman (1974) argue that, in reality, the likelihood that performance in one lesson will properly predict future career prospects is relatively small. Tversky and Kahneman (1974) do not address the fact that, even when point estimates for predictions of a student's future career success coincide, that does not mean that doubt is absent because doubt is captured via wider confidence intervals, not different point estimates for predictions of future career performance: that is, a judgment of a probability is not the same as its weight, but they introduce weighting functions into their analysis of prospect theory.

Illusion of validity and over-confidence

Interviewers will often overestimate their ability to judge the calibre of a candidate from a selection interview, even if they know and/or have prior experience of unreliable interpretations of character and performance from selection interviews. Another illustration of this problem is that the internal consistency of a pattern is judged to have more reliability than a less internally consistent pattern: the internal consistency leads to a judgment of representativeness. For example, the application of intuitive, heuristic principles leads a teacher to conclude that a student with an exam record of BBBBB is more obviously representative of a B-class student than another student with an exam record of ACBAC. Tversky and Kahneman (1974) argue that this is another form of bias, because highly consistent patterns are more likely to contain redundant elements and/or strong correlations between elements; for example, for a student who gets two Bs in Spanish and Italian: both these scores are picking up similar things and are more likely to be correlated. Yet an A in maths and a C in history are likely to be independently determined, and these independent elements combined are giving more reliable information overall that the student is, on average, a B-standard student. Predictions based on a set of independent, uncorrelated elements are more likely to give an accurate answer than predictions based on a set of related, highly correlated elements, but people judge a set of correlated elements as being more reliable because they are more representative.

The illusion of validity may create other biases, such as over-confidence, a particular problem in financial markets, and self-serving bias. These will mean that a person will be more likely to claim responsibility for successes than for failures. Over-confidence is especially a problem for extreme probabilities (close to 0 per cent and 100 per cent) which people tend to find hard to assess. Other evidence shows that over-confidence is linked to herding and social learning; specifically, over-confidence is associated with a propensity to lead herds rather than follow them (Bernardo and Welch 2001).

Camerer and Lovallo (1999) analyse over-confidence in the context of business planning mistakes, particularly excessive business entry. In experiments in which success depends on relative skills, most participants expect total profits to be negative but their own profits to be positive – without seeming to recognize that someone has to lose if total profits are negative. Overall, this inconsistency remains even when financial incentives are offered for correctly judging their own skill levels and skills are defined more clearly. Their hypothesis is that the high rate of business failure reflects over-confidence and also reference group neglect: everyone knows that payoffs depend on skill, and they know that everyone else knows that too. They should infer that others are self-selecting into the projects because they perceive their own skill levels are high, and yet there is still excess entry. This phenomenon could also link into emotional reasons for participating, for example as captured by Keynes's entrepreneurial animal spirits: the 'spontaneous urge to action', explored in more detail in chapters 8 and 12.

Misconceptions of regression

Misconceptions of regression link into Galton's fallacy about regression towards the mean and Galton's (1886) empirical observation that tall men are more likely to have sons shorter themselves. This is because there are random elements in the determination of a man's height (as well as nonrandom aspects such as genetic makeup). Outliers are outliers partly because of large random errors. So if the very tall man is an outlier reflecting a large positive error component in his height, then his son's height is unlikely to reflect the same magnitude of error and the son will be shorter than his father. Mean reversion and convergence do not reflect causal mechanisms; they are just statistical tendencies.

Tversky and Kahneman (1974) apply this insight to heuristics and biases. If a child performs very well in one test, then his performance in the next is likely to be disappointing, but people will assign spurious causal explanation, reflecting the fact that the output (for example, a prediction about a child's performance) should be representative of the input (the child did well in a previous test). In reality, a bad performance after a good performance just reflects a statistical tendency, just as very tall fathers will have shorter sons.

Tversky and Kahneman (1974) argue that there will be some worrying behavioural implications for punishment and reward. If someone is rewarded for doing well, but then is just statistically more likely to do less well, rewards will be associated with deteriorating performance; on the other hand, if someone is punished for poor performance, and their performance improves just because of mean reversion, then punishments will be associated with improving performance. Iterating to the impacts on the person who is rewarding and punishing: punishment is rewarded and reward is punished.

This interpretation of Galton's fallacy does not allow that there will be some deterministic relations affecting performance, rewards and punishments. The illustrations of biases that Tversky and Kahneman (1974) have identified in the context of Galton's fallacy are assuming that statistical errors overwhelm deterministic forces.

Representativeness and the conjunction fallacy

Another illustration of the representativeness heuristic, which interferes with the objective application of statistical rules for a conjunctive event, is the conjunction fallacy. There are many illustrations of the conjunction fallacy, and a classic is the 'Linda problem'.

> Linda is 31 years old, single, outspoken and very bright. She majored in philosophy. As a student, she was deeply concerned with issues of discrimination and social justice, and also participated in anti-nuclear demonstrations. Please check off the most likely alternative:
>
> 1.   Linda is a bank teller.
> 2.   Linda is a bank teller and is active in the feminist movement.
>
> (Tversky and Kahneman 1983, p. 297)

Here there is an interaction between representativeness and the conjunction fallacy. In experiments, a large proportion of people will judge it to be more likely that Linda is a bank teller active in the feminist movement than that she is an unspecified sort of bank teller, even though the former is a subset of the latter and therefore statistically can be, at most, equally probable. If this problem is framed as a statistical question, then most people with a basic knowledge of probability would realize that the conjunction of two events is less probable than each event alone.

People are better at dealing with this problem if it is expressed purely in probabilistic/ statistical terms: is event 1 more likely or not than a conjunction of event 1 with event 2? Most people with a basic knowledge of probability would realize that two events happening together is less probable than each event happening irrespective of whether the other occurred. However, when confronted with the details about Linda, most people find the second option more likely than the first, simply because the description appears to be more representative of a feminist stereotype, and hence more plausible.

This is a conjunction fallacy: the former option is the most likely since the probability of the conjunction of two events can never be more probable than either event independently. That is, a more detailed scenario is always at best equally (and usually less) probable than a simple scenario. The problem of bias in judgments about conjunctive versus disjunctive events is explored in more detail in the context of anchoring and adjustment, as discussed below.

Availability heuristic

Availability is the heuristic of judging an event to be more likely if occurrences of the event can be easily recalled; for example, large, more frequent classes of events are easier to recall (Kahneman and Tversky 1974). The availability heuristic will also lead to primacy and recency effects in which the first and last events in a series have a disproportionate impact on current judgments. The availability heuristic introduces a role for memory in economic analysis too – for example, Mullainathan (2002) analyses memory and bounded rationality. The role of memory in decision-making has been studied extensively by cognitive psychologists including Alan Baddeley (2002). The role of memory in cognitive bias more generally has been studied in the context of financial investment: Goetzman and Peles (1997) studied mutual fund investors' perceptions of their performance. Using questionnaires, they explored the investors' recollection of their performance and found a positive bias in investors' recollections, the investors overestimated their own performance. The degree of bias also reflected previous choices, suggesting a degree of cognitive bias in investors' assessments as well as their recollections.

Kahneman and Tversky (1974) outline a number of biases that emerge from the misapplication of the availability heuristic, including retrievability bias, imaginability bias and illusory correlation.

Retrievability bias/familiarity bias

This bias emerges from the fact that some classes of events are recalled more easily and, if they are easier to recall, then they will be judged as more numerous. This also links to a familiarity bias; we recall more easily people and events that are more familiar to us. For example, subjects were asked to listen to a list of names, including a mixture of unfamiliar names and celebrity names. After they'd heard the list they were asked to judge whether the lists included more men or women. When there were more male celebrity names, the subjects erroneously judged that there were more males in the group; when there were more female celebrity names, the subjects erroneously judged that there were more females in the group. This was perhaps reflecting the fact that when they tried to remember the names on the list, they recalled the celebrity names more easily because they were more available.

Effectiveness of search

If people are searching for instances of events and they can identify instances quickly and easily, then this effectiveness of search will lead to an upward bias in the probability judgment. For example, if people are asked to decide whether or not it is more common that words have 'r' as a first letter or as a third letter, they will be able to search more effectively recalling instances of words that begin with 'r', and this will lead them to judge that words beginning with 'r' are more frequent than words with 'r' as a middle letter, even though English words with a middle letter 'r' are more common than those with a starting letter 'r'. Similarly, people find it easier to recall abstract words such as 'love' than concrete words such as 'door', and Kahneman and Tversky argue that this is because people can more easily recall contexts including love than contexts including a door – though perhaps emotional salience is playing a role here too.

Imaginability bias

Events that can be generated or 'imagined' are easier to recall and, via the availability heuristic, will be judged more likely. Kahneman and Tversky illustrate with an example of an adventurous expedition. If people are asked to judge the risk of an expedition, if they can imagine many dangerous, uncontrollable contingencies then they will judge the trip to be very risky. If they cannot easily conceive of the dangers involved then they will judge the trip to be less risky. The evaluation of risks will not necessarily coincide with any objective likelihood. For example, if people are comparing the likelihood of the relative risks of a trip to Antarctica or a trip to the jungle, then they may be able to imagine many more dire contingencies for the latter and therefore will judge a jungle trip to be more risky than an Antarctic trip just – because they don't know much about the risks in Antarctica.

Illusory correlation

This bias occurs when people imagine correlations between events because the features of the events fit together. Tversky and Kahneman cite evidence from a study in which experimental subjects are presented with two sets of information about patients: a drawing and a clinical diagnosis. Afterwards the subjects were asked to judge the frequency with which a diagnosis such as paranoia or suspiciousness coincided with particular features from the drawings (for example, 'peculiar eyes'). Subjects significantly overestimated the actual frequency of some coincident events: for example, if they were asked how many times they had seen a picture of someone with peculiar eyes and a diagnosis of paranoia, they would significantly overestimate that set of coincident events, but the positive correlations reported by subjects, for example between suspiciousness and peculiar eyes, were illusory. Kahneman and Tversky attribute this to an 'associative bond' between events: for example, suspiciousness is popularly associated with peculiar eyes.

Attention bias

Another bias emerging from the misapplication of the availability heuristic is attention bias. Earl (2005), in developing some axiomatic foundations for psychological economics, focuses on the impact of attention bias, meaning that attention cannot be allocated optimally. In this case choices will be fickle and susceptible to random influences and context: for example in the case of fashions and fads. Attention bias may emerge from a misapplication of the availability heuristics leading to misjudgments including primacy and recency effects.

Attention bias can also lead people into misguided predictions about the future. If events have recently caught people's attention, then they will affect perceptions of the likelihood of similar events in the near future. This is why insurance companies do well after a spate of disasters. Attention bias will also affect perceptions of terrorist attacks (Gigerenzer 2004). Similarly, attention bias and the availability heuristic may cause researchers to recall the most interesting, attractive or complex field examples rather than those that are most often encountered, biasing their future interpretation. There may also be limits on attention: for example, a limited attention bias may lead to overbidding in auctions or when supermarket shopping (Malmendier and Lee 2011).

The affect heuristic

Affect is the experience of feeling an emotion and will have an impact on decision-making via the affect heuristic, in which emotions are used to guide decision-making. Sometimes, as Antonio Damasio explains in the context of his somatic marker hypothesis, emotions can be a reliable guide. At other times emotions can lead to significant biases if they distort objective perceptions. Emotions and affect may also have an indirect impact via availability heuristics: emotions are more available than objective facts and figures because they are often highly salient, vivid and easily recalled. Emotional factors can dominate cognition, especially as they are associated with quicker, more automatic responses.

Finucane *et al.* (2000) observe that the affect heuristic can distort judgments of probability and risk: when people are feeling optimistic about a situation, this will lead to misplaced perceptions of lower risk and larger benefits. For example, emotional responses from the public to journalistic accounts of murder arrests can lead to significant injustices when people's emotional responses interact with a misapplication of heuristics, including the representativeness heuristic. As illustrated by journalists' treatment of Christopher Jefferies during the hunt for the murderer of Jo Yeates in 2010: in disseminating emotionally misguided opinions about someone's guilt, journalists sometimes describe traits that are associated with the stereotype of a murderer rather than objective facts.

Emotional salience also affects retrievability and availability. It will also interact with the attention bias outlined above. Someone watching a car-crash scene will draw on these emotionally salient images, affecting their perception: they will judge it more likely that *they* will be involved in a car crash even though objective information about the frequency of car crashes has not changed. Similarly, headline news of airplane crashes will be brought to mind more readily than bike accidents because of vivid reports from air-crash sites, even though bike accidents are far more frequent.

So, whilst availability enables quick decision-making, it will lead to biases if the prominence of recent events does not reflect the actual frequency with which events usually occur, especially if the events are associated with vivid emotional cues.

The somatic marker hypothesis and other connections between emotions, affect and decision-making are explored in more depth in chapter 8.

Anchoring and adjustment

Anchoring and adjustment is a single heuristic that involves making an initial estimate of a probability called an anchor, and then revising or adjusting it up or down in the light of new information (Tversky and Kahneman 1974). This typically results in assessments that are determined by an anchor value or reference point (as explored in chapter 7 in the context of Kahneman and Tversky's prospect theory). For example, in deciding about an appropriate wage demand to make in the face of an uncertain economic environment, workers will tend to anchor their demands around their existing wage. Anchoring effects may operate in a social dimension, too, if one individual's judgments is 'anchored' to others' opinions.

Kahneman and Tversky (1974) identify three specific biases associated with anchoring, including insufficient adjustment, biases in evaluation of conjunctive and disjunctive events, and anchoring biases.

Insufficient adjustment

This bias occurs when probability judgments are anchored to prior information or events, and are not adjusted as the information or context changes. Kahneman and Tversky illustrate this with an example of incomplete numerical tasks. Two groups of school students were given five seconds to estimate the answer to a numerical question: one group was given the task of estimating $8 \times 7 \times 6 \times 5 \times 4 \times 3 \times 2 \times 1$; the other group was given the task of estimating $1 \times 2 \times 3 \times 4 \times 5 \times 6 \times 7 \times 8$. Their time allowance of five seconds was not enough for most to have time for reflection. The group with the first problem estimated 512; the second group 2250. The correct answer is 40,320. The estimate for the first expression was higher than for the second, and Kahneman and Tversky argue that this reflected anchoring onto the first number: the group anchoring onto the starting value of 8 came up with higher estimates that the group anchoring on a starting value of 1. Both groups underestimated the true answer by a substantial degree, reflecting incomplete adjustment – they hadn't had time to extrapolate to the large correct answer.

Evaluation biases

Tversky and Kahneman (1974) discuss biases that emerge when people are asked to evaluate conjunctive and disjunctive events. One illustration of evaluative biases is the conjunction fallacy, illustrated above with the example of the Linda problem in the context of the representativeness heuristic. Further problems with probability estimates from conjunctive and disjunctive events reflect anchoring and adjustment. For example, Tversky and Kahneman give an example of an experiment in which subjects could place bets on events. There were three types of event:

A   A simple event of drawing a red marble from a bag containing 50 per cent red marbles and 50 per cent white marbles. The objective probability of this event is 0.50.

B   A conjunctive event specifically drawing a red marble seven times in a row from a bag containing 90 per cent red marbles and 10 per cent white marbles, with replacement of the marble after each draw. The objective probability of this event is 0.48.

C   A disjunctive event specifically drawing a red marble at least once at some stage in seven draws (with replacement) from a bag containing 10 per cent red marbles and 90 per cent white marbles. The objective probability of this event is 0.52.

Then the subjects were offered two sets of choices

1.   When offered a bet between the simple event and the conjunctive event, subjects preferred to bet on the conjunctive event, even though the conjunctive event was less likely.
2.   When offered a bet between the simple event and the disjunctive event, the subjects preferred the simple event, even though the simple event was less likely.

The subjects' intuitive judgments of probabilities inverted the objective probability ranking. Kahneman and Tversky attribute this to anchoring and adjustment, asserting that people are judging the probabilities relative to a starting point with incomplete adjustment downwards or upwards towards the reference point. In the case of choice 1 (between event A and the conjunctive event B), the probability of the elementary event in event B (a red ball) is 90 per cent; this is the anchor point event and adjustment *downwards* from 90 per cent to 48 per cent (the true probability) is incomplete, leading subjects to decide event A is a better bet.

For choice 2 (between event A and the disjunctive event C), the elementary event is event C (again a red ball), but in this case the bag was biased towards white balls and so the probability of the elementary event (a red ball) was 10 per cent; adjustment *upwards* from this point is incomplete, leading subjects to decide that event A is more likely.

Kahneman and Tversky describe the directions of the anchoring bias in terms of metaphors of funnels and chains: the chain-like structure of conjunctive events leads to overestimation of probabilities; the funnel-like structure of disjunctive events leads to underestimation. Bar-Hillel (1973) explains: in the same way that the probability of events compounded using the logical 'AND' is often overestimated, the probability of events compounded using logical 'OR' is often underestimated. This sort of bias leads to an unbounded probability problem: subjects tend to overestimate each probability in a set of exhaustive and mutually exclusive scenarios, and do not correct their probability estimates when the set of exhaustive but mutually exclusive outcomes is augmented. These biases lead people implicitly to infer that the total probability of the set of possible events is greater than one, that is, greater than certain (Anderson 1998, p. 15). On the other hand, probabilities of disjunctive events are underestimated, and this means that people will erroneously judge that the sum of probabilities of a set of mutually exclusive and exhaustive outcomes is less than one.

These evaluation biases have implications for planning, in particular when people are judging the likely success of investment strategies. Some investment strategies involve a step-by-step process of success or failure – an example would be new product development in the pharmaceutical industry, in which there is a chain-like series of events: a trial is successful, the drug is successfully patented, then it is effectively marketed, and so on. This series of events is conjunctive, and Kahneman and Tversky predict that investors will be overoptimistic because they overestimate the likelihood of this series of related events. However, if it is a disjunctive event then there will be a number of unrelated risks which do not develop sequentially over time. The new technology of 'fracking' or rock-blasting to extract shale gas is an example. There are a series of risks involved in fracking. Fracking might cause an earthquake. It might contaminate groundwater. There may be industrial accidents. These events are not sequential and chain-like, and together they form a disjunctive event. So, applying Tversky and Kahneman's analysis, the overall risk may be underestimated.

Assessment biases

Assessment biases reflect inaccurate calibration. If a person is asked to construct a subjective probability distribution around their judgments, for example that the Dow Jones average will take some value, their probability distributions will reflect overly narrow confidence intervals. If a subject is calibrating probabilities on percentiles, then values below the first percentile should be seen 1 per cent of the time and values above the 99th percentile should also be seen 1 per cent of the time. Overall, true values should fall within a 98 per cent confidence interval. But experimental evidence reveals large, systematic departures with subjects revealing overly narrow confidence intervals. This phenomenon is seen in naïve and sophisticated subjects, and is not eliminated by incentives or scoring.

Tversky and Kahneman attribute this to anchoring. There is insufficient upward adjustment from the mean to the 99th percentile and insufficient adjustment downwards from the mean to the first percentile. Overall, this leads to confidence intervals that are too narrow. They describe a study in which quantities, for example air distances from New Delhi, were presented to subjects who were then asked to judge the 10th or the 90th percentile. Another group was given the median judgment from the first group and asked to assess the odds that the given value exceeded the true value. The first group was too extreme: they judged a probability of 10 per cent for event that occurred 24 per cent of the time. The second group was too conservative: events that they judged 34 per cent likely occurred in only 26 per cent of cases.

Problems also emerge with the anchoring heuristic when people anchor onto misleading or irrelevant reference points. Tversky and Kahneman give an example of a wheel-of-fortune experiment. For each subject, the wheel was spun to reveal a number and each subject was then asked to estimate the number of African nations in the United Nations. Their estimates were anchored on the number they spun: subjects spinning a low number gave low estimates for the number of African countries in the UN; subjects spinning a high number gave high estimates. Ariely *et al.* (2003) identified similar evidence of 'coherent arbitrariness' in a series of consumer experiences in which arbitrary anchors affected product valuations and hedonic experiences. Their experimental subjects were shown six products, including computer accessories, wine, chocolates and books. They were asked if they would buy these products for an amount equal to the last two digits of their social security number (SSN). Then they were asked to reveal their level of willingness to pay (WTP). Subjects with an SSN above the median reported significantly higher WTP than subjects with an SSN below the median. For example, a subject with an SSN in the top quintile was willing to pay $56 on average for a cordless computer keyboard versus a WTP of $16 on average for subjects with bottom quintile SSNs.

Loss aversion, endowment effects and status quo bias

Thaler (1980) identified the endowment effect as a loss of utility from giving up a valued good greater than the gain in utility from acquiring the same good. This creates a divergence between WTP and willingness to accept (WTA). Knetsch (1989) conducted an experiment to capture endowment effects. Students were asked to choose between mugs and pens. Imagine a choice in which you won a mug and then were given the chance to trade it for five pens, and you decided to keep the mug. Imagine if this choice is reversed: you have five pens and are offered a mug; if your preferences are consistent and reversible, then you will again choose the mug. Knetsch found students' choices were not consistent and reversible. He divided a group of students into two groups, which essentially captured different incarnations of their indifference curves: a WTA curve and a WTP curve. In standard theory, these curves should coincide. The WTP group started with $4.50; the WTA group started with five pens. The students were offered a series of trades: the WTP of the first group was assessed by giving the students opportunities to buy a pen at a range of prices; the WTA of the second group was captured by giving the students the opportunity to sell their pens at a range of prices. Knetsch found that preferences were determined by initial endowments: those who started with more pens on average valued pens more highly than those who started with money. The WTP and WTA versions of the indifference curves were intersecting, violating the standard assumption of transitivity. This behaviour could not be attributed to subjective preferences for pens, because those who started with pens did not rate pens more highly than the group that started with money. Environmental valuation will also be affected by disparities between WTP and WTA. Knetsch observes that in valuing the loss of duck habitat, WTP is appropriate only if the duck habitat is absent; stated WTP will undervalue environmental resources and WTA should be used instead (Brown and Hagen 2010; Knetsch 2010).

Endowment effects link to *status quo* bias. This is a phenomenon identified by Samuelson and Zeckhauser (1988), capturing preferences for the current state of affairs. Samuelson and Zeckhauser use an example of an economist who owns an expensive bottle of Bordeaux wine. He does not want to buy another bottle, nor does he want to sell the bottle he has. Kahneman *et al.* (1991) explore these effects in the context of car insurance in New Jersey and Pennsylvania: two policy options are offered – a cheap option with restricted right to sue; and an expensive option with unrestricted right to sue. In New Jersey, the cheap policy was the default option. In Pennsylvania, the expensive policy was the default option. When offered the chance to buy the right to sue, only 23 per cent of people in New Jersey took that option; they preferred to stay with the *status quo*. On the other hand, 53 per cent of Pennsylvanians retained the right to sue, and Kahneman *et al.* also attribute this inconsistency to *status quo* bias.

Kahneman *et al.* (1990, 1991) and Kahneman and Tversky (1991) developed this analysis, linking endowment effects to *status quo* bias and loss aversion. They carried out a range of experiments to test the endowment effect. In one set of experiments they divided a group of seventy-seven students randomly into three treatment conditions: seller, buyer or chooser. The sellers were given mugs and asked if they were prepared to sell those mugs at a range of prices from $0.25 to $9.25. The buyers were offered the mugs at the same set of prices. The choosers were given a choice, at the same prices, between the money and the mug, for example, at $p = \$0.25$ they could either have a mug or keep $0.25. The sellers and buyers are, in objective terms, in the same position, yet there was a large divergence in reservation prices: the sellers' median price was $7.12 and the choosers' median price was $3.12. They attribute this inconsistency to the endowment effect.

Aside from loss aversion and *status quo* bias, Kahneman *et al.* (1991) assert that loss aversion and related endowment effects can affect a wide range of decision-making, including job choice. They designed experiments in which people were choosing between jobs with two main aspects: commuting time and social opportunities for contact with others. If people start with a job that has many social opportunities, then they are more averse to losing them even with considerable extensions of commuting times; if people start with a job with shorter commuting times then they are averse to losing this, even at considerable cost in terms of social life.

Other experiments illustrate *status quo* bias too. Kahneman *et al.* also study *status quo* bias in the context of money illusion in wage adjustment. Subjects were asked to consider a scenario in which a company is making a small profit. Subjects are asked to consider two options:

A   Given no inflation, a company manager decides to decrease wages and salaries by 7 per cent.
B   With inflation at 12 per cent, a company manager decides to increase salaries by only 5 per cent.

More subjects (78 per cent) thought that option B was acceptable, whereas only 37 per cent thought that option A was acceptable. This is a classic nominal wage-resistance result seen in macroeconomics – attributed by some economists as an example of money illusion, but explained by Keynes (1936) as reflecting the fact that workers are worried about their relative, not absolute positions. In terms of real wages, everyone suffers equally from inflation, but nominal wage falls may affect one group disproportionately relative to others.

Kahneman *et al.* link *status quo* bias and endowment effects together as manifestations of the deeper tendency towards loss aversion, arguing that people are adjusting to *changes* from a reference point given by the current *status quo*. The links between reference points and loss aversion are explored in more detail in chapter 7.

Thaler (1980) identifies other manifestations of divergences between WTA and WTP, including the fact that people are willing to pay for a vaccine to eliminate small chance of death from a virus, but less willing to accept money by participating in medical experiments when there is the same small chance of death. Viscuis *et al.* (1987) describe an experiment in which consumers are shown cans of insecticide and asked about their WTP to eliminate health risks, for example from poisoning. Then they are asked their WTA if the insecticide was fine initially, but they could have a price reduction if they were prepared to take an increased risk of poisoning. Divergences reflect more complex motivations – including legal distinctions between relationships between risk, and failures of omissions versus commission, an aspect that can be captured to an extent within regret theory (see chapter 7). See also Plott and Zeiler (2005, 2007, 2011) and Isoni *et al.* (2011) on gaps between WTP and WTA.

Some studies attribute the endowment effect to experience, learning and context rather than to bounds on rationality and cognitive capacity. For example, List (2003) explores the impact of market experience on the endowment effect, finding that behaviour converges to standard predictions as market experience increases. He concludes that market experience plays a significant role in eliminating the endowment effect, and his findings are robust to institutional change. Endowment effects reflect people treating opportunity costs and monetary costs in different ways: 'foregone gains are less painful than perceived losses'. This focus on actual losses rather than potential gains fits with legal principles: in tort law, a loss in expenditure is often given more legal weight than the failure to make a gain.

Biases and heuristics in expert judgment

Tversky and Kahneman argue that accumulation of experience does not stop people from systematically misapplying heuristics if they do not have an opportunity to discover their own mistakes. They identified some of these biases amongst experts as well ordinary decision-makers. Experts will be susceptible to heuristics and biases even when they have had extensive statistical training. This reflects the fact that consistency in judgments does not necessarily reduce the chance of systematic mistakes. The gambler's fallacy, for example, involves an assumption that a long run of red wins on the roulette wheel will make a black win more likely on the next spin. Gamblers do not change their minds about this fallacy, and so the gamblers' fallacy is not an internally inconsistent belief. The gambler's belief is not unstable and so it does not violate standard economic rationality axioms. Nonetheless, it is not compatible with the more general objective belief that a roulette wheel has no memory and so cannot deliver a black win just because there has been 'too long' a series of red wins.

Curtis (2012) notes that the background and experience of geologists correlates with their ability successfully to interpret geological information; nonetheless, experts are still susceptible to a range of biases reflecting subjectivity in expert decision-making. Baddeley *et al.* (2004) and Curtis (2012) have identified a number of biases in expert judgment, including over-confidence, anchoring and motivational bias. In many cases where experts are involved in the elicitation of knowledge, the experts are individually over-confident about their knowledge, and multiple experts undergoing the same elicitation procedure will produce estimates of elicited parameter values that barely overlap. One way to overcome bias might be to collect a range of opinions simultaneously from a number of experts, but in this setting the experts are susceptible to herding and social influences, which may reflect the application of the availability heuristic as the judgments of others are often easily accessible. Polson and Curtis (2010) conducted an experiment in which experts were asked to interpret geological data and assess the probability of a geological fault. They were asked for their judgments before, during and after group meetings, and opinions changed significantly through the process even though there was no change in the objective information available to the experts.

Weisberg and Muldoon (2009) use modelling techniques to assess the efficacy of different learning strategies amongst scientific experts, contrasting follower strategies with maverick strategies. With the follower strategy, experts followed other experts rather than making their own tracks, and as a consequence large parts of the epistemic landscape remained unexplored. Conversely the maverick strategy, which involved avoiding the research approaches of other experts, was considerably more successful and ensured that a larger area of the epistemic landscape was explored.

Choice overload and cognitive dissonance

The heuristics and biases discussed above focus on decision-making when people are using information to obtain approximate answers; sometimes the reasoning processes are incomplete or incorrect, but information processing continues, albeit in an imperfect fashion. Sometimes, however, the reasoning process breaks down completely because of deeper limits on cognition. Two ways in which this can happen are choice overload and cognitive dissonance.

Choice overload

The standard model in economics focuses on the importance of choice, and implicitly it is assumed that the more choices we have, the better we will be. Psychological research has shown, however, that too much choice – choice overload – can have negative impacts on our emotions and motivation.

Iyengar and Lepper (2000) describe findings from three experimental studies illustrating the negative impacts from having too much choice. For all studies, participants were more satisfied with their selections and performed better when their set of options was limited. The first study examined the behaviour of shoppers at an upmarket grocery store. A tasting booth displayed either a limited choice of six jam flavours or an extensive choice of twenty-four flavours. Motivation was explored in two ways: the number of shoppers drawn to the booth, and the number of jams they bought. For 242 subjects exposed to the extensive choice treatment, 145 stopped at the booth but only four bought jam. On the other hand, for 260 subjects exposed to the limited choice treatment, 104 stopped but thirty of those bought some jam. The study revealed that there was no correlation between the two forms of motivation: 40 per cent of shoppers stopped at the booth displaying a limited range and 30 per cent of them subsequently bought some jam. For the group encountering a booth with an extensive selection of jams, 60 per cent of customers stopped but only 3 per cent of them bought jam.

For the second study, students were offered six or thirty potential essay topics for optional credit. Motivation was assessed in terms of number and quality of essays written; for the limited choice condition, 74 per cent wrote an essay and the mean grade for these essays was 8.09; in the extended choice condition, 60 per cent wrote essays with a mean grade of 7.69. For the third study, Iyengar and Lepper studied the choices of university students choosing chocolates and extended their experimental design by introducing three treatment conditions: no choice, limited choice (from six types of chocolate) and extensive choice (from thirty types of chocolate). The subjects in the extensive choice group reported feeling that they had been offered too much choice, and those who had a limited set of choices experienced more satisfaction.

The extent to which people perceive themselves to be overloaded with choices will also depend on the time frame within which they must make their decisions. Gabaix and Laibson (2000) construct a model of decision-making that blends together insights about bounded rationality, satisficing and heuristics. If people have plenty of time to decide then they can reach the correct answer, but real-life situations often involve time constraints. Gabaix and Laibson tested their hypotheses using experiments on 259 Harvard undergraduates and found that their subjects decided by identifying representative scenarios. In contrast to the backward induction hypothesized in standard game theory models, their evidence shows that people economize by simplifying decisions using heuristics to identify feasible paths.

Cognitive balance and cognitive dissonance

Other distortions in decision-making identified by economists develop insights from cognitive psychology and cognitive balance theory. Cognitive balance theory explores cognitive functioning, including interactions of cognition and emotion, and cognitive dissonance. Heider (1958) developed cognitive balance theory to analyse the extent of congruence between expectations and outcomes, an issue also of central interest in economics. People seek consistent patterns and cognitive balance. When there is cognitive imbalance, people will act to return themselves to a state of psychological balance. For example, if you respect your friend but your friend likes the watching *The X Factor* (which you hate), then you will adjust your perceptions so that either you respect your friend less, or like *The X Factor* more.

Festinger's (1957) analysis of cognitive dissonance draws on similar themes, developed by Hirschman (1965), who defines cognitive dissonance as occuring when that 'a person who, for some reason, commits himself to act in a manner contrary to his beliefs, or to what he believes to be his beliefs, is in a state of dissonance. Such a state is unpleasant, and the person will attempt to reduce the dissonance'. When unexpected or undesirable events occur, people reinterpret events and information to fit their prior beliefs about how the world is, or should be. When people behave in a way that is contrary to their beliefs about themselves, this creates cognitive dissonance between their beliefs and experience. In response, they act to try to remove the dissonance. This creates belief biases, for example when we interpret events and information to fit our preconceived notions as a device to overcome cognitive dissonance. This is done unconsciously. If we believe something, then we will perceive that it has a logical basis, even if that logical basis is imagined.

A type of cognitive dissonance also affects political attitudes when perceptions of the logical basis for an assertion are determined by beliefs in the conclusion, not necessarily the objectivity of the assertion; for example, if a Republican voter believes that healthcare should be privatized then they are more likely than a Democrat to perceive that 2012 Presidential candidate Rick Santorum's critiques of the UK's National Health Service had a logical, objective basis. Similarly, if a person is religious and believes that God created the Earth then they are more likely than an atheist to believe that the theory of intelligent design has an objective basis.

Akerlof and Dickens (1982) apply psychological insights about cognitive dissonance to an economic model based on three basic preferences: first, people have preferences not only over states of the world, but also over their *beliefs* about states of the world; second, people have some control over their beliefs; and third, beliefs persist over time. The cost of the belief is the cost associated with mistakes made because of the belief. For example, people have a preference for believing that their workplace or environment is safe. The cost of their belief relates to the mistakes that emerge when reality and beliefs are mismatched. Believing that you're safe may lead people to behave in a reckless way by not wearing radiation safety badges in nuclear plants, or by failure to buy earthquake insurance when living in an earthquake zone. People in dangerous jobs must rationalize their choices: working in an unsafe place is not smart, therefore working in an unsafe place creates cognitive dissonance. This can be reconciled if the worker adjusts beliefs towards thinking that the workplace is safe.

Akerlof and Dickens describe a range of experimental evidence that supports their three basic premises. In one study, students were asked to insult other students by describing them as 'shallow, untrustworthy and dull'. The students making the insults adjusted their attitudes towards their victims, reflecting cognitive dissonance: they believed themselves to be nice people, nice people don't insult other students without justification, so the other students must have been shallow, untrustworthy and dull. People who engage in anti-social, aggressive or violent behaviour may reconcile their behaviour with their fundamental belief that it is wrong to behave violently by rationalizing and believing that they were provoked. Akerlof and Dickens cite another study of cognitive dissonance in weight reduction: if dieters are set difficult tasks for weight reduction, then they must justify why these difficult tasks as worthwhile, otherwise it would be foolish to undertake them. This generates persistence in beliefs. Weight-watchers with difficult goals are more likely to have sustained weight loss than groups with more modest goals, because they had to modify and reconcile their beliefs to achieve the initial weight loss, and their modification of beliefs persists.

Neuroeconomic analyses

Neuroeconomic studies can illuminate the biases that underlie decision-making in uncertain situations by identifying the neural correlates of analytical thought and assessing the extent to which these areas are engaged during ordinary decision-making. For example, Yoshida and Ishi (2006) use functional magnetic resonance imaging (fMRI) techniques to analyse how people navigate under uncertainty and how they adapt their existing beliefs using Bayesian reasoning. They find that areas of the prefrontal cortex are engaged during Bayesian updating, and this evidence is consistent with standard models of Bayesian decision-making.

Some neuroeconomic studies have captured different neural responses to WTP. Knutson *et al.* (2007) used fMRI techniques to analyse buyers' decisions when they were exposed to a range of prices. They found that items purchased were associated with greater activations in the ventral striatum (associated with reward processing) and the ventromedial prefrontal cortex (associated with risk and decision-making). Anterior insula activations were lower for items purchased.

Assessing endowment effects, Lakshminaryanan *et al.* (2008) find evidence that the choices of capuchin monkeys when trading treats given in the form of chunks of fruit are prone to endowment effects. The monkeys required higher compensation to forego a treat they already had than to forego an equivalent treat that they did not have. Lakshminaryanan *et al.* postulate that this evidence may show that biases are evolved behaviours.

Sharot *et al.* (2007) used fMRI methods to examine overoptimism whilst subjects imagined the contrast between positive and negative future events. They found that that optimism is associated with differential activations in the amygdala and the anterior cingulate cortex, both areas associated with emotional processing. Abnormalities in these areas are also associated with depression and pessimism.

Reutskaja *et al.* (2011) use neuroscientific eye-tracking techniques to develop Iyengar and Lepper's (2000) insights about choice overload, summarized above. Eye tracking monitors the direction of a person's gaze and uses this information to make inferences about which objects are attracting a person's attention. Reutskaja *et al.* assessed the choices of hungry consumers choosing snack items but making their decisions within a strictly limited time frame. They found that the experimental subjects assessed objects according to their appeal, and this assessment correlated strongly with willingness to pay. However, the eye tracking evidence revealed that people had a tendency to look and choose according to the spatial placements of items within shop displays, not the characteristics of the specific goods.

Case study: heuristics and biases in real-world decision-making

Heuristics and biases affect a wide range of real-world decision-making by households and firms. This case study focuses on online behaviour and decisions about energy and the environment.

Online heuristics and biases

For computing decisions, an absence of meaningful and available information about security threats leads to overoptimism and vulnerability to identity theft. For security and human behaviour, Acquisti (2004) and Acquisti and Grossklags (2006) explore a number of other biases specifically affecting online behaviour, including *status quo* and familiarity biases when people prefer the current situation (also explored by Thaler and Sunstein 2008). Some of these biases can be manipulated to encourage people to engage in more efficient behaviour. When online, status quo bias means that people tend favour the existing situation and will avoid the effort involved in changing their choices. Setting online default options cleverly can exploit this bias. If the default option applies the maximum privacy protection, then a large number of consumers may be too lazy to change these options, thus protecting them from security violations.

Heuristics will also be used when online. For example, when thinking about buying new software, an ordinary person may have little real knowledge about what is going to happen in the future. Given this limited information, they will adopt the heuristic of following the crowd in buying what their friends are buying.

For internet security and human behaviour, the availability heuristic combined with an overoptimism bias may lead people to decide that security is not a problem because they haven't had a problem with it in the recent past. On the other hand, if recent news stories have focused on security risks then people may be disproportionately focused on protecting their security. Stories about destructive viruses and malware such as firesheep and/or perils of cloud computing/unsecured information-sharing might encourage more people to be careful about how they use privacy settings on *Facebook* and *Twitter*.

Anchoring may also be relevant: if someone's friends and colleagues are all talking about the benefits of some new software, then a person's judgment of that software may be anchored around these opinions. Another type of decision-making bias that deserves particular attention is the present bias, explored in more detail in chapter 9. People's behaviour may be inconsistent over time: plans to do something constructive (for example, backing up files) change as the future becomes the present, because people procrastinate and lack self-control reflecting present bias.

Bias is not necessarily irrational and may reflect a procedurally rational approach. People may treat different financial decisions in different ways using different 'mental accounts', for example, online buying is put into 'fast' account. Acquisti and Grossklags also build on the behavioural economics literature on procrastination and self-control (e.g. O'Donoghue and Rabin, 1999, 2001; DellaVigna and Malmendier 2006). When using the internet, people will procrastinate about setting up effective security systems in much the same way as many ordinary people procrastinate about backing up files. Procrastination is potentially a key policy issue, particularly if the most effective privacy and security solutions are to be driven by individual choices. Assuming that people suffer biases, but are sophisticated enough to realize that this might generate security and privacy problems in the future, then they can be encouraged to set up pre-commitment devices such as identity-verification systems and/or computer default options which exploit the *status quo* bias (Acquisti 2004; Acquisti and Grossklags 2006). Employing these devices enables sophisticated users to pre-commit to protecting themselves from security violations in the short term when they might be tempted to act impulsively.

The problem for internet security is that people do not necessarily learn quickly about their biases. Emotions have an impact because they are quick and impulsive, and engage automatic decision-making systems. To enable faster learning, if group leaders can be identified and encouraged to adopt appropriate online protections, then others may follow their example. Alternatively, if information about the adoption of safeguards by others is prominent in information provided, then this normative influence will encourage people to do what others are doing. Cooperation between self-seeking individuals will lead to the evolution of new social norms (Axelrod 1990).

The impact of social norms and social influence has been identified in the context of household energy choices (Schultz *et al.* 2007; Thaler and Sunstein 2008; see chapter 5). Similar influences may operate in the online environment too. In understanding these issues, the roles of social capital, cooperation, trust and reputation are crucial. For security and human behaviour, decisions are made in a multidimensional space and reflect contradictory goals, and so trust and control are central; effective security and privacy systems will allow transparent communication between trusted parties but will be closed to the 'bad guys' (Clark 2010). Attitudes to privacy and security are changing; for example, it is widely believed that the younger generation are more vulnerable to identity theft because they are far more willing to reveal important personal information. In terms of policy implications, perhaps people can be encouraged to take more care in their online decision-making if learning leads to new social norms via advertising, social networking and other forms of social interaction.

Heuristics, biases and folk wisdom in environmental decision-making

Social information is used when households anchor their energy consumption decisions around socially determined reference points. Without a reference point, information about embedded emissions is of little use to the consumer because they do not know what it means, but social information can be used in setting reference points around social comparisons; for example, the French supermarket chain E. Leclerc is introducing carbon labelling which includes not only information about carbon emissions per kg for specific products, but also total carbon footprints for each trolley of food alongside a social comparison with the average trolley footprint (*The Economist* 2011b, p. 14).

Environmental behaviour takes place in a world of bounded rationality in which there are constraints on information, knowledge and learning. Shogren and Taylor (2008) draw on Mullainathan and Thaler (2000) in identifying three aspects to limits on rational behaviour as seen in environmental behavioural economics: bounded rationality, bounded willpower and bounded self-interest. Just increasing the availability of information is not necessarily the simple solution it seems; Leiserowitz *et al.* (2012) note that often behaviours that would be most effective (for example, driving cars less often) are neglected in favour of less arduous behaviours such as switching off lights. Knowledge and belief are not enough – just because people have knowledge about the benefits of environmental actions, that does not mean they will engage in those actions.

One fundamental constraint on rationality is lack of knowledge, though Stern (2000) argues that knowledge is just a necessary component in engineering environmental behaviour change and is not sufficient in itself. Pongiglione (2011) emphasizes the role of knowledge in behavioural analyses of climate change and individual decision-making. In risky situations, deep psychological mechanisms propel people towards inaction and apathy, and this constrains pro-environmental behaviour. Behaviour change requires a combination of understanding, procedural knowledge and self-interest. To an extent this can be explained in terms of standard economic models which incorporate transaction costs.

Problems emerge because self-interest interacts with subjective perceptions and limited knowledge/imperfect information. Procedural knowledge, including practical information about ways to reduce environmental impact, is particularly important as it enables people to turn subjective beliefs into concrete actions (Kaiser and Fuhrer 2003). Similarly, Reynolds *et al.* (2010) focus on knowledge deficits to explain environmental inaction and empathy gaps. Pongiglione argues, however, that it is not all about knowledge deficits. The main obstacles to behaviour change reflect interplaying factors: perception, self-interest and limits to knowledge, where knowledge includes awareness, understanding and procedural practical common-sense knowledge about energy efficiency and the environment.

Biases in environmental decision-making are exacerbated by uncertainty about the future, which, together with limited knowledge about the present, has a dampening impact on decisions about energy and the environment. Decisions between risky alternatives will affect both firms and households: firms in their investment decisions, and households in their energy consumption decisions and in purchases of lumpy consumption goods such as refrigerators and boilers. Uncertainty will have a profound impact on consumption and investment decisions. Carbon labelling can reduce consumers' uncertainty about the impact of their purchases, but although labelling can provide some guidance to environmentally conscious consumers, the question of how emissions should be measured and reported remains. Best practice would involve calculating emissions over the life cycle of a product – in its manufacture as well as its end use – but for many products, life-cycle emissions are uncertain. How do you calculate the end-use emissions from shampoo, given the variability in its use? Here, end-use emissions will depend on how long someone spends in the shower and how hot the water is (*The Economist* 2011b).

Decisions affecting the environment are also affected by heuristics and biases. Sunstein (2006) analyses the role played by the availability heuristic in people's intuitive cost–benefit analysis of climate change. He argues that if people have recently experienced serious tangible harms from climate change, then climate change will be perceived as a more salient problem. People are also affected by bounded rationality and cognitive limitations when assessing quantitative information about the environment.

Hartman *et al.* (1991) explore *status quo* bias in household energy consumption. They conducted a survey of electricity consumers who were asked about their preferences for reliability and rates. Their responses fell into two groups: those with a reliable service and those with an unreliable service. They found that 60.2 per cent of the high reliability group wanted to retain their current contract even when the low reliability contract came with a 30 per cent rate decrease; 58.3 per cent of the group with the less reliable supplier wanted to stay with their existing supplier when offered the opportunity to switch at a 30 per cent increase in rates. Whilst to some extent their original choices may reflect underlying preferences, learning and/or habits, nonetheless Kahneman *et al.* attribute limited switching to a *status quo* bias (Hartman *et al.* 1991; Kahneman *et al.* 1991).

Status quo biases will lead people to stick with old habits and avoid change, and – to an extent – this may be an economically rational way of avoiding the transaction costs associated with change (McNamara and Grubb 2011; Pongiglione 2011). However, there is evidence that it is not just about transaction costs. For example, in the UK switching energy supplier is a quick and easy process: cost-comparison websites are easily accessible, and if a customer decides to switch, the new supplier contacts the old supplier, so overall the risks and transaction costs associated with a switch are small. Yet, even in the face of rising energy prices from the UK's big six energy suppliers, households do not necessarily apply competitive pressure by switching supplier. A 2011 YouGov poll commissioned by Anglian Home Improvements showed that 51 per cent of respondents are likely to delay switching energy supplier and would prefer instead to ration energy, for example, by wearing warmer clothing (YouGov 2011). This reluctance to switch may partly reflect a *status quo* bias/familiarity bias.

Kempton and Montgomery (1982) and Kempton *et al.* (1992) analyse the use of heuristics and 'folk methods' in energy consumption decisions, and observe that miscalculations can lead to underinvestment in energy efficiency. Information about energy efficiency is often presented in a way that is intelligible to experts but esoteric to ordinary consumers. Research has shown that, in encouraging drivers to be aware of their fuel use, gallons-per-mile is more effective than miles-per gallon (Loewenstein and Ubel 2010). Also, bounded rationality leads to reliance on heuristics – for example, people will adapt old methods to new situations when old methods will not provide the optimal solution. Consumers will use everyday reasoning, including heuristics, to speed up and simplify their measurement of residential energy decisions. The use of these folk methods is reasonable in the sense that it saves time and effort in computation, but it does also lead to mistakes.

Kempton and Montgomery (1982) analysed folk quantification via interviews with thirty Michigan families, ten of whom were using energy-saving devices. These families also used 'folk units' – familiar absolute measures such as gallons, dollars and months – to gauge their energy use. One householder conceptualized his energy consumption in terms of how many times per month he had to fill his oil tank. He did not conceptualize his energy decisions in terms of kilowatt-hours. People also focused on peak consumption – a woman describing to her husband that insulation had reduced gas bills noted that they were no longer getting large $100 gas bills as they had before.

Kempton and Montgomery also identified a tendency to overemphasize certain forms of consumption. People overemphasized lighting as a drain on energy, and were more likely to turn the lights off than they were to use less hot water – even though the latter had a larger impact. This overemphasis on lighting could reflect historical factors (lighting used to be the biggest energy user) and/or problems of perception and categorization. Lighting output is more salient (we notice it more); it is also a prototype representing the broad general category of electricity use. People also focused on first-hand experiences and experiences of friends rather than impersonal, but objective, data summaries from organizations. Kempton and Montgomery found that householders focused on the dollar amount of their energy bills, neglecting the fact that consumption measured in dollars reflects price as well as volume. They also identified biases when people did not recognize that behaviour changes had had an impact on their bills. They were not recognizing that their bills reflected not only their water consumption changes but also price increases.

Households were also using folk methods to calculate savings from reducing energy consumed, and by focusing just on dollar amounts to make comparisons they neglected the impact of rising prices. This failure to incorporate rising prices led to underestimation of the savings from reduced consumption. These problems also affected energy investments – by using simple payback methods without adjusting for price increases, folk methods led householders to overestimate how long it would take them to pay off their energy-efficient investments.

Overall, whilst heuristics are cognitively efficient in the sense that they are quick and easy to learn and useful for household budgeting, they also lead to systematic errors in quantification, ineffective energy conservation, underestimation of benefits of investments in energy efficiency, and increased vulnerability to online fraud.

Conclusions and policy implications

The studies explored in this chapter show that human decision-making is limited by the power of human cognition. The need to make quick decisions efficiently leads to the adoption of a number of heuristics, and in many cases these can lead to systematic biases in behaviour and choice. These biases cannot be explained in terms of standard assumptions, though alternative behavioural approaches to decision-making can capture some of the heuristics and biases that characterize everyday decision-making.

Earl (2005) encourages policy-makers to recognize that people do not competently use statistical techniques and, whilst this can distort perception and judgment, psychological economics can play a normative role by promoting better decision-making techniques. Thaler and Sunstein (2008) also explore the fact that, whilst biases can create problems for the policy-maker, often biases can be exploited to encourage more socially beneficial behaviours. For example, too few people donate their organs, give blood, or save properly for their retirement, but the *status quo* bias can be exploited using default options. If donating blood or organs is the default, then people will be less likely to opt out of donating, and overall donations will increase. A wide range of policy lessons from the application of ideas about heuristics and biases is explored by Thaler and Sunstein (2008) in the context of policy nudges. Nudges can work well when behaviour is nonmaximizing. In situations of choice overload, policy-makers can also focus on the architecture of choice to ensure choices are more manageable and so constructive decisions can be made.

In developing an analytical framework for heuristics and biases, Kahneman and Tversky's prospect theory provides an alternative to standard theory and can capture some biases, particularly those related to loss aversion and framing effects. Prospect theory and the related literature are analysed in detail in chapter 7.

7   Prospects and regrets

Introduction

The previous chapter explored some of the limits on rationality which explain heuristics and biases seen in everyday decision-making. This literature is discursive and intuitive in style, and so vulnerable to a criticism that it lacks objective rigour. In response, Kahneman and Tversky (1979) developed these insights to construct their own alternative to the standard approach to decision-making captured by expected utility theory (EUT). Kahneman and Tversky argue that a number of behavioural paradoxes cannot be explained by EUT, but these can be reconciled using their prospect theory, which analyses how people choose between 'prospects' – defined as sets of risky alternatives. Prospect theory can reconcile behavioural inconsistencies without abandoning rigorous analysis.

There are two elements to prospects – their risk and their utility. This chapter starts by exploring some behavioural paradoxes that led to a rethinking of standard approaches in the evolutions of Kahneman and Tversky's prospect theory. Some of the limits on statistical reasoning that might explain these behavioural paradoxes are then discussed, leading into Kahneman and Tversky's critique of EUT. Then Kahneman and Tversky's alternative to EUT is analysed, including its limits, developments and alternatives, including cumulative prospect theory, Thaler's mental accounting model, and Loomes and Sugden's regret theory.

Behavioural paradoxes

Standard economic models are dependent on assumptions of rational consistent preferences and so they cannot easily explain some behavioural paradoxes: instances in which people violate basic rationality axioms such as transitivity and consistency. In this section, a selection of these paradoxes is explored, including the Allais paradox, the Ellsberg paradox, the Monty Hall paradox and the St Petersburg paradox, as discussed by Allais (1953), Ellsberg (1961), Samuelson (1977), Bar-Hillel and Falk (1982), Nalebuff (1987) and Conlisk (1989), amongst others.

St Petersburg paradox

The St Petersburg paradox is described by Samuelson (1977): Peter and Paul are playing a coin-toss game. Peter suggests to Paul that he toss a fair coin an indefinite number of times. Paul will be paid two ducats if heads come up at the first toss, four ducats if he tosses a head at the second toss, eight if he tosses a head at the third toss. Overall Paul's payment will be 2^n where n is the number of coin tosses. The paradox in this game is that Paul's expected reward will be infinite: assuming a fair coin, his chance of a head on the first round is $1/2$ so his payoff for a head in round 1 will be $1/2 \times 2 = 1$. For round 2, his payoff will be $(1/2 \times 2) +$

$(^1/_4 \times 4) = 1 + 1 = 2$, and for round 3 his payoff will be $(^1/_2 \times 2) + (^1/_4 \times 4) + (^1/_8 \times 8) = 1 + 1 + 1 = 3$, and so on. If Paul plays an infinite number of rounds, then his expected payoff will be ∞. Therefore a fair stake for Paul to place on this game is also ∞, but he is unwilling to do this. He will avoid a finite fair bet. This paradox is resolved by assuming that marginal utility is a decreasing function of wealth, that is, by assuming that Paul is risk averse. The dependence of EUT on the assumption of risk aversion is one of the key elements of Kahneman and Tversky's (1979) critique, as explained below.

Allais paradox

Allais's (1953) paradox describes inconsistencies in choice when people are deciding between options in two gambling games, one of which involves a certain outcome. Conlisk (1989) describes a set of gambles in which people choose between lotteries.

Gamble 1: choose A or A*

Lottery A $1 million with certainty
Lottery A*   1 per cent chance of zero; 89 per cent chance of $1 million; 10 per cent chance of $5 million

Gamble 2: choose B or B*

Lottery B   89 per cent chance of zero; 11 per cent chance of $1 million
Lottery B*   90 per cent chance of zero; 10 per cent chance of $5 million

Standard economic theory predicts that a person with consistent preferences will choose B if they chose A, and B* if they chose A*; which of these pairs they choose will depend on their risk aversion. The expected value for A is less than the expected value for A*, but the chance of zero is eliminated. Similarly, the expected value for B is less than the expected value for B*, but there is a smaller chance of nothing. However, experimental evidence shows that real people commonly choose the inconsistent combinations A*B and B*A. Choices are not completely random, however, and Conlisk observes a systematic pattern: violations of EUT more commonly involve the combination AB* than A*B. Kahneman and Tversky (1979) attribute the violations to a 'certainty effect', as discussed below.

Ellsberg paradox

Ellsberg's (1961) paradox can be illustrated with an urn game. An urn contains ninety balls: thirty are red balls and the remaining sixty balls are some unknown combination of black and yellow balls. Subjects were asked for their preferences over two gambles.

Gamble 3: if one ball is drawn from the urn, will you bet on:

(a) red? or
(b) black?

Gamble 4: if one ball is drawn from the urn, will you bet on:

(c) red or yellow? or
(d) black or yellow?

Subjects were given plenty of time to make their choices. Ellsberg found that many people prefer to bet on red in gamble 1 and on black or yellow in gamble 2.

Ellsberg observes that this is a violation of the 'sure thing principle', which requires that if (a) is preferred to (b) then (c) should be preferred to (d), because the same change has been made to both choices: a yellow ball has been added to each option. For a strictly rational person, if they prefer red to black in gamble 3, then they should also prefer red to black in gamble 4 too; the inclusion of yellow in the second pair of choices should not affect the outcome. Ellsberg attributes this inconsistency to ambiguity aversion in the face of Knightian uncertainty. As defined by Knight (1921), Knightian uncertainty describes fundamental uncertainty about unknowable probabilities. Knightian risk describes probabilities that can be quantified because they capture observable, repeatable events, which can be measured using frequency ratios or, in the case of Ellsberg's urn game, are given as prior information about proportions. In the case of Ellsberg's paradox, the subjects know that the probability of a red ball is 0.33, because they are told that thirty of the ninety balls are red. This is a case of Knightian risk. On the other hand, they are given no information about the probability of a black ball versus a yellow ball. All they know is that the sixty remaining balls are either black or yellow, and this is a case of Knightian uncertainty. There is no objective information based on which people can form an objective, quantifiable probability judgment. Ellsberg observes: 'it is impossible to infer even the qualitative probabilities of yellow versus black'. Abdellaoui *et al.* (2011) observe that when uncertain events are associated with probabilities that cannot be quantified, something else is needed to resolve the paradox. They give a tractable quantitative method in which subjective probabilities are converted into a willingness to bet.

Monty Hall/three prisoners paradox

Nalebuff (1987) describes a number of paradoxes including the Monty Hall paradox, which is interesting because it raises much controversy. Even statisticians struggle to understand why the correct answer is correct, because the answer is counterintuitive. This paradox emerges in the context of a TV show, *Let's Make a Deal*, hosted by Monty Hall. Contestants are shown three curtains. A large prize is hidden behind one curtain, and small prizes are hidden behind the other two. The contestant makes a choice and then Monty Hall opens the curtain to reveal what's behind one of the curtains not chosen, and asks the contestant if they want to change their mind. If people are reasoning in a Bayes rational way (as described in chapter 4), then they should decide to change their mind. If they don't, then they are making a decision based on a misplaced updating of prior probabilities. They are not updating their probabilities using a Bayesian reasoning process. Bar-Hillel and Falk (1982) show why this is the case in describing essentially the same problem set in a different context – the Three Prisoners problem. Tom, Dick and Harry are held in a jail. The next day, one of them will be executed and the other two will be set free. Tom, Dick and Harry's prior probabilities of being executed are $\frac{1}{3}$. The guard is not allowed to reveal to the individual prisoners their own fate, but Dick is anxious and asks the guard to tell him just whether Tom or Harry will be set free. The guard tells Dick that it is Harry who will be freed. No new information has been revealed about the probability that *Dick* will be executed, and so his chance of execution remains $\frac{1}{3}$. The fact that this result seems counterintuitive to most people reflects the fact that human intuition is not probabilistic; often people struggle intuitively to understand statistical problems. An intuitive response to this question reflects confusion, at least in terms of Bayes's rule, of posterior and conditional probabilities. Bar-Hillel and Falk explain the correct answer using Bayes's rule, as shown in Box 7.1.

Box 7.1   Bar-Hillel and Falk's solution to the Three Prisoners problem

The events D, H and T are the hanging of Dick, Harry and Tom, respectively, and the probabilities of each are given by:

$P(D) = P(H) = P(T) = \frac{1}{3}.$

The guard reveals to Dick only that Harry will be freed, and the conditional probabilities of event $\overline{H}_g$ – denoting that the guard designated Harry as the prisoner to be freed – are given by:

$P(\overline{H}_g \mid D) = \frac{1}{2}, P(\overline{H}_g \mid H) = 0, P(\overline{H}_g \mid T) = 1.$

If Dick is to be hanged, then Harry and Tom are equally likely to be designated by the guard as the prisoner to be freed:

$P(\overline{H}_g) = P(\overline{T}_g) = \frac{1}{2}.$

This gives the conditional probability that Dick will be hanged, conditional on the guard designating Harry as the prisoner to be hanged:

$$P\left(D \mid \overline{H}_g\right) = \frac{P(\overline{H}_g \mid D)P(D)}{P(\overline{H}_g \mid D)P(D) + P(\overline{H}_g \mid H)P(H) + P(\overline{H}_g \mid T)P(T)} = \frac{\left(\frac{1}{2}\right)\left(\frac{1}{3}\right)}{\left(\frac{1}{2}\right)\left(\frac{1}{3}\right) + 0\left(\frac{1}{3}\right) + 1\left(\frac{1}{3}\right)} = 1/3$$

Expected utility theory

A fundamental aspect of Kahneman and Tversky's analysis of prospect theory is their critique of EUT. Concepts of expected value and expected utility were developed by Bernoulli and others from the eighteenth century onwards, but found their way into mainstream economics only in the mid-twentieth century, most famously in von Neumann and Morgenstern's (1944) analysis of EUT.

To enable an understanding of Kahneman and Tversky's critique, a summary of some of the basic principles of EUT are outlined in Box 7.2. The von Neumann and Morgenstern preference axioms include transitivity, completeness, substitution, continuity and invariance. Transitivity means that if A is preferred to B and B is preferred to C, then A is preferred to C. Completeness means that, in a choice between A and B, an individual will either prefer A, prefer B, or be indifferent between A and B. Substitution implies that if two alternatives are identical, then they can be substituted for each other – for example, if an individual is indifferent between two alternatives, then they will also be indifferent between the alternatives if these are offered with equal probabilities. Continuity implies that if $A \leq B \leq C$, then B can be expressed as a weighted sum of A and C. Invariance implies that the expected utility function can be scaled up without affecting the ordering of preferences.

Overall, these EUT axioms generate a theory in which people have stable, consistent risk preferences. By including an assumption of risk aversion, the standard concave utility function is specified, expected utility will increase at a decreasing rate, and individuals will prefer averages to extremes. Given these axioms, Savage (1954) shows that expected utility

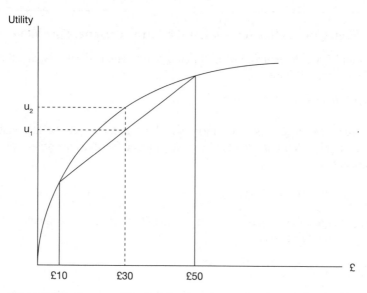

Figure 7.1 A concave utility function

is the product of a subjective utility function and a Bayesian subjective probability distribution (Savage 1954; Kahneman and Tversky 1979).

As noted above, EUT makes particular assumptions about risk aversion, and these define the concave shape of the utility function, as illustrated in Figure 7.1.

Figure 7.1 shows an example of a choice between £10 and £50. If a person is offered a choice between a 50 per cent chance of £10 and a 50 per cent chance of £50, then the expected value of this gamble is £30, but this gives utility at u_1 whereas a guaranteed £30 has a utility of u_2 and $u_2 > u_1$. To put another way, if a person requires a certainty equivalent (the amount which makes them indifferent between the gamble and a guaranteed amount) of less than £30 to take a gamble with an expected value of £30, then they are risk averse. EUT assumes that people are risk averse, and the more bowed the utility function, the higher risk aversion will be. This is captured by the Arrow–Pratt measure of absolute risk aversion, which captures the curvature of the utility function using the change in marginal utility relative to its level. The coefficient of relative risk aversion weights the risk parameter by monetary accounts. Further variants of absolute risk aversion and relative risk aversion include constant absolute risk aversion and constant relative risk aversion. Ultimately all these measures assume stable, measurable risk preferences.

Kahneman and Tversky's critique of expected utility theory

Kahneman and Tversky provide a critique of Savage's (1954) approach to analysing decisions between uncertain outcomes – the set of risky alternatives that Kahneman and Tversky call 'prospects'. People do not necessarily reason using mathematical/statistical tools, and this explains some of the behavioural paradoxes described above. Kahneman and Tversky set out some of the problems with EUT and then devise their own solution in the form of prospect theory – a model that enables us to better understand various anomalies in human decision-making.

In developing prospect theory, Kahneman and Tversky (1979) start with a critique of standard EUT and explain how real-world behaviour is better explained by prospect theory. Expected utility theory aims to be both a normative theory – capturing how rational people *should* behave, and a positive/descriptive theory – capturing how people *do* behave. Many people probably would, in principle at least, prefer not to plan their lives in an illogical, inconsistent way, so as a normative theory EUT has more merit – even normative issues can be incorporated within it, as seen in models of inequity aversion (see chapter 5). Normatively, if utility functions can be broadened properly to incorporate preferences for nonmonetary sources of utility such as equity, then most people would like to act in a way predicted by EUT.

According to Kahneman and Tversky, the most profound problem with EUT is its legitimacy as a positive theory. The problem is that people don't/can't act as predicted by EUT, which means that it lacks predictive power and its role as a positive descriptive theory is compromised. Kahneman and Tversky argue that EUT does not provide an adequate description of human behaviour in the real world.

Some of the mathematics underlying Kahneman and Tversky's critique of EUT are outlined in Box 7.2. In their critique, Kahneman and Tversky focus on the Savage axioms underlying EUT of expectation (overall utility is the sum of the expected utilities); asset integration (acceptable prospects are those that integrate with wealth to give a utility greater than the utility of the wealth alone); and risk aversion (which holds if, and only if, the utility function is concave, as illustrated in Figure 7.1).

Illustrating the asset integration axiom with an example: if you have wealth of £10 and an uncertain prospect is offered to you, that prospect is acceptable only if its expected utility plus the utility of £10 exceeds the utility of £10 on its own. So if a friend suggests a poker game in which you have to put down a stake of £1 for a 10 per cent chance of winning £10, then that poker game is an acceptable prospect for you if, and only if, the utility of your new wealth (£10 – £1 = £9) plus the utility of a 10 per cent chance of winning £10 is greater than the utility of £10 alone. According to Kahneman and Tversky, a key feature of the asset integration assumption is that utility is about final stages, not changes. One of the key features of prospect theory, as will be seen below, is the assumption that utility is determined by *changes*, not levels.

Kahneman and Tversky present experimental evidence showing a range of phenomena showing real-world violations of EUT assumptions. They do acknowledge that reliance on evidence from hypothetical choices may not be valid. In particular, experimental results – especially as many of the experiments use university students as subjects – may lack external validity and may not be generalizable to the wider population. However, Kahneman and Tversky defend the experimental approach on the grounds of simplicity: in investigating real choices, you need to see those choices either in the field or in lab experiments, and the problem with field experiments is that probabilities and utilities cannot easily be measured, whereas measurement is relatively straightforward in lab experiments because experimental conditions can be tightly controlled.

Kahneman and Tversky present evidence from Israeli, Swedish and US experiments in which students and faculty members were given a series of questionnaires that asked them to make hypothetical choices between a range of prospects. They found that people's choices were not consistent with EUT, and this finding was similar across all the samples. There were some common anomalous effects in people's decisions: the certainty effect, the isolation effect and the reflection effect.

Box 7.2 Kahneman and Tversky's critique of expected utility theory

Developing von Neumann and Morgenstern (1944) and Savage (1954), Kahneman and Tversky (1979) focus their critique of EUT on Savage's axioms:

Expectation:

$$U(x_1p_1; x_2p_2; \ldots ; x_np_n) = p_1u(x_1) + p_2u(x_2) + \ldots + p_nu(x_n)$$

– total utility is equal to the expected utility of each outcome where x is the payoff and p is its probability.

Asset integration:

$$U(x_1p_1; \ldots ; x_np_n \mid w) \text{ if}$$

$$U(w + x_1p_1; \ldots ; w + x_np_n) > u(w)$$

– a prospect is acceptable at asset position w if, and only if, its utility exceeds the utility of w alone.

Risk aversion:

$$u'' < 0$$

that is, total utility is increasing at a decreasing rate; total utility is concave.

According to Kahneman and Tversky, the risk aversion tenet of EUT implies that people will prefer probabilistic insurance (PI) to contingent insurance (CI). Assume a person starts at a position of indifference between no insurance and contingent insurance:

$$u(w - y) = pu(w - x) + (1 - p)u(w)$$

where x is a negative prospect (i.e. a loss), p is the probability of loss, and y is the contingent insurance premium paid to avoid the loss.

To simplify, Kahneman and Tversky assume:

$$u(w - x) = 0, u(w) = 1$$

which gives:

$$u(w - y) = 1 - p.$$

Kahneman and Tversky assume that a person will be willing to reduce their premium by a factor r to reduce their insurance cover, and therefore:

$$(1 - r)pu(w - x) + rpu(w - y) + (1 - p)u(w - ry) > u(w - y).$$

This represents the amalgamation of risks characteristic of PI. In addition to the risk of a loss, there is also a risk with the PI policy: in the case of a loss, you have some chance of being covered by insurance and some chance of facing the full loss yourself.

Again assuming:

$$u(w - x) = 0, u(w) = 1$$

and:

$$u(w - y) = 1 - p$$

gives:

$$rp(1 - p) + (1 - p)u(w - ry) > 1 - p$$

thus

$$u(w - ry) > 1 - rp$$

Kahneman and Tversky conclude that EUT implies people should favour PI, yet in reality they favour CI.

Certainty effect

This effect can be illustrated with Kahneman and Tversky's example of two sets of choices: Gamble 1: a choice between A and B; and gamble 2: a choice between C and D. This is essentially the same as the Allais paradox choice, described above.

Gamble 5: choose A or B

Prospect A   a 33 per cent chance of $2500, a 66 per cent chance of $2400, and a 1 per cent chance of 0

Prospect B $2400 with certainty

Gamble 6: choose C or D

C   a 33 per cent chance of $2500 and a 67 per cent chance of 0
D   a 34 per cent chance of $2400 and a 66 per cent chance of 0

The consistent choices are to pick C if you picked A, or pick D if you picked B. Either of these sets of choices is justifiable under EUT. Which pair you choose will depend on how risk averse you are. However, the real choices were inconsistent. Kahneman and Tversky found that actual choices were broadly similar to Conlisk's (1989) finding as outlined above, and 18 per cent of people picked A but 83 per cent of people picked C; similarly, 82 per cent picked B but only 17 per cent picked D. A substantial proportion of people picking B switched to C when they were no longer offered a certain prospect.

More precisely, for the choice between C and D, unless you are very risk averse it would be sensible to pick C, and indeed a large proportion of people (83 per cent) did pick C; only 17 per cent of people were sufficiently risk averse to take the slightly reduced chance of getting nothing. You would expect a similarly low proportion of highly risk-averse people were confronting the choice between A or B. With A, there is just a very small (1 per cent) chance of getting nothing, yet many more people avoided it, suggesting extreme risk aversion. Only 18 per cent of people preferred A to B, and 82 per cent of people chose the certain outcome of 2400. This suggests that people are overweighting certain outcomes – people behave very differently when offered a guaranteed outcome relative to how they behave when offered an outcome that is only slightly less likely (i.e. very highly probable). Kahneman and Tversky call this effect the certainty effect and its existence is inconsistent with EUT.

The certainty effect is a violation of the substitution axiom and a further illustration of the Allais paradox. Experimental evidence also reveals other violations of the substitution axiom. When the probability of one outcome is double the outcome of another, choices will depend on whether the probabilities are low or high. Kahneman and Tversky illustrate this with the following choice pairs:

Gamble 7: choose A or B

 A a 45 per cent chance of $6000
 B a 90 per cent chance of $3000

Gamble 8: choose C or D

 C a 1 per cent chance of $6000
 D a 2 per cent chance of $3000

For Gamble 7, 85 per cent chose B. For Gamble 8, 73 per cent chose C. Note that the amounts are the same. The probability of B is double the probability of A. The probability of D is double the probability of C. Even if the risk-aversion assumption is relaxed, EUT predicts that a risk-averse person would pick the more likely outcome; a risk seeker would pick the larger payoff, but Kahneman and Tversky's evidence shows that people are not consistent in their choices between risky prospects: people's choices shift depending on whether they're choosing between low probabilities or high probabilities. When probabilities are small, 73 per cent of Kahneman and Tversky's subjects were picking the bigger but less likely payoff; when probabilities are large, 86 per cent were choosing the smaller but more likely payoff. This suggests a nonlinearity in the *value function* – the function that captures the relationship between expected utility and the magnitude of payoffs, as explained below.

Reflection effect

Kahneman and Tversky find further evidence of nonlinearity in the value function in experimental evidence about losses. Following Markovitz (1952), who identified the tendency to seek risk when confronting losses, Kahneman and Tversky set up choices in which their experimental subjects are choosing between losses, not gains. These experiments provide more powerful evidence against EUT because risk preferences shift when people are choosing between losses. Preferences for losses are a mirror-image reflection of preferences for gains, whereas EUT would predict that a risk-averse person is just as averse when confronting losses as when looking at gains. To illustrate Kahneman and Tversky compare the following choices:

Gamble 9: choose A or B

 A an 80 per cent chance of $4000 gain
 B a certain gain of $3000

Gamble 10: choose C or D

    C   an 80 per cent chance of a $4000 *loss*
    D   a certain loss of $3000

For gamble 9, Kahneman and Tversky's experimental evidence showed that 80 per cent of subjects chose B. For gamble 10, 92 per cent of subjects chose C. Preferences for negative prospects (i.e. losses) were a reflection of preferences for positive prospects: Kahneman and Tversky's subjects avoided risk in the domain of gains, but they were risk seeking in the domain of losses. Kahneman and Tversky call this phenomenon the reflection effect, and it reveals people taking greater risks to avoid losses, a phenomenon also linked to loss aversion – as discussed below.

Preferences for losses and gains were a completely symmetrical mirror image, which is a clear violation of the EUT expectation assumption, and so eliminates risk aversion as the explanation for the certainty effect identified above. If people are ambiguity averse, then a certain outcome has zero variance – so no ambiguity at all; and if someone is extremely risk averse, perhaps they will avoid outcomes associated with any sort of positive variance at all, no matter how small. But the reflection effect demonstrates unequivocally that risk aversion is not the explanation because people are not risk averse when confronting losses.

Isolation effect

The isolation effect is about the fact that people disregard common components in alternatives, whether those common components are in the payoff or the probabilities. Kahneman and Tversky compare some choices in which preferences are altered by different representations of probabilities, even though objectively the choices are identical. For example, they analyse choices to a two-stage game, as follows.

Gamble 11: choose A or B.
Given a 75 per cent chance of getting nothing and a 25 per cent chance of moving to a second
    stage of choices, choose between A or B:

    A   an 80 per cent chance of $4000
    B   a certain payoff of $3000

Gamble 11 is a two-stage version of the following one-stage gamble:

Gamble 12: choose C or D

    C $4000 with probability 20 per cent
    D $3000 with probability 25 per cent

For gamble 11, the chance of getting to stage 2 is only 25 per cent, and so all second-stage payoffs must be quartered. If A delivers 4000 in the second stage, then the probability of 4000 is 0.25×80 per cent = 20 per cent; and if B delivers 3000 in the second stage, then the probability of 3000 is $0.25 \times 1 = 25$ per cent.

Gamble 11 and gamble 12 are essentially the same choice, yet Kahneman and Tversky's subjects approached these gambles in different ways. For gamble 11, 22 per cent of subjects chose A and 78 per cent B, but for gamble 12, 65 per cent chose C and 35 per cent chose D. Their preferences were inconsistent and depended on the way in which the gambles were framed. According to EUT, people should focus on the probabilities of the final states, but people are treating the sequential game as if it is a standard game. In the second stage game they are ignoring the first stage.

Similarly, when the same payoffs are represented in different ways, people will make inconsistent choices, as illustrated by the next set of prospects.

Gamble 13: choose A or B
Imagine that you start with a positive endowment of 1000 and have the following choice:

A   a 50 per cent chance of 1000
B   a certain payoff of 500

Kahneman and Tversky compare gamble 13 with gamble 14:

Gamble 14: choose C or D
Imagine that you start with a positive endowment of 2000 and then choose between:

C   1000 loss with 50 per cent probability (50 per cent chance of 2000; 50 per cent chance of 1000)
D   500 loss with certainty (1500 with certainty)

For gamble 13, the net payoffs from A are 1000 with 50 per cent probability and 2000 with 50 per cent probability. The net payoff from B is 1500 with certainty. For gamble 14, the net payoffs from C are a 50 per cent chance of 1000 and a 50 per cent chance of 2000, and the net payoff from D is a certain 1500. The payoffs in the two gambles are identical. Gamble 13 and gamble 14 are identical, yet choices were variable. For gamble 13, 16 per cent chose A and 84 per cent chose B. For gamble 14, 69 per cent chose C and 31 per cent chose D. Preferences were not invariant. These experimental results were also consistent with the reflection effect because the preferences for losses were the mirror image of preferences for gains, and with the insight from prospect theory, as explained below, that people respond to changes in payoffs, not levels of payoffs.

Kahneman and Tversky's prospect theory

Kahneman and Tversky's (1979) experimental results do not fit easily with the predictions of EUT, and Kahneman and Tversky construct prospect theory to reconcile some common behavioural anomalies. They argue that choices are made as the outcome of two separate, sequential processes: an editing phase and an evaluation phase.

Editing phase

The editing phase is about simplifying the representation of prospects. There are a number of ways in which this is done, including coding, combination and cancellation.

Coding

When prospects are coded as either gains or losses relative to a reference point, this reference point is not necessarily set at zero. In fact, the reference point is more often set by the status quo, for example a person's current asset position.

Combination

Probabilities associated with identical outcomes are combined. If a set of prospects includes a 25 per cent chance of 200, another 25 per cent chance of 200 and a 50 per cent chance of zero, the 200 payoff will be combined into a 50 per cent chance of 200.

Cancellation

Cancellation occurs when people disregard common elements in a set of choices for, example, ignoring first stages in sequential decisions, or ignoring a common bonus, as outlined in the isolation effect examples above. Other editing operations include simplifications such as rounding-up probabilities and payoffs to approximate amounts and discarding outcomes that are very unlikely. Editing will also involve the deletion of dominated prospects.

Editing does create the possibility of inconsistency and intransitivity, because differences in prospects that are eliminated in the editing process may change the preference ordering of prospects, especially as the outcome of simplification will depend on the editing sequence and context. Kahneman and Tversky give the example of a choice between one prospect involving a 500 payoff with 20 per cent probability versus a 101 payoff with 49 per cent probability, and another prospect involving a choice between 500 with probability 15 per cent and 99 with probability 51 per cent. The second choices in both prospects might be simplified to a 50 per cent chance of a 100 payoff, then the first prospect will appear to dominate the second, whereas it would not have dominated if the choices had not been simplified in the editing phase.

Evaluation

After editing the prospects, the next stage is to evaluate the prospects so that the decision-maker can choose the prospect with highest expected value. In this Kahneman and Tversky develop insights from previous analyses, for example Markowitz (1952), who identified nonlinearities in utility functions rather than strict concavity, and proposed a model in which values are assigned to changes not final states. The process of evaluation will depend on the nature of the prospects available, and specifically whether the prospect is strictly positive (all choices are gains and probabilities sum to 1); strictly negative (all choices are losses and probabilities sum to 1); or regular (a combination of gains and losses and/or probabilities that sum to less than 1). Kahneman and Tversky state explicitly that this will lead to a model in which choices violate normative principles of choice, and choices made may be inconsistent, intransitive and/or dominated by better alternatives. This is the point of Kahneman and Tversky's theory: they are aiming to explain the anomalies in real-world choices that cannot be explained by EUT.

The value function

In prospect theory, there are two elements to the value of the edited prospect: the decision weight of each probability and the subjective value of the outcomes. According to prospect theory, subjective value is determined by changes in utility, specifically the subjective value of deviations from the reference point.

With loss aversion, people will overweight losses, and the value function for losses is steeper than the value function for gains. The mathematics of prospect theory are summarized

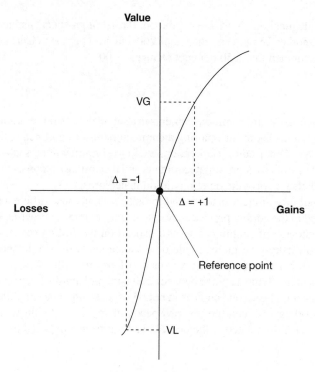

Figure 7.2 Prospect theory value function

in Box 7.3 and the essential features of the prospect theory value function are:

(i)　value is determined by deviations from a reference point;
(ii)　generally the value function is concave for gains and convex for losses;
(iii)　the value function is steeper for losses than for gains.

It follows from (ii) and (iii) that the value function will be steepest at the reference point and Kahneman and Tversky's hypothetical value function has an S-shape, as depicted in Figure 7.2.

Reference points

Reference points play a central role in prospect theory as the anchor of the value function. In prospect theory, the reference point is the status quo, for example the current asset position, but shifts of reference points may lead to mismatches between the reference point and current assets, altering preference orderings. If someone receives an unexpected tax bill, then it may take them a while to adjust reference points and may lead to people accepting gambles that might otherwise be unacceptable, and their preferences will seem inconsistent.

　　Reference points link into the anchoring and adjustment heuristic explored in chapter 6, and prospect theory can help to explain these effects. Abeler *et al.* (2011) discuss experimental evidence from subjects working on a tedious task: counting the number of zeros in tables of randomly ordered zeros and ones. The incentives were a 50 per cent probability of a fixed payment and a 50 per cent probability of a piece-rate payment. The differential reference points were established using two treatments – LO, in which the fixed payment was €3; versus HI, for which the fixed payment was €7. They found that effort provision was reference dependent: the subjects in the HI treatment worked harder and for longer than the subjects in the LO treatment.

Drawing on biological/physiological metaphors and physiological principles, Kahneman and Tversky argue that, physiologically, we are adapting all the time to change. Biologically the reference point is homeostasis, the internal bodily equilibrium. Generally, physiological responses are a concave function reflecting diminishing marginal responses. If we hold our hand in cold water, for example, then the initial impact on our comfort of a single degree change in temperature is likely to be large. As the water gets warmer, however, our comfort will increase at a decreasing rate, at least until the shape of our utility function shifts again, for example when the water temperature starts to approach boiling point. Feelings of pleasure and pain reflect departures from the homeostatic set point.

Perception adjusts to restore homeostasis via a process of alliesthesia – the temporary distortion of preferences that occurs as the body attempts to restore equilibrium: for example, placing a hand in warm water feels good in cold weather but uncomfortable in very hot weather (Camerer *et al.* 2004a, 2005). Overall, biological principles of homeostasis and alliesthesia reflect the fact that perceptions are relative, and Kahneman and Tversky argue that the same principle applies to people's evaluation of monetary changes. Economic choices are driven by changes in the same way that perception and judgment are driven by changes. Kahneman and Tversky are saying that a similar phenomenon affects thinking and decision-making, which means that changes are more important than levels.

Whilst reference points are central to prospect theory, Kahneman and Tversky do allow a role for special circumstances too. If someone needs £60,000 to pay off some gambling debts, then their evaluation of a prospect to get some money will be particularly steep around £60,000, but will flatten off beyond that point. This raises the issue of framing, addressed in developments of prospect theory, for example Thaler's mental accounting model, as explained below.

Loss aversion

Gains and losses are defined with respect to the reference point, and Kahneman and Tversky emphasize that losses affect value more than gains. This means that the value function will be steeper for losses than it is for gains. This can be seen in the illustration of the prospect value function in Figure 7.2. For a positive change $\Delta = +1$, the increase in value is given by VG. With losses of the same magnitude, $\Delta = -1$, the decrease in value is given by VL. In absolute terms, VL > VG; losses 'loom larger' than gains.

Again special circumstances may come into play. Homeowners' aversion to losses may be particularly steep just at the point when a house is at risk of repossession because that loss will be associated with a larger, wider range of other losses. In this way, attitudes to money are not 'pure'; they are complex and determined by a whole range of factors and consequences, meaning that value functions can shift from concave to convex regions and may even be linear in some regions. Building on empirical evidence from five independent studies of thirty decision-makers, Kahneman and Tversky (1979, p. 280) identified concave utility functions for gains and convex utility functions for losses, and utility functions were usually steeper for losses than for gains.

Box 7.3   Mathematics of prospect theory

Kahneman and Tversky (1979) define a prospect as a set of probabilistic outcomes for example, $(x_1,p_1; \ldots ; x_n,p_n)$. To capture some the essential elements of prospect theory Kahneman and Tversky compare very simple prospects for example, (x,p,y,q) in which a person receives x with probability p and y with probability q or nothing with probability $1 - p - q$ where $p + q \leq 1$.

A strictly positive prospect involves positive outcomes, a strictly negative prospect involves only negative outcomes. A regular prospect involves both losses and gains, for example, (x,p,y,q) is a regular prospect if $p + q < 1$, $x \geq 0 \geq y$, or $x \leq 0 \leq y$.

Kahneman and Tversky observe that their prospect theory involves relaxing the expectation principle of EUT. The value of a prospect is captured by the subjective value of the outcome $v(x)$ and its decision weight, $\pi(p)$.

The value function

Kahneman and Tversky's value function captures the values and weights of the prospects as follows:

$$V(x,p,y,q) = \pi(p)v(x) + \pi(q)v(y)$$

This value function is illustrated in Figure 7.2. It has three main features:

  (i)   it captures deviations from a reference point not final states (i.e. gains and losses relative to the reference point);
  (ii)   it is usually concave above the reference point (i.e. for gains) and convex below it (i.e. for losses): $v''(x) < 0$ for $x > 0$; $v''(x) > 0$ for $x < 0$;
  (iii) it is steeper for losses than for gains: $v'(x) < v'(-x)$.

The weighting function

A probability weighting function can be described as:

$$\pi(p) + \pi(1 - p)$$

It will exhibit the following properties, given $0 < r < 1$:
  – subadditivity: $\pi(rp) > r\pi(p)$
  – overweighting: $\pi(p) > p$ for low probabilities
  – subcertainty: $\pi(p) + \pi(1 - p) < 1$
  – subproportionality $[\pi(pq)/\pi(p)] \leq [\pi(pqr)/\pi(pr)]$

The weighting function

Kahneman and Tversky assign weights to the probabilities of prospects, as captured by the weighting function and explained mathematically in Box 7.3.

The weighting function is steep at its extremes and is discontinuous when probabilities are close to 0 or 1, because people do not know how to comprehend extreme events. They do not know how to weight extreme probabilities, or even if they should weight them at all. This can be captured by recognition that in prospect theory, the scaling of the value function is complicated by the introduction of the weighting function. Decision weights can capture the complexity of decision-making. They can transform linear value functions into non-linear ones to capture risk aversion and risk seeking. The concept of probability weights has received attention elsewhere, but Kahneman and Tversky emphasize that their weighting function is not about degrees of belief. Instead, decision weights measure the relationship between the likelihood of events and their probability. In EUT, the focus is on simple problems, but in prospect theory other factors beyond simple probability, such as ambiguity, determine desirability.

The weighting function has a number of properties, including overweighting, subcertainty and subproportionality. Overweighting means that weights are an increasing function of probabilities. The subcertainty property captures the fact that probabilistic outcomes are given less weight than certain outcomes, and this feature captures the Allais paradox. Subcertainty will be more pronounced for vague probabilities than for clear probabilities. Subproportionality captures the fact that the ratio of decision weights is closer to unity for small probabilities than for large probabilities.

Once the weighting of probabilities is incorporated into prospect theory, in contrast to the nonlinear utility functions from Markowitz, the expectation principle of EUT no longer holds. There will be violations of dominance reflecting the nonlinearity of the prospect theory weighting function. The editing phase has significant implications here: simplification of prospects during editing leads to very low probabilities being treated as if they are impossible and very high probabilities being treated as if they are certain.

Evidence from game shows

Post *et al.* (2008) note that empirically testing EUT and prospect theory against each other is complicated by the joint hypothesis problem. There are two sets of unknowns: the true probability distribution is unknown to the subject, and the subjects' beliefs are unknown to the researcher. Game shows can resolve this problem in providing natural experiments that enable an experimenter to infer the players' beliefs because the subjects are told the probability distribution, and the game itself requires minimal skill and strategy.

Post *et al.* analyse evidence from *Deal or No Deal* (*DOND*) games played between 2002 and 2007 by 151 contestants from the Netherlands, Germany and the USA. The games were played in slightly different ways in the different countries, but a typical version of the game involves each contestant picking one suitcase from a selection of twenty-six suitcases; each suitcase contains a sum of money varying between €1 and €5 million. Having selected her own suitcase, in round 1 the contestant is invited to select one or more of the other suitcases to be opened. Once these other suitcases have been opened, the game's banker offers to buy the contestant's suitcase. The banker's offer will reflect the average value of the unopened suitcases. If the contestant agrees on a deal to sell her suitcase to the banker, then the game finishes. If not, and the contestant decides 'no deal' in response to the offer for her suitcase, then the contestant can see the contents of more and more suitcases (except her own) and the banker continues to make offers to buy the contestant's suitcase. The game lasts up to eight or nine rounds and, in the final round, the choice is reduced to a simple binary choice in which the contestant faces a 50 per cent chance of winning the larger sum when she decides between 'deal' or 'no deal'.

Post *et al.* find that the contestants' choices reflect moderate levels of risk aversion and also exhibit reference dependence and path dependence, a result consistent with prospect theory. They predict contestants' choices using EUT and prospect theory, and then compare the predictions. EUT predicts 76 per cent of outcomes, but it fails to capture the evidence of path dependency seen in the contestants' choices. A simple version of prospect theory predicted 85 per cent of choices and captured the reference dependence and path dependence observed in the contestants' choices. On the basis of this evidence, at least, prospect theory outperforms EUT.

Cumulative prospect theory

Kahneman and Tversky admit that their theory has limitations. It cannot capture complex choices. Prospect theory does not give insight into more complex tasks when more than two prospects are available, for example bidding processes. And it does not capture more complex factors affecting attitudes towards prospects, including social norms, security, prudence and misinformation.

Kahneman and Tversky's prospect theory has also been criticized because it leads to violations of stochastic dominance. Whilst violations of dominance can be removed in the process of editing, prospect theory then leads to violations of transitivity. Whilst for some the point of prospect theory is to capture the fact that people are not always consistent in their choices, it nonetheless rests uneasily with an attempt to devise a structured account of decision-making. For this reason, Kahneman and Tversky developed cumulative prospect theory, incorporating rank-dependent weightings in which only extreme unlikely events were overweighted, not all unlikely events (Tversky and Kahneman 1992).

Mental accounting and framing

Tversky and Kahneman (1981) analyse the issue of framing in the context of prospect theory and introduce the notion of 'psychological accounts' to capture the processes via which people frame and evaluate different outcomes. Thaler (1990, 1999) builds on this insight and also on other elements of Tversky and Kahneman's prospect theory, including reference points, loss aversion and the nonlinear value function, to propose a model of mental accounting that analyses how people economize on time and thinking by framing and bracketing their decisions and choices. Thaler (1999) connects mental accounting and framing, arguing that people's perceptions of different types of transactions will depend on the context in which they are made.

Mental accounting

Thaler defines mental accounting as 'the set of cognitive operations used by individuals and households to organize, evaluate, and keep track of financial activities'. The mental accounting approach captures the cognitive process via which people think about their transactions and sort them in their mind, depending on the type of expenditure involved. Thaler notes that individuals and households record and analyse their spending as businesses do, in order to track their money and keep spending under control. In the mental accounting model, they do this not only using conventional methods such as computer and written records, but also using psychophysical methods via which they sort expenditures into different mental accounts.

Mental accounts provide a hedonic frame for 'coding, categorizing and evaluating events', and this framing of choices means that decision-making is piecemeal and topical, affected by context. Mental sorting means that not all spending is perceived in the same way: 'mental accounting matters' because the allocation of expenditures to different mental accounts has a significant impact on decisions and utility. Household spending violates the standard assumption of fungibility: expenditure in one mental account is not a perfect substitute for expenditure in another; and money cannot be costlessly reallocated between the mental accounts. The process of mental accounting is not neutral and will affect the utility gained from choices.

Thaler postulates three aspects to mental accounting, all designed to promote hedonic efficiency and maximize utility. The first aspect captures the process of evaluating decisions and outcomes using both *ex ante* and *ex post* cost–benefit analyses. Expenditures are grouped into categories, sometimes constrained by explicit or implicit budgets. The second aspect involves the assignment of expenditures to different accounts and involves labelling and sorting spending into categories; sometimes the different types of spending are constrained by implicit or explicit budgets. Stocks of cash, wealth and housing equity are separated from flows of regular income and windfall gains. The third aspect relates to the frequency with which accounts are balanced and the bracketing of choices.

In terms of evaluating decisions and outcomes, people distinguish acquisition utility from transaction utility. Acquisition utility is similar to the concept of consumer surplus, and captures the difference between the value of a good and its price. It is separated from transaction utility, which will be affected by perceptions of the value of a deal. In a sale, for example, people will buy things not so much on the basis of their acquisition utility, but because of transaction utility; they derive utility from snaffling a bargain.

Thaler gives an example of a woman buying a quilt: she finds that quilts are on sale and all quilts (double, queen and king size) are on sale for the same price. The woman buys the biggest quilt even though it is too large for her bed. Some expenditures will be assigned to the mental equivalent of petty cash: framing a person's choice, for example a charity donation, in terms of pennies per day rather than annual fees will mean that a cost will be less salient and therefore perceived as more manageable. Mental accounts are managed to maximize the utility of consumption and minimize the pain of expenditure. For example, a colleague of Thaler's set up a charity account – he assigned a target donation to this regular account but then, when he experienced unforeseen losses, he drew from his charity account. In this way, unexpected costly expenditures can seem less painful than if they come out of regular expenditure accounts.

In sorting expenditures into mental accounts, choices may be bracketed broadly or narrowly. Choice bracketing draws on insights from Read *et al.* (1999), who analyse the way in which people combine choices – either broadly by assessing the consequences of groups of choices, or narrowly by assessing each choice on its own. In gambles, the attractiveness of two bets may be increased if they are bracketed together. Thaler gives the example of Paul Samuelson offering a colleague a bet by suggesting that they toss a coin: if the colleague won the toss they would get $200; if they lost the toss they would pay $100. The colleague offered to take the bet, but only if it was offered 100 times. This counter-offer does not make sense in terms of EUT, but it can be explained in terms of mental accounting, bracketing and prospect theory. If the bets are combined, the expected value of losses will be reduced and, given loss aversion, this will reduce the disutility of losses. Similarly, narrow framing, focusing on each potential loss in isolation, will lead to myopic loss aversion and inhibit risk-taking.

Choices will be updated and evaluated over different periods (daily, monthly, annually). The frequency of evaluation can explain the equity premium puzzle of persistent differences between the rate of return on equities versus bonds. Thaler argues that this reflects the fact that investors evaluate their stock purchases and update their reference points too frequently, preventing them from adopting suitably long-term financial strategies.

The mental accounting model is closely related to prospect theory, and Thaler formulates some 'hedonic editing' hypotheses to capture how gains and losses are sorted. Given the concavity of the value function in the region of gains, he hypothesizes that it will be hedonically efficient to segregate gains to increase the sum of marginal value from separate gains. Similarly, it would make people happier to integrate losses because, given the concavity of the value function in the regions of losses, the sum of negative marginal values from losses will be less than if the losses are separated. Evidence shows that these hypotheses are supported for gains, for example, people prefer to win two lotteries paying $50 and $25 over winning one lottery paying $75. Separation of gains does seem to produce more happiness. However, people are also happier to separate losses, and Thaler postulates that this is because loss aversion is even more pronounced than prospect theory allows: prior losses make people more sensitive to future losses and intensify the feeling of disutility.

Mental accounts are opened and closed to minimize the pain of loss, and this explains the fact that investors are more likely to sell rising stocks than losing stocks. Sunk costs influence future decisions. Spending on an expensive pair of shoes will affect how many times the shoes are worn, how long they are stored unused, and how long it takes before someone throws them away. Payments may be decoupled to reduce the perceived cost of a transaction, and this explains credit card usage: paying for something using a credit card disconnects the buyer from the cost of the transaction by temporally separating purchase and payment, and a credit card bill represents an amalgamation of many payments for different things, again reducing the salience of the cost of each particular purchase.

The violations of fungibility seen in mental accounting can reflect complex motivations. For example, people may underspend on particular categories for complex reasons, such as to enable self-control. Consumers may pay premiums for smaller quantities of luxuries such as wine. People will accumulate money in funds that they mentally consider to be 'off limits', thereby accumulating illiquid wealth whilst simultaneously running up credit card debts in order to prevent consumption splurges, as explored in chapter 9. Sources of income will affect how it is spent. Windfall income from a lottery win is often spent in a more frivolous way, on holidays for example, than income earned from work.

Understanding some apparent inconsistencies in choices can be enabled by recognizing that different expenditures are being assigned to different mental accounts depending on perceptions of the context in which the transaction was made. Thaler (2000b) gives an example of Mr and Mrs L and Mr and Mrs H, who went on a fishing trip, caught some fish and air-freighted them home. The fish were lost by the airline, which gave them $300 compensation, but they spent this on a dinner in a fancy restaurant at a cost that would be beyond their normal budget. In this case, the $300 was put into the 'windfall account' and so could be spent in a way in which the couples would not spend from normal expenditure accounts. Mental accounting approaches can also explain some apparent anomalies in intertemporal decision-making; mental accounting in this context is explored in chapter 9.

Framing and bracketing

In mental accounting models, decisions are evaluated relative to a person's value function and its reference point – capturing the person's perceptions of pleasure. This process of mental accounting is affected by context, but at the core is Kahneman and Tversky's value function from prospect theory. As explained above, this value function is assessed in terms of gains and losses relative to a reference point and assuming that people exhibit loss aversion, as discussed above. Then events are coded into a frame reflecting whether the transaction refers to the present or the future, whether it is a windfall gain, etc.

The mental accounting approach emphasizes the context in which transactions are made, and this raises the issue of framing and bracketing. Thaler introduces the concept of hedonic framing, in which people code joint outcomes to make themselves as happy as possible. They segregate gains and losses, as explained above – they separate acquisition utility from transaction utility. They may be reluctant to open and close these mental accounts depending on the context, for example, traders are reluctant to close accounts that are in the red because of loss aversion. Opening and closing accounts also affects advance purchases: sunk costs and payment depreciation are treated separately. For example, people do not treat sunk costs in the way predicted by standard economics. Arkes and Blumer (1985) ran an experiment in which people could buy theatre season tickets: one group paid full price, another group got a 13 per cent discount, and another got a 47 per cent discount. Those who paid full price attended more plays in the first half of the season, but all groups attended approximately the same number of plays in the second half of the season. Thaler interprets this as people taking time to adjust to sunk costs.

Framing effects are a key source of cognitive bias, and capture how people's responses will be determined by the way/context in which questions or problems are framed. For example, people may exhibit disproportionate aversion to losses relative to their appreciation of gains, and so if warnings about the consequences of careless behaviour are framed in terms of the losses of irresponsible behaviour rather than the gains from being responsible, then they may be more effective. Also, there will be individual differences in personality traits and other characteristics, leading some people to be over-confident about their knowledge and overoptimistic about future events.

Kahneman and Tversky (1991) analyse endowment effects in the context of reference dependence: they argue that utility judgments are made with respect to changes from a reference point and to perceptions of advantages and disadvantages. Kahneman and Tversky (1984) fit framing effects within a critique of standard assumptions, but they find that choices from sets of gambles will depend on whether the gamble is framed as a gain or a loss (for example, disease outbreaks). This violation of EUT rationality assumptions is seen in sophisticated as well as naïve subjects.

Regret theory

Loomes and Sugden (1982) formulate regret theory as a 'simpler', 'more intuitive' alternative to Kahneman and Tversky's prospect theory. They analyse the behaviour of an individual facing a finite number of alternative states of the world. Each of these states has a probability which can be interpreted as either an objective probability or, if knowledge is absent, a subjective probability. The individual must choose between actions where each action is some multiple of consequences broadly defined. Loomes and Sugden develop their model in terms of consequences captured by changes in wealth, but emphasize that this is not essential for their theory. An innovation relative to prospect theory is that there is a clear link between actions, consequences and states of the world, whereas the concept of prospects does not associate consequences with states of the world. In regret theory there is one consequence for each state of the world, whereas in prospect theory a number of different actions may correspond with each prospect.

Loomes and Sugden's mathematical model is summarized in Box 7.4. They construct a choiceless utility function which captures the utility, the 'psychological experience of pleasure', derived from a consequence in the absence of choice, for example, the utility a person gets from housing allocated by government may differ from the utility from housing that has been chosen. Intuitively, the concept of choiceless utility introduces the possibility of regret: a person has a choice between two actions, A and B, with consequences x and y dependent on the state of the world (which is not known beforehand). If the person chooses action A, they will experiences consequence x, but they will nonetheless be aware that if they had chosen B, they would have got y. Their pleasure will depend not only on the consequences they chose via their action, but also on the consequences from options not chosen. Loomes and Sugden illustrate with an example: an increase in tax rates leading to an increased tax bill of £100 is a choiceless consequence, but losing £100 in a horse race is the outcome of a choice. Loomes and Sugden postulate that the decrease in pleasure will be greater in the latter case because it generates regret.

Assume that a person chooses option A with an *ex post* payoff x and rejects option B with a payoff y. If x is less than y, they will experience regret from choosing A and that will reduce their pleasure. On the other hand, if x is greater than y, they will experience 'rejoicing': their pleasure will increase. Using these insights about rejoicing and regret, Loomes and Sugden construct a modified utility function which incorporates pairs of consequences for each state of the world. In regret theory, the utility function captures not only 'what is' but also 'what might have been'.

These insights are combined into a restricted version of their model – the regret–rejoice function – which captures the rewards from a chosen strategy and also the differential between chosen and unchosen utility, as explained in Box 7.4.

Box 7.4   Mathematical summary of Loomes and Sugden's regret model

Loomes and Sugden start by assuming that there are many states of the world j and each state of the world j has a probability $0 < p_j \le 1$ with $p_1 + p_2 + \dots p_n = 1$. People choose an action i, and its consequences x (defined for the purpose of illustration as changes in wealth) are determined by j. Choiceless consequences are used as a benchmark, and the pleasure from choiceless consequences is given by $C(x)$.

Given uncertainty, for actions $i = 1,2$ if the person chooses action 1 (i.e. $i = 1$) then, in addition to the direct pleasure derived from x_{1j} there are additional emotional sources of pleasure i.e.:

– Regret when $x_{2j} > x_{1j}$
– Rejoicing when $x_{2j} < x_{1j}$

A modified utility function is constructed by defining $C(x_{ij}) = c_{ij}$ to give:

$$m_{ij}^k = M(c_{ij}, c_{kj})$$

Simplifying the modified utility function gives a regret–rejoice function:

$$m_{ij}^k = c_{ij} + R(c_{ij} - c_{kj})$$

$R(.)$ captures the differential rewards from choosing action i. $R(.) = 0$ is the limiting case consistent with EUT, but Loomes and Sugden assume that $R(.)$ is strictly increasing and three times differentiable.

Loomes and Sugden assume that people maximize expected modified utility, but do not claim that maximization is only objective consistent with rationality. Employing Friedman's (1953) defence of positivism, they use this assumption because it gives predictions consistent with empirical evidence. Loomes and Sugden explain that experimental evidence from Kahneman and Tversky's (1979) analysis of prospect theory, including the Allais paradox, isolation effects, reflection effects and preferences for contingent insurance, are all consistent with regret theory. Regret theory is also one of the early attempts to incorporate emotional factors into economic models. The role of emotions in economic decision-making is explored in more detail in chapter 8.

Neuroeconomic analyses

Neuroeconomic analyses of prospect theory have analysed the evolutionary roots of decision-making by exploring the behaviour of our close relatives. Chen *et al.* (2006) examine the behaviour of capuchin monkeys, exploring whether or not they behave according to the law of demand and also assessing the degree of reference dependence and loss aversion in their choices. The capuchins were given a fiat currency in the form of coin-like discs, which they were conditioned to associate with food rewards; they could exchange these coins for rewards. They found that the capuchins did adjust their purchases to wealth and price shocks, and in this way the capuchins' behaviour fitted with standard economic models.

However, when the information was framed in terms of gains and losses, the capuchin monkeys' choices exhibited signs of reference dependence and loss aversion, as predicted by prospect theory. They chose gambles in which payoffs were framed as gains but rejected gambles in which payoffs were framed as losses – even though the actual payoffs were identical in both scenarios. A similar study identified a reflection effect. When presented with a potential gain in terms of food rewards, the monkeys preferred to avoid risk, but when facing a potential loss, they were more prepared to gamble and take risks (Santos and Chen 2009). The fact that monkeys and humans behave in similar ways suggests that some common evolutionary mechanisms underlie behaviour in both species.

Fox and Poldrack (2009) explore a range of methods for eliciting the parameters of the value function from prospect theory and review some of the key neuroeconomic findings from the application of prospect theory. de Martino *et al.* (2006), in an fMRI study of reference dependence in gambling tasks, analysed the responses of people offered a choice between a sure loss versus a gamble and a sure gain versus a gamble. The reflection effect was observed confirming the predictions of prospect theory. In addition, the fMRI imaging results showed differential amygdala activations for sure gains and risky losses, suggesting that amygdala is associated with the coding of value (see chapter 3).

Windmann *et al.* (2006) studied the Iowa gambling task (IGT) in standard and inverted form. For the standard IGT, subjects are presented with decks of cards: each time they pick a card they usually win a small reward, but for some cards they incur a punishment. The decks are constructed so that there are some bad decks (incurring a net loss in the long run) and some good decks (awarding a net gain in the long run). Normal subjects usually learn to identify the good decks reasonably quickly.

Windmann *et al.* studied subjects playing the standard IGT, in which good decks involved taking small constant rewards to avoid large punishments, and also an inverted IGT, in which the good decks involved taking large constant punishments for large rewards.

They used fMRI to capture activations and identified asymmetries in orbitofrontal cortex activations. For the inverted IGT incorporating large constant punishments to obtain large rewards, orbitofrontal cortex activations, associated with emotional processing of reward, were greater for rewards than punishments. In some cases for the standard IGT the activations were reversed, with differential orbitofrontal activations for rewards versus punishments. This suggests similar value responses for rewards in the inverted IGT and punishments in the standard IGT, and this result is consistent with the S-shaped form of Kahneman and Tversky's prospect theory value function, as illustrated in Figure 7.2.

Case study: buying insurance

In theory, insurance can be offered in two forms: probabilistic insurance (PI) and contingent insurance (CI). An example of PI would be an insurance policy for which you pay a lower premium, but the probability that the insurance company will cover your losses is reduced. For example, you pay half the regular premium and in return there is a 50 per cent chance that the insurance will cover your loss, regardless of how that loss occurred. Your policy might cover you for any sort of loss, but only on odd days of the month, not on even days of the month. Kahneman and Tversky argue that people generally don't want PI but prefer CI: they want to be covered for losses contingent on a specific set of events. You insure your car in case of fire and theft, so if your car is stolen you are covered, but this does not eliminate the risk: there is still a chance that you will lose your car. For example, you might have an up-to-date fire and theft insurance policy, but if your car rolls down the hill and crashes because you forgot to put the handbrake on, then that contingency is not covered. You bear the losses yourself.

In EUT, people insure themselves against a wide range of risks involving both small and large losses. This reflects general risk aversion and a concave utility function, but this cannot explain why people would prefer to insure themselves against a small set of specific contingencies. As explained in Box 7.2, Kahneman and Tversky (1979) argue that EUT together with the assumption of risk aversion leads to the prediction that people should prefer PI to CI. In terms of risk, CI is no more of a guarantee against loss than PI, yet experimental evidence shows that real people seem to prefer CI.

Kahneman and Tversky asked ninety-five students at Stanford University about their preferences for CI versus PI. They gave the students some information about a standard contingent policy which covered the policy-holder against losses from fire and theft. The students were also given information about the premiums and risks for particular events. The students were asked to start by imagining that they were at their indifference point, that is, indifferent between taking out CI or no insurance at all.

Then they were asked to consider an alternative PI deal. They would pay a 50 per cent premium upfront, and if they suffered a loss then two possibilities followed:

A   a 50 per cent chance that the insurance company would request the remaining 50 per cent of the premium and cover the loss, regardless of how that loss occurred
B   a 50 per cent chance that the insurance company would refund the premium and not cover any of the loss.

The experimental results revealed that 80 per cent of students rejected the PI offer, preferring to stick with a CI policy. Kahneman and Tversky argue that these choices cannot be explained using EUT. Kahneman and Tversky argue that the preference for CI over PI reflects a nonlinearity in preferences for risk and insurance captured within the prospect theory probability weighting function. Overweighting of probabilities of loss leads people to prefer CI over PI.

The preference for CI over PI also illustrates a number of the biases and heuristics explored in chapter 6. People may buy CI because they are suffering an illusion of control and believe that they have more control over some contingencies than others. It might also reflect a *status quo* bias because CI is the standard policy and people are more familiar with it. It may also link to availability and affect heuristics. People can imagine losing their car or house through theft or fire because the news is full of stories about fire and theft. Similarly, they can imagine being involved in accidents when they have been exposed to emotionally salient images of planes crashing and boats sinking.

Overall, people can draw on examples of the contingencies offered in standard CI policies, but are not affected by the thought that there might be causes of loss that they can't imagine.

On the other hand, they may suffer from choice overload. For example, there is a wide range of uncertainties surrounding health insurance, including the chances of contracting a wide range of different illnesses, and uncertainties about the monetary and nonmonetary costs involved, means that it is difficult for people to form a clear judgment about whether they need health insurance and, if so, what sort of insurance is needed (Liebman and Zeckhauser 2008). This sort of choice overload can lead people to decide they want a simple, transparent policy that is easy to understand.

Conclusions and policy implications

Expected utility theory is difficult to reconcile with some of the heuristics and biases outlined in chapter 6, and Kahneman and Tversky's prospect theory offers an alternative that captures many of the essential features of heuristics and biases. Some of the key insights include that losses are avoided more than gains are pursued, and that people adjust to reference points, focusing on changes rather than utility levels. Prospect theory is not without its limitations, however, and alternative theories, including Loomes and Sugden's regret theory, capture some of the features of nonstandard decision-making that Kahneman and Tversky's prospect theory does not capture.

In prospect theory and regret theory, models are constructed to capture behavioural paradoxes and limits to EUT. These models suggest that human thought is not well adapted to processing probabilistic and statistical information. As discussed in chapter 6, research has shown that most ordinary people make common mistakes when they judge probabilities. Some biases may reflect a lack of data, an issue addressed in economic analyses that focus on incomplete and/or asymmetric information, uncertainty and risk, but mistakes may also reflect cognitive limits on processing if human brains are not well adapted to the format of data inputs and/or algorithms needed effectively to process data.

In terms of policy, it is important to recognize that changes are important, and that people decide according to their reference points. If policies can be designed to reset these reference points, this may lead to more effective decision-making, via defaults to exploit *status quo* bias, for example. In addition, framing effects will have significant impacts, and reference points can be reset by changing the framing of a choice; for example, expressing desirable choices in terms of potential gains instead of potential losses may lead to more effective decision-making by encouraging positive behaviours. Similarly, expressing undesirable choices in terms of potential losses instead of potential gains may deter those behaviours. This connects with some of the nudge policies introduced in chapter 6 and advocated by Thaler and Sunstein (2008), although it is important to emphasize that nudges can lead to only limited behaviour changes, and deeper policy approaches will also be required.

There could also be a greater focus in policy-making on communicating information in a way that suits our cognitive capacities. Anderson (1998) analyses the impact and nature of memes. Memes are the cultural equivalent of genes, and a unit of imitation (Dawkins 1976; Blackmore 1999). Successful memes survive (are remembered) and reproduce (are transmitted) effectively in three cases: when they map effectively onto human cognitive structures; incorporate a standardized decision structure; and have been reinforced by dominant members of the scientific community. By drawing parallels between memes and genes, evolutionary approaches can be applied to the analysis of how memes spread knowledge and information. Lynch (1996, 2003) applies these insights in his analysis of the evolutionary replication of ideas, and argues that 'thought contagion' affects a wide range of human behaviours and beliefs.

These insights can be incorporated into policies that enable more effective decision-making. As noted above, if students are asked to judge the probability of two coincident events within the context of a statistics class, then they know how to apply their knowledge of statistical principles. Outside their classes, however, when presented with essentially the same problem, they may be unable to answer correctly because they misapply heuristics, using instincts and intuition in a misleading way. To overcome these problems, Anderson suggests that Bayesian approaches can be refined using the advantages of a frequentist approach, for example by using more mental/visual imagery to guide decision-making. If frequency ratios could be communicated to people in a more clear and accessible way, then human cognition might be able to process subjective probabilities more effectively. For example, probabilistic information about the risks of different alternatives (taking a train versus driving, for example) could be represented in graphical or pictorial form. In presenting information, attention could be paid to devices for cognitive interpretation. When prompted by clear signals and steers, the human brain may be able to deal with probabilities more effectively.

8   Personality, moods and emotions

Introduction

In this chapter we bring subjective psychological factors into behavioural economics by exploring the role played by personality, moods, emotions and visceral factors (VFs) in economic and financial decision-making. Rational choice theories in standard economic models assume homogeneous, self-interested individuals using logical methods to make their choices. A representative agent captures the average behaviour of everyone and there is no obvious role for psychological factors. Many models in behavioural economics reflect this approach to some extent, and the analyses in previous chapters, whilst admitting that subjectivity and behavioural bias have important impacts on beliefs and expectations, have generally focused on observable influences and choices, usually in an experimental context. Therefore individual differences and largely unobservable phenomena such as moods and emotions have been assumed away.

This chapter deepens the analysis by exploring the impacts on economic behaviour of heterogeneity and individual differences, including demographic characteristics, personality traits and cognitive/noncognitive skills. Personality will have an impact on emotions because it determines an individual's predispositions; for example, a person with an optimistic personality will be more inclined to feel cheerful. Emotions, moods and decision-making are intertwined in the economic and financial world but, until recently, emotions have been neglected in economic analysis. As well as moods and emotions, decision-making will also be affected by VFs which include basic drives and urges. This chapter also outlines a range of ways in which moods, emotions and VFs can be incorporated into economic analysis.

Personality and individual differences

Personality can be defined as 'patterns of thought, feelings and behaviour' (Borghans *et al.* 2008). Personality can affect economic decision-making in a number of ways. Some personality traits affect cognitive functioning via their impact on cognitive skills. Personality traits may also be associated with standard economic preference parameters including time preference, social preferences, risk aversion and preferences for leisure. For example, personality will be a determinant of a person's rate of time preference, and so will have an impact on life-cycle choices such as savings: a conscientious person is inclined to be more patient, for example, and so is more likely to save for the future and/or invest in their own human capital. Personality traits also determine emotional predispositions and so are a crucial link between emotion and behaviour: if an impulsive person is more likely to feel anger quickly, then they are also more likely to act aggressively. The links between personality, cognitive/noncognitive skills and preference parameters is explored below, and the relationship between personality, predispositions and emotions in the following section on emotions.

Introducing personality traits into economic analysis is complicated by the difficulties in defining personality traits clearly in economic terms. If personality traits are constraints, then standard economic preference parameters can be conceived as the product of those constraints. They can also be described as goods and/or inputs, and Borghans *et al.* analyse the public good and private good aspects of traits. Some traits may be excludable and rivalrous, and if more of a trait is devoted to one task then this means that there may be less available for another. A person may devote their conscientiousness to their work and so will be less able to be conscientious about their social life, for example.

Introducing personality into economic analysis requires instruments for personality measurement. As explained in chapter 2, there is a range of tests available, but measuring personality is not as straightforward as measuring standard economic variables. Most economic studies of personality use the Big Five OCEAN model, focusing on the broad, higher level traits of openness to experience, conscientiousness, extraversion, agreeableness, and neuroticism (versus emotional stability) (McCrae and Costa 1989; Costa and McCrae 1992, 2005), but there are a range of other personality testing instruments available, including the Eysenck tests (Eysenck and Eysenck 1975, 1978) as explained in chapter 2.

There is substantial empirical evidence that individual differences and personality traits predict socio-economic outcomes, including academic achievement and job performance. Borghans *et al.* (2008) present a comprehensive analysis of the economics and psychology of personality traits and individual differences using the big five model to capture personality traits. The Big Five trait of conscientiousness, perhaps because it links to self-control and perseverance, is a good predictor of academic achievement and also many other aspects of socio-economic performance, including years of education, job performance, leadership and longevity (Borghans *et al.* 2008).

The concept of comparative advantage can be applied to personality traits in the workplace. Individuals differ in their capacities, and this may reflect the role of specific traits. Some traits, including trustworthiness, perseverance and extraversion, are generally valuable in the workplace (Osborne *et al.* 2001). Technological changes have increased the importance of social skills, and these will be affected by personality traits and individual differences (Borghans *et al.* 2006). The value of specific characteristics will vary across tasks and occupations, and some personality traits will be more important to particular jobs, for example, extraversion is a desirable trait for a salesperson (Borghans *et al.* 2008).

These differences will affect job matching too. Dohmen and Falk (2011) use the Big Five model to assess the impact of individual differences on worker self-selection. Using lab experiments, they assess the impacts of different incentive schemes, including piece rate, revenue sharing and tournament schemes. They find that the different incentives attract different personality types, with gender, social preferences and risk preferences also playing a role.

Statistical problems such as endogeneity, reverse causality and measurement error will affect econometric estimations incorporating personality. Measured traits will be imperfect proxies for actual traits. It will be difficult to untangle cause and effect. Measurement errors will emerge because of the subjectivity involved when personality assessment is based on the observations and judgments of others, with the additional problem of self-report bias reflecting deception, over-confidence and/or lack of self-insight in tests involving self-assessment (Borghans *et al.* 2008).

Personality and cognition

The interplay between personality and cognition has an impact on a range of socio-economic phenomena, including wages, education, crime and longevity. Borghans *et al.* (2008) define cognition as the use of thought to overcome obstacles. It is determined by a person's ability to understand, adapt and learn. There are different aspects to cognition and different ways of measuring it, but it is important to allow for the impact of personality traits on cognition, particularly 'quasi-cognitive' traits including emotional intelligence.

Common tests of cognitive ability, including IQ tests, do not capture maximum potential intellectual performance. Cognition is enabled by reflection and impulsivity will lower performance in tests of cognitive reflection (Frederick 2005). Performance incentives are important too, and Borghans *et al.* (2008) cite studies showing that performance on IQ tests increases when people are offered incentives including money or candy. These findings can be attributed to the impact of personality traits on a person's response to incentives: cognitive test performance reflects the interplay of intellectual ability and personality traits. This is because IQ tests require effort, and so poor performance may reflect a lack of motivation as much as a lack of ability. Anxiety may also affect performance, and so a person with a high neuroticism score may do less well because of that aspect of their personality and not because of lower intelligence. In terms of the impact of incentives on cognitive test performance, these will increase motivation for some personalities, but those with high emotional stability and conscientiousness are less likely to be affected by external incentives. This suggests that there is a role for personality in the analyses of extrinsic and intrinsic motivation (discussed in chapter 5).

Personality and preference parameters

There are a number of potential links between personality traits and preference parameters. Personality traits such as empathy will affect social preferences such as altruism, for example. Experimental evidence using Eysenck's personality tests shows that psychological traits associated with sociability including conformity and extraversion, along with personality traits associated with time preference including impulsivity and venturesomeness, will interact to affect subjects' susceptibility to social influence in financial decision-making (Baddeley *et al.* 2007, 2010, 2012. Dohmen *et al.* (2008) analyse the links between trust, reciprocity and the Big Five. Personality will also affect risk attitudes, time preference and preferences for leisure.

Dohmen and Falk (2011) analyse the relationships between risk aversion, ambiguity aversion, cognitive skills and personality traits, and find that higher IQ is associated with more risk tolerance (see also Dohmen *et al.* 2007). Gender may also play a role, and some studies show that women are more risk averse and less ambiguity averse (Barsky *et al.* 1997). Measured risk tolerance is positively related to risky behaviours including smoking, drinking, failing to have insurance, and holding stocks rather than Treasury bills. These relationships are both statistically and quantitatively significant, although measured risk tolerance does not capture a large proportion of the variance in behaviour.

Personality also affects time preference, although there can be problems with separating time preference and risk attitudes (Borghans *et al.* 2008). Green and Myerson (2004) assert that risk attitudes and time preferences belong to different psychological processes and will react differently to the same effect. Increases in size of reward decrease discount rates but increase risk aversion, for example. Risk preferences are multidimensional, and people will have different risk preferences across different domains. A person may be risk loving with financial decisions but risk averse with health decisions, or *vice versa*. Perceptions of the risk–return trade off are domain-specific (Borghans *et al.* 2008).

There is also a link between personality and rates of time preference as captured by the discount rate. One of the problems with establishing a link between individual differences and the rate of time preference is that self-report measures ignore problems of over-confidence and lack of insight. Someone may think that they are more patient than they actually are, and so hypothetical choices are not a reliable test of time preference. There is also evidence that time preference parameters are not constant as postulated in standard economic approaches, and people often use higher discount rates for real rewards rather than hypothetical rewards (Kirby 1997). Frederick *et al.* (2002) explore a wide range of empirical studies of time preference and find a wide range of estimated discount rates, and also identify within subject inconsistencies.

There are a number of studies linking individual differences and discount rates, as explored in more detail in chapter 9. Harrison *et al.* (2002) used a stratified sample of 268 19–75-year-olds from the European Community Household Panel Survey (ECHP). They asked participants to make decisions across 6-, 12-, 24- and 36-month time horizons, with real monetary rewards allocated as a redeemable certificate. They identified an overall discount rate of 28.1 per cent. There were no gender-significant differences, but they did identify a role for individual differences: discount rates declined with age, educational attainment and skill level, for example. Similarly, Warner and Pleeter (2001) analysed evidence from US military personnel payments. Military personnel were asked to decide between a voluntary separation incentive giving a regular payment over time, and a lump-sum selective separation benefit: 30 per cent of officers and 90 per cent of enlisted personnel took the lump sum, implying relatively high discount rates with a mean discount rate of 26 per cent. They also found that discount rates varied inversely with the size of lump sum payments. They also found that white, female, college-educated personnel were less likely to take the selective separation benefit. There were links with cognitive ability, and military personnel in the top two 'mental groups' had lower discount rates, which might reflect the fact that people in these groups have a better understanding and/or more experience of quantitative decision-making. This evidence suggests that time preference is not a stable parameter, as assumed in standard economic analysis. Borghans *et al.* (2008) postulate that time preference has a 'tri-dimensional' association with personality traits and is affected by impulsivity, compulsivity (sticking with plans) and inhibition (ability to override automatic responses and emotions).

Individual differences and human capital investment

Individual differences in personality traits and cognitive skills have implications for human capital investment. Identifying when and if traits can change is an important question. The returns from investment in education, for example, will depend on the relative impact on a child's development of nature and genes versus nurture and the environment. If environmental factors play a significant role, then parental investment in a child's learning environment can enable the evolution of productive traits. Early childhood interventions may also play a role because developing complex skills requires effort, practice and exposure to productive learning opportunities.

One relevant issue is the extent to which personality traits and cognitive skills can change over a lifetime. Are personality and cognition plastic and flexible? Or are they rigid and set in stone? If personality is rigid, then the returns on investment in enhancing cognition and social skills are likely to be relatively low. The malleability of personality can be captured empirically by exploring mean level changes and rank order stability. Mean level changes are generally thought to reflect the impact of environmental factors, and genetic factors are thought to be responsible for the stability of traits, although there are some key exceptions.

Borghans *et al.* (2008) explore the evidence on mean level changes and rank order stability, and identify a number of significant mean level changes in traits over a lifetime. Different traits evolve at different speeds over the life cycle, with cognitive processing speed developing rapidly to peak in late adolescence. Conscientiousness, social dominance (part of extraversion), and emotional stability increase steadily over a person's lifetime. Social vitality (another aspect of extraversion) and openness rise, then fall. Personality change in adulthood also reflects social roles. Female workforce participation increases confidence, and identity (explored in chapter 5) may also play a role in this.

Rank order stability in traits increases steadily over a lifetime and, although stability is often attributed to heritability, environment also plays a role. A range of individual differences can be ascribed to genetic factors. Cesarini *et al.* (2009a) use evidence from twin studies to show that genetic differences capture about 20 per cent of the variation in preferences for giving and also risk-taking. Cesarini *et al.* (2009b) use another set of twin studies to show that over-confidence in cognitive ability, measured as the difference between perceived and actual rank scores in a general intelligence test, is affected by both genetic and environmental differences, with genetic factors explaining 16–34 per cent of the variation in over-confidence. Cesarini *et al.* (2010) also identify a genetic component to risk-taking: they analyse evidence about the pension fund choices of Swedish twins and find that genetic variations empirically capture around 25 per cent of the variation in portfolio risk. IQ also reflects an interaction of genetic and environmental factors. It is a relatively stable trait with strong genetic links, but gains in IQ between generations suggest that environmental factors also play a role (Dickens and Flynn 2001).

Personality and cognition are particularly malleable in very early childhood. An early critical period for intellectual development may reflect neurobiological factors and the development of neural connections (Borghans *et al.* 2008). Children adopted by parents with high socio-economic status have larger gains in IQ points, also suggesting that environmental factors are important (Borghans *et al.* 2008). Early interventions, such as enriched childcare centres and home visits, can alleviate disadvantage and, whilst designed to improve cognitive skills, succeed mostly in boosting personality skills.

Heckman *et al.* (2010a, 2010b) analyse evidence from a controlled childhood intervention via the HighScope Perry Preschool Study. For the children in the treatment group, the scheme was designed to educate children from disadvantaged African American backgrounds by exposing them to a curriculum tailored to facilitate the development of cognitive and socio-emotional skills via active, open-ended learning and problem-solving. The participants were selected on the basis of IQ scores and family socio-economic status. This reflected not significant gains in IQ, but improvement in other areas. Treatment and controls were followed to age forty and assessed a range of factors, including academic achievement and social skills. Heckman *et al.* conclude that personality and motivation are as crucial to early success as cognitive ability and IQ.

Cunha and Heckman (2007) and Cunha *et al.* (2010) have used insights about the role of personality and cognitive skills in attainment to develop production models that incorporate the technology of skill formation. Using these models, they determine the optimal level of targeting for interventions. Returns to investment in cognitive/noncognitive skills formation decline as children develop, and marginal returns are higher for disadvantaged groups. This suggests that investment in skills formation should be targeted towards very young children from underprivileged socio-economic groups.

Overall, these findings suggest that investment in early childhood interventions can generate benefits not only for the individuals involved, but also for society as a whole. Heckman *et al.* estimate that the overall social rate of return for the treatment group – in terms of reduced criminality and benefit dependency together with increased educational attainment, earning power and employability – was around 7–10 per cent.

Moods

Mood and emotion are considered separately because there are crucial differences between them. In some ways mood can be included within a standard approach because it may affect all people equally, for example, if mood is affected by weather. Individual differences do not necessarily complicate the analysis of moods. Behavioural economists and economic psychologists distinguish mood from emotions. Elster (1996) describes emotions as having 'an intentional object or target' whereas moods are more diffuse in character: they are 'undifferentiated and untargeted states of contentment or discontentment'. Moods are more general phenomena, often experienced collectively, in which case they will be less affected by differences in personality and predisposition.

Moods and weather patterns

The impact of moods on markets has been explored by analysing moods in financial markets. Kamstra *et al.* (2003) analyse links between depressive moods, risk aversion and financial market activity, focusing on the analysis of data on seasonal affective disorder (SAD) – a depressive state linked to the reduced hours of sunlight experienced during winter seasons. Kamstra *et al.* hypothesize that SAD is associated with increased risk aversion. They adopt the insight from prospect theory (explained in chapter 7) that people respond more to changes than to levels, and hypothesize that changes in risk aversion prompted by the changing seasons will translate into changes in stock market returns. Returns will be lower in the autumn as hours of sunlight decline and higher in the winter when days are starting to get longer again. Kamstra *et al.* estimate stock market returns for markets at different latitudes using lagged returns, an autumn dummy variable, a SAD measure capturing hours of darkness, plus range of weather variables (for example, cloud cover, precipitation, temperature) as explanatory variables. They find that their SAD variable has a strongly significant impact on stock market returns and attribute this pattern to the impact of seasonal depression on risk aversion.

Hirshleifer and Shumway (2003) make a more general prediction that hours of sunlight are associated with a positive mood. They analyse weather data, specifically hours of sunshine and their impact on stock market returns between 1982 and 1989 for twenty-six international stock exchanges. Similarly to Kamstra *et al.*, they find that daily stock returns correlate positively with hours of sunshine, but other aspects of the weather, for example snow and rain, do not correlate with stock market returns. They suggest that weather derivatives could be devised to exploit this weather-related pattern of returns.

Social mood in socionomic analyses

A relatively novel area of behavioural economics, focusing almost entirely on the role of mood in decision-making, is socionomics. In socionomic analysis, mood is the ultimate causal factor and is experienced collectively in the form of 'social mood'. Socionomic analysis is developed by Prechter (2003) from Elliott's wave principle, which focused on deterministic cyclical fluctuations. Insights have been applied specifically to financial market fluctuations by Prechter and Parker (2007). Casti (2010) surveys the socionomic literature and outlines some of the key facets of socionomic analysis. The central hypothesis focuses on interactions between individuals via social networks and herding – generating a collective 'social mood' which has impacts on events depending on the 'mood polarity'. A negative, pessimistic mood polarity will lead to financial instability, conservatism in fashion and consumer purchases, and insularity in government policy leading governments to favour policies such as protectionism. With a positive social mood polarity, people will be optimistic and hopeful: fashions will reflect the positive mood (hemlines will go up) and politicians will do well. Attributing causality to these events is complex, but Casti rules out feedback effects between events and social mood: mass psychology determines events, but no event can feed back into social mood because mood is the ultimate independent variable. As support, Casti notes that the events of 9/11 had a minimal impact on financial markets because overall the social mood was positive.

Emotions and affect

Elster (1996, 1998) explains that, whilst there is no one distinguishing feature of emotions, most emotions do have the following features: they are formed on the basis of cognitive antecedents and beliefs, involve intentional objects, and are associated with physiological arousal and expression. They have valence – that is, they may be positive or negative. Psychologists make a distinction between emotions and affect. Emotions are biological, innate and instinctive responses to stimuli and involve the recall and cognitive processing of affect. Affect is the experience of *feeling* an emotion. Elster (1996, 1998) also distinguishes emotions and visceral factors (VFs), the former being triggered by beliefs and the latter reflecting basic drives and instincts. However, VFs are biological, innate and instinctive. Incorporating an evolutionary perspective, VFs reflect basic, primitive responses. Emotions, especially social emotions, are more highly evolved.

Psychologists tend to focus on 'action tendencies'. In focusing on these tendencies to act, they identify the cause of emotions rather than their impact on behaviour (Elster 1998). Generally, positive emotions are passively undergone and not chosen, though negative emotions can be blocked or the situations that cause them can be avoided. This reflects a distinction between 'occurrent emotions' (emotions that occur in a particular situation) and 'emotional dispositions'; for example, the occurrent emotion of anger is more likely if a person has an irascible predisposition. The occurrent emotion can be avoided, assuming a person has some insight into their own irascibility, if a person can avoid situations that might trigger an angry response. Some of these features are difficult to establish empirically, but physiological responses can be measured during economic experiments; for example, Smith and Dickhaut (2005) use heart rate data to infer emotional states in auction experiments.

Elster (1996) argues that emotions do not necessarily interfere with rationality. Emotions may be important 'tie-breakers' when outcomes are indeterminate and reason is an insufficient guide to decision-making. Emotion 'serves as a functional equivalent for the rational faculties it suspends' (Elster 1998, p. 60). Visceral factors and emotions are often very efficient because they can operate quickly and with minimal cognitive intervention, but people may nonetheless underestimate their influence, leading to self-destructive behaviours such as addiction (Le Doux 1996; Loewenstein 1996, 2000), an issue that is addressed in Loewenstein's analysis of VFs and also in some analyses of addiction (see chapter 10).

These emotional factors affect economic and financial decisions in a range of ways. Risk can be characterized as a feeling (Loewenstein *et al.* 2001, 2007; Slovic 2010). Feedback effects can intensify fear responses to evaluations of risk, precipitating panics. Emotional factors such as nervousness or euphoria can induce shifts in aggregate demand in a way that cannot be explained just using economic analysis (Katona 1951). Other emotions will affect economic decisions more broadly; for example, the irrational exuberance seen in bullish markets reflects interactions between fear, hope and greed.

Ifcher and Zarghamee (2011) analyse self-reported levels of happiness from the US General Social Survey and find that positive affect increases patience and makes people less likely to 'live for today'. They confirm the association with a random assignment experiment: a 'positive affect' treatment group was shown a mood-enhancing film clip, for example from a stand-up comic routine, and moods were measured to confirm the effect. A 'neutral affect' control group was shown clips of landscapes and wildlife. Both groups were asked to state their present value equivalents of a payment in the future, and the subjects in the positive affect group were significantly more patient.

Emotions and heuristics

Emotions and affect influence decision-making directly via the affect heuristic (explored below and in chapter 6). Emotions and affect may also have an indirect impact via availability heuristics: emotions are more available than objective facts and figures because they are often highly salient, vivid and easily recalled. Emotional factors can dominate cognition especially as they are associated with quicker, more automatic responses.

Emotional responses have an impact on other heuristics too. When people are in a happy mood, they are more likely to use heuristics associated with top-down processing, relying on pre-existing knowledge with little attention to precise details. By contrast, people in a sad mood are more likely to use bottom-up processing heuristics, paying more attention to precise details than to existing knowledge (Schwarz 2000, p. 434). Minsky (1997, p. 519) analyses some of the emotional constraints in the case of expert knowledge, arguing that the 'negative knowledge' associated with some emotional states may inhibit whole strategies of expert thought.

Emotions can also be linked to heuristics, bias and prospect theory in describing the impact of fear and greed in financial decision-making. Shefrin (2002) argues that frame dependence means that decisions will be affected by the context in which they are taken, and this will reflect interplay of cognitive and emotional factors. Emotion and cognition also interact in responses to ambiguity aversion, described by Shefrin as fear of the unknown. Emotion will affect the use of the 'availability heuristic'. This heuristic involves using information that is most readily accessible (i.e. most easily remembered): emotions affect memories and so on will determine what is remembered and what is forgotten.

The somatic marker hypothesis

As explained in chapter 6, the affect heuristic involves using emotions to guide decision-making. This can lead to bias because emotions may distort objective judgments. For example, hopefulness can lead people to underestimate risks and overestimate benefits, and despondency can lead them to overestimate risk and underestimate benefits (Finucane *et al.*

2000). Emotions are also very vivid and salient and so can have a disproportionate impact; for example, if people have witnessed horrific car crashes then that will affect their perceptions of the risk of driving a car.

Damasio (1994/2006) extends the role of emotions well beyond the affect heuristic. He postulates that emotions and affect are integral to all decisions, not just to decisions in emotionally charged contexts. In the interplay of cognition and emotion, affect gives important physiological cues enabling efficient thinking. These cues are based on somatic markers – the bodily signals we perceive as affect/emotion provide important guides to action, complementing rational action. Somatic markers may be the outcome of conscious thought – for example, the gut feel of entrepreneurs represents conscious feelings about choices and plans. Knowledge communicated via emotions, either explicitly or implicitly, enables people to make fast and efficient decisions (Bechara and Damasio 2005; Damasio 1994/2006).

In developing the somatic marker hypothesis, Damasio and his colleagues focus their research on patients with brain damage, and find that damage to specific neural areas usually associated with emotional processing can adversely affect decision-making. The best-known lesion patient is probably Phineas Gage, whose case is described in chapter 3. Phineas Gage was wounded by an iron rod which damaged his frontal lobe and impaired his decision-making abilities. Damasio (1994/2006) describes a range of other lesion patient cases, including his own patient, Elliot, who had suffered damage to the frontal lobes after an operation to remove a brain tumour. As a consequence Elliot suffered a reduction of affect and emotion and, whilst tests showed that he retained a wide range of cognitive functions, these did not enable him to make wiser or more judicious decisions. Instead he became obsessed with the details of specific tasks, hampering his ability to manage his job. Damasio observes that the reductions in his ability to process emotions made Elliott unable to differentiate between options: 'his decision-making landscape [was] hopelessly flat . . . cold-bloodedness made his mental landscape too shifty and unsustained for the time required to make response selections'.

Adolphs *et al.* (1995) find similar absence of affect in patients suffering amygdala damage. They analysed the behaviour of a group of eighteen lesion patients and seven normal patients. Of the subjects with brain lesions, six had suffered amygdala damage; the remaining twelve, with brain damage to other areas, were used as experimental controls alongside the seven normal subjects. Adolphs *et al.* asked their experimental subjects to judge facial expressions from a series of black-and-white slides; for example, they were shown a face and asked 'How happy does this person look?' They found small differences between the controls and the subjects with unilateral amygdala damage, but one particular patient (subject SM-046) had suffered severe bilateral lesion damage as the result of the genetic Urbach–Wiethe disease, leading to bilateral calcification and atrophy of her amygdala. SM-046's ratings for 'afraid' faces were significantly lower than the ratings from the other subjects. When asked about her responses to the fearful faces, she said that she was aware that an emotion was being expressed, but was unsure what that emotion was.

The subjects were also asked to draw representations of various emotional states, including fear. The patients with unilateral amygdala damage, whilst experiencing difficulty relative to the control subjects, were able to represent fear, anger and disgust. For patient SM-046, most of her drawings were skilful and effective representations of the various emotions, but she represented fear as a crawling baby. In explaining her responses she explained that 'she did not know what an afraid face would look like'. Adolphs *et al.* conclude that the amygdala plays a key role in processing emotions, particularly fear, and this may impair social decision-making. Subject SM-046 also experienced some difficulties with social decision-making, confirming findings from other studies showing that the amygdala is activated during social interactions. The amygdala may play a role in interpreting social cues and/or processing fear of social sanctions.

Basic instincts and visceral factors

The somatic marker hypothesis's emphasis on emotions as bodily cues links into analyses of VFs, reflecting basic instincts, although VFs play a less constructive role than emotions. Visceral factors can propel individuals towards acting in ways that are contrary to their own self-interest, but Elster (1996) emphasizes that VFs are a-rational because they are not the outcome of choice and they can operate efficiently at low levels of cognitive intervention.

Loewenstein (2000) develops a model of VFs: his main premises are that VFs crowd out all other goals, and people underweight or ignore their own past/future VFs as well as other people's VFs. Visceral factors have direct hedonic impacts even when actual consumption is unchanging, so they resemble consumption not tastes, and also often generate an aversive experience (for example, fear, pain). Changes in VFs correlate predictably with external circumstances and do not reflect a permanent change in people's dispositions. Visceral factors change more rapidly than tastes because tastes are much more stable in the short run. Tastes and VFs draw on different neurophysiological mechanisms: VFs are associated with stable steady states and homoeostasis, whereas tastes draw on memory and experience.

Loewenstein develops his model to put forward seven main propositions, as follows.

1. Discrepancies between actual versus desired rewards from consuming a particular good increase with the intensity of the VFs immediately relevant to the consumption of this good.
2. Future VFs produce little discrepancy between the value we plan to place on a good and its desirable value.
3. Increasing VFs (e.g. by creating vividness) increases the rewards from immediate consumption relative to delayed consumption.
4. Current VFs will have a mild effect on future decisions.
5. People underestimate impact of VFs on their future behaviour.
6. People forget the influence of past VFs and so may be perplexed by past behaviours driven by VFs.
7. Drawing a parallel between interpersonal and intrapersonal interactions, VFs affect interpersonal comparisons (self versus others) and intrapersonal comparisons (current self versus delayed self) in the same ways. We are more short-sighted and selfish when VFs take hold, for example: we are less altruistic when VFs are intense; when deciding for others, we ignore/underweight their VFs; parallel increases in VFs in oneself and another lead to decreased altruism; we imagine that others experience VFs when we experience them; and people underestimate the impact of others' VFs on others' behaviour.

Visceral factors and emotions will also affect the trade-offs people make in pursuing different goals. Visceral factors will compromise the stability of preferences, particularly in the short term, because internal bodily states can change so rapidly. Whilst VFs are essential to human survival and basic daily functioning, they may conflict with higher-level cognitive processes. The extent of the conflict between cognition and VFs will depend on the intensity of the VFs. Visceral factors are overwhelming in 'hot' states, but in 'cold' states cognitive factors will exert more influence. Misjudgments can occur when individuals underestimate the impact of VFs in a cold state.

Visceral factors are often neglected in standard economic models because these tend to focus on rational motivators of behaviour. More recently, there has been an increasing recognition of VFs, for example in models of addiction and in analyses of emotional factors, such as fear in situations of risk and uncertainty (see e.g. Laibson 2001; Loewenstein 2000, 2007; Bernheim and Rangel 2004).

Social emotions

Social emotions are associated with more highly evolved decision-making systems than VFs and basic instincts, especially with social decision-making. Simon (1967) emphasizes the role of emotion in social interactions. Humans are socialized to acquire sophisticated sets of cues enabling appropriate responses to interactions with others. Given the complexity of these human interactions, there will be a large number and range of social stimuli, and these will increase the emotionality of social situations. Emotions will also interact with social motivations and preferences, including inequity aversion: social emotions may reinforce external sanctions by inducing negative emotional states when behaviour is antisocial (Elster 1998). In this way, social norms will regulate and sustain certain emotions in encouraging conformity to particular social and economic norms.

Social emotions may also be associated with collective behaviour, for example herding in financial markets. Acting with a group may moderate fear, but has the unintended consequence of generating speculative bubbles. Responses in uncertain social situations will differ from responses in isolated situations and/or when outcomes are more certain. Uncertainty in financial markets, for example, will generate unconscious, nonrational herding as an instinctive response to endogenously generated volatility. When individual panics precipitate 'social panics', this may reflect interplay between risk, anxiety and fear (Loewenstein *et al.* 2007). Markets will fluctuate erratically, reflecting social mood and contributing to financial instability (Prechter and Parker 2007).

Emotions are affected by social context, although there is some evidence that emotional responses are suppressed in extreme circumstances. Erber *et al.* (2004) postulate that social constraints affect mood regulation and processing. Social norms may constrain the expression of usual human emotions in extreme institutional settings. In the degrading conditions of Abu Ghraib or the Stanford Prison experiment, as described in chapter 2, the dehumanization of prisoners was exacerbated by the prisoners' suppression of their own socio-emotional responses, pity for example, thus compromising the essence of their own 'humanness' (Haney *et al.* 1973; Zimbardo 2007). Personality can play a role too. For the Stanford Prison experiment, individual predispositions were shown to affect preferences for anti-social opportunities. The students participating in the experiment were initially asked to volunteer for a prison treatment versus a control treatment, and those who had self-selected into the prison treatment scored less highly in measures of sociability such as altruism and empathy. They scored more highly in measures of antisocial tendencies such as Machiavellianism, aggression, authoritarianism, narcissism and social dominance (Carnahan and McFarland 2007).

Empathy, theory of mind and mentalizing

Theory of mind involves inferences about the beliefs, feelings and action of others (Frith and Frith 2003; Camerer *et al.* 2005). 'Mentalizing' involves guessing what others will do. Social emotions such as empathy play a role in theory of mind. Theory of mind may be associated with a special 'mentalizing' area controlling reasoning about others' beliefs and actions, associated with increased activation in Brodmann area 10 when playing games involving trust, cooperation and punishment (McCabe *et al.* 2001). Autistic patients are thought to have deficits in Brodmann area 10, and about a quarter of autistic adults offer nothing in ultimatum games, perhaps because of empathetic deficiencies (Sally and Hill 2006). There is also evidence that cognitive control has evolved within a social context. Research shows that human children and chimpanzees use similar cognitive skills when dealing with physical tasks, but human children have more sophisticated cognitive skills when dealing with social tasks, including social learning and theory of mind (Herrmann *et al.* 2007).

A lot of economic action, especially in a strategic context, involves mentalizing. Similarly, empathetic behaviour may lead to herding and imitation when people make decisions on the basis of mentalizing responses, and there is some experimental evidence to support this. Singer and Fehr (2005) argue that mentalizing and empathizing explain people's responses to situations involving incomplete information. Singer *et al.* (2004) reveal that empathizing with the pain of others activates areas associated with the affective processing of pain. They also confirmed that individual differences can play a role. They found heterogeneity in empathetic abilities across people.

It is possible that humans have a 'mirror system' that helps us to understand the actions of others, and the analysis of mirror mechanisms parallels elements of the analysis of sympathy and empathy in Adam Smith's (1759) *Theory of Moral Sentiments* (Sugden 2005). There are different conceptions of sympathy: Smithian sympathy draws on insights from *The Theory of Moral Sentiments*, especially ideas about the role played by feeling sympathy in ensuring societal stability. Introspection in games can also be explained in terms of sympathy: sympathy allows the individual introspectively to consider actions of others.

Experiments on monkey imitation show that monkeys' socialized instincts are propelled by the activity of mirror neurons. These ideas have been extended to describe human instincts to follow others as the outcome of mirror neuron activity (Rizzolatti *et al.* 2002; Rizzolatti and Craighero 2004; Iacoboni 2005), although analysis of the role played by the mirror system in a human context is limited by the fact that the single-neuron experiments required to verify mirror neuron theories cannot easily be conducted on human subjects for ethical reasons. Rustichini (2005a) focuses on sympathy, drawing on ideas from neuroscience about mirror neuron systems, as explored above. Sympathy is an affective state but it is also sophisticated, not naïve (see also Glimcher *et al.* 2005).

Cognition and emotion in dual-system models

Dual-system models bring together emotion and cognition, and can also provide a basis for neuroeconomic analysis of interactions between cognition and affect. Dual-system models focus on interactions of affect and reason. For example, Kahneman (2003, 2011) devises maps of bounded rationality and emphasizes the separation of an intuitive system 1 from a reasoning system 2 in maps of bounded rationality, as explained below. Similarly, Romer (2000) distinguishes decisions based on thoughts from decisions based on feeling.

Some analyses of interacting systems have focused on the impact of emotions on performance. For example, Ariely *et al.* (2009b) postulate that generous incentive schemes can have unintended emotional impacts. Too much arousal can impair performance. Generous incentives may shift attention from automatic to controlled systems; for example, people tend to play sports better if they are not thinking too hard about their movements. Increased incentives also narrow people's focus and dampen creativity. Drawing on these insights from psychology, Ariely *et al.* (2009b) postulate that generous payments can lead to 'choking under pressure'. They conducted a set of experiments in the USA and in India. Subjects worked on different tasks and received performance-contingent payments varying in amount from small to very large relative to their typical levels of pay. One set of experiments was conducted in Indian villages: the villagers performed a series of cognitive tasks involving memory, creativity and motor skills. The villagers were sorted into three incentive conditions: one group was offered small incentives of up to 4 Rupees (Rs); another moderate payment group received up to 40 Rs; the high payment group received up to 400 Rs. As 400 Rs is the average monthly wage, the latter group was playing for a significant sum of money.

Within each condition, good performance was rewarded with a relatively high level of reward: very good performance led to high rewards; good performance to substantial rewards; and average performance gained no reward at all. Ariely *et al.* identified a perverse impact from large incentives: higher rewards adversely affected performance. In terms of the shares of average earnings relative to maximum earnings for each treatment group, these were 35.4 per cent in the lowest group; 36.7 per cent in the medium group and 19.5 per cent in the highest payment group. They attributed this to choking under pressure, and identify similar results from US studies. With some important exceptions, very high reward levels had a detrimental effect on performance, perhaps because emotional responses to generous rewards lead to choking under pressure, reflecting conflicts between affect and cognition.

Behavioural models of dual processing move away from the focus on purely rational behaviour, and can help to explain a number of behavioural conundrums in terms of interactions between cognition and emotion and between controlled versus automatic systems (Schneider and Shiffrin 1977). Kahneman (2003) maps the brain into two different systems: system 1 (automatic, quick, intuitive) and system 2 (cognitive, deliberative, controlled). There are different systems for emotion and deliberation, and these are associated with automatic versus controlled processing. Emotions are the low-level physiological processes that rapidly elicit stereotyped, valenced behavioural responses and engage different neural structures from those engaged during cognitive processing (Sanfey *et al.* 2006). The operation of these different systems is not a manifestation of irrationality: emotional and cognitive systems can operate together, and emotional systems may have evolved as effective adaptations to past environments and circumstances.

Neuroeconomic models are being developed that analyse economic decisions as the outcome of dual-systems processing, focusing on the neural correlates of interactions between deliberative/cognitive and automatic/affective systems (Camerer *et al.* 2004a, 2005; Loewenstein and O'Donoghue 2004; Rustichini 2005a; Camerer 2007). Also, Glimcher and Rustichini (2004) focus on the dual roles of emotion and reason as manifested in the consilience of economic and neuroscientific approaches to decision-making. Frith and Singer (2008) develop ideas about the interaction of reason and emotion in a socio-economic context. When social motivations and emotions compete, they affect our sense of fairness, altruistic punishment, trust and framing effects. Sanfey *et al.* (2006) also argue that economic behaviour can be understood in terms of 'dual-process models' which make a distinction between emotion and deliberation.

Dual systems can also be understood in evolutionary terms by analysing which areas of the brain are associated with particular functions. Higher-level, recently evolved cognitive functions are more general and flexible, are used for reasoning and planning, and may be a 'critical substrate for the standard economic conception of a rational *"homo economicus"*' (Cohen 2005). Cohen also postulates that increased capacity for reason and control is associated with the development of particular areas of the brain, in particular the prefrontal cortex, and that this reflects adaptations to profound changes in the social as well as physical characteristics of human environments.

Ironically, this may have generated social and evolutionary instability, because ancient emotional responses are less well adapted to modern conditions than to ancient environments: the development of technologies may have accelerated the mal-adaptation of old emotional processes. For example, limbic structures in the brain are often associated with impulsive emotional responses, and these may have been appropriate in a world in which immediate rewards were important. In primitive environments, basic resources were scarce and perishable, so quick, instinctive action was essential to avoid starvation; but in a modern context these instincts may not serve a useful purpose and may in fact generate perverse behaviour such as addiction. Cohen argues that more recently evolved areas of the brain, including the prefrontal cortex, have developed to interact effectively with older structures in circumstances to which our emotional mechanisms are not well suited. In this way we can override inappropriate emotional responses using control and reasoning. Evolution has 'vulcanized' the brain, increasing its strength and resilience. Reason and control have balanced primitive emotional responses, for example by allowing humans to develop pre-commitment devices such as savings plans and nicotine gum to moderate the influence of impulsive, self-destructive emotional decision-making (Cohen 2005).

Lee *et al.* (2009) test the relationship between emotions and quick decision-making within a dual-system model, using experimental evidence. Experimental subjects were given a set of binary product choices alongside the name, picture and a short description of the products they were offered. Emotions and affect were manipulated in different ways. Firstly, pictures were given in colour versus black-and-white photos, assuming that coloured images are more vivid and therefore more emotionally salient. Secondly, the subjects were asked to remember two versus ten occasions when their feelings and emotions gave them the right instincts, and this was done in order to prime the subjects to have either high or low trust in their feelings. It was assumed that those subjects given the more difficult task (remembering ten occasions) would be more doubtful about the trustworthiness of their feelings. Thirdly, subjects were primed to form beliefs about their cognitive capacity by being asked to remember ten versus three numbers. Using the same insight as for the second treatment, this was done to manipulate the subjects' judgments of their own cognitive ability: it was assumed that if the subjects found it hard to recall positive examples of cognitive success, then they would have less faith in their cognitive capacity.

The results consistently indicated that greater reliance on emotional reactions during decision-making is associated with greater preference consistency and less cognitive noise. Additionally, the results of a meta-analysis based on data from all five experiments show that products eliciting a stronger emotional response are more likely to yield consistent preferences. For all the manipulations, greater reliance on emotions led to increased preference consistency. When subjects had low trust in their cognitive capacity, they relied more on emotions. When they had high trust in their feelings, they relied more on emotions. When they had colour photos, they relied more on emotions. The positive impact of emotions on preference consistency supports dual-system models and also models emphasizing the positive impact of emotions in decision-making.

Neuroeconomic analyses

Analysing emotion is closely connected to neuroscientific analysis, and so some of the theo-retical work of neuroeconomists ties directly into the essential concepts outlined above. This section focuses on some specific empirical findings. Neuroscientific evidence can help us understand the roles played by socio-psychological factors in economic decision-making. Developing ideas from psychology, evolutionary biology and neuroscience, neuroeconomists argue that understanding brain organization and function can help us to understand economic and financial behaviour. As explained above, Damasio (1994/2006) pioneered the neurosci-entific analysis of the role of emotion in economic and financial decision-making, arguing that the impact of emotional factors does not necessarily preclude rational thought. Mood and emotion do not necessarily work against reason; instead, they may work in concert with it. Lesion patient studies established that brain lesions associated with damage to emotional processing led to constraints on rational behaviour.

As also explored in chapter 11, the role of affect in financial decision-making is confirmed in a functional magnetic resonance imaging (fMRI) study showing that risk-seeking and risk-aversion mistakes in financial decision-making are associated with activation of neural circuits associated with affect and emotion (Kuhnen and Knutson 2005). The role of emotions in economic decision-making has been confirmed by other neuroscientific evidence which shows that emotional circuits in the brain operate in response to ambiguity and during learning/information processing (Glimcher and Rustichini 2004; Houser *et al.* 2005; Shiv *et al.* 2005; Naqvi *et al.* 2007).

Sanfey et al.'s *fMRI study of social emotions*

One of the pioneering neuroeconomic studies of social decision-making was Sanfey *et al.*'s (2003) study of the neural basis of decision-making in the ultimatum game. Incorporating experimental design elements from Guth *et al.* (1982), and linking this into social utility models outlined in chapter 5 (including models from Fehr and Schmidt 1999 and Bolton and Ockenfels 2000), Sanfey *et al.* study the ultimatum game using fMRI imaging to investigate neural substrates of cognitive and emotional processes involved. As explained in chapter 2, fMRI captures changes in the blood oxygen level-dependent (BOLD) signal as blood passes through an area of the body and the signal variation is detected by the fMRI scanner.

Sanfey *et al.* cite experimental evidence from ultimatum games showing modal offers by 'proposers' of around 50 per cent of total amount, with moderately low offers rejected by respondents in approximately 50 per cent of cases. But why would people knowingly reject monetary reward? It's not a failure to understand or conceptualize, because the ultimatum game is very simple. Sanfey *et al.* hypothesized that objecting to unfair treatment is a funda-mental adaptive mechanism to reinforce social reputation, but this generates conflict between motivations: cognitive processes push towards acceptance; emotional processes push towards rejection. So the interaction of these processes when respondents reject unfair ultimatum game offers will be represented in brain areas associated with cognition, emotion and medi-ation of conflicting goals. Sanfey *et al.* are careful to use the intuitively accessible word 'cognitive' rather than 'rational' because they argue that emotional responses may have a rational basis too, as emphasized in Damasio's somatic marker hypothesis, as explained above. A fear response is often rational in the face of physical threats, for example. They acknowledge that tighter, consistent use of terminology must develop as the field develops.

Experimental design

Sanfey *et al.*'s experiment was designed so that nineteen subjects met ten people before playing in the scanner. They were playing for a split of $10. Subjects were told that they would play a one-shot game, and each subject completed thirty rounds with three 'treatments' (of ten rounds each). In the first round they would play against the humans they had met earlier. In the second round they would play against a computer. The third treatment was the control: the subjects received money just for pressing buttons. This was to capture responses to monetary reinforcement independently of social interaction. For all treatments (including those against humans), offers made were the same, and were determined by an algorithm designed to generate offers mimicking those typically made in an ordinary experimental context. For each round, the offer algorithm generated fair splits of $5:$5 for five offers and uneven splits for the remaining five offers in each round. The uneven splits were further divided into two offers of $9:$1, two offers of $8:$2 and one offer of $7:$3.

   As noted in chapter 1, Sanfey *et al.*'s fMRI study is somewhat controversial because it uses a contrived offer algorithm that involves limited deception. Subjects were told that they were responding to decisions by real people when they were responding to offers artificially generated by the experimenters. In experimental economics, incorporating deception is often regarded as taboo because of fears that it might lead to 'dirty' experiments. Sanfey *et al.* argue in defence of their experimental design that their deception was necessary given the 'heavy logistic demands' of fMRI studies, and demonstrate that their limited deception has not affected the interpretation of results. As noted in chapter 1, limited deception may be unavoidable in neuroimaging studies because of the technical, logistical and financial constraints.

Behavioural results

The behavioural results (ignoring the fMRI findings for the moment) showed that unfair offers from human proposers were rejected more frequently than unfair offers from computers, perhaps reflecting a stronger response during human interaction. Participants' reports from the debriefing stage revealed that standards of fairness were salient: when participants were asked what they thought would have been an unfair offer, 58 per cent said that an offer less than 50 per cent would be unfair; 42 per cent said that an offer less than 30 per cent would be unfair. Subjects reported feeling angry when they were made an unfair offer, and they were prepared to sacrifice financial gain to punish their partner.

   For the fMRI analysis, Sanfey *et al.* specifically studied three main areas of potential activation. For these they found that unfair offers elicited activity in the bilateral anterior insula – a brain area often associated with emotional processing; the dorsolateral prefrontal cortex (DLPFC) – an area often associated with cognitive processing, goal maintenance and executive function; and the anterior cingulate cortex – associated with conflict resolution.

Insula activations

The magnitude of activation in the insula was significantly greater for unfair offers from humans versus computers, perhaps because activations were not solely a function of the amount of money offered, but were also sensitive to the context (perception of unfair treatment). The responses in the bilateral anterior insula were also sensitive to degree of unfairness in the offer. There was greater activation for unfair offers and the magnitude of activation scaled monotonically: activations for $9:1 were stronger than for $8:2, which were stronger than for $5:5. Insula activation also correlated with subsequent decisions to reject: participants with stronger insula activations rejected a significantly higher proportion of unfair offers. The left anterior insula showed the strongest reaction to the most unfair offers. Overall findings from analysing insula response are consistent with a general hypothesis that neural representations of emotional states guide behaviour. Activation of the anterior insula is associated with negative emotional states such as pain, distress, hunger, thirst, anger and disgust, and Sanfey *et al.* suggest that there may be links between the physical and social catalysts to emotional states. Unfair treatment, including insultingly low offers in the ultimatum game, generate 'moral' disgust and anger and engage the same neural structures in the anterior insula as are engaged when someone smells a bad smell.

DLPFC activations

In the DLPFC, there was activation to unfair offers but not to fair offers, and DLPFC activation was relatively constant across the unfair offers. There was no significant simple correlation with acceptance rates so DLPFC activation is not sufficient to explain acceptance of unfair offers, but a differential comparison of brain areas shows that unfair offers subsequently rejected are associated with relatively greater anterior insula activation relative to DLFPC activation. Unfair offers subsequently accepted had relatively greater DLFPC activation versus anterior insula activation.

Sanfey *et al.* emphasize that it is not possible to make meaningful *quantitative* comparisons across different brain regions, but they nonetheless analyse the patterns *qualitatively*. They found no significant simple correlations with acceptance rates for DLPFC activation. DLPFC activation alone cannot explain accepting unfair offers. However, a differential comparison of brain activations for unfair offers subsequently rejected showed relatively high anterior insula activation relative to the DLFPC activations. Unfair offers subsequently accepted had relatively greater DLFPC activations relative to the anterior insula activations. Overall, heightened DLPFC activation in response to unfair offers in the ultimatum game may suggest that unfair offers are more difficult to accept because they impose higher cognitive demands in overcoming the emotional tendency to reject.

Anterior cingulate cortex activations

There were also significant activations in the anterior cingulate cortex, an area associated with conflict resolution (as noted above). Sanfey *et al.* suggest that this may reflect a conflict between the twin goals of resisting unfairness and accumulating money. The anterior cingulate cortex may be implicated in resolving the conflict between twin goals of resisting unfairness – associated with emotional responses and insula activation; and accumulating money – associated with cognitive processing and DLPFC activation.

Overall, Sanfey *et al.*'s findings suggest that emotional influences are an important, vital, dynamic component of decision-making. Sanfey *et al.* conclude that the evidence from neuroeconomic studies provides a quantitative analysis that 'may be useful in constraining the social utility function', but more research is needed on characterizing emotional responses, their neural substrates and the social context.

Neuroeconomic studies of empathy

As explained above, mirror neurons may be implicated in theory of mind and mentalizing. There have been a number of neuroeconomic studies of mirror neurons. Mirror neurons are located in the pre-motor areas of primate brains. They are activated without conscious control and generate imitative behaviour in primates. The discovery of human mirror neurons has lent some scientific support to biological explanations for imitative behaviour (Rizzolatti *et al.* 2002). If so, then the mirror system may be the neural basis for Smithian sympathy: observing others involves internally reproducing the mental processes of the observed person. Single-cell recordings in monkeys have identified mirror neurons in the pre-motor cortex (prefrontal cortex) that fire as monkeys perform grabbing movements and also when they observe similar movements performed by experimenters (Rizzolatti *et al.* 2002). Baddeley *et al.* (2004) suggest that such mirror neuron activity may explain imitation and herding in socio-economic contexts. There is evidence that socialized instincts to imitate in humans are associated with mirror neuron activity (Rizzolatti and Craighero 2004; Iacoboni 2005). The fact that similar responses are seen in our primate ancestors may indicate that herding behaviour is automatic and 'hard-wired', and the outcome of primitive emotions such as impulsiveness.

Functional magnetic resonance imaging and transcranial magnetic stimulation studies have tested hypotheses about theory of mind and empathy: empathy allows us to understand and share emotions; theory of mind allows us to understand others' beliefs and desires. When experimental subjects observe their partner receiving painful electrical shocks, their empathetic responses engage automatic emotional processing circuits such as the insula. Furthermore, empathetic responses seem to be generated by making representations of our own internal feeling states in response to pain observed in others, and heterogeneity in brain activation across subjects is strongly correlated with heterogeneity in the responses to empathy questionnaires (Singer *et al.* 2004; Singer and Fehr 2005).

Avenanti *et al.* (2005), using evidence from transcranial magnetic stimulation experiments, identified motor responses associated with empathetic inferences about others' pain. Other research shows that children with autism or Asperger's syndrome have trouble understanding emotions and social cues, and this has been linked to relatively low activations in the medial prefrontal regions and relatively high activations in the ventral prefrontal cortex for Asperger's patients. Higher activations in the ventral prefrontal cortex may suggest that some compensation is being made in patients who realize that their ability to empathize is constrained (Camerer *et al.* 2004, 2005).

Case study: emotional trading

In standard financial models, market fluctuations are the outcome of decisions by rational agents in free markets using objective information. These theories focus on a view of people as atomistic, independent, forward-looking and self-interested agents; they do not make systematic mistakes and they use all available information efficiently. It is difficult fully to reconcile these models with the existence of speculative bubbles, including Tulipmania, one of the more colourful episodes in financial history. For three to four short months starting in November 1636, demand for tulip bulbs in Holland spiralled out of control and tulip bulb prices exploded; price rises of up to 6000 per cent were recorded for the rarer tulip bulbs. At the height of Tulipmania, a single bulb from the exotic Semper Augustus tulip cost as much as a three-storey house in central Amsterdam (Baddeley and McCombie 2004). Speculative bust followed the speculative frenzy in a way that was just as dramatic. By February 1637, most bulbs became impossible to sell at any price and many tulip speculators lost their fortunes.

There are many other examples of speculative bubbles, for example the South Sea Bubble, the dot.com bubble of the late 1990s, and today's global/regional financial crises. These and the many other speculative episodes from history have undermined standard financial theories grounded on assumptions of rational expectations and efficient financial markets. Whilst there are models of rational speculative bubbles, these cannot fully explain systematic trends in financial markets.

One of the problems with the standard accounts is that they fail to incorporate emotions. Emotions play an important role in financial trading. Keynes (1936) focused on the irrational propellants of financial market movements, analysing the role of factors such as crowd psychology, herding and market conventions. More recently, economists such as Shiller and Shleifer have focused on irrational forces in financial markets, developing the insights about irrational exuberance following Federal Reserve governor Alan Greenspan's comments about the dot.com bubble of the late 1990s. Hirshleifer and Shumway (2003) analysed the relationships between mood, sunlight and financial trading activity, and Kamstra *et al.* (2003) investigated the impact of seasonal depression (SAD) on stock market activity (see above).

Neuroeconomics can add some valuable additional information to the debate because tools are developing that enable us to identify particular neural areas associated with emotion. As explained in more detail in chapter 11, some neuroeconomic studies explore the impact of emotions on financial trading. Lesion patient studies show that damage to emotional processing areas can improve performance in restricted scenarios. Shiv *et al.* (2005) studied the performance of lesion patients with damage to emotional processing areas in the brain in twenty rounds of investment decisions, and compared the performance of the lesion patients with performance by normal subjects. The normal subjects learnt quickly to select more conservative, less risky strategies, but the disconnection of emotional responses enabled the lesion patients to perform better. They earned significantly greater rewards from the investment games because they did not feel risk. Shiv *et al.* interpret this as evidence that when the processing of negative emotions, including fear of loss, is disconnected, people are more likely to adopt risk-seeking strategies which earn them higher returns. Similarly, Lo *et al.* (2005), in a study of eighty-day traders, found that trading performance was significantly hampered for those with more intense emotional reactions. Also, there is evidence that more primitive emotions, in the form of VFs, are implicated in some self-destructive behaviour, as explained below.

Kuhnen and Knutson (2005) and Knutson and Bossaerts (2007) use fMRI techniques to analyse choices by traders between safe and risky stocks. They found that the mistakes the subjects made linked to emotional processing areas. Activations in the striatum, implicated in reward processing, were correlated with risk seeking mistakes. Activations in the anterior insula, implicated in the processing of negative emotions including fear of loss, are associated with risk aversion mistakes. Hormonal factors may also play a role in emotional trading via their impact on risk. Coates and Herbert (2008) and Coates *et al.* (2010) examine the impact of testosterone (implicated in risk-taking and associated with anti-social behaviour), and cortisol (associated with stress responses). Taking saliva samples from London day traders to measure hormonal levels, they correlated the hormonal data with traders' returns and found that morning testosterone levels correlated with performance later in the day, perhaps suggesting a link between testosterone, risk and ruthlessness.

Tuckett (2011) analyses traders' emotions using a psychoanalytical approach. As explained further in chapter 11, Tuckett argues that financial assets are not perceived just as stores of value; they are pursued as 'phantastic objects' – objects with superlative qualities. This creates emotional conflict because the excitement from expectations of potential profits is separated from the panic and fear induced by potential losses. During a speculative bubble, traders forget quickly about the losses from previous busts, and construct stories to rationalize their impulsive behaviours. Bubbles and busts are generated as path-dependent emotional sequences. Euphoric booms are followed by emotional oscillations concluding in spectacular collapses of confidence as bubbles burst.

Ultimately, if these studies show that people do not necessarily use objective information in a systematic way, then rational expectations and efficient markets will no longer be at the core of theoretical analyses of financial markets. On the other hand, if behavioural economists and neuroeconomists can show that economic and financial decision-making is associated with logical, rational cognitive responses, then we could conclude that the emphasis on rationality and market efficiency may be justifiable, at least as an approximation.

Conclusions and policy implications

Personality, mood and emotions affect economic and financial decision-making in a wide range of ways. Personality traits, together with individual differences such as age and gender, will have an impact on economic preference parameters including risk attitudes, time preference, social preferences and preferences for leisure. Personality will also interact with cognitive ability to determine socio-economic outcomes including educational ability, job performance and unemployment history. Emotions and personality will interact when specific personality traits create predispositions making some people susceptible to specific emotions and moods.

The impact of personality can be quantified, though there are important limitations. Personality tests may give imperfect proxies for personality traits, meaning that quantitative analyses will be prone to measurement errors. Unravelling cause and effect between personality traits and socio-economic outcomes can be difficult too, especially as some personality traits may be affected by events and experience, creating problems of reverse causality. Overall, the literature on personality in economic decision-making is underdeveloped, and there are many opportunities to further economic understanding in this area.

Emotions are more difficult to measure than personality, though neuroeconomic studies have illuminated some of the neural correlates and identified ways in which cognition and affect can interact. Emotions can have an overwhelming impact on decision-making, and sometimes that impact is positive. They can play a positive role in guiding decision-making as they may enable people to make decisions quickly and efficiently. They also play an important role in social decision-making, and the various manifestations of sociality explored in chapter 5 can be understood as the product of social emotions. In other circumstances, however, emotions – together with VFs – can have a destructive impact and are often implicated in impulsive, unwanted behaviours such as addiction, as explored in chapter 10.

Introducing personality, mood and emotions into economic analysis leads to some relatively novel economic policy implications. The insight that personality is malleable in early childhood but becomes more rigid in adulthood suggests that more resources could be devoted to early childhood interventions, because those interventions can have an impact not only in developing cognitive ability, but also in enabling children to acquire the skills to enable them to maximize their potential in adulthood. At a microeconomic level, recognizing that traits and predispositions can create comparative advantages suggests that when employers pay attention to personality as well as skills, this will enable them to operate more efficiently because they will be effectively matching their employees/potential employees to specific jobs and tasks.

When moods, emotions and VFs undermine people's best long-term intentions, then policies based on models incorporating an assumption of strict rationality are less likely to be effective. In some cases, policies should focus on limiting the role of emotional factors in specific situations – for example, taxes to limit impulsive, risk-seeking behaviours such as rogue trading on financial markets, consumption of addictive substances and/or gambling. There have also been policy initiatives focused on designing gadgets to help people to recognize when emotions are overwhelming reason; for example, Thaler and Sunstein (2008) describe the Ambient Orb technology, which glows a specific colour depending on energy use: it glows red for high levels of energy use, giving a quick, emotionally salient signal to the householder to reduce their energy use. This sort of technology is now commonly used in domestic 'smart' meters. Similar technology is available to monitor trading decisions: General Electric and ABN-Amro have developed the Rationalizer, which monitors traders' physiological states and produces alerts when a trader is overexcited.

Overall, recognizing that personality, moods, emotions and VFs can have a profound impact on behaviour leads to the implication that firms' and governments' policies should allow for the fact that people are not always making reasonable, logical calculations. Policies designed to slow down decision-making in situations where people are likely to be misled by mercurial moods and emotions are likely to be as effective – sometimes more effective – than standard policy tools.

9   Time and plans

Introduction

Standard economics assumes that people are consistent when they plan their decisions over time. For a rational, consistent person it should make no difference whether they are choosing between something today versus tomorrow, or between something in a year versus a year plus a day. In macroeconomics, Friedman's permanent income hypothesis and Modigliani's life-cycle hypothesis both postulate that people plan consumption over their lifetimes and so their decisions about the future should not change unless information changes. However, ordinary observation tells us that few people are able to plan consistently and/or over long time horizons, and one of the major contributions from behavioural economics comes in theories and principles that capture time inconsistency and preference reversals. People change their minds. They aren't necessarily very good at making decisions today about choices with consequences for the future, and they are prone to temptation and procrastination.

Exponential discount functions

People's intertemporal planning is affected by the rate of time preference, and this is captured in economic models via a discounting assumption. Following from Fisher's impatience principle, Samuelson (1937) assumed exponential discounting with the discount rate (ρ) as a stable preference parameter. Within exponential discounting the discount rate is a positive number measuring impatience. A patient person will have a lower discount rate and so will have larger discount factors; they will value future rewards by a larger amount. With exponential discounting, the discount function declines at a constant rate over time, but a choice between something today and tomorrow will be the same as a choice between something in a year versus a year and a day.

People's choices will be stable over time. Deviations from rationality come when time preferences shift, when people are impatient in the short run but patient in the long run or vice versa. Samuelson explicitly emphasized that his exponential discounting assumption was not realistic, but exponential discounting is now the standard discounting assumption seen in almost all modern economic theory.

Individual differences with exponential discounting

The exponential model can capture differences in preferences. If someone has a high discount rate and so values future outcomes less strongly, then they can still be described as (impatiently) rational if their impatience is stable over time. For example, if someone is choosing between chocolate cake today versus chocolate cake tomorrow, then their choice will be the same as if they are instead choosing between chocolate cake in a year versus a year and a day. Exponential discounting can capture impatience, and if someone cannot wait even an hour for their piece of chocolate cake, that may just reflect a high discount rate. As long as they would make the same choice for chocolate cake in a year's time, then their choices are still rational and consistent.

There may nonetheless be individual differences in discount rates. One study illuminating these differences was conducted by Harrison *et al.* (2002). They tested two standard hypotheses: first, discount rates do not differ across socio-demographic characteristics; second, for a given individual, discount rates do not vary over time. They used surveys conducted in June–July 1997 from a stratified sample of 268 19- to 75-year-olds, all of whom had participated in the European Community Household Panel Survey (ECHP). They also collected demographic, health and financial information. They asked the subjects to make decisions across four possible time horizons (6, 12, 24 and 36 months), with real monetary rewards allocated as a redeemable certificate. They were told that one of them would be randomly chosen to receive large sum of money and, if they won, they would choose either option A (a smaller amount in one month) or option B (a 'menu' of twenty possible higher payments to be made in seven months).

They analysed the responses and found an overall discount rate of 28.1 per cent, which did not vary significantly across the time horizons. There were no gender-significant differences, but discount rates declined with age, and discount rates were lower for those of higher educational levels, skilled people, those who were not students, people who had invested more in education, those owning houses, people before retirement, the employed (versus unemployed) and/or good credit risks. They estimated a distribution of discount rates that was roughly normal.

There is also evidence from natural experiments about individual differences in people's forward planning. As also discussed in chapter 8, Warner and Pleeter (2001) analysed evidence from real-world decisions about pension choice using data on US military personnel payments upon voluntary separation. Military personnel were given two contract choices: a voluntary separation incentive giving a regular annuity over time, versus a selective separation benefit (one lump-sum payment). They found that 30 per cent of officers and 90 per cent of enlisted personnel took the lump sum, implying relatively high discount rates with a mean discount rate of 26 per cent. Analysing the data using probit techniques, they found that discount rates varied inversely with size of lump-sum payment (in contrast to exponential discounting models, in which the discount rate is assumed to be a constant, reflecting stable preferences). They also found significant demographic variation in discount rates, with white, female, college-educated personnel being less likely to take the selective separation benefit.

Cognition also plays a role in determining time preference. Warner and Pleeter identified lower discount rates in the top two 'mental groups', perhaps reflecting the fact that these groups are better able to understand/process information about intertemporal choices and/or perhaps just had access to better financial education. They argue that their evidence has external validity given that the military are representative of the average American. Individual differences will also lead to differences in attitudes towards social security programmes (Heckman 2001).

Behavioural discount functions

Behavioural anomalies

Frederick *et al.* (2002) identify a number of anomalies that cannot be captured within models incorporating exponential discounting of utility: gains are discounted more than losses; small outcomes are discounted more than large ones; choices are affected by delay–speed-up asymmetry: for example, when buying video recorders people's discount rates are higher if they want to speed-up delivery than if they want to delay it. People also have preferences for improving sequences, for example they prefer to see their salary increasing over time; this is inconsistent with a standard exponential discounting assumption, but instead may reflect some of the heuristics and biases outlined in chapter 6.

Angeletos *et al.* (2001) also give some examples of time inconsistency. Workers prefer a twenty-minute break in 101 days rather than a fifteen-minute break in 100 days, but exhibit preference reversals if they are asked to decide in the immediate future: if asked for a decision today, they prefer a 15-minute break today over a 20-minute break tomorrow. Smokers are another example: on Monday they may prefer to quit smoking on Tuesday, but on Tuesday change their mind and prefer to quit smoking on Wednesday. Another example that affects almost everyone is the alarm clock: when planning the night before an early start, people will choose an extra 15 minutes of wakefulness over 15 minutes of sleep, but by 5:30 am the following morning, they will choose an extra 15 minutes of sleep over an extra 15 minutes of wakefulness. Overall, in many of our decisions we exhibit more patience when we are making long-run choices.

Animal models

A large volume of experimental evidence shows that people do not show consistency of choice over time. Early evidence about the consistency of people's decisions over time comes from animal models and experiments. Early in experimental psychology, the Bischof–Köhler hypothesis was put forward – that only humans can dissociate themselves from current motivations to take actions for future needs; however, there is significant evidence against this hypothesis. Mulcahy and Call (2006) find that animals plan over time: for example, bonobos and orang utans select, transport and save tools to use 1 hour later and 14 hours later, and they infer that planning skills may have evolved in earlier species. Raby *et al.* (2007) find that scrub jays make provision for future needs by storing food when that food/food type will not be available in the morning.

Ainslie (1974) analysed impulse control in pigeons. The pigeons were placed in a sound-proof chamber with single key illuminated by red or green lights. If they pecked when the red light was on, they got a smaller, sooner reward. If they pecked when the green light was on, they got a larger reward later. Overall, the pigeons were impulsive, choosing small short-term gains at the expense of large long-term losses, and the tendency to seek shorter access to immediately available food remained strong for up to as many as 20,000 trials. The more interesting finding was that their preferences for reinforcement at different delays changed with elapsing time, leading to preference shifts. Some pigeons learned to peck at a key at an earlier time if, and only if, this made them unable to obtain the smaller reinforcement, so perhaps the pigeons were binding their own future freedom of choice by learning to use a pre-commitment device of pecking the green light.

Behavioural discounting models

Frederick *et al.* (2002) outline a number of ways in which models of choice can be enriched to capture time inconsistency. A major innovation is in adjusting discounting assumptions, for example using hyperbolic or quasi-hyperbolic discounting assumptions in place of the standard exponential discounting assumptions.

Frederick *et al.* (2002) also explain how time inconsistency can be captured by enrichments of standard discounted utility models, for example by allowing habit formation and/or allowing utility to be affected by anticipation as well as current consumption. Similarly, given time inconsistency, temptation utility models can be constructed in which sophisticated decision-makers anticipate lack of self-control and therefore pre-commit to responsible strategies. When temptation is a problem, people have preferences for commitment.

Time inconsistency can also be explained as the outcome of interactions between multiple selves. Strotz (1955) outlines a model in which more proximate satisfactions are overvalued relative to more distant ones. The optimal plan of future behaviour may be inconsistent with optimizing future behaviour, generating an 'intertemporal tussle', and if this tussle is not recognized, spendthrift or miserly behaviour will be observed. On the other hand, these inter-temporal conflicts may be recognized and resolved via strategies of pre-commitment and/or consistent planning. Similarly, Ainslie (1991) describes hyperbolic discounting as an inter-temporal 'internal prisoner's dilemma', and the best choice will depend on how far a person can predict their future perceptions. Conflict between a far-sighted responsible self versus an impetuous, myopic and short-sighted self has Freudian connotations of conflicts between the id and the ego; Ainslie and Haslam (1992) develop this interpretation in the context of Freudian themes of 'ego-splitting'.

Visceral factors, described in chapters 8 and 10, will also have an impact. Bernheim and Rangel focus on the impact on intertemporal choices of hot, emotional versus cool, rational states of mind. Similarly, Rick and Loewenstein (2008) suggest that examples of time incon-sistency may reflect trade-offs between tangible and intangible rewards. Tangible rewards tend to arrive more quickly (e.g. smoking a cigarette), whereas distant outcomes (e.g. getting healthy) are less tangible. When decisions are triggered by immediately salient emotional factors, then immediate tangible rewards will be preferred to later intangible rewards. Other behavioural factors will have an impact too. Cognitive bias can generate time inconsistency if a projection bias leads people to underestimate the impacts of future changes. Choice fram-ing or bracketing, in which only a small subset of choices is considered at any one time and/ or reference point, produces models in which people's decisions are anchored to prior choices.

These insights can be incorporated into discount functions that decline more rapidly in the short run than in the long run. There are two main families of behavioural discount function that capture this phenomenon: hyperbolic and quasi-hyperbolic discount functions, explained in Box 9.1.

Laibson (1997) and O'Donoghue and Rabin (1999) show that the quasi-hyperbolic discount functions generate discount factors which decline over time, as for exponential discount functions, but with the rate of decline distorted by the degree of present bias – β. Quasi-hyperbolic discount functions converge on exponential discount functions as β approaches 1, as explained in Box 9.1.

Harris and Laibson (2001) compare exponential discount functions with quasi-hyperbolic discount functions. With exponential discounting, from the perspective of self at time t the intertemporal marginal rate of substitution (the ratio of discounted marginal utilities between two choices with equal time intervals) should be the same. In present value terms, the marginal rate of substitution of consumption in period $t + 1$ relative to $t + 2$ will be equal to marginal rate of substitution in period $t + k + 1$ and $t + k + 2$. Quasi-hyperbolic discounting splices together the standard exponential discounting model with the present bias parameter. This generates models in which marginal rates of substitution differ over equivalent time intervals, and the marginal rate of substitution in period $t + 1$ relative to $t + 2$ will be greater than the marginal rate of substitution in period $t + k + 1$ relative to $t + k + 2$.

Box 9.1   Some mathematics of discount functions

Exponential discounting

The standard exponential discount factor $D(t)$ is given by:

$$D(t) = \delta^t = [1/(1 + \rho)]^t$$

Hyperbolic discounting

With hyperbolic discounting, the discount function is constructed to be a function only of time, in its simplest form as:

$$D(t) = \gamma/(1 + \alpha t)$$

This version of hyperbolic discounting incorporates γ into the numerator, but some versions assume $\gamma = 1$, which bounds the discount factors between the empirically plausible bounds of 0 and 1 and also enables meaningful comparison with other discount functions.

Quasi-hyperbolic discounting

Discounted utility is derived from the intertemporal Euler relation:

$$U_t = E_t\left[u(c_t) + \beta\sum\delta^\tau u(c_{t+\tau})\right]$$

where τ is the number of periods of delay relative to the current period, t.
    The discrete time discount function evolves over time as:

$$\{1, \beta\delta, \beta\delta^2, \beta\delta^3, \beta\delta^4, \ldots\}$$

where β captures present bias. If $0 < \beta < 1$, this discount structure mimics the qualitative features of the hyperbolic discount function; but if $\beta = 1$ the discount function reverts to the standard discount function as seen in exponential discounting models.

The consequences of these different assumptions for the evolution of discount factors over time, including exponential discount factors, hyperbolic discount factors and quasi-hyperbolic discount factors, are captured diagrammatically in Figure 9.1.
    This embeds specific assumptions about the magnitude of the various parameters. For exponential discounting $\rho = 0.04$, $\delta = 0.96$. For hyperbolic discounting $\gamma = 1$, $\alpha = 0.07$. For quasi-hyperbolic discounting factor $\rho = 0.02$, $\delta = 0.98$, $\beta = 0.70$. It is important to note that the paths of the discount factors are very sensitive to the magnitudes of these parameters, as shown in Figure 9.2.
    Another interpretation of the evidence on time inconsistency is provided in models of subadditive discounting. Read (2001) argues that subadditive discounting can explain

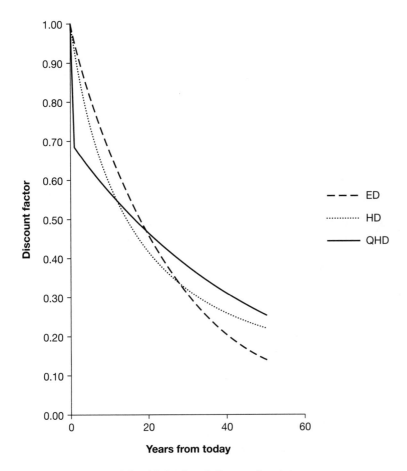

Figure 9.1 Exponential and behavioural discount functions

declining impatience because discounting over a delay depends on the subdivision of intervals. People are less patient over shorter subintervals, and so when the delay is divided into subintervals outcomes will be more heavily discounted than if the interval is left undivided. Using three choice experiments, he found no significant evidence that impatience declines over time, and he explains that the apparent preference reversals attributed to hyperbolic discounting can also be explained as the outcome of subadditive discounting. Apparently anomalous choices do not reflect impulsivity, but instead are about the delays between rewards – the issue is not whether people are choosing between today and a year's time; the same patterns would be observed if people were making choices between having something in a year versus two years. They are less patient over shorter spaces of time regardless of when the choices occur.

Time inconsistency in the real world

Time inconsistency can affect a range of real-world decision-making. DellaVigna and Malmendier (2004) explore how firms respond to consumer bias by analysing a firm's contract design given partially naïve consumers with time-inconsistent preferences.

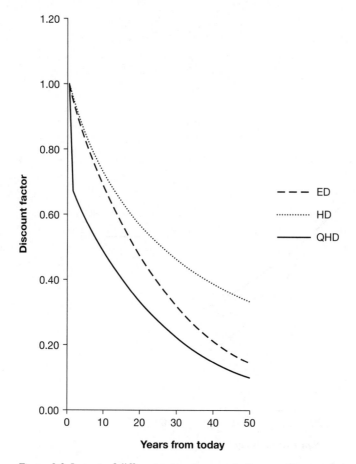

Figure 9.2 Impact of different parameter assumptions on discount factors

DellaVigna and Malmendier compare two types of purchase: investment goods with immediate costs and delayed benefits; and leisure goods with delayed costs but immediate benefits, for example consumption funded using credit cards. This generates a number of inefficiencies, including price distortions: leisure goods are priced above marginal cost and investment goods are priced below marginal cost. Empirical evidence from credit cards, gambling, life insurance, mail order, mobile phone and time-share businesses show that time inconsistency lowers consumer welfare for naïfs but not sophisticates. (DellaVigna and Malmendier's (2006) analysis of health club behaviour is explored in chapter 10.)

In behavioural development economics, Duflo *et al.* (2011) link time inconsistency to procrastination in agrarian working capital investment. Duflo *et al.* (2011) hypothesized that the failure of Kenyan farmers to buy fertilizer reflects not only liquidity constraints but also poor intertemporal planning affected by time inconsistency and procrastination. Duflo *et al.* constructed a randomized controlled trial to test the differential impact of a savings and fertilizer initiative programme (SAFI). Farmers were offered access to SAFI in two ways: in the simple version the farmer was offered fertilizer on the spot at harvest time; in the second version farmers were visited before the harvest season and were offered the option to buy fertilizer at a later point in time. Both versions of SAFI led to a significant increase in fertilizer use. If farmers were rational in a standard sense then, for the second version of SAFI, they would order the fertilizer for a future date and invest their money in the meantime. If they were time inconsistent and naïve, then they would overestimate their ability to save for future fertilizer purchases and would agree to buy it at a later delivery date. A way to overcome this problem is to offer small, time-limited subsidies for fertilizer purchases as a way to overcome the problem of procrastination.

Behavioural life-cycle models

Behavioural life-cycle models incorporate insights about time inconsistency and present bias into otherwise standard approaches to life-cycle planning, constructing models to capture households' financial planning over a lifetime, including decisions about consumption, savings, pensions and investments. Overall, hyperbolics smooth consumption and savings less successfully than is assumed in the standard economic model incorporating exponential discounting. People tend to hold high levels of credit card debt alongside high levels of retirement wealth (especially in the form of housing). This approach cannot account for conflicts between short-run and long-run discount rates, reflecting simultaneous patience and impatience (Angeletos *et al.* 2001). Behavioural models have greater external consistency in explaining the simultaneous existence of high stocks of illiquid wealth and large credit card debts: models incorporating quasi-hyperbolic discount functions can incorporate parameters which predict that people will be more willing to hold savings in the form of illiquid wealth. At the same time, the costs of holding illiquid savings are balanced by the benefits of illiquid savings as a crude commitment technology preventing impulsive consumption splurges. Nonetheless, intertemporal tussles will emerge when hyperbolics are holding little liquid wealth and are more tempted to take on credit card debt to fund instantaneous gratification.

Following Laibson (1997) and Harris and Laibson (2001), Angeletos *et al.* (2001) and Laibson *et al.* (2007) use the quasi-hyperbolic discount function within a structural modelling approach. They adopt a modelling approach in preference to an experimental approach because they are concerned that there are different results between different sets of experiments. Whilst experimental studies have some advantages (they can reveal the extent of individual socio-economic and demographic differences), experimental findings may confound time preferences with other factors. Also, subjects may behave perversely because they doubt the trustworthiness of the experimenter; experimental tasks are often too abstract and external validity may be limited, especially as experimenters are often reliant on student volunteers when conducting their experiments.

Angeletos *et al.* focus on some stylized facts, including that US households accumulate relatively large stocks of wealth before retirement, yet borrow actively on credit cards and consumption is excessively sensitive to predictable income changes. Bernheim *et al.* (2001) found that consumption growth rates close to retirement do not vary with retirement wealth (versus Modigliani), and that there are discontinuities in consumption at retirement (versus consumption smoothing). They conclude that there is little support for standard life-cycle models; their evidence is more consistent with rules of thumb, mental accounting and hyperbolic discounting in intertemporal decision-making.

Angeletos *et al.* (2001) and Laibson *et al.* (2007) develop these insights in constructing a structural buffer stock model analysing consumption/wealth patterns building on Strotz (1955), in which intertemporal decision-making is modelled as an intrapersonal strategic game between selves. They develop a standard economic theory of life-cycle planning (following Phelps and Pollak's 1968 analysis of intergenerational time preferences) by incorporating buffer stocks, but blended with a psychological model of self-control. Rational players are engaged in intrapersonal and intertemporal strategic tussles. Angeletos *et al.* incorporate three principles: labour income and liquidity constraints are uncertain; households can simultaneously borrow on credit cards whilst investing in illiquid investment assets (though simultaneously holding liquid assets and credit card debt is precluded). Quasi-hyperbolic discounting allows time-variant discount functions in which short-term preferences favour immediate gratification whilst long-run preferences are to act patiently.

Quasi-hyperbolic discounting is consistent with predictions of quasi-hyperbolic discounting for 'sophisticates' who can anticipate conflict with earlier selves' preferences so they will accumulate illiquid wealth sooner and hold it longer to protect themselves from future consumption splurges. This insight is consistent with Strotz's observations about pre-commitment devices. It is also consistent with Laibson's (1997) 'golden eggs' hypothesis: it is not wise to kill the goose that lays the golden eggs; similarly, illiquid assets accrue benefits only if you can hold them for a long time (Harris and Laibson 2001). Limits on liquid wealth prevent consumption smoothing and co-movements between income and consumption are particularly pronounced around retirement, which conflicts with Hall's hypothesis that consumption follows a random walk and therefore exhibits no systematic tendencies or correlations. There may be high levels of credit card borrowing to fund instantaneous gratification. Whilst they focus their analysis on sophisticates, the behaviour of 'naïfs' will be broadly similar, contrasting with O'Donoghue and Rabin's analysis (1999) in which naïfs and sophisticates adopt radically different behaviours.

The agents in Angeletos *et al.*'s model are assumed to be intertemporal utility maximizers, though not necessarily with stable intertemporal preferences. The agents are assumed to be high school graduates with a ninety-year maximum life and a working life extending from twenty to sixty-three years old, and household size will vary over a lifetime. Labour income is autocorrelated with shocks. Liquid assets are used as buffer stocks to enable riding out of transitory shocks. Illiquid assets yield a relatively high rate of return, but transaction costs of $10k + 10$ per cent of value of asset prevent easy sale, making the assets illiquid, paralleling some features of housing wealth, a major source of household wealth. Transactions costs are made large enough to prevent the sale of illiquid assets before wealth is bequeathed to increase computational tractability, but also because there are many partially illiquid consumers given transactions costs and delays. With quasi-hyperbolic discounting, even small transaction costs generate complete illiquidity. Illiquid assets earn interest yielding an annual consumption flow of 5 per cent, but no capital gain occurs. Credit card debt attracts higher rates of interest (but adjusted for bankruptcy and inflation). There is a credit limit on credit card debt of 30 per cent of mean income for each age cohort.

No analytical solution can be derived from the theoretical model, so the model is calibrated and simulated in two forms to allow the comparison of predictions from two possible discounting strategies: exponential discounting versus a quasi-hyperbolic discounting. Calibration involves incorporating prior information into the equations to give forecasting equations that are matched with consumption and asset allocation data from the US Panel Study of Income Dynamics and Survey of Consumer Finances (SCF). Labour income shocks are calibrated to match empirical data on labour income; the degree of present bias is assumed to be $\beta = 0.7$, as typically measured in lab experiments and, consistent with SCF data, the discount factor is 0.944. The age-dependent survival rate is calibrated from US National Center for Health Statistics data, and the willingness to save is equalized to match real savings with quasi-hyperbolic and exponential discount factors used to ensure a match with SCF data on retirement savings stock. Stochastic elements are incorporated using random number generators. Finally, equilibrium strategies are computed numerically using these assumptions and prior information.

Angeletos *et al.* (2001) find co-movement of income and consumption in their simulations, with marginal propensities to consume from predictable income changes ranging from 0.19 to 0.33 for both exponentials and hyperbolics. This contrasts with Hall's random walk hypothesis, and reflects the fact that low income early in life holds down consumption because of borrowing constraints. Consumption peaks in mid-life when household size is largest. 'Hyperbolics' are more willing to hold illiquid wealth because, whilst illiquidity is costly for both hyperbolics and exponentials, these costs are balanced by the benefits of illiquidity for the hyperbolics. In comparison with the exponentials, hyperbolics have higher discount factors in the *very long run* and, if rational, will use a crude commitment technology to prevent splurging behaviour. This explains why they invest in illiquid assets whilst simultaneously running up credit card debt. With a perfect commitment technology, exponentials would match hyperbolics. Exponentials are better at using buffer stocks and are more likely to accumulate liquid assets pre-retirement. Hyperbolics hold little liquid wealth and more credit card debt to fund instantaneous gratification. Overall, sophisticated hyperbolics smooth consumption less successfully than the exponentials, but they accumulate more illiquid assets earlier as a commitment device and because their very long-run discount factor is relatively high.

Similarly, Laibson *et al.* (2007) impose and reject the restriction associated with exponential discounting ($\beta = 1$). This restriction is rejected at a 1 per cent significance level. Their model is consistent with different discount functions in the short run versus the long run, implying a high short-run discount rate (39.5 per cent) alongside a low long-run rate (4.3 per cent). Overall, they find that the short-run and long-run discount factors are not equal, leading Laibson *et al.* to reject the exponential discounting hypothesis. Exponential discounting cannot account for high levels of credit card debt alongside high levels of retirement wealth accumulation, and cannot account for conflicts between short-run and long-run discount rates and simultaneous patience and impatience. Quasi-hyperbolic discounting explains why illiquid wealth is accumulated at real interest rates of about 5 per cent, but the same households accumulate credit card debt at 12 per cent.

Limitations of the Angeletos et al. *behavioural life-cycle model*

Whilst Angeletos *et al.* and Laibson *et al.* claim that their model fits better with real-world data, the differences in correlation are not large – using their data on the proportion of the population with relatively high liquid assets, the correlation coefficients between the exponential model and real data are 0.39 to 0.87; coefficients between the (quasi-)hyperbolic model and real data are 0.44 to 0.87. Also, the finding that exponential and hyperbolic/quasi-hyperbolic discount functions intersect (implying that people are simultaneously prone to consumption splurges and patient with their 'golden eggs') is sensitive to the parameter values selected. Comparing with Figure 9.1, Figure 9.2 shows the evolution of discount factors using parameter values for the hyperbolic and quasi-hyperbolic functions that more closely match the parameters used in calculation of the exponential discount factor (exponential discount factor, $\rho = 0.04$, $\delta = 0.96$ (as before); hyperbolic discount factor, $\gamma = 1$, $\alpha = 0.04$; quasi-hyperbolic discount factor, $\rho = 0.04$, $\delta = 0.96$, $\beta = 0.70$). The golden eggs result no longer holds for these parameter values, and the hyperbolic discount factor gives consistently higher discount factors.

More work needs to be done in establishing the relative empirical merits of different behavioural life-cycle models and parameter estimates, and this could be a rich seam for further research.

Temporal mental accounting and bracketing

Thaler's general mental accounting model (introduced in chapter 7) can also be applied specifically as an explanation for time inconsistency and present bias. Thaler (1981) conducted an early behavioural laboratory experiment with University of Oregon students, testing for time inconsistency by finding implicit time-variant discount rates. His hypothesis was that discount rates are time-variant; that they vary inversely with size of payoff because waiting for reward requires mental effort and self-control. He also postulates that the implicit discount rate for losses will be lower than for gains. The experimental design involved questionnaires: three for gains and one for losses. For gains, subjects were told that they had won money in a lottery held by their bank – they could take the money now or wait, and were asked to say how much they would need to make waiting equivalent to getting payments now. For losses, they were told that they had a traffic ticket that they could pay now or later.

Thaler found very large median implicit discount rates. The median response for the equivalent of $15 in a year was $60, implying a (compounded) discount rate of 139. Implicit discount rates dropped sharply with size of prize and over time. The median discount rate for an early prize of $15 versus the same payment in three months was 277 per cent; for a prize in three years it was 63 per cent. Overall, choices between a $15 prize today versus a larger prize in three months suggested implicit discount rates of up to 277 per cent; for a $3000 prize today versus a larger prize in three years, responses suggested an implicit discount rate of 12 per cent. Thaler also found sign effects. Implicit discount rates were higher for gains than they were for losses, and this fits with Kahneman and Tversky's prospect theory (chapter 7). In explaining these anomalies in intertemporal decision-making, Thaler's interpretations included the role of arithmetic errors in exponential calculations and self-control – differences in rewards over time need to be substantial and noticeable for individuals to expend effort on self-control.

Bracketing in labour supply

Time inconsistency can also lead to violations of the standard assumption about intertemporal substitution of labour for leisure, as seen alongside an exponential discounting assumption in real business-cycle models. Standard approaches assume that people work when wages are high and consume leisure when wages are low, reflecting the marginal rate of intertemporal substitution. In this case there should be a positive labour supply response, with more labour supplied when wages are high. Camerer *et al.* (1997) assess this hypothesis using a natural experiment capturing the working patterns of New York City cab drivers. They argue that this is a good data set with which to study intertemporal labour supply, because there will be considerable fluctuations in wages day-to-day, reflecting fluctuations in demand on holidays, or when the subway breaks down, for example.

If cab drivers are rational intertemporal maximizers in the sense presented in standard models, then they will work harder on busy days and less hard on quiet days. Camerer *et al.* collected data from 192 trip sheets for NYC cab drivers and estimated labour supply functions from the trip sheet data. Fare rates were fixed by the Taxi and Limousine Commission. Their estimated labour supply curves were downward-sloping because cab drivers made less effort on busier days, giving negative wage elasticities. They found little evidence of intertemporal substitution: drivers tended to stop work sooner on busy, 'high-wage' days, perhaps consistent with target-setting. They address the potential of measurement error on endogeneity by using wages of other drivers as an instrument, using instrumental variable estimation with fixed effects. They conclude that, in general, there are significantly negative wage elasticities for NYC cab drivers.

Camerer *et al.* list a few possible explanations but, according to them, the most compelling explanation is daily income targeting – a type of bracketing. As explained in chapter 7, bracketing is used to simplify decisions by isolating them from a stream of more complex decisions, so daily targeting means that people do not have the cognitive challenge of thinking over long time horizons. They don't have to worry about what it will be like tomorrow or remember what it was like yesterday. This is also consistent with comparisons against a reference point or aspiration level, and gives a simple decision rule to use in the face of choice overload. Quitting early on some days may also ameliorate self-control problems. The cab drivers who stop early but at the same time every day are pre-committing to a steady level of effort. Developing this habit stops them feeling tempted to quit early even on quiet days. Also, they might be tempted to fritter away the windfalls earned on the good days if they worked too hard on those days, if windfall income is more likely to be spent on luxuries.

Neuroeconomic analyses

As explored in chapter 8, Damasio (1994/2006) developed the somatic marker hypothesis to capture the impact of emotions on decisions. Emotions provide important physiological cues that can help decision-making. This links to temporal discounting because Damasio's early study focuses on the fact that damage to emotional processing circuits impairs people's ability to make wise financial decisions: for example, brain lesions associated with damage to emotional processing lead to constraints on rational planning over time (see also Bechara and Damasio 2005).

McClure, Laibson, Loewenstein and Cohen's fMRI evidence

McClure *et al.* (2004) look at fMRI evidence on the neural correlates of time discounting. Experimental subjects are offered a series of monetary reward choices varying by delay to delivery. McClure *et al.* test for the involvement of two separate neural systems: first, the limbic system including the midbrain dopamine system, particularly the paralimbic cortex which is preferentially activated for decisions involving immediately available rewards; second, the lateral prefrontal cortex and posterior parietal cortex activated for all intertemporal choices (irrespective of delay). They find greater relative activation of the fronto-parietal cortex when subjects choose longer-term options.

In constructing their analysis, they draw on one of Aesop's fables – the story of the ant and the grasshopper. The ant works hard all summer long collecting food for the winter whilst the grasshopper sings away the summer amusing himself. This fable illustrates the conflict between impulsive desires to consume now versus recognizing the future benefits of patience. As explained above, existing evidence shows large discrepancies between time discounting in humans versus other species. There is limited evidence that other animals make intertemporal choices deliberatively (according to McClure *et al.*). Consumers behave impatiently today but are prepared to plan for the future: if given the choice between $10 today and $11 tomorrow, most choose the former; but given a choice between $10 in a year and $11 in a year and a day, most choose the latter. This generates dynamic inconsistency: intertemporal choices are not discounted exponentially, and rewards available in the immediate future are valued disproportionately consistent with impulsive preference reversals.

In terms of background neuroeconomic evidence, lesion patient studies show that damage to the prefrontal cortex is associated with more impulsive behaviour. As explained above, quasi-hyperbolic discounting functions that splice together two different discounting functions by incorporating the present bias parameter β into an exponential discounting specification provide a good fit to experimental data. McClure *et al.* develop this approach to assess the role of different neural systems involved in intertemporal decision-making. They set out their β – δ model following Phelps and Pollack (1968) and Laibson (1997). The present discounted value of a future reward is equal to the standard discount factor multiplied by the present bias parameter, β. This means that more immediately available rewards are valued relatively highly. Their neuroeconomic evidence shows how the discrepancy between short-run and long-run preferences reflects differential activation of distinguishable neural systems, and they hypothesize that distinct neural processes are interacting in the following way: short-run impatience is associated with a *beta* system and is mediated by limbic structures associated with the midbrain dopamine system, including the ventral striatum, medial orbitofrontal cortex and medial prefrontal cortex, which are also implicated in processing of reward expectation/delivery; long-run patience is associated with a *delta* system and is mediated by the lateral prefrontal cortex and associated structures – with higher cognitive functions associated with evaluation of trade-offs between abstract rewards.

They tested their hypothesis using an fMRI imaging study in which they scan participants making intertemporal choices between early and later monetary rewards. Immediate rewards activated the beta areas. Choices involving delayed rewards (the delta system) were associated with activations in the lateral prefrontal cortex and also in primary visual and motor cortices. These delta areas were differentially activated for longer-term choices but not for more immediate rewards. As expected, visual/motor cortices were activated as in most decisions.

They also screened delta areas for the difficulty of tasks by comparing activations when the intertemporal differences in monetary amounts were relatively small and so harder to process. They identified differential activations in the frontal and parietal cortex – areas implicated in higher-level cognitive functioning. This is consistent with findings about the role of the prefrontal cortex in deliberation and of the parietal cortex in mathematical processing. They also found significant activations in the inferior parietal cortex, an area that is also engaged during numerical processing.

Their interpretation draws on insights from evolutionary biology, and suggests that intertemporal decision-making in humans, our capacity to postpone reward, is associated with higher cognitive functioning engaging the delta system. Overall, intertemporal choice is the outcome of competition between lower-level, automatic processes reflecting evolutionary environmental adaptations (engaging the *beta* system) and a more recently evolved, uniquely human capacity for abstract planning (engaging the *delta* system).

Glimcher, Kable and Louie's analysis of delayed choices

Glimcher *et al.* (2007) present an alternative neuroeconomic interpretation and analysis of discount functions. They analyse hyperbolic/quasi-hyperbolic discounting, and agree with McClure *et al.* that it gives a better understanding of intertemporal choice than exponential discounting models. However, they reject McClure *et al.*'s β–δ model, arguing that intertemporal decision-making is not the outcome of an intrapersonal conflict between a patient long-term self and an impulsive short-term self.

They conduct two experiments. For their first experiment, they use ten human subjects making 576–720 binary intertemporal choices between payments with different waiting times. The responses were used to construct individuals' indifference curves, and Glimcher *et al.* (2007) found that these were consistent with hyperbolic discounting. Glimcher *et al.* arranged payment via debit cards because these are nationally accepted, it is easy to monitor consumption with debit card information and transactions costs are negligible. One set of data included three behavioural sessions per subject, each facing 144 choices between certain, immediate gains of $20 versus larger gains but with a delay of between six hours and six months. They scanned one or two additional sessions in a brain scanner.

From the behavioural sessions they identified the amount of money at which each subject was indifferent to an immediate reward of $20. Hyperbolic discount functions gave a better fit for these choices. They found considerable variation, up to an order of magnitude, in rates of discounting between the most patient and most impatient subject. They used their estimates of the discount function to calculate the discounted utility of each delayed option for each subject. This was correlated with brain activation, and they found a clear correlation between estimates of discounted utility and brain activation in the medial prefrontal cortex, the ventral striatum (associated with processing reward) and the posterior cingulate cortex. But they found no evidence of differential activation in the beta areas identified by McClure *et al.*

Glimcher *et al.* conducted another experiment to investigate further. They used the same design as for their first experiment, but with a sixty-day front-end delay to prevent impulsive decision-making. The results from both the behavioural and scanning data were the same as for their first experiment, showing significant activations in ventral striatum and anterior/posterior cingulate cortex, but no differential activation in the limbic system. Immediate, potentially impulsive choices were no more hyperbolic than choices involving delayed rewards of at least sixty days. Their study does not support the hypothesis that discount functions are the product of multiple selves within the human brain. Glimcher *et al.* argue that dynamic inconsistency is not about impulsiveness, it's about getting things as soon as possible – perhaps reflecting temptation rather than impatience. More generally, they argue that neurobiology is most useful in helping us to understand the revealed preference approach in terms of the algorithmic structure of the brain.

Case study: intertemporal planning and the environment

Climate change and resource depletion are problems that will intensify over time. Similarly, decisions about energy-efficient consumption/investment involve costs now for benefits in the future. Given the importance of time to decisions affecting energy and the environment, the behavioural literature on intertemporal decision-making offers a number of relevant insights. McNamara and Grubb (2011) observe that energy is an abstract commodity – invisible and intangible – and so learning about substituting towards more energy-efficient consumption is delayed by perceptions of risk and procrastination. In resolving these problems, habits and planning will play a crucial role.

Behavioural discount functions for environmental decision-making

Environmental decisions are often taken with a view to the future, and in judging future consequences people will be affected by present bias. This links to dual-self models, explored above. Thaler and Sunstein (2008) argue that intrapersonal conflicts between a 'doer' self and a 'planner' self make people unwilling to take action if the costs are immediate and the payoffs more distant, because the doer prefers to spend less in the present. This can lead to an excessive focus on current costs/benefits relative to future costs/benefits, encouraging procrastination and overindulgence. In an environmental context, it may also lead people to underestimate the benefits of environmental actions. For example, even when long-term incentives and payoffs are substantial, only 19 per cent of Europeans opt for home insulation and only 6 per cent opt for eco-friendly cars (Pongiglione 2011, citing Special Eurobarometer Survey 75.1).

Hepburn *et al.* (2010) apply hyperbolic discounting to a fishery model: the fishery collapses because, at minimum viable population, the marginal rate of return is lower than the relatively high early discount rate, and this may explain the demise of Canadian cod and Peruvian anchoveta fisheries. Allcott and Mullainathan (2010) also argue that environmental decision-making is affected by procrastination: attention wanders and peripheral factors subconsciously influence decisions and perceptions, though commitment devices and default options can influence constructive choices and enable effective planning.

Brutscher (2011b) analyses temporal inconsistencies in energy decision-making using data from the Northern Ireland Continuous Household Survey. He analyses pre-payment for household electricity consumption, and finds that upfront payments are associated with higher electricity consumption than *ex post* payment, even when transaction costs are higher and feedback is given about electricity use. Using data from 10,124 households, he explores links between top-up behaviour of households using pre-payment meters. Households will balance the costs and benefits of top-ups – topping-up is costly because of foregone interest, but this is balanced by the benefit of convenience. Topping-up a pre-payment meter means that the household does not have to make a payment every time they use electricity. (See also Gourville and Soman 1998 on temporally separating payments from consumption.)

Brutscher identifies two behavioural anomalies in households' electricity consumption. People top up more often with smaller amounts than optimal, and increases in tariff do not lead to equal changes in number and amounts of top-ups; they just lead to increases in the number of top-ups. These anomalies cannot be explained by learning because there is little adjustment in months following a change in tariff, so learning is slow or nonexistent. Top-ups may be used as a pre-commitment device enabling households to save electricity and resolve the conflict between an impatient present self and a patient future self. A sophisticated agent will look for a pre-commitment device, but this does not explain the asymmetrical adjustment of number versus amount of top-ups. If the behaviour reflects pre-commitment, then there should still be a unique optimal top-up amount, but the survey evidence shows people adjusting by choosing different top-up amounts depending on the timing.

Another explanation draws on Thaler's mental accounting model (explored in chapter 7). People perceive costs differently, and whilst each £10 payment seems trivial, one larger £100 payment does not. To test the mental accounting model, Brutscher uses data from a natural experiment to analyse the impact of an exogenous increase in minimum top-up amount. An increase in minimum top-up amount from £2 to £15 was implemented in May 2009 and this did lead to decreases in electricity use: electricity consumption decreased by around 15 KWh as a result of the change in minimum top-up, consistent with mental accounting models in which people treat small amounts as trivial even when paid more frequently (Brutscher 2011b).

Goals, planning and feedback

Intentions do not always translate into action, and often there are conflicts between declared intentions and actual action, which may reflect preference reversals and/or naïve intertemporal decision-making. A survey by Fondazione Eni Enrico Mattei indicated that whilst 70 per cent of Italians surveyed were willing to increase energy savings, only 2 per cent are currently reducing their use (Pongiglione 2011). People may want to reduce emissions in principle, but will not approve if this has tangible consequences for themselves. American survey evidence shows that 78 per cent of Americans oppose gasoline tax and 60 per cent oppose business energy taxes (Leiserowitz 2006). Even though people may express concerns about climate change, there is limited real commitment to environmental action by Americans: 52 per cent of Americans claimed to support the Kyoto Treaty in principle, but if they had to pay an extra $50 per month then they would oppose it (Sunstein 2006).

Goals modify behaviour; ambitious goals lead to greater and more prolonged effort (Locke and Latham 2002). Planning is also important because effective behaviour is not just about intention; behavioural control, including self-confidence, guides action (Ajzen 1991). Whilst standard economics emphasizes the role of monetary incentives, Bamberg (2002) analyses two environmental behaviours – using a new bus route and shopping in a bio-shop. He finds that forming intentions about implementing the new behaviours increases their likelihood, and so implementation intentions can substitute for monetary incentives. Monetary incentives alone increase the likelihood of environmentally sensitive behaviour, but additional implementation incentives do not increase the likelihood of environmentally sensitive behaviour any further. Intentions can be reinforced when people make concrete pre-commitments to conserving energy, and commitments may endure even when the initial incentive to commit is temporary. Cialdini (2007) describes the enduring impact of 'lowball' tactics in promoting changes in habits – a lowball being a tempter offer which is later withdrawn.

Pallak *et al.* (1980) analysed the gas-consumption behaviour of a sample of Iowan households. A control group of households were given some energy-saving tips but the advice had no significant impact on their energy use. Then a matching sample of households was told that they would receive positive publicity for their efforts – they would be identified as energy-saving citizens in local newspaper articles. The publicity treatment had a significant, positive effect, with each homeowner saving on average 422 cubic feet of natural gas, equivalent to first-month savings of 12.2 per cent in gas consumption. But the most interesting result occurred when the households were sent a letter telling them that they would not receive any positive publicity after all – on average, these households increased their fuel savings to 15.5 per cent in the second month. Pallak *et al.* found similar results in an analysis of air-conditioning use. These apparently anomalous results have been attributed to the fact that the initial promise of publicity encouraged householders to pre-commit to energy reduction, and this commitment did not disappear when the promise of positive publicity was withdrawn.

Becker (1978) emphasizes the importance for intertemporal planning of feedback alongside hard goals. He analysed the behaviour of US families in identical three-bedroom houses. Eighty families were asked to set goals for reducing energy consumption during the summer: half were set an easy goal, the other half a difficult goal. Half of each group were given regular feedback three times per week. An additional twenty families were used as a control group. The group with the difficult goal and regular feedback was the only group to consume significantly less electricity: they reduced their electricity consumption by at least 13 per cent.

Thaler and Sunstein (2008) emphasize the importance of salient and frequent feedback in energy planning. Hargreaves *et al.* (2010) found that information feedback on electricity consumption leads to decreased use. Darby (2006) also emphasizes the importance of direct feedback with information presented clearly, using computerized tools; indirect feedback is more effective in addressing larger impacts, for example, seasonal impacts on energy consumption. Direct feedback via self-meter reading, direct displays, consumption displays and interactive feedback lead to savings of up to 15 per cent; indirect feedback, including frequent bills and information leaflets, can generate up to 10 per cent savings (Darby 2006; Brophy Haney *et al.* 2009). This suggests that regular feedback may help to lower discount rates and enable better planning.

Conclusions and policy implications

The theories and evidence outlined in this chapter demonstrate that the standard assumption of exponential discounting has a number of limitations and does not effectively capture empirical patterns observed in natural and lab experiments. Evidence from simulations of models calibrated using some parameter estimates from experimental studies also generates predictions about consumption, savings and investment that match real-world behaviour more effectively than exponential discounting models, though these models do suffer from the limitation that they have no analytical solution, and therefore the parameterization process is somewhat subjective. Time inconsistency and preference reversals can also be explained in terms of psychological factors including emotions and visceral factors, as explained in chapter 8. The literature on time inconsistency and emotions links up in explaining bad habits, including addictive behaviours, as explored in chapter 10.

Time inconsistency, preference reversals and present bias can distort effective decision-making in a number of domains. Overall, policies could be designed to accommodate the extent of sophistication in people's understanding of their own susceptibility to time inconsistency. If many consumers are naïfs, time inconsistency not only creates problems for the individual affected, but also has implications for the allocation of resources more generally, and can generate negative externalities. Policies to ameliorate time inconsistency are not just about interfering with the free choices of individuals, but are about getting more efficient outcomes for the economy more widely, depending on the proportion of naïfs and sophisticates in a population.

Time inconsistency is particularly problematic in the context of financial decision-making and pension planning because time plays a crucial role in these decisions. For savings, Ashraf *et al.* (2006) discuss the role of commitment devices in banking: they examined savings decisions in an experimental treatment allowing people an option to open a savings account at the same time as they started a bank account. They were paid the same interest rate on the money in their savings account, but their money was locked in. People who opted for this increased savings rates by 82 per cent. This evidence suggests that pre-commitment devices may be an essential part of enabling people to save.

The issue of present bias over long time horizons is particularly pressing in the context of pension provision. To prepare properly for retirement, people may have to make decisions that will not affect their standard of living for forty years (or more as retirement ages increase). Increasing pressures on government finances alongside increases in life expectancy mean that most governments will struggle to help their ageing populations, and individual responsibility will become a stronger theme in pension provision. Whilst governments may not be able to provide retirement incomes to people, Thaler and Sunstein (2008) argue that governments could nonetheless adopt an approach of 'liberal paternalism', allowing people the freedom to choose whilst also nudging them in a constructive direction. With greater attention to the 'architecture' of choice, people may be able to plan more effectively over their lifetime. In planning for retirement, present bias and time inconsistency may interact with other forms of bias, including *status quo* and familiarity biases.

The current standard default for many people is that they make no contributions automatically; they have to opt-in to make pension contributions. Madrian and Shea (2001) analyse the impact of adjusting these pension defaults. The architecture of choice could be adjusted to set default options so that individuals contribute automatically, and if they would prefer not to contribute they have to opt-out. Madrian and Shea found that pension participation increased by 65–98 per cent with opt-outs rather than opt-ins. Similarly, Thaler and Benartzi (2004) show that their Save More for Tomorrow scheme – in which people allocate a set proportion of their salary rises towards their pension – can also be very effective in encouraging people to save for retirement.

Overall, recognizing the interplay of present bias with other behavioural biases can enable governments to design policies not only to enable effective financial decision-making, but also in other spheres, including moderating the impact of behavioural factors on destructive behaviours and bad habits such as addiction, as explored in chapter 10.

10 Bad habits

Introduction

Within standard economic approaches based on assumptions of rational, forward-looking agents, self-destructive habits and addictions are anomalous. Behavioural economics offers some deeper insights into what motivates people to do things that adversely affect their future wellbeing. Potentially, bad habits and addiction can bring together models of time inconsistency and preference reversals (chapter 9) with insights about the role of emotions and visceral factors (chapter 8). So far, however, the analysis in economics has tended to focus on rational addiction models based on exponential discounting assumptions.

This chapter explores rational addiction models and related empirical evidence. The rational addiction analyses suggest that bad habits and addictive behaviour are rational choices but may still be associated with negative externalities and other market failures. Other models relax rationality assumptions to allow that environment and context will affect vulnerability to addictive behaviour, for example, the cue-trigger consumption models of Laibson, and Bernheim and Rangel. Some approaches focus on emotional, visceral and neurobiological factors, for example analyses by Loewenstein, and Tasnádi and Smith.

Evidence about smoking is covered extensively in empirical studies of addiction, perhaps because smoking is a legal activity; its consumption is easy to measure, and it has been well known for a long time that smoking is very bad for you. The health effects from smoking cost governments a lot of money. For these reasons good data that are relatively easy to interpret are widely available. For other bad habits, more data and analyses are becoming available; bad lifestyle habits and their impacts on health are covered in the case study section of this chapter.

Rational addiction models

Standard approaches to analysing addiction are associated with rational addiction models initially developed by Becker, Grossman and Murphy (BGM). Generally these models and analyses are applied to smoking habits, but similar concepts will apply to other bad habits, and some of these are explored in more detail below. Rational addiction theories confront the conventional wisdom about addictive consumption, which asserts that addictive substances are not price responsive because they reflect irrational impulses.

Becker, Grossman and Murphy's model

The theoretical background to the model of rational addiction is outlined in Becker and Murphy (1988) and also Becker *et al.* (1991, 1994). BGM assume that consumers are rational and forward looking with time-consistent preferences so addiction is not myopic. Rational consumers anticipate the future consequences of current actions, and this can be captured by relaxing the assumption of separable utility, instead allowing utility in each period to depend on previous and future consumption.

Addictive capital stock

A central element of the model is the stock of addictive capital, and for this reason some of the analytical features of BGM's model resemble features in Solow's macroeconomic model of growth. The stock of addictive capital builds up with past consumption of addictive substances and stressful life-cycle triggers such as divorce. Once the steady state is reached, the stock of addictive capital will be stable and unchanging.

Adjacent complementarity, tolerance and reinforcement

Intuitively, the adjacent complementarity condition holds when consumption of goods in adjacent periods is complementary. This reflects some basic characteristics of addictive behaviour, including tolerance and reinforcement. Addicts need to consume more of an addictive substance as consumption increases, generating tolerance: past consumption lowers current and future utility, leading to a decrease in current utility as the stock of addictive capital increases. Addicts realize that their behaviour builds up a stock of addictive capital that will harm them in the future. Reinforcement captures the fact that increases in past consumption lead to increases in the stock of addictive capital, increasing present consumption.

Putting these together, BGM outline the adjacent complementarity condition. Addiction is consistent with rational utility maximization given expectations of future harm from addiction, but only if there is adjacent complementarity, that is, only if positive impact of increased addictive stock in reinforcing the marginal utility of current consumption exceeds the negative effect of higher addictive stock on tolerance. In this case, past (current) consumption will lead to greater current (future) consumption, as explained mathematically in Box 10.1.

Box 10.1   Mathematics of Becker, Grossman and Murphy's rational addiction model

Becker, Grossman and Murphy (BGM) assume that consumers are rational and forward looking with time-consistent preferences. In the rational addiction model, addiction is not myopic.

Dynamics of stock of addictive capital

Past consumption of addictive substance (c) and life-cycle events will build up the stock of addictive capital (S), which will evolve as follows:

$$\dot{S}(t) = c(t) - \delta S(t)$$

In steady state, S will be stable and the steady-state condition is $c = \delta S(t)$.

Addicts need to consume more of the addictive substance as consumption increases, and this is associated with tolerance and reinforcement.

Tolerance

Tolerance reflects the fact that past consumption lowers current and future utility and so current utility decreases as the stock of addictive capital increases:

$$\partial u/\partial s = u_s < 0$$

Tolerance can be explained in terms of addicts realizing that their addictive behaviour builds up a stock of addictive capital that will harm them in the future.

Reinforcement

With reinforcement, increases in past consumption lead to an increase in the stock of addictive capital stock, and this raises present consumption:

$$\partial c/\partial s = c_s < 0$$

Adjacent complementarity

With adjacent complementarity, past (current) consumption is reinforcing and leads to greater current (future) consumption. The necessary and sufficient condition for reinforcement near steady state is:

$$(\sigma + 2\delta)u_{cs} > -u_{ss}$$

where σ is the rate of time preference and δ is the rate of depreciation in S. This gives:

$$u_{cs} = \partial^2 u/\partial c \partial s, \; u_{ss} = \partial^2 u/\partial s^2$$

When the adjacent complementarity condition holds, reinforcement as captured by the discounted, depreciated marginal utility of consumption with respect to increments to the stock of addictive capital, will dominate tolerance and past consumption will be associated with increases in future consumption.

Using this model, BGM predict that consumption of addictive goods is likely to be price responsive and strong addictions will be associated with a more price-elastic response in the long run. Multiple equilibria and unstable steady states will mean that addiction is sensitive to initial stock of addictive capital. The mechanisms underlying BGM's rational addiction model are illustrated in Figure 10.1.

Figure 10.1a illustrates that there are multiple equilibria in the rational addiction model. There is an unstable steady state at point [0]: consumption is relatively low so addictive stock is depreciating faster than it accumulates. Even if consumption is initially positive, eventually the consumer will stop addictive consumption and return to zero consumption.

At point [2] consumption is stable. If consumption decreases, it is still greater than replacement rate so the addictive stock will increase again. If consumption rises, it will be less than needed for replacement so it will fall again. Either way, consumption will return to point [2].

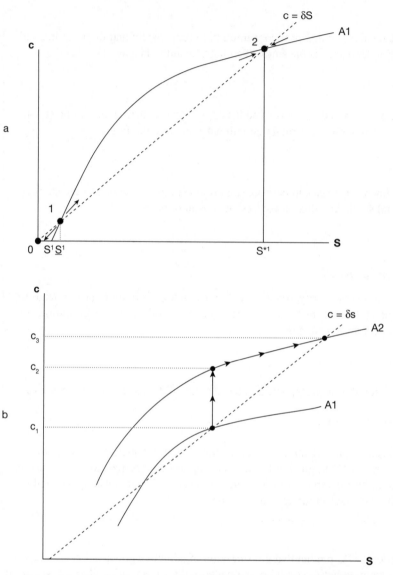

Figure 10.1 Becker, Grossman and Murphy's rational addiction model

On the other hand, [1] is locally and globally unstable: small perturbations rightwards will lead to increasing contributions to the stock of addictive capital until the consumer converges on point [2]. Similarly, decreases in consumption will lead to insufficient replacement of the stock of addictive capital and the consumer will converge on [0].

The existence of these different equilibria explains the unstable behaviour seen amongst many consumers of additive substances. In steady states, the same person can use heavily and at other times give up because impacts are multiplied; for example, if the price decreases, consumption shifts from $[0] < c < [1]$ to $c > [1]$ and the impacts of the price decrease will be magnified, leading to increased demand as consumer shifts to a new steady state at [2].

In terms of the dynamic, intertemporal aspects of addictive consumption, BGM allow that addiction is more likely if a consumer discounts the future heavily, and/or pays less attention to future consequences. In this case, the effects of reinforcement will outweigh those of tolerance. If there is rapid depreciation of addictive stock, current consumption has smaller negative effects and harmful effects will disappear. There will be different responses in the short run versus the long run, as illustrated in Figure 10.1b. Given a fall in prices, demand for the addictive substance rises from A1 to A2 in two stages: in the short run consumption rises from c^1 to c^2; in the long run it rises from c^2 to c^3. It follows therefore that long-run impacts will exceed short-run impacts. Initial increases in addictive consumption flow into stocks of addictive capital stimulating further growth in consumption.

Becker and Murphy's empirical evidence

BGM put forward a number of empirical hypotheses which follow from their model. The long-run price elasticity of demand (LRPED) of smoking consumption will be sizeable and larger than the short-run price elasticity of demand (SRPED). High future and past prices will reduce current consumption, reflecting adjacent complementarity. People on lower incomes will tend to have higher discount rates and will respond more to price changes than people on higher incomes with lower discount rates. People on higher incomes will respond more to future harmful effects and younger people will be more responsive to price changes than older people.

It follows from BGM's models that current and past consumption will be complementary, and consumption in this period will be affected both by consumption in the last period and by consumption in the future period. Consumption in all periods will be correlated. In contrast to BGM's approach, myopic models of addiction are explored by Pollak (1970, 1976) and Yaari (1977), who explain that myopic individuals fail to consider impacts of current utility on future utility and consumption; because they ignore future effects, consumption becomes entirely backward-looking. Myopic addicts would not increase consumption in the face of expectations of price increases.

BGM construct an empirical test to separate models of rational addiction from models of myopic addiction. If the parameter on past consumption is significantly greater than zero and the parameter on future consumption is not significantly different from zero, then this confirms a hypothesis that addiction is myopic. Similarly, if the parameter estimate on future prices is insignificantly different from zero, then future prices are not affecting current consumption, which again would be consistent with myopic addiction.

On the other hand, if the parameters on past and future consumption are both significantly greater than zero, then consumption across time periods is complementary across time. Past, present and future consumption are affected by each other, and this is consistent with BGM's model. If lower prices today lead to increased consumption today and tomorrow, this again is consistent with complementarities in consumption over time, consistent with rational addiction. For rational forward-looking agents, if price falls are anticipated then consumption in the past and current periods will both rise; similarly, rises in consumption in the future period will lead to rises in consumption in future periods.

Some empirical hypotheses about permanent versus temporary price changes can also be formulated. Permanent price falls will have a larger effect on current consumption than temporary falls, because they involve a fall in all future prices and therefore a rise in all future consumption; it follows – as noted above – that the LRPED will be greater than the SRPED.

BGM (1994) test these hypotheses using various econometric techniques. They make the basic rational addiction model more tractable by setting out an empirical model in which current consumption is a function of past and future consumption, current prices and life-cycle events (captured within an error term). To test their hypotheses, BGM use data on cigarette sales and prices for US state cross-sections from 1955–85 for fifty US states. Some data points are missing, so overall they have a panel data set with 1581 observations.

They capture price variability using state excise taxes; variation in tax rates leads to substantial variation in retail prices. They note a number of limitations in the data. The impact of health education will change the temporal patterns, but they hope this will be captured by time dummies. Demographic differences may affect patterns, so they assume these do not correlate with interstate tax/price differentials. Smuggling of cigarettes across state borders will mean that sales do not necessarily correlate with consumption, so they use tax differentials to construct smuggling incentive variables for exports/imports. One key problem is that they are using aggregate data and so cannot study the decision of each individual smoker, and this issue is addressed in analyses of smoking using microeconomic data, for example Chaloupka's (1991) study (discussed below).

BGM do not use ordinary least squares estimation because of potential endogeneity problems. The error term capturing life-cycle events will probably be serially correlated, and even if it is not, it will affect consumption at all dates and given the inclusion of both leads and lags on variables, it will create endogeneity. Instead they use instrumental variable estimation with lead and lagged prices as instruments. They use fixed effects with two-stage least squares and incorporate the fixed effects to resolve heterogeneity bias.

Using this data set, BGM estimate SRPEDs between −0.436 and −0.355, and LRPEDs between −0.734 and −0.788. They conclude that findings are consistent with addiction generally. They note that their results are consistent with myopic addiction because lagged consumption is a significant determinant of current consumption and, whilst the future consumption parameter is significant, it has not been reliably estimated because it implies implausible discount factors of between 56.3 and 222.6 per cent.

Overall, BGM's results were mixed; partly the findings are consistent with the hypotheses from the BGM model, but the econometric problems are significant. Hausman tests suggested that the estimates were inconsistent; the data were not rich enough to pin down the discount factor accurately. A source of potential measurement error came from using actual future prices rather than *expected* future prices, which could generate another source of endogeneity. BGM admit that their results are mixed: 'The conclusions to be drawn from these tests of the estimates in Tables 3 and 5 depend on one's priors.'

Other econometric studies of addiction

BGM's analysis triggered a range of econometric analyses of smoking patterns, and some of these studies incorporated additional elements to address some of the limitations in BGM's approach. As explained below, Gruber and Köszegi recognize that time inconsistency may play a role; Baltagi and Griffin use a wider range of econometric techniques to resolve endogeneity problems; and Chaloupka uses microeconomic data to overcome potential aggregation problems. Other studies test the rational addiction model on other forms of addiction, including alcoholism, caffeine addiction and gambling.

Gruber and Köszegi's analysis

In analysing addiction, Gruber and Köszegi (2001) use consumption as well as sales data. Price increases may lead to stockpiling and this leads to an implication similar to that identified by BGM: increased sales does not equal increased consumption. Whilst Gruber and Köszegi's model is about rational addicts in the sense that it incorporates forward-looking decisions, they do relax the assumption about time consistency, allowing that addiction reflects time inconsistency. They note that many psychological experiments have revealed evidence of time-inconsistent preferences. Also, the fact that so many people buy quitting aids is evidence that future behaviour does not always coincide with current desires.

To resolve the problems of endogeneity bias, Gruber and Köszegi assume that true exogenous variation comes from taxes, and they analyse consumers' responses to tax changes using data on consumption as well as sales. Gruber and Köszegi's analysis relies on the assumption that people forecast prices in advance, but policy changes aren't always announced in advance; only eight of 160 tax changes from 1973 to 1996 had been announced a year before. They analyse behaviour in response to legislative changes in tax rates between the time when the tax rate change was enacted and when it was effective, to capture consumption period in the period between announcement and implementation. In this way they test forward-looking behaviour by examining consumption in the period between enactment of legislation and when changes became effective.

Using panel fixed-effects estimation techniques incorporating time and state dummies to capture time invariant effects and spatial heterogeneity, they examine data from 1973 to 1996. During this period there were thirty-six tax changes enacted and effective in the same month; forty-four tax changes enacted and effective in consecutive months; and sixty-eight tax changes with at least one month between enactment and implementation. Gruber and Köszegi justify their assumption of no omitted variable bias on the basis that they are using high-frequency monthly data, and preference structures would not have time to change over such a short period. For consumption data, they use the Vital Statistics Detailed Natality Data 1989–96 on mothers' smoking habits, averaged to give state average monthly consumption per capita.

Gruber and Köszegi find that the coefficient on the pre-announced rate is positive and highly significant. This suggests a hoarding effect – a type of forward-looking behaviour. These results are consistent with other analyses, and partly confirm the findings from BGM's analyses of rational addiction. Consumption does jump in anticipation of tax rises, also suggesting that rational hoarding is taking place, though they do note that it is difficult empirically to separate addiction models with rational time-consistency versus models with myopic/time-inconsistent preferences.

In terms of implications, Gruber and Köszegi emphasize that policy-makers should worry about internalities as well as externalities. With time-consistent preferences, smoking generates externalities. With time-inconsistent preferences, internalities are generated too: individual smokers impose costs on their future selves, reflecting future health problems. So Gruber and Köszegi argue that policy-makers should adjust cigarette taxes to reflect these internalities as well as externalities. At standard values of life measures, internalities were $30.45 per pack in lost life expectancy (i.e. 100 times the externalities from smoking). Significant internalities mean that optimal tax rates should be at least a dollar higher even for modest time inconsistency.

Baltagi and Griffin's analysis

Baltagi and Griffin (2001) are strongly critical of empirical findings from BGM given the econometric problems with their analysis. They study smoking using a dynamic panel analysis with data set for forty-six US states from 1963–92 and estimate the relationship between consumption, prices, income, and prices in neighbouring states. They experiment with a range of estimation procedures and instruments to resolve the potential endogeneity problems, including combinations of two-stage least squares with fixed effects and generalized method of moments.

Their dependent variable is current consumption, and they find that the parameters on lagged and future consumption are positive and significant. There is less evidence that prices have a significant impact – the impacts vary depending on the estimation technique used. Their estimates for SRPED range from –0.69 to –0.42 and for LRPED between –1.39 and –2.04, though, as BGM found, the discount rate is not sharply estimated which undermines the robustness of the results. Whilst they do use a more careful econometric approach than other studies, and their results are broadly consistent with other studies, they admit that macroeconomic analyses are vulnerable to significant econometric limitations because of aggregation problems and endogeneity. Microeconomic empirical studies have the potential to deliver more reliable results.

Chaloupka's microeconomic analysis

Chaloupka's (1991) analysis is a significant advance on the previous studies because he uses microeconomic data. He assumes rationality by assuming that addicts consider the future consequences of current and past behaviour, but allows that discount rates will be higher for some groups. One innovation in Chaloupka's analysis is that he also incorporates a variable to capture addictive capital stock. He also introduces the concept of 'relaxation' (the psycho-logical and physiological benefits from addiction) reflecting tolerance (when past consump-tion lowers the marginal utility of current consumption, as in BGM's model) and reinforcement (when past consumption increases current consumption, also seen in BGM's model).

His econometric analysis builds on micro-level data from the second US National Health and Nutrition Examination Survey, examining responses from 28,000 people from six months to seventy-four years over the period 1976–80. As for other studies, he uses instrumental variable estimation to resolve potential endogeneity problems. Chaloupka finds that price impacts are negative and past prices have a greater impact than future prices, consistent with rational addiction because the future price parameter incorporates a discount factor. He finds that lagged consumption is usually significant and positive. The findings are mixed, so offer no clear lessons about myopia versus forward-looking addiction.

The coefficient on addictive stock is significant and positive, confirming the reinforcement hypothesis. The estimates of the LRPEDs are lower than in Becker *et al.* and for current/former smokers lie between –0.48 and –0.35. Individual differences are significant: the less educated are more price-responsive, with LRPED estimates between –0.62 and –0.57. More educated smokers are unresponsive to price, as are young adults and the elderly. In middle age (25–64-year-olds), LRPEDs range between –0.46 and –0.31.

Other studies

There are a number of other studies of addiction which are broadly consistent with BGM's hypotheses. Lewit and Grossman (1981) and Lewit and Coate (1982) found that youths respond more than adults to price changes. Townsend (1987) and Farrell and Fuchs (1982) analyse smoking data to show that information since the 1960s about harmful consequences has had more effect on smoking by the rich/more educated than on the poor/less educated.

Olekalns and Bardsley (1996) study caffeine consumption, a habit which is strongly addictive but legal, so they were easily able to use data on coffee prices. They exploited the fact that the commodity price cycle leads to price fluctuations, and argue that this gives a good natural experiment for analysing coffee consumption responses to price changes. Using US data on per capita caffeine consumption from the US Department of Agriculture Economic Research Service, they find positive associations between current consumption and past and future consumption, consistent with rational addiction. Negative associations were found between current consumption and current prices, but positive associations between current consumption and past and future prices. The long-run price elasticity is poorly estimated/ wrong sign, perhaps reflecting the fact that they were working with a very small sample. There are a number of econometric problems with their study, but their results are broadly consistent with the other econometric studies discussed.

For other addictions, Cook and Tauchen (1982), in a 1962–77 cross-sectional analysis of alcoholism in US states, found that excise taxes led to significant, negative impacts on cirrhosis deaths. There is also evidence about gambling. Mobilia (1990) conducted an experimental study of gambling at horse-racing tracks in the period 1950–86. Paralleling the analysis of effects of changes in cigarette prices on smoking, for horse-racing the demand variable is the number of bets per person (known as the 'handle' per person), and the price variable is the takeout rate (the fraction of the bet retained by the track). Mobilia finds, with results similar to smoking results, that an increase in the takeout rate lowers the future handle per person, and estimates an LRPED of –0.7 and SRPED of –0.3, not dissimilar to the estimates for the smoking studies.

Rational addiction models: summary of evidence and implications

The econometric studies explored above, including BGM's study, show that rational addiction models can be empirically distinguished from myopia by introducing lead variables to capture expectations. This empirical evidence shows that future prices/consumption have an impact on current consumption, which supports rational addiction models based on assumptions of forward-looking addicts.

Overall, these studies show that, in controlling addiction, money price is more important to poorer, younger people because they often place smaller value on future costs from health problems and other future harms, reflected in the fact that younger, poorer people have higher discount rates. Addicts with higher discount rates respond more to price changes, and so reductions in price will have a substantial positive impact on consumption, particularly amongst the young. It follows that doubling federal excise tax on cigarettes would lead to increase of 15 per cent in price and therefore a 6 per cent fall in average cigarette consumption.

For hard drug use, there is no direct evidence from the econometric studies above but, assuming that patterns are similar, if drugs are legalized then a fall in prices will expand use. Within poorer, less educated groups (where discount rates are higher), consumption is more responsive to price, so drug addiction amongst the poor is likely to become more significant as prices fall with legalization. Similarly, addiction would become more of a problem amongst younger age groups. Temporary policies won't work: the effects of 'wars' on drugs are limited because only current (not future) prices rise; there will be no complementary fall in current use from a fall in future use. Addicts with lower discount rates respond more to changes in harmful future consequences, and education programmes are more likely to be effective with these groups, including richer, older people.

BGM also outline some industrial policy implications, focusing on monopoly and addiction. The cigarette industry is highly concentrated, with a large proportion of output produced by two firms – British American Tobacco and Philip Morris International – so these companies have significant monopoly power. A monopolist can set price at a point where the marginal revenue is less than marginal cost, and whilst that won't lead to profit maximizing in the short term, if consumption is addictive, then increases in current consumption in the short term will lead to increases in future consumption in the long term, then the monopolist can raise future prices to increase future profits. Lower prices get consumers hooked.

Similarly, Gruber and Köszegi (2001) argue that inelastic demand for addictive substances allows oligopolistic producers to raise prices. Adler and Freedman (1990) note the 'magic trick' from production of addictive goods. Cigarette producers are able to increase profits in an industry in which demand is falling rapidly because past and present consumption interact via adjacent complementarity. This habit persistence amongst smokers explains why cigarette companies post big profits despite better education about negative health consequences.

One overall remaining problem with the econometric analyses of rational addiction models, identified by Gruber and Köszegi, is that they cannot empirically distinguish models of addiction with time-consistent versus time-inconsistent preferences when the difference might be important. Does evidence about heterogeneity across demographic groups suggest that younger/less educated people are myopic? Or have time-inconsistent preferences? Or just higher discount rates? Everyday observation of smokers suggests that their behaviour is time-inconsistent because many people do use quitting aids that would not be consistent with future intentions to smoke. The experimental evidence does not justify assumptions of exponential discounting and time consistency often seen in the econometric analyses. Behavioural experimental techniques, including neuroeconomic studies, can move beyond these constraints and, as explored below, can provide a richer understanding of what really propels addictive habits.

Cue-triggered consumption

Cue-triggered consumption models develop from the insight from psychology that resistance to temptation is determined by context and environment. As mentioned in chapter 2, Walter Mischel and colleagues conducted experiments on self-imposed delay of gratification, to test resistance to temptation.

Mischel and Ebbesen (1970) manipulated children's attention to delayed rewards in a number of contexts. They studied thirty-two preschool children waiting for a preferred but delayed reward. They were studied in four settings in which they were in a room with: (1) a delayed reward; (2) a less preferred but immediately available reward; (3) both rewards; or (4) no reward. Mischel and Ebbesen found that the amount of time the children were able to wait for the preferred reward before it was forfeited was affected by context. Voluntary waiting time increased substantially when they were outside the presence of the preferred rewards. This finding foreshadows cue-triggered consumption models focusing on the importance of contextual cues.

The study of contextual cues was developed further by Mischel *et al.* (1972) in the famous marshmallow experiment using a group of ninety-two three- to five-year-olds. They were allowed to eat one marshmallow (or some other treat). Many resisted the temptation to eat the first marshmallow in order to get the second, but the most interesting finding was that they were able to wait longer if they were distracted. On the other hand, thinking about the treat, and also negative thoughts, led to decreases in waiting times. The children used a range of techniques to distract their own attention from the treats, perhaps as a form of pre-commitment device. Metcalfe and Mischel (1999) postulate that delay of gratification involves interactions between a cool, cognitive 'know' system, which is slow and strategic; and a hot, emotional 'go' system, which is impulsive, innate and undermines efforts at self-control. (This approach also links with Kahneman's (2003) analyses of system 1 and system 2 thinking, as discussed in chapters 6 and 8.)

Laibson's cue theory of consumption

Cue-triggered consumption models develop these insights from social learning theory and also incorporate insights from behavioural psychology about the links between stimuli, reinforcement and behaviour. Laibson (2001) develops a model of cue-triggered addiction based on psychological analyses of learning and conditioning.

As explained in chapters 2 and 4, the experimental psychologist Thorndike constructed some psychological laws to capture the progress of conditioning. He found that animals made associations between stimuli, actions and rewards, and from this devised some laws of conditioning: the law of effect – actions which produce pleasure will be repeated and so behaviour responds to pleasure and reward; the law of exercise – actions are more likely to be used if they produce positive associations and less likely to be used if they produce negative associations; and the law of recency – experiences from recent events will have more salience. We are more likely to repeat recently learned responses and the impacts of prior rewards and punishments will decay over time.

Laibson (2001) captures some of these conditioning effects in an analysis of cue-triggered consumption and the role of environmental factors in addiction. He describes the case of a man with cocaine/heroin dependence who weaned himself off drugs whilst in prison. He was able successfully to resist temptations whilst in prison but, upon his release, he was exposed to environmental cues that reminded him of his drug-addicted state. He was not able to resist those cues, and so relapsed.

Cue-based complementarities are created when a cue by itself leads to increases in the marginal utility of consumption. Impulsivity plays an important role and, when exposed to immediately available rewards, cues will trigger physiological changes that prime the consumer to consume immediately. Laibson argues that his model provides biological foundations for rational addiction models: the BGM model is a special case of Laibson's more general cues model, applying when the adjacent complementarity condition holds. Laibson also embeds pre-commitment into his analysis, arguing that, in a restricted cues version of his model, people may decide to reduce their set of choices in order to enable cue management.

Bernheim and Rangel on hot–cold systems

Bernheim and Rangel's (2004) analysis of addiction was foreshadowed by Metcalfe and Mischel's (1999) psychological analysis of hot/cool systems, as explained above. Bernheim and Rangel (2004) contest Becker and Murphy's (1988) models of rational addiction and form three main postulates: firstly, using addictive substances is a mistake; secondly, individuals are sensitized by exposure and hot states trigger mistaken usage; and thirdly, addicts are nonetheless sophisticated and attempt to manage their addictions by using pre-commitment devices.

Bernheim and Rangel (2004) identify a number of behavioural patterns which cannot be explained by rational addiction models. First, addicts often try unsuccessfully to quit their addiction; second, exposure to cues is associated with recidivism; third, when describing their past drugs use, addicts often describe it as a mistake; fourth, addicts attempt self-control via pre-commitment and will voluntarily remove options to consume in the future; and fifth, behavioural and cognitive therapies, partly by teaching cue avoidance, reduce addictive behaviour. None of these patterns is consistent with an assumption of rational addiction.

Cues in natural addiction models

Smith and Tasnádi (2007) use insights from neurobiology to construct a biological model of cue-triggered 'natural addiction'. They start with the evolutionary/biological foundations of addiction: for example, in foraging for food we have evolved to respond to cues such as sweetness, which might convey something about the nutritional value of foods. So a proximate mechanism develops in which cues become satisfying themselves. The problem is that in modern settings, where many foods have unnaturally high sugar content, these cues can lead to destructive, unhealthy behaviours.

Smith and Tasnádi focus on the role of endogenous opiods in optimal foraging. Rats will self-administer morphine to the point of addiction, and administration of opiates leads to increased food intake. Smith and Tasnádi explore the biological process: opiate molecules bind with opiate receptors and activate them, leading to physiological and behavioural changes.

In particular, endogenous opioids play a role in influencing perceived palatability. When endogenous opioids are released they reinforce the consumption of the food, stimulating the dopaminergic pathways. As discussed in chapter 3, dopamine plays a key role in the neurobiology of learning, and if consumption of a good (e.g. sugar) gives pleasure by stimulating these neurobiological reward structures, then more of that good will be consumed in the future. Endogenous opioids make food taste good, and the consumption of sweet foods leads to release of endorphins, producing similar effects to opioids. In this way, eating sweet things generates a 'biochemical cascade', causing us to eat more irrespective of calorific needs. This also links to drug addictions because heroin and other drugs mimic the effects of these endogenous opioids. Optimal foraging involves responding to environmental cues indicating nutritional value. In nature very sugary foods occur rarely, and, as noted above, in a primitive foraging environment sweetness signals highly nutritious foods. In a modern context, however, sugary foods are a lot more common and human physiology is not adapted to cope with their abundance.

In a modern version of Stigler's (1945) diet problem (which was about the volume of specific foods that would have to be eaten to satisfy a range of nutritional needs), Smith and Tasnádi construct a model of 'natural' addiction which involves optimizing for a balanced diet. They postulate two states of the world: a no-cue balanced diet problem when people have to forage for food without specific cues; and a positive-cue balanced diet problem when positive cues give clues about the concentration of nutrients in an addictive good.

Consumption is propelled by cues. If a positive cue is received, then the consumption of the addictive good increases and consumption of other goods will fall. A simplified interpretation of Smith and Tasnádi's model is illustrated in Figure 10.2. Increments to consumption of an addictive good will generate two effects: an ε benefit reflecting the *subjective* beliefs about the nutritional value of the addictive good – shown by area B; and an ε loss reflecting the impact on nutrient intake of a decrease in consumption of relatively nutritious ordinary good – shown by area L. If B > L then the perceived benefits of the addictive good will outweigh the perceived losses and the person will increase their consumption of the addictive substance.

Smith and Tasnádi assert that Bayesian learning generates adjacent complementarity: a positive cue in one period increases a person's judgment of the posterior probability of a

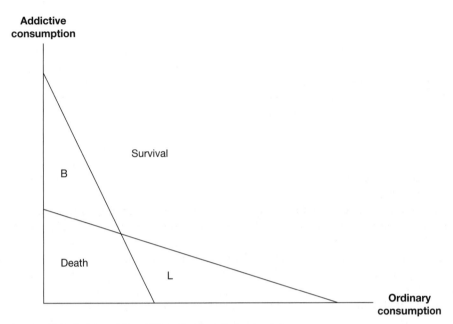

Figure 10.2 Smith and Tasnádi's rational addiction model

positive cue in the next period. However, the process of consumption is still not fully rational. Visceral factors, and bodily responses, are important because it is subjective, psychological factors that determine the magnitude of B relative to L. In addition, as explained above, the cues may be misleading if they stimulate the dopaminergic pathways even when the potential nutritional value of an addictive substance is limited or nonexistent.

Giving-up strategies might harness the learning elements of addiction: quitting 'cold turkey' may stop the arrival of hedonic 'false clues' about benefits of use. On the other hand, uncertainty, incomplete information and time inconsistency suggest a role for paternalism. Overall, Smith and Tasnádi suggest that conceptions of rationality should recognize that we are affected by sophisticated biological systems which are adapted to a pre-industrial environment. These systems can be 'hijacked' by technological advances, and we have not (yet) evolved to cope. They conclude that pleasure and satiety from smoking (and overeating, etc.) is derived from bodily effects and, whilst there is a role for habits, bodily urges are an important aspect of addiction. Quitting therapies could be designed accordingly. Sensory replacements such as inhalers and de-nicotinized cigarettes could be made more cheaply and widely available to allow addicts to satisfy their bodily 'needs' to smoke.

Visceral factors

Loewenstein (1996) offers an alternative to the rational addiction models by analysing the impact of bodily, visceral influences on addiction. He observes that discrepancies between knowledge and action lead to people feeling 'out of control'. As noted in chapters 2 and 8, this can be attributed to the impact of visceral factors (VFs), which are basic drives and instincts, for example thirst and hunger. Visceral factors are not bad in themselves, but self-destructive behaviour reflects the excessive influence of VFs.

Intensity is important in reconciling interactions between cognitive and affective factors, and this is similar for VFs. At low levels VFs can be accommodated; at medium levels they can be moderated via effortful self-control; at high levels VFs take over and rational deliberation is overridden. If a driver is sufficiently tired, then a visceral need to sleep will overwhelm the cognitive processes such as concentration that are engaged during driving, and the driver will fall asleep at the wheel.

Rational choice requires that VFs be taken into account, and addiction occurs when VFs have excessive influence – it represents the overriding of rational deliberation by VFs. Loewenstein argues that Becker and Murphy's model does not fit the facts because it does not capture the hedonic aspects of addiction, including the downward 'hedonic spirals' observed as cocaine addictions develop when people fail to notice small, incremental negative effects. Addicts don't use information aside from their personal experience even though it is widely available.

Addiction is as much about avoiding pain as pursuing pleasure. Pain from habituation comes in two forms: pain of withdrawal and cravings from conditioned associations. These are captured by two propositions from Loewenstein's schema: people underestimate impact of future VFs and so exaggerate their ability to give up; and future pains seem unreal to the currently pain-free self. Loewenstein concludes that the problems generated by failure to embed VFs and emotions into decision-making paradigms means that the problem has been underestimated. Irrationality as failure to adhere to axioms of choice doesn't fit with our personal experiences. When VFs are overwhelming, behaviour becomes 'a-rational' – it is not a conscious decision to do something stupid.

Neuroeconomic analyses

Smith and Tasnádi's (2007) study emphasizes the role of dopaminergic pathways. They also note that insula plays a role in conscious feeling by anticipating bodily effects of emotional events, so the insula may play a role in propelling addiction by anticipating the bodily effects of addictions such as smoking. Animal studies show that addiction in rats resembles human addictions, and this suggests that human addiction is propelled by primitive reward circuitry engaging the dopaminergic pathways. Evolution may also play a role, raising the question: do addictive substances hijack primitive reward circuitry to create phenomena of reinforcement, tolerance, craving and withdrawal? There have been a range of neuroeconomic studies of addiction which illuminate some of these issues.

Naqvi et al.*'s lesion patient study*

McClure *et al.* (2004) (whose study of the neural correlates of time inconsistency was discussed in chapter 9) make the connection between present bias and addiction. Immediacy, impulsivity and drug addiction lead to similar activations of dopaminergic limbic structures.

This is explored in more detail in a neuroeconomic study of lesion patients by Naqvi *et al.* (2007). They argue that addiction reflects long-term adaptations. Many brain systems are implicated in addiction, including the amygdala and nucleus accumbens. Citing fMRI evidence, Naqvi *et al.* observe that exposure to drug-associated cues activates the anterior cingulate cortex, the orbitofrontal cortex and the insula. They hypothesize that the insula is a critical neural substrate for addiction and therefore damage to the insula will disrupt addiction. Their focus on the insula is justified by the fact that it plays a key role in processing emotion and is associated with representation of bodily states/conscious urges/

emotional feelings. Also, activity in the insula is shown to correlate with subjective cue-induced drug urges.

To test their hypotheses, Naqvi *et al.* conducted a study of sixty-nine lesion patients, all smokers, nineteen of whom had insula damage – six patients with right insula damage and thirteen with left insula damage. The remaining fifty smokers had lesions but no insula damage. From patients' responses to questionnaires about their habit, they found that there were significant disruptions to smoking in four situations: first, if the subject had reported quitting less than a day after lesion onset; second, if they did not start smoking again after they quit; third, if they had low ratings on difficulty of quitting; and fourth, if they reported no urges to smoke since quitting. They estimated the probability of smoking disruption for insula damage patients and noninsula damage patients with an odds ratio of 22.05 a probability value of $p = 0.0005$. Smoking disruption was twenty-two times more likely if a patient had an insula lesion versus a lesion elsewhere.

Specifically for the extent of smoking disruption in quitters, twelve of thirteen insula patients had smoking disruption and four of nineteen patients with noninsula damage had smoking disruption, giving an odds ratio of 136.46 ($p = 0.00008$). The insula damage patients were 136 times more likely to give up smoking. Some patients also had damage to adjacent areas, and there were also significant effects if they had suffered damage to the dorsal striatum (putamen). There were no similar results for other behaviours such as eating, perhaps because smoking is a learned response and people have to learn to overcome the aversive effects. Overall, patients with insula damage were significantly more likely to quit smoking easily and to remain abstinent. One patient observed that he quit because his 'body forgot the urge to smoke'. Naqvi *et al.* conclude that the insula is a critical neural substrate in nicotine addiction

Post-mortem studies

Hope *et al.* (2007) analysed post-mortem brain tissue from human smokers and former smokers, looking at enzyme levels in different areas of the brain. They found elevated levels in the nucleus accumbens (part of the ventral striatum) and ventral midbrain dopaminergic regions. Enzymes are associated with activation of the reward system and stimulate dopamine receptors in the nucleus accumbens. They found higher enzyme levels in ventral midbrain dopaminergic regions for smokers and former smokers, which suggests that repeated use of addictive drugs caused changes in the dopamine system and target neurons in the nucleus accumbens. This also suggests that smoking-induced brain neuro-adaptations can persist for long periods, which would explain frequent relapses in former smokers.

Case study: healthy lifestyles

One of the key policy issues of our time is declining health reflecting lifestyle choices, including bad eating habits, excessive alcohol consumption and insufficient exercise. These problems reflect the fact that we are not always good at doing things that are unpleasant in the short term, even when they deliver good outcomes in the long run. We are susceptible to present bias, lack of self-control, temptation and procrastination.

Parkin *et al.* (2011) estimate the fraction of cancers in the UK in 2010 that could be attributable to exposures to lifestyle and environmental risk factors, and therefore were to some extent preventable. As shown in Figure 10.3, tobacco was the major risk factor, but diet and lifestyle factors, including low consumption of fruit and vegetables, excessive consumption of alcohol, salt and red meat together with insufficient exercise and being

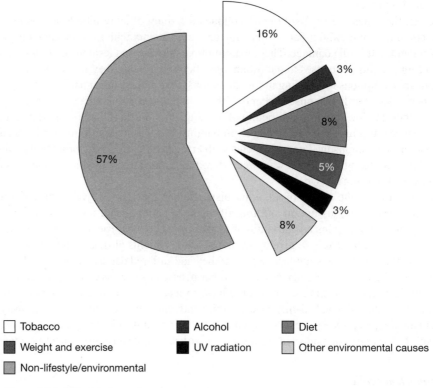

Tobacco

Alcohol

Diet

Weight and exercise

UV radiation

Other environmental causes

Non-lifestyle/environmental

Figure 10.3 Life style impacts on cancer rates

overweight/obese were also major risk factors.[1]

The data depicted in Figure 10.3 are probably not too much of a surprise. We all know which bad habits we should avoid: smoking; eating too much fat and sugar; drinking too much alcohol and/or caffeine; not getting enough exercise – a sedentary habit. There have been numerous studies of unhealthy behaviours that have significant impacts on people's lives. Social norms play a key role, for alcohol and marijuana consumption as well as cigarette smoking (Hansen and Graham 1991; Haines and Spear 1996; Thombs *et al.* 1997).

Adler and Stewart (2009) identify a range of factors affecting obesity, including an 'obesogenic' environment: areas where healthy fresh food is difficult to find but unhealthy takeaway food is quickly available. In addition, this unhealthy food is often advertised using cues designed to exploit impulsive visceral instincts. These insights add weight to Laibson, Loewenstein, and Smith and Tasnádi's analysis of the impact of environment cues on addictive behaviours. Solutions focus on making healthy food more widely available, particularly for children. A range of initiatives have emerged, including healthy school meals campaigns in the UK and USA, championed by UK chef Jamie Oliver and focusing on providing children with access to healthy school food.

Belot and James (2009) analysed the impacts of Jamie Oliver's campaigns by studying the impact of diet on educational performance. They compared the performance of primary school children at schools in Greenwich, London. Jamie Oliver's 'Feed Me Better' school meals campaign was launched in some Greenwich schools. The quality of school meals was improved by reducing the volume of processed foods and increasing the provision of fruit, vegetables and water and healthy, freshly cooked food. The performance of children at these schools was compared with performance by a control group of children at schools not participating in the Feed Me Better campaign. For children in the treatment group, educational outcomes improved significantly and absenteeism fell. Jamie Oliver's campaigns had similar beneficial effects elsewhere, including in the USA, and focused not only on increasing the quality of food, but also on changing some of the social norms surrounding people's attitudes towards food and healthy eating.

Bad health habits: not going to the gym

For most people, getting enough exercise is one aspect of a healthy lifestyle that can be particularly hard to maintain. One potential solution is to buy a gym membership, and this is usually offered in the form of a contract. Standard economic approaches to contract choice assume that people choose from a 'menu' of contracts using a rational, optimizing approach incorporating exponential discounting. But DellaVigna and Malmendier's gym evidence shows that this does not happen in the real world. DellaVigna and Malmendier's (2006) study of gym membership/use shows people paying far more for annual and monthly gym membership plans than is justifiable given their infrequent attendance. They analyse a natural experiment on gym membership which showed that people seem to be willing to pay *not* to go the gym.

DellaVigna and Malmendier assess data from three New England health clubs including detailed attendance data for 7752 and 8273 enrolment spells, focusing their analysis on the first enrolment spell. They also assess survey evidence from ninety-seven health clubs. They analyse three choices facing people signing up for gym membership: pay-as-you-go; an annual flat-rate contract; or a monthly flat-rate contract. Standard theory would predict that price per expected attendance should be lower for those signing up to a flat-rate contract than for those using pay-per-visit. If gym-goers are perfectly rational then the expected number of visits under the annual contract should exceed the expected number of visits under the monthly contract; average forecasts of attendance should equal average actual attendance; low attenders should delay cancellation for a few days at most; people signing up for an annual contract should have larger survival probabilities, i.e. should remain as gym members for longer.

From their analyses of health club data, DellaVigna and Malmendier found limited evidence to support predictions of a rational gym-goer. The average price per visit was over $17 for monthly contracts and $15 on annual contracts, yet the pay-per-visit fee was significantly lower at $10. Consumers choosing monthly membership paid on average 70 per cent more than if they were on the pay-as-you-go contract. Average attendance in months two to four was 10 per cent higher under the annual contract than the monthly contract. The average *forecast* of attendance was more than twice as large as *actual* attendance for monthly contracts. The average cancellation lag was 2.31 months between last attendance and cancellation for monthly members. Survival probability (share still enrolled at fifteen months) was estimated using probit (conditioned on gender, age, etc.). People on a monthly contract were 17 per cent more likely to stay enrolled beyond a year, even though they paid higher fees (than for the annual contract) for the option to cancel each month. Most of these findings were inconsistent with a rational optimizing approach.

DellaVigna and Malmendier suggest a number of behavioural explanations for the apparently anomalous behaviour of gym-goers. Their decisions may have reflected risk aversion: a flat-rate contract minimizes variance of payments. Transaction costs of daily payments may have created a preference for flat-rate contracts. For flat-rate contracts, there were additional membership benefits including psychological benefits. Preferences varied over time, and whilst there was rational updating, it was slow. Limited memory might have meant that people forgot to cancel their memberships. If health club employees are incentivized to sell the more expensive flat-rate contracts, then persuasion might also have had an impact on the gym-goers' choices.

The behaviour can also be explained using different assumptions about intertemporal decision-making. Seemingly paradoxical choices may reflect pre-commitment strategies. Sophisticated consumers may have realized that they were vulnerable to problems of time inconsistency and so tied themselves using a pre-commitment devices. By paying relatively large sums of money up front, they were hoping to encourage their future selves into going to the gym more often. Time inconsistency may also explain the results for the naïve gym-goers. If initial attendance reflected over-confidence about future self-control then they overestimated net benefits, perhaps reflecting projection bias and the anchoring heuristic.

At the same time, there may be heterogeneity in over-confidence. Users paying a high price per visit on monthly contract are also the ones with a longer cancellation lag. Overall, DellaVigna and Malmendier's findings suggest that observed health choices do not match actual behaviours, generating biases in decision-making. An important policy implication is that in the fight against obesity, it isn't enough just to subsidize health clubs because there is no guarantee that, just because people have a gym membership, they will actually go to the gym.

Conclusions and policy implications

Addiction and other bad habits reflect a complex interaction of economic and psychological factors. In the rational addiction models of Becker, Grossman and Murphy, addiction is a voluntary choice but does nonetheless generate externalities and other forms of market failure. Rational addiction models do not, however, rest easily with our intuitions about addiction. The fact that addicts are often very keen to kick their habits suggests that the roots of addiction are more complex than rational addiction theorists allow. Addiction is more likely to be the product of present bias and lack of self-control, exacerbated by neurobiological factors which increase a person's susceptibility to visceral cues.

In terms of policy implications, the rational addiction theorists have analysed a range of policy implications, as discussed above. Becker *et al.* (1994) assert that poorer and less educated groups are more responsive to prices, and if legalization lowers prices then addictions will get worse, not better. Richer, more educated groups with lower discount rates are more likely to respond to information campaigns about future consequences. Wars on drugs may lead to temporary price rises but, given expectations of future price falls once the war on drugs is over, impacts will be limited. Monopolistic tobacco manufacturers should be regulated because they are able to exploit addictive behaviour to increase long-term profits. Gruber and Köszegi explain that optimal taxation should be designed to remove externalities from smoking, but if 'internalities' are also generated, then optimal excise taxes on tobacco should be higher to reflect these internalities.

Bernheim and Rangel suggest a range of policy implications following from their analysis of cues and hot–cold systems, as described above. They do not advocate limits on planned use because this reflects voluntary, reasoned choice. Instead, they focus on policies that control the influence of the cue triggers precipitating impulsive consumption, particularly for people in hot, emotionally charged states. Alongside standard policy approaches focusing on reducing externalities and improving information and education about addictive substances, they advocate some more novel policy prescriptions. Uncertainty is a particularly profound problem for addicts because it is impossible to predict environmental cues that might trigger self-destructive behaviour, and this generates significant monetary risks in terms of the financial consequences from random environmental events. Universal insurance policies would reduce these risks. Rehabilitation should be subsidized and distribution should be controlled via prescription. Advertising and marketing restrictions alongside controls on public use will reduce the frequency of cues and will help to reduce impulsive use of addictive substances. Counter-cues, such as including photographs of diseased lungs on cigarette packaging, may also be effective.

Another approach is to use tools developed from standard economic approaches adapted to take into account some of the behavioural and psychological factors discussed in this chapter. Loewenstein and Ubel (2010) argue that too much is claimed for behavioural economics, and suggest policies that blend insights from the rational addiction theorists with those from the behavioural economists. Behavioural economics might provide some guidance about the need to subsidize unsweetened drinks or tax sugary ones, but standard economics will tell us that we need a large price difference between the two.

Different addictions and self-destructive behaviours may need different solutions. Taxation may play an important role, but social influences may also have a significant influence. Policies such as smoking bans will have positive impacts for a number of reasons, not only because they reduce the incidence of passive smoking and reduce the cues that might trigger a relapse in an ex-smoker, but also because smoking is removed from a social context facilitating the evolution of a new nonsmoking social norm. Overall, if we can develop a deeper understanding of the complex roots and causes of self-destructive behaviours, then this will enable governments to tailor policies more effectively to the particular features of specific addictions.

Note

1 Some of the factors will contribute jointly to cancer incidence; for the purposes of the pie chart, the environmental/lifestyle factors were weighted as a proportion of total lifestyle/environmental cancer risk in order to ensure the risks sum to 1.

Part 3

Macroeconomics and financial markets

11 Financial instability

Introduction

Financial instability is one of the most pressing problems of our time and is affected by a complex nexus of financial, economic and political forces. From the 1960s onwards, standard approaches focused increasingly on assumptions of rational expectations and efficient financial markets (Muth 1961; Fama 1965). The actions of homogeneous, independent, self-interested individuals were assumed to be coordinated effectively via the 'invisible hand' of the price mechanism. Traders were assumed to use information efficiently, systematically and consistently, forming expectations rationally by avoiding systematic mistakes. Asset prices would equilibrate towards the true fundamental values, where the fundamental value is defined as the discounted stream of expected future returns: for example, in the case of a stock/share this is the discounted stream of expected future dividends. Given the liquid, fast-moving nature of financial markets, it was also assumed that speculative noise trading would have no significant impact because arbitrage would eliminate it and asset prices would adjust fully to reflect all currently available information. Allowing for differences in risk across assets, an asset's price was assumed to be an unbiased indicator of its fundamental value given its risk profile.

Financial crises have always been common and are difficult to reconcile with assumptions of rational expectations and efficient markets. From the 1990s, a growing number of economists were working on innovations in financial theory, particularly focusing on asymmetric information and principal–agent problems. In addition, economists including Kindleberger, Shiller and Shleifer were analysing problems of mob psychology, panics and irrational exuberance to explain the roots of financial crisis focusing on phenomena such as herding alongside problems of policy mismanagement (Shiller 2000; Shleifer 2000; Kindleberger and Aliber 2005). These endeavours were given extra momentum following the bailout of Northern Rock in 2007, the collapse of Lehman Brothers in 2008 and the ensuing financial crises. It became clear to almost everyone that approaches based on strict assumptions of rational expectations and efficient markets were unlikely to deepen our understanding of financial crisis, and analysis shifted to focus on a wider range of explanations for financial crises, including regulatory failures, leveraging enabled by excessive liquidity, asymmetric information and fundamental uncertainty.

At the same time, behavioural finance explanations received a boost because erratic financial market fluctuations can be captured more easily by admitting that behavioural and psychological factors place limits on rational trading. Speculative bubbles – persistent deviations in asset prices away from fundamental long-term value – are an essential feature of financial instability. If markets are efficient and people are rational, then mistakes should cancel out on average, and asset prices will track fundamental values. Behavioural finance can explain how and why speculation emerges and spreads to create financial instability.

In this chapter, a range of concepts from behavioural economics and finance are used to analyse the forces underlying financial instability. This analysis will focus on the microeconomic behavioural foundations outlined in chapters 4 to 10, including herding, learning and social influence; heuristics, biases and prospect theory; moods and emotions; and poor intertemporal planning.

Herding, learning and social influences

Herding is endemic within financial markets, especially during uncertain times, and will lead to asset bubbles/trending in asset prices because speculative decisions are disproportionately focused on short-term outcomes: the long-term value of an asset is unimportant if you intend to sell the asset quickly (Keynes 1936, p. 156). This insight is important because it suggests that if time horizons are short, discount rates are high and financial markets are very liquid, then speculative bubbles generate negative herding externalities, in which case the social costs of liquid financial markets may be disproportionately high.

In standard approaches, new information rather than group behaviour influences changes in asset prices (Muth 1961; Fama 1965). Herding in financial markets generates speculative bubbles when traders are tracking the decisions of others, not the fundamental value of assets. This phenomenon undermines strict assumptions of efficiency and rationality, but complementary macroeconomic analyses build on rationality assumptions to construct models of herding and imitation, for example Topol's (1991) analysis of mimetic contagion in financial markets.

Weaker rationality assumptions can be maintained if herding is still the outcome of calculations based on mathematical algorithms. In Bayesian models, for example, prior probability judgments are being updated systematically and logically using others' actions as new information arrives (see chapter 4; Banerjee 1992; Bikhchandani *et al.* 1992; Chamley 2003). From a Bayesian perspective, a rational agent will use every bit of available information, including social information about the actions of others. Herding can be understood as an extension of principles of rational behaviour whilst nonetheless allowing that human actions are not necessarily independent.

Bayesian models explain herding in the form of information cascades, as a process of sequential learning on a microeconomic scale with people updating probabilities sequentially as the decisions of other individuals are revealed. On a macroeconomic scale, financial herding cannot easily be explained as the outcome of a sequential Bayesian process, and is a more general phenomenon occurring when people respond to social influences by following the group or herd. This will necessarily generate a violation of strict forms of the efficient markets hypothesis, because this hypothesis precludes the systematic trends generated by herding in assuming that all changes are unpredictable and asset prices follow random walks.

Keynes (1936, 1937) pioneered the study of social influences in financial markets, perhaps partly a reflection of his financial trading expertise. He blended economics, psychology and finance, explaining financial instability as the outcome of the socio-psychological forces, focusing on three main reasons why people follow the crowd in a world of uncertainty: social learning, beauty contests and reputation.

Social learning

Keynes (1930, 1936, 1937) described herding in financial markets as a response to uncertainty and individuals' perceptions of their own ignorance. Herding will be the outcome of social learning when people follow the crowd because they think that the rest of the crowd is better informed. In this way, market fluctuations are driven by conventional beliefs rather than fundamental values. Instability emerges because herding affects the general state of business confidence and also generates self-fulfilling prophecies and speculative episodes. Keynes argues that, during financial speculation, people will purchase an asset at a seemingly exorbitant price not because they independently believe that the object is worth the cost, but because they believe that other people think that it is.

Whilst herding means that conventional beliefs will hold sway for sustained periods, during episodes of extreme uncertainty financial markets will become very fragile. Investors and speculators will respond in a volatile way to ephemeral changes in information because decisions and choices do not have a substantive basis (Keynes 1936, pp. 153–54). This generates social costs: whilst it may be rational for individuals to copy others, if copying and herding spreads through large groups of people, then volatile speculative episodes will become more likely. Given uncertainty, if people are learning about financial assets from looking at others' trades, then herding may be the outcome of a rational learning; but it may also be irrational if it is propelled by blind convention and unreasoning speculative frenzies.

Beauty contests

Financial beauty contests were first used by Keynes to describe the second-guessing that characterizes financial speculation. Keynes's beauty contest is a newspaper competition: competitors are asked to select from a series of photos not who they think is prettiest, but who they think others will think is prettiest, or who they think others will think others will think is prettiest. It is a metaphor for the iterated reasoning that characterizes financial speculation. Speculators are not worrying about what they think an asset is worth; they are more interested in tracking short-term judgments of others and so are more focused on average opinions of average opinion.

Given the fast, liquid nature of financial markets, speculators have no reason to worry about the long-term fundamental value of an asset because they intend to sell it quickly. To make money out of speculation in highly liquid and fast-moving markets, it is important to judge what the crowd is thinking, and to follow it when you think that market valuations of assets are going to increase in value, even though you may privately think that they are over-priced. So people buy assets at seemingly exorbitant prices not because they independently believe that the asset is fundamentally worth its price, but because they believe they can sell it to someone else for an even higher price. This helps to explain why, throughout history, people have frequently been observed buying seemingly over-priced assets, whether tulip bulbs during Tulipmania, houses during housing booms, or dotcom shares during internet bubbles.

As explained in chapter 4, analyses of beauty contests have been used in microeconomic models of learning to capture the links between imitation and iterative thinking, for example see Camerer and Weigelt (1991); Camerer (1997, 2003b); Ho *et al.* (1998); Bhatt and Camerer (2005). Similar models of imitation explain irrational imitative behaviour as an outcome of the expectation that *others* will behave irrationally (Porter and Smith 1995). With beauty contests, financial instability will increase because asset prices will be susceptible to feedback loops and, if borrowings are used to fund asset purchases, instability will be magnified by leverage. Leveraging can have a destabilizing impact even on experienced traders. Porter and Smith (2008) devise experiments that incorporate increases in liquidity and dividend uncertainty as shocks to the environments of experienced subjects. By introducing credit into asset markets in this way, experienced subjects can be repeatedly jolted away from equilibrium rekindling and sustaining speculative bubbles.

Beauty contests can also be linked to payoff externalities and reflexivity. When a person buys an asset, this contributes to rising demand and increasing prices, and these generate payoff externalities for all holders of the asset, including the buyer. Reflexivity describes a related phenomenon characterizing systems affected by feedback loops and simultaneity. Cause and effect cannot be separated, and markets will be prone to endogenously determined market fluctuations. Soros (1987) applies the concept of reflexivity to financial markets; in financial systems, reflexivity is manifested in speculative episodes in which rises in asset prices lead to further rises. When financial traders herd behind others, trends will develop, propagating mistakes through financial markets and changing individuals' perceptions of market fundamentals. Mistakes will not be random but instead will feed on themselves, generating self-fulfilling prophecies. When speculators follow trends, these biases will spread: for example, share prices fall because speculators believe they will fall, and so they do fall.

Reputation

Herding often emerges as the outcome of reputational concerns. If a trader takes risks and performs poorly, they will be less likely to lose their job and/or bonus if other traders have been taking the same risks. There is job security in numbers. Keynes postulated that it is rational to follow the crowd and herd if it helps you to maintain a good reputation, observing that it is better to fail conventionally than to succeed unconventionally (Keynes 1936, pp. 157–58). Scharfstein and Stein (1990) apply this insight to explain herding by investment managers.

Following in Keynes's footsteps, other influential economists (including Minsky 1975; Shiller 1995, 2000; Kindleberger and Aliber 2005) have analysed the socio-psychological impacts of emotional contagion and financial fragility, identifying the speculative euphoria which spreads through groups of investors during manic phases as a crucial catalyst in economic and financial booms; in turn, excessive pessimism and extreme risk aversion precipitate bust phases.

Heuristics, biases and prospect theory

Speculative bubbles and financial instability reflect an incomplete process of arbitrage: assets do not trade and markets do not clear at prices reflecting assets' fundamental values. There are a number of observed market phenomena confirming that excess returns are not arbitraged away, including seasonality effects, January effects, Monday effects, Labor Day effects, etc. Specifically in the context of equity markets, Barberis and Thaler (2005) describe a series of puzzles that characterize the historical performance of US stock markets: the equity premium puzzle – stocks have earned disproportionately high returns and yet investors are relatively unwilling to hold them; the volatility puzzle – stock returns are very variable with large dispersions; and the predictability puzzle – stock returns are predictable, suggesting that persistent profits are not being eroded by arbitrage.

These puzzles would not persist if financial markets were efficient because asset price changes would be inherently unpredictable. A rational arbitrageur would spot opportunities for profit, would buy assets that were undervalued and, because financial markets move so quickly, any potential gains would quickly disappear leaving asset prices to follow a random walk.

Overall, limits to arbitrage can be explained in terms of misapplied heuristics and/or prospect theory.

Anufriev and Hommes (2007) explore bounded rationality in financial trading experiments, and observe that traders use a small set of simple heuristics, including adaptive expectations, trend following and anchoring/adjustment. With learning, selection of simple forecasting heuristics evolves reflecting the forecasting performance of those heuristics, and this generates path dependence. Developing these insights, Thoma (unpublished, 2011) finds that increases in herding parameters generate speculative bubbles.

Thaler and others analyse behavioural financial anomalies using insights from Tversky and Kahneman's (1974) analysis of heuristics and biases, and Kahneman and Tversky's (1979) prospect theory. (The finer details of these general approaches are explained in chapters 6 and 7.) There is a wide range of heuristics and biases specifically affecting financial markets, and some of the more commonly identified financial biases are explored below. For a fuller analysis of heuristics and biases in financial markets, see Thaler (2005) for a comprehensive compilation of analyses.

Over-reactions and under-reactions

de Bondt and Thaler (1985) identify empirical evidence about over-reactions in financial markets. They analysed monthly returns between 1926 and 1982 for portfolios of thirty-five New York Stock Exchange common stocks. They sorted these portfolios on the basis of historical performance into winner and loser portfolios. Standard assumptions of rational agents and efficient markets generate a prediction that there should be no systematic tendency for either a winner or loser portfolio to outperform other portfolios because all relevant information should already be captured by asset prices. Yet de Bondt and Thaler identified that loser portfolios outperformed the market by 19.6 per cent on average, and winner portfolios earned 5 per cent less than the market on average. The over-reaction observed was asymmetric and was larger for loser portfolios than for winner portfolios. Also, de Bondt and Thaler found turn-of-year effects and seasonality, consistent with other analyses: over-reaction was most common in the second and third years of the test period. They conclude that these anomalies reflect over-shooting of fundamental values as a reaction to dramatic and unexpected news about particular stocks, with the over-shooting followed by a gradual reversion to mean.

Over-confidence and over-reactions

Hong and Stein (1999) draw on attribution theory in attributing over-reactions to over-confidence and self-attribution biases. People tend to ascribe success to their own talents and ability, but will attribute adverse events to 'noise and sabotage'. Similarly, Barberis and Thaler (2005) identify two aspects to over-confidence in financial markets: people underestimate the variance of asset returns, leading to confidence intervals that are too narrow; and probabilities are poorly calibrated, with people overestimating the probabilities of events that are very likely and underestimating the probability of events that are relatively improbable. Barberis and Thaler also note that over-confidence can reflect hindsight bias as well as self-attribution bias: after an event, people believe that they had predicted it beforehand (a common phenomenon in the fallout from recent financial crises). Barberis and Thaler also observe that confirmation biases may lead people to falsely assess contradictory evidence as confirmation of their prior hypotheses; in academic finance, people start with a belief in the efficient markets hypothesis and continue to believe it even in the face of contradictory evidence. Tuckett also addresses this type of effect in the context of a psychoanalytical approach to emotional finance, described below.

Over-reaction and over-confidence is observed not only in the decisions of financial traders, but also amongst householders when they overestimate their future ability to repay mortgages/payday loans/credit card bills, even though they are struggling to pay their bills today. When this pattern is repeated on a macroeconomic scale and interacts with other financial market rigidities, then it can precipitate financial instability, as was seen during the US subprime mortgage crisis.

Under-reactions and the representativeness heuristic

Barberis *et al.* (1998) also analyse *under-reactions* to good news and attribute them to conservatism and/or misapplications of Tversky and Kahneman's (1974) representativeness heuristic. With conservatism, people are slow to change their beliefs in response to new information, and so whilst individuals may use Bayes's rule to adjust their expectations, they adjust too slowly. Conservatism may lead people to disregard publicly available information, especially if it contradicts their private beliefs.

As explained in chapter 6, the representativeness heuristic can also lead people into gambler's fallacy and/or neglecting sample sizes and base rate probabilities, exacerbating biases in financial decision-making. Barberis *et al.* (1998) identify the representativeness heuristic as a source of under-reaction occurring when people focus disproportionately on recently observed prices or prices paid by others because they perceive them to be more representative of expected future prices. As well as leading to under-reactions, representativeness may lead people into a gambler's fallacy in which they expect a particular asset to 'win' just because it has been a loser in the past. Sample size neglect may encourage traders to focus on spurious patterns in very short series or small samples of financial data; for example, people may over-rate the advice of a financial analyst who has picked a small, unrepresentative number of winning stocks (Barberis and Thaler 2005).

Diversification biases and the availability heuristic

Financial instability may also be exacerbated by misapplications of Tversky and Kahneman's (1974) availability heuristic, also described in chapter 6. People base decisions on recently available information and forget more distant, less salient events. During speculative episodes, they may remember only recent high prices, intensifying speculative euphoria. The availability heuristic and related familiarity biases can also lead to insufficient diversification, and a common manifestation of this is home bias – the tendency for investors to hold a disproportionate number of domestically denominated assets in their portfolios. Various studies have identified home bias. French and Poterba (1991) found that Japanese, UK and US investors held 98, 82 and 92 per cent, respectively, of their equity investments in domestic equities. Barberis and Thaler (2005) attribute home bias to the role played by familiarity in the availability heuristic: information about domestic markets is more immediately available, familiar and salient.

Diversification biases can also emerge from choice bracketing. Thaler (1999) describes an experiment exploring children's behaviour during Halloween trick-or-treating. Children were offered opportunities to pick two treats, either simultaneously at one house or sequentially at two different houses. More diversification was observed if the children were picking two treats simultaneously. Thaler concludes that when choices are bracketed together, people will opt for diversification. Benartzi and Thaler (2001) assert that a similar approach of naïve diversification characterizes financial markets when people apply the '$1/n$ heuristic'. When there are n investment opportunities, people will spread their budgets evenly with $1/n$ of their funds allocated to each opportunity; the relative merits of the opportunities and/or investor's initial preferences will be ignored.

In financial decisions, when people are offered a range of investment vehicles then they will apply the $1/n$ heuristic by dividing their funds evenly across the investment vehicles even when one consistently outperforms the others. Benartzi and Thaler (2001) analysed the $1/n$ heuristic using experimental techniques. They asked their experimental subjects to make choices in three different experimental treatments. In the first treatment, subjects chose between a stock fund and a bond fund; in a second treatment, they chose between a stock fund and a balanced fund, the latter comprising 50 per cent stocks and 50 per cent bonds; and in the third treatment, the subjects chose between a bond fund and a balanced fund. Benartzi and Thaler observed naïve diversification across the two choices offered regardless of what those two choices were, and so the proportion of funds allocated to stocks varied depending on the pair of choices offered. With a simple choice between stocks and bonds, 54 per cent was invested in stocks; with a choice between stocks versus a balance of stocks on bonds, 73 per cent was invested in stocks; with a choice between bonds and a balance of stocks and bonds, 35 per cent was invested in stocks. Standard financial theory predicts that people's stock allocations will be determined purely by a person's preference for stocks and, whilst these preferences will be shaped by risk attitudes, they should not be affected by the arbitrary pairing of choices.

Momentum trading

Bounds on rationality may lead traders to adopt simple heuristics in their trading decisions, and this can fuel momentum trading in which traders respond to market momentum rather than fundamental values, for example by buying into rising markets. Hong and Stein (1999) analyse momentum trading assuming two types of traders: news-watchers, who make their decisions on the basis of private information and news, ignoring past prices; and momentum traders, who engage in positive feedback trading and buy assets in response to increasing prices in those assets. With positive news stories, momentum may start to develop in the market, partly reflecting the impact of good news on the trading of news-watchers; however, given the presence of momentum traders, price rises will be magnified and will last long past the point at which prices attain fundamental values. Once doubt sets in amongst the momentum traders, the bubble will burst and price reversals will precipitate destabilizing over-reactions as traders rush to sell.

Prospect theory, loss aversion and ambiguity aversion

Some of the biases seen in financial markets can be explained in the context of Kahneman and Tversky's (1979) prospect theory. As explained in chapters 6 and 7, Tversky and Kahneman (1974) analyse anchoring and adjustment around reference points and these insights are incorporated into Kahneman and Tversky's (1979) prospect theory. Prospect theory postulates that perceptions of value are affected by changes relative to a reference point. Anchoring to subjectively determined reference points will mean that people's expectations will be slow to adjust, leading to sustained speculative episodes. Subjective perceptions will also be prone to framing effects: choices are determined by the context or frame within which decisions are made, and this is consistent with Thaler's (1985, 1999) analysis of framing within mental accounting models (also explored in chapter 7) and Shefrin's (2002) analysis of frame dependence in financial markets.

Loss aversion and the equity premium puzzle

In prospect theory, loss aversion occurs when judgments made relative to a reference point, and losses are disproportionately painful relative to the pleasure from gains. Kahneman and Tversky's prospect theory value function reflects the fact that losses are overweighted relative to gains and, in financial markets, this may lead investors and traders to hold onto assets even as asset prices are falling in order to avoid loss. When the current state of the world is used as a reference point, loss aversion will interact with anchoring, generating *status quo* bias and familiarity bias favouring the current state of the world and/or things that are already familiar. Endowment effects will also distort people's valuations of objects (see chapters 6 and 7). People will over-value things that they already own, leading to divergences between willingness to pay and willingness to accept: they will pay less for an object that they don't yet own than they will accept when selling the same object that they already own.

Loss aversion and endowment effects will have impacts on sale decisions within financial markets and also in housing markets. Traders/speculators will not sell shares and homeowners do not sell their houses even when, financially, it would be wise to do so (Odean 1998; Genesove and Mayer 2001). Shefrin and Statman (1985) also identify a tendency for people to sell winning stocks too easily whilst riding losers to too long, which may be a reflection of loss aversion. Benartzi and Thaler (1995) analyse short-termism together with loss aversion in an analysis of myopic loss aversion as an explanation for the equity premium puzzle, defined above as the persistence of relatively high returns on equities. Mehra and Prescott (1985) observe that, over the period 1889–1978, the average yield on Standard & Poor's 500 Index was 7 per cent, six points higher than the yields on short-term debt, which were less than 1 per cent over the same period.

Thaler *et al.* (1997) analyse myopic loss aversion, arguing that it reflects a disproportionate sensitivity to losses relative to gains combined with frequent evaluations of outcomes. They formulate two hypotheses. First, with myopic loss aversion, investors will accept risks more willingly if the frequency with which they can evaluate investments is limited, and they may accept more risk if they evaluate their investments less often. Second, if all payoffs are gains and losses are eliminated, then investors will accept more risk.

Thaler *et al.* test these hypotheses experimentally using a task in which investors have the opportunity to learn from experience. They find that investors who can access feedback and information more frequently are more likely to avoid risk, but these risk-averse investors earned the lowest returns. Gneezy and Potters (1997) also argue that myopic loss aversion can explain the equity premium puzzle and the marketing strategies of fund managers. When investors evaluate returns more frequently, they become more risk averse. This is consistent with myopic loss aversion: people focus on short-term patterns when evaluating outcomes over time and are more sensitive to losses than to gains. Myopic loss aversion can help to explain the equity premium puzzle.

Ambiguity aversion and the Ellsberg paradox

Ambiguity aversion and the Ellsberg paradox (described in chapter 7) can also be captured within prospect theory. In the probability weighting function of Kahneman and Tversky's prospect theory, ambiguity is discounted, and certain probabilities are overweighted. Barberis and Thaler (2005) observe that ambiguity aversion will be a particular problem for financial markets because the probability distribution of asset returns is unknown. Condie *et al.* analyse ambiguity aversion in the context of Knightian uncertainty using simulation techniques. Ambiguous information is often ignored within financial markets because traders exit or various forms of bias lead traders to ignore ambiguity in the data.

Condie and Ganguli (2011) explore models incorporating ambiguity aversion when partial information is revealed. These insights can be applied to show that ambiguity aversion in financial markets leads to phenomena not observed in standard models, including increased trading volume and volatility, large price swings, and 'bad' signals not revealed to the market.

Overall, the range of biases and heuristics identified above will mean that financial markets do not automatically correct to fundamental values in the face of shocks. Various behavioural biases will lead to persistence and path dependency in asset prices. DeLong *et al.* (1991) show that noise traders can dominate markets, and their errors are not necessarily corrected. This can have a strong impact because there will be no tendency for real-world traders to correct their errors. These biases may interact with socio-economic factors such as herding, as explored above, and also with psychological and emotional factors, as explored below.

Time and instability

In addition to other forms of bias, financial instability will be exacerbated by present bias and distortions to intertemporal preferences. In mainstream analysis, short-termism/impatience can be captured by high discount rates, but recent developments in behavioural economics and finance have developed a richer understanding of preference reversals and time inconsistency. Present bias can be captured by replacing the conventional assumption of exponential discounting with an assumption of 'hyperbolic' or 'quasi-hyperbolic' discounting – as explored in chapter 9 (see also Laibson 1997; Thaler and Shefrin 1981; Angeletos *et al.* 2001; Frederick *et al.* 2002). Angeletos *et al.* (2001) construct behavioural life-cycle models based on quasi-hyperbolic discounting, capturing the fact that people hold onto large stores of illiquid wealth (often in the form of housing) whilst simultaneously running up large credit card debts at punitive interest rates.

In a computerized world, people may procrastinate in protecting themselves from exploitation and fraud, for example, they may procrastinate about setting up proper protections when using the internet for financial transactions. In terms of saving for the future, a person may have good intentions but, in the short term, may be unable to resist immediately available alternatives, reflecting problems of temptation and procrastination. The problem will be magnified when present bias reacts with other forms of bias, particularly overoptimism, leading people to be tempted into financial choices that are too good to be true, such as payday loans.

A large volume of experimental evidence from experimental psychology as well as economics shows that individuals' discount functions are not stable and people tend to exhibit disproportionate impatience in the short run. The standard exponential discounting model predicts that if a person is making a choice in two situations, then those choices should be stable over time. Experimental evidence shows people preferring to take rewards sooner when choosing for the short term than when deciding over longer time horizons. For example, Warner and Pleeter's (2001) study of financial choices by US military personnel shows preferences for lump sum payments over annuities, reflecting present bias. Warner and Pleeter also find that different choices correlate with individual differences in age, education and military rank.

The consequences of short-termism in household decision-making are not confined to the householder alone. It may have consequences for financial stability more generally when the aggregated build-up of household debt becomes unsustainable in the short term. Short-termism, time inconsistency and cognitive bias may limit people's ability to make judicious financial decisions, and if macroeconomic factors further undermine their ability to service their debts, either because they lose their job and/or they have taken on unsustainable forms of debt, such as payday loans, then this will exacerbate and prolong household financial problems, making default more likely. As householders default, the contagion spreads to their lenders and financial institutions more widely, with negative impacts for the financial system and macroeconomy, as was seen in the fallout to the subprime crisis in the USA and also as housing bubbles burst in other OECD countries during the credit crunch of 2007/08 onwards.

Moods, emotions and personality

As explored in chapter 8, decision-making, emotion and affect (the experience of feeling an emotion) are all intertwined in the economic and financial world, but until recently economic analysis has neglected the role of emotions in economic decision-making (Elster 1996, 1998). Emotions will affect financial decision-making, and will contribute to volatility if they weaken the link between asset prices and fundamental values and thereby increase susceptibility to bullish asset bubbles and bearish busts.

The emotions most commonly identified as contributing to financial fragility include greed, hope and fear (Shefrin 2002). Slovic *et al.* (2004) and Slovic (2010) characterize risk as a feeling, and the risk felt during financial trading can be characterized as a feeling of fear with feedback effects and reflexivity intensifying fear responses and precipitating panics. Other emotions will affect financial decisions more broadly, for example, the irrational exuberance seen in bullish markets may reflect an interaction of hope and greed (Shiller 2000, 2003). Financial markets are also susceptible to social influence, as explained above, and tendencies to herd may reflect socialization processes reinforcing group pressure and instinctive, inbuilt mechanisms to imitate. When individual panics precipitate 'social panics', this may reflect interplays of risk, anxiety and fear (Loewenstein *et al.* 2007).

Emotional factors will also play a role via heuristics, particularly the availability and affect heuristics. In a fast-moving environment, the vividness of emotions will make them more salient: they are remembered more easily. Emotions also connect with other forms of bias, including ambiguity aversion, described by Shefrin (2002) as fear of the unknown. This dominance of emotions may reflect interactions between decision-making systems. Financial traders are often making decisions at great speed which involve very high stakes, and in this sort of context hot, intuitive, automatic emotional systems are more likely to prevail over cold, reasoning, deliberative cognitive systems.

Lo *et al.* (2005) separate the impact of mood and personality on financial decision-making by day traders by correlating responses to daily surveys of emotions and personality with traders' profit-and-loss records for day traders. Subjects with more intense emotional reactions to monetary gains and losses performed less well. Lo *et al.* conclude that extreme moods impair trading performance, but that good trading performance is not significantly associated with particular personality traits. They focus on mood as a reflection of exogenous factors rather than individual differences, and conclude that any individual can be a good trader if they have the appropriate training and experience.

Similarly, Prechter and Parker (2007) identify social mood as the ultimate independent variable, affecting trends in all markets, particularly financial markets. There is also some evidence that financial markets are affected by exogenous weather-induced changes in mood rather than individual differences (Hirshleifer and Shumway 2003; Kamstra *et al.* 2003). Other studies focus on the role of individual differences and personality traits on trading behaviour and performance. Baddeley *et al.* (2007, 2010, 2012) find that financial herding tendencies correlate with individual differences including gender and age, and psychological traits including impulsivity, venturesomeness and conformism.

An emotional finance model

Tuckett (2009, 2011) brings together some of these insights about the role of emotion in financial decision-making using psychoanalytical principles and insights from psychological interviews of real-world fund and portfolio managers. He argues that financial instability is created by emotional conflicts as people perceive financial assets as 'phantastic objects' – objects imbued with superlative qualities and powers to perform. In pursuit of phantastic objects, whether these be tulip bulbs, houses or dotcom shares, traders are susceptible to a divided state of mind in which the excitement of potential gains is separated from the anxiety, panic and fear induced by potential losses. In a euphoric phase, traders quickly forget the losses from previous busts.

In this divided state, traders construct stories to exaggerate positive potential and rationalize negative experiences. This generates biases of overoptimism leading to underestimation of risk and overvaluation of opportunities. Speculation, especially speculative frenzies such as Tulipmania, may be propelled at least partly by unconscious instincts. These generate bubbles and busts as path-dependent emotional sequences in which euphoric booms are followed by a period of emotional oscillation as people struggle to reconcile reality with their beliefs, culminating in 'spectacular' collapses of confidence as the bubble bursts.

These tendencies are exacerbated by 'groupthink' within a 'basic assumption group', that is, a group connected by a common belief in some fundamental assumption(s); for financial markets, the basic assumptions are rational agents and efficient markets. Mirroring psychological insights about cognitive dissonance, Tuckett postulates that the basic assumption group in financial markets does not challenge assumptions of rational expectations and efficient markets. Instead, contradictory information is rationalized or dismissed as noise; stories are constructed to ameliorate doubt and distrust. This means that no-one takes responsibility for past failures and so learning from past mistakes is limited or nonexistent.

Tuckett emphasizes that the impact of emotional factors does not reflect irrationality. Emotions are often valuable guides to effective decision-making. The problem is that financial market institutions have been distorted by emotional conflicts, and this partly reflects the essential characteristics of financial assets. Financial markets are volatile; financial assets are abstract and intangible; and it is difficult for a trader to judge their own performance. Leveraging has exacerbated the potential for overinvestment during euphoric phases. Also, a lot of financial market activity has been directed towards securing comfort and reassurance rather than identifying the real reasons why things went wrong. Tuckett suggests solutions that focus on extracting the glamour and excitement from people's perceptions of financial trading. Developing statistical barometers of financial market temperature can be used to restrict financial innovations or increase capital ratios during fragile times when markets are heating up.

Akerlof and Shiller's animal spirits

Akerlof and Shiller also analyse emotional factors, arguing against models that assume efficient processing of information in financial markets. Pretending that asset prices reflect rational expectations of future payoffs is like 'hiring a weather forecaster who has gone berserk' (Akerlof and Shiller 2009, p. 132). In the place of standard assumptions of rationality and efficient markets, Akerlof and Shiller (2009) develop a more broadly based analysis of psychological and emotional factors, developing Keynes's insights about animal spirits. According to Akerlof and Shiller, markets are propelled by animal spirits, not by rational forecasts.

Originally, Keynes analysed animal spirits just in the context of entrepreneurship, arguing that uncertainty about the future prevents entrepreneurs from properly calculating the future benefits of their business decisions. In the absence of a basis for rational calculation, entrepreneurs' decisions will be propelled by spontaneous urges to act and to do something positive (Keynes 1936, 1937).

For financial trading, Keynes focused on the relationships between psychological forces and instability, including psychological waves of optimism and pessimism that affect financial markets and the social conventions that anchor speculators' expectations. Keynes analysed speculators responding to sociological forces, especially socially propelled conventions. When uncertainty prevents speculators from using information to form their own clear judgments, conventions will take hold and will encourage speculators to believe what others believe and to do what others do.

Akerlof and Shiller define their animal spirits more broadly than Keynes and analyse the impact of their animal spirits on all economic agents, not just entrepreneurs. Their animal spirits include confidence, fairness, corruption, money illusion and storytelling. These are approximations of other aspects of Keynes's analysis of financial markets, specifically the forces of spontaneous optimism and pessimism in financial markets.

Akerlof and Shiller also suggest a connection between instability and social preferences in observing that one of their animal spirits – corruption – will exacerbate financial instability: throughout history, corruption has accompanied the business cycle – from the Prohibition and the Great Depression of the 1930s, to the Savings and Loan crisis associated with the 1991 recession, to the Enron scandal associated with the 2001 recession, and to the subprime mortgage crisis which precipitated today's recession.

Corruption implies reductions in other-regarding preferences, cooperative social norms and trustworthiness, and these are all aspects of sociality (as discussed in chapter 5). Corruption grows during boom times, perhaps when evidence of inequality is less available and salient, but it also creates fragility within the financial system, and exposures of fraudulent activity can exacerbate financial downturns.

Akerlof and Shiller also identify other social influences as the product of animal spirits: market confidence is a form of social information, and stories about financial market trends, including naïve folk wisdoms, are communicated via social interactions. Akerlof and Shiller use an example of house prices: the story that spread before the collapse in US housing markets was that house prices could only go up, they could never go down. Markets fluctuate erratically, reflecting social mood, and waves of euphoria, optimism and over-confidence will be followed by slumps of pessimism and crises of confidence, all spreading through the economy via herding and contagion. These are fed by word of mouth and false intuitions (such as that prices don't fall), and perturbed by a wide range of catalysts, from dramatic news stories to unexpected sporting results.

All Akerlof and Shiller's animal spirits have the potential to play a role in magnifying financial instability. If confidence is high and people are optimistic, then financial systems and the macroeconomy more generally will be vulnerable to emotions of euphoria, optimism and over-confidence, precipitating herding and speculative bubbles. When confidence is weak and people are pessimistic, then the macroeconomy will be prone to slumps and financial crises. Asset prices will be susceptible to feedback loops, with instability further magnified by leverage. The real economy will be affected too: herding and speculative bubbles will exacerbate instability and depress wealth, the availability of finance, investment, employment and consumption.

Neuroeconomic evidence

Neuroeconomic analyses of financial markets have tended to focus on cognition and emotion in financial decision-making, developing insights about the importance of emotions, as discussed above. This focus by many neuroeconomists on interactions of cognitive and emotional decision-making systems links to Keynes's early insights about decision-making as a reflection of interactions of deliberation and emotion: 'it is our innate urge to activity which makes the wheels go round, our rational selves choosing between the alternatives as best we are able, calculating where we can, but often falling back for our motive on whim or sentiment or chance' (Keynes 1936, pp. 162–63). In the context of financial instability, in a world of fundamental Knightian uncertainty, emotional factors will interact with socio-economic forces, increasing the susceptibility of financial markets to fluctuations in optimism and pessimism.

Elster (1996) and Loewenstein (1996) emphasize that emotions and visceral factors are neither rational nor irrational because they cannot be chosen. Emotions do not necessarily interfere with rationality, but may be important 'tie-breakers', for example when outcomes are indeterminate in rational choice models. The influence of visceral factors varies in intensity, exerting overwhelming influences when in a 'hot state' but with cognitive factors exerting more influence during 'cold' states (Bernheim and Rangel 2004).

In terms of the impact of emotions on financial decisions, some of the earliest neuroeconomic studies of emotion analysed financial decision-making by lesion patients with damage to emotional processing areas, as discussed in chapter 8. From these studies, Bechara and Damasio (2005) and Damasio (1994/2006) developed the somatic marker hypothesis that emotions provide important physiological cues that can help decision-making.

The role of emotions in economic decision-making has also been confirmed by recent neuroscientific evidence showing that emotional circuits in the brain operate in response to ambiguity during learning/information processing (Glimcher and Rustichini 2004; Houser *et al.* 2005; Naqvi *et al.* 2007). Whilst Damasio (1994/2006) emphasizes that emotions play a valuable role in a lot of decision-making, they may also intensify some of the behavioural biases discussed above.

Lo and Repin (2002) used neurophysiological techniques to monitor the responses of ten professional derivatives traders by measuring skin conductance, heart rates, muscular responses, blood pressure, respiration rates, and body temperature. They analysed the differences in physiological response between traders with high levels of experience versus traders with low to moderate levels of experience. In most cases the experienced traders were better at controlling emotions, though Lo and Repin emphasize that this does not suggest that emotions are not valuable inputs to decision-making. They postulate that experienced professional traders often draw on intuition in decision-making and, consistent with Damasio's somatic market hypothesis, intuitive decision-making rules are often propelled by emotions. The implication of their findings is that experienced traders have learned not to over-react emotionally – which does not imply that they do not react emotionally at all.

Risk, impulsivity and fear

Risk seeking and impulsivity will affect instability in financial markets. Shiv *et al.* (2005) studied the behaviour of lesion patients with amygdala, orbitofrontal and insula damage, and found that damage to neural emotional circuitry was associated with an increased willingness to take risks. Patients with lesions in areas associated with emotion were more willing to take risks by investing money in gambling tasks and were able to make larger profits than normal controls, perhaps because decreased affect ameliorates the problems of myopic loss aversion.

Christopoulos *et al.* (2009) also identified links with risk aversion. They used functional magnetic resonance imaging (fMRI) to analyse participants' choices between risky and safe options. They found changes in blood oxygen level-dependent (BOLD) responses in the inferior frontal gyrus, an area commonly implicated in risk aversion. BOLD responses in the striatum increased with the probability of a risky choice, and inferior frontal gyrus responses decreased with the probability of a risky choice.

Coates and Herbert (2008) and Coates *et al.* (2010) identify a role for steroid hormones including testosterone – often associated with risk-taking, and cortisol – often associated with stress. They postulate that cortisol encodes risk and testosterone encodes rewards. They studied hormonal profiles by taking saliva samples from seventeen day traders from a London trading floor. They correlated the hormonal data with traders' profit-and-loss accounts and also with market events, and found that when a trader's morning testosterone level was relatively high, this correlated with better profit-and-loss performance over the day. In addition, average daily cortisol levels correlated with the volatility of traders' profit-and-loss accounts and also with market volatility overall. These findings are mirrored in Coates *et al.*'s (2009) study of pre-natal androgens, associated with success in competitive sports. Finger length, specifically the 2D:4D ratio capturing the ratio of the lengths of the second finger and fourth finger, are markers of pre-natal androgen levels. Coates *et al.* (2009) measured the 2D:4D ratio for high-frequency traders and found that traders' long-term profitability correlated with their 2D:4Ds.

Kuhnen and Knutson (2005) and Knutson and Bossaerts (2007) explored the role of affect in financial decision-making using event-related fMRI techniques. Kuhnen and Knutson examined the behaviour of nineteen volunteers offered safe stocks and risky stocks. The subjects had to learn which were the riskiest choices, and Kuhnen and Knutson identified two types of mistake associated with risk seeking and risk aversion. These correlated with activations in neural circuits associated with emotion and affect. They found that distinct anticipatory affect circuits are associated with different types of financial choice. Activations in the nucleus accumbens, which forms the main part of the striatum and is associated with reward learning, were correlated with risk-seeking mistakes. Conversely, activations in the anterior insula, associated with negative emotions and fear of failure and loss, are associated with risk-aversion mistakes.

Risk seeking may reflect impulsivity if short-termism or time inconsistency lead people into wanting too much too soon. The disproportionate focus on the short term is captured in behavioural models of time preference. As explored in chapter 9, neuroeconomic analyses have unravelled some of the neurological correlates of time inconsistency, with implications for financial decision-making. McClure *et al.* (2004) present brain imaging evidence which shows that time-inconsistent preferences correlate with brain activations in 'delta' areas (associated with sophisticated decision-making and mathematical processing) and 'beta' areas (more primitive and emotional neurological areas).

Slovic (2010) connects the feeling of risk with impulsivity and addiction. Neuroscientific evidence has established that money stimulates the same dopaminergic reward-processing systems as are activated with more basic rewards, including food, sex and drugs. Reflecting evolutionary processes, hard-wired, instinctive emotional responses may dominate even though they are not well adapted to modern conditions. The rapid development of technologies such as computerization may have accelerated the mal-adaptation of ingrained emotional processes. For example, primitive limbic structures in the brain are often associated with impulsive emotional responses appropriate in a world in which immediate rewards were important. In primitive environments, basic resources were scarce and perishable, and so quick, instinctive action was essential to avoid starvation. In a modern context, these instincts may not serve a useful purpose and may in fact generate perverse behaviours such as gambling addictions.

In financial markets, risk seeking by financial traders may reflect interactions between neurological systems. If emotional systems encourage risk-prone traders to take impulsive decisions, then the amplification of impulsivity in modern computerized markets will increase the fragility of the financial system. As explained in chapter 10, in some contexts, impulsive behaviours, such as over-consumption of addictive substances, can be overridden by pre-commitment devices, but with traders' returns focused very much on short-term performance there is little incentive for traders to rein in impulsive instincts if institutional safeguards limiting impulsivity are not in place.

Financial herding and social emotions

As explained above, socio-economic forces affect investors: for example, the socially propelled conventions that, in times of uncertainty, encourage speculators to believe what others believe and to do what others do (Keynes 1930, 1936, 1937). Following this approach, other economists, most famously Hyman Minsky, analyse emotional contagion, identifying the speculative euphoria that spreads through groups of investors during manic phases as a crucial catalyst in economic and financial booms. In turn, excessive pessimism and extreme risk aversion precipitate bust phases (Minsky 1978, 1986; see also Davidson 1997, 2008).

Neuroscientific techniques can enable the identification of the neural correlates of these social influences. Various studies have tested hypotheses about theory of mind and empathy, and these have implications for understanding herding in financial markets. There is evidence that socialized instincts to imitate are associated with mirror neuron activity (Rizzolatti and Craighero 2004; Iacoboni 2005). This may suggest that herding responses are automatic and 'hard-wired', and are the outcome of impulsiveness. Single-cell recordings in monkeys have identified mirror neurons in the premotor cortex (prefrontal cortex) which fire not only when monkeys perform grabbing movements, but also when the monkeys observe similar movements performed by experimenters (Rizzolatti *et al.* 2002). Extending this finding, experiments show that monkeys' *socialized* instincts are also propelled by the activity of mirror neurons, and these insights have been extended to describe human instincts to follow others (e.g. Rizzolatti *et al.* 2002; Rizzolatti and Craighero 2004; Iacoboni 2005). Baddeley *et al.* (2004) suggest that mirror neuron activity may explain imitation and herding in socio-economic contexts too.

Herding can also be conceptualized as the outcome of interacting thought processes, linking into neuroeconomic insights about the interaction of the cognitive, controlled, emotional and automatic responses (Baddeley 2010). Learning from others using Bayes's rule would be an objective way of deciding, but a cognitive impression formed via Bayesian reasoning may interact with less objective emotional processing. If economic behaviour (herding and other forms of social influence included) reflects interactions of different neurological systems, then a neuroeconomic approach blending economics, psychology and evolutionary biology with social neuroscience may provide an explanation of herding as the product of both cognition and emotion. An inter-disciplinary approach is essential to understanding how and why herding and social influence evolve in an economic and financial context.

In distinguishing social learning from social influence more generally, there are a number of neuroeconomic studies that explore some of the neural correlates of social influence. Berns *et al.*'s (2005) fMRI studies of visual mental rotation tasks incorporate Asch's ideas about social conformity (described in chapter 2). Berns *et al.* found that conformity is associated with activation in the occipital–parietal network, particularly when following incorrect signals from others. On the other hand, amygdala and caudate activation is associated with independent decision-making.

Klucharev *et al.* (2009) identify a link between social conformity and learning using an fMRI study to show that conformity draws on mechanisms that reflect reinforcement learning principles. They found that individual conflicts with social opinions led to differential activations in the rostral cingulate and the ventral striatum, areas also activated in models of reward-prediction error, as explored in chapter 4. Klucharev *et al.* (2011) extend these insights in a study of social influence applying transcranial magnetic stimulation (TMS) techniques. As explained in chapter 3, these techniques involve applying electromagnetic induction for temporary, benign stimulation of specific neural areas.

Klucharev *et al.*'s subjects were sorted into three groups: a control group; a 'sham' TMS group receiving subthreshold levels of TMS; and a TMS group. Then they were asked to participate in a two-stage 'seeing beauty' task: they were asked to record their perceptions about the attractiveness of a series of photos of female faces. In the first stage, they were asked for an initial rating of the attractiveness of the faces on an eight-point scale. They were then given social information about others' perceptions of attractiveness using the average ratings from all the experimental subjects. In the second stage, the subjects were asked again to rate the attractiveness of faces. The TMS group received TMS, inhibiting the activity of the neurons in the posterior medial frontal cortex – an area involved in reward prediction – before they gave their second-stage ratings. Overall, Klucharev *et al.* found that the ratings from the control and sham groups were responsive to the information about average percep-tions; however, the TMS group experienced significant reductions in conformity in their ratings of attractiveness after receiving TMS. Klucharev *et al.* conclude that this confirms the link between social conformity and reinforcement learning.

Burke *et al.* (2010b) develop these neuroeconomic analyses of social learning and conformity specifically in the context of financial herding. They used fMRI techniques to analyse social influence in financial decision-making. They showed that when subjects were offered the opportunity to buy versus reject a stock, the ventral striatum was differentially activated if subjects' decisions coincided with the decisions of a group. Furthermore, when subjects were balancing social information about a group's decisions against private information in the form of stock charts capturing a stock's historical performance, the probabilities of buying conditioned on social information correlated with differential activations in the ventral striatum – an area associated with emotional processing of reward.

The emotion of fear will have a particularly profound impact on financial decision-making, and some studies have shown that areas associated with the processing of fear are activated during financial herding. Burke *et al.* (2010b) and Baddeley *et al.* (2012), again using fMRI evidence, analyse differential activations for herding decisions (decisions to buy a stock when the group buys and to reject it when the group rejects) versus contrarian decisions (decisions to reject when the group buys and to buy when the group rejects). As shown in Figure 11.1, herding is associated with differential activations in the amygdala and anterior cingulate cortex.

These differential activations suggest a role for fear because the amygdala is commonly associated with aversive learning and the emotional processing of fear. Overall, the evidence about the differential activations in the ventral striatum and amygdala suggest that there may be interactions between fear, social reinforcement learning and reward in financial decision-making.

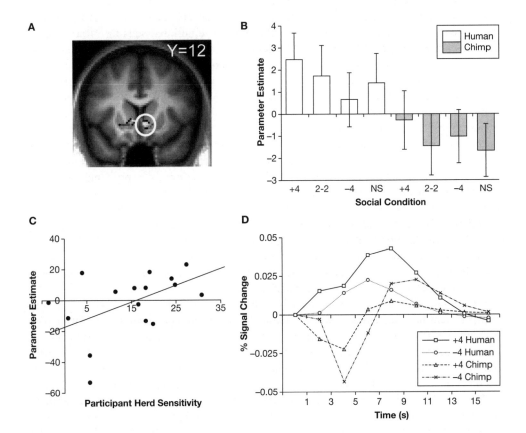

Figure 11.1 Neural activations during financial herding

Conclusions and policy implications

This chapter has shown that a wide range of psychological factors and behavioural biases affect financial decisions – including social influences, biases and heuristics, animal spirits and emotions. With herding and reflexivity, these biases can spread through financial markets via speculative trading, generating financial instability.

In terms of broader implications, if herding and speculation are rational responses to uncertainty and informational constraints, then policies to ensure the quick and efficient dissemination of information will be justified. But if herding is the outcome of more emotional and impulsive responses, then there would also be a role for government in controlling financial instability. Baseline versions of standard models based on assumptions of rational expectations and efficient markets will have limited relevance, though adaptations to standard models which incorporate asymmetric information and principal–agent problems do offer some useful insights about encouraging transparency, improving information transmission and correcting misaligned incentives.

A greater understanding of how psychological traits affect economic and financial decision-making will inform policies designed to control financial risk-taking at a microeconomic level. Excessive risk-taking can be controlled if firms can construct incentives to encourage traders to take a more long-term view. Rogue trading can be reduced if people work within teams and traders have to report to a manager who takes a longer-term view. Other policy suggestions have included hiring more women or older men because they have lower testosterone levels and are less inclined to take risks (Coates *et al.* 2010). Technical innovations have also been devised, including the emotional-sensing 'Rationalizer' system – a machine promoted by Royal General Electric and ABN-Amro, designed to provide an 'emotional mirror' by monitoring online traders' galvanic skin response (a measure of skin conductance reflecting sweat rates), producing alerts when a trader is over-excited.

It is not clear how feasible these microeconomic solutions might be, particularly as it would be difficult to enforce their adoption by private firms. Designing effective macroeconomic policies is crucial, especially as financial instability can be a socially driven, aggregate phenomenon. Effective macroeconomic polices are also important because of financial instability's impact on the macroeconomy more generally. Externalities from financial instability have implications for the real economy and growing, bursting asset price bubbles affect wealth, investment and the availability of finance. There will be feedback effects between speculation and entrepreneurship via equity markets because, as identified within Tobin's *q* models of fixed asset investment, asset market valuations will affect new investment directly if market capitalization is used as a proxy for future profitability. There will also be indirect impacts if stock market buoyancy is interpreted as a signal of wider business confidence. Overall, if financial markets are struggling, then this will lead to declines in fixed asset investment with knock-on effects for employment, consumption and growth.

Designing effective financial policies is a challenge, and Keynes's analysis of financial markets identifies the central policy dilemma. On one hand, unregulated financial markets encourage a liquidity 'fetish', exacerbating financial instability. Whilst speculation does no harm as 'bubbles on the steady stream of enterprise', a problem emerges when 'enterprise becomes a bubble on a whirlpool of speculation. When the capital development of a country becomes a by-product of the activities of a casino, the job is likely to be ill-done' (Keynes 1936, p. 159). On the other hand, Keynes writes that the 'spectacle of modern investment markets has sometimes moved me towards the conclusion that to make the purchase of an investment permanent and indissoluble, like marriage, except by reason of death or other grave cause, might be a useful remedy. . . . But a little consideration of this expedient brings us up against a dilemma, and shows us how the liquidity of investment markets often facilitates, though it sometimes impedes, the course of new investment' (Keynes 1936, p. 160). In reconciling this dilemma, Keynes believed that financial markets should be supported, but with government intervention to control and slow market excesses (Keynes 1936; see also Backhouse and Bateman 2011).

One potential policy solution receiving a lot of attention recently is the Tobin tax, initially proposed by James Tobin as a way to 'throw sand in the wheels' and moderate volatility in currency markets (Tobin 1974, 1978). It has also been developed as a potential solution to restraining short-termism in financial markets more generally, but it is problematic because it would require a high level of international policy coordination to prevent the shift of financial services to tax havens. Domestic political constraints are likely to compromise international attempts to coordinate financial policy.

Akerlof and Shiller (2009) emphasize that the impact of psychological factors on financial markets means that governments have an important role to play in complementing capitalism. 'Capitalism must live within certain rules [and] the government must set those rules' (Akerlof and Shiller 2009, p. 173). They recommend that governments should adopt a two-target approach in which fiscal and monetary stimuli are complemented by targeted financial flows smoothed using lending and capital injections to ensure that they are consistent with full employment.

Government regulations – particularly those involving stress-testing of banks, capital controls to limit international movement of capital, minimum capital reserve ratios and institutional changes to separate retail and investment banking – could limit the spread of consequences from impulsive risk-taking, and have been the focus of recent changes in financial policy, for example in the UK and in response to Basel III.

From a modern behavioural finance perspective, if economic behaviour is the outcome of psychological forces such as impulsive risk-taking rather than logical, objective decision-making thought processes, then government intervention has a particularly important role to play, particularly as computerization, globalization, and increased leveraging enabled by financial deregulation in the 1980s and 1990s have amplified the speed and liquidity of modern financial markets.

12 Behavioural macroeconomics, happiness and wellbeing

Introduction

Behavioural economics is mostly about microeconomic phenomena, and the concepts focus on the motivations underlying individual behaviour. Applying these microeconomic principles to macroeconomic analysis is complicated by the limits to aggregation, which are particularly profound once behavioural principles are introduced into the mix. Whilst standard models aggregate, by assumption, from atomistic representative agents, behavioural economics focuses on individual differences, social interactions, behavioural biases and nonrational forces, including emotions and visceral factors. These are difficult, if not impossible, to aggregate. Behavioural influences mean that the macroeconomy cannot be a simple sum of its parts.

These obstacles explain why the modern literature on behavioural macroeconomics is so scant – with the key exception of Akerlof's analysis of behavioural macroeconomics (Akerlof 2002) and Akerlof's work with Shiller on animal spirits (Akerlof and Shiller 2009), explored below. This work draws on insights from John Maynard Keynes, who constructed a psychological analysis of the macroeconomy, though (for better or worse) without the logic and internal consistency that characterizes modern macroeconomic approaches.

Whilst little has been done on behavioural macroeconomics, it is nonetheless important to understand how and why behavioural factors affect macroeconomic outcomes. This chapter attempts to put together some ideas and insights from behavioural economics to enable a better understanding of how and why the psychology of individuals affects the macroeconomy. Keynes (1936, 1937) offers some key insights into the behavioural analysis of macroeconomies and, whilst his approach was generally intuitive rather than mathematically rigorous, it nonetheless it provides a good starting point. Keynes's approach was developed by Akerlof and Shiller (2009), in particular by extending the concept of animal spirits to a wider range of macroeconomic agents and phenomena. Building on Keynes and Akerlof and Shiller, this chapter presents a behavioural analysis of macroeconomic interactions, drawing on the behavioural economic principles developed in earlier chapters of this book to capture the psychology of the various actors in the macroeconomy – including firms, workers/households, speculators and policy-makers,

Another complication for behavioural macroeconomics is that the goals of macroeconomic policy are changing. Governments are shifting focus away from standard monetary measures of economic progress such as GDP and GNP towards socio-economic goals defined more broadly. Whilst broader measures of economic progress, including indexes such as the Human Development Index (HDI), have been around for some time, governments and policy-makers are increasingly interested in broadening macroeconomic measurement further – for example, by using survey instruments to capture people's perception of their own quality of life. The second part of this chapter addresses some of these issues and explores the literature on happiness and wellbeing.

Keynes's psychology of the macroeconomy

Keynes's macroeconomic analysis draws on insights that he developed early in his career, in *A Treatise on Probability* (Keynes 1921). In this book, rather than constructing a model of rationality and assuming that all economic agents behave accordingly, Keynes explores the limits of individual rationality and the impact of socio-psychological forces. Psychological motivations mean that different people will behave in different ways. Some economists conclude that Keynes's analysis is based on an underlying assumption of rationality given uncertainty, reflecting themes developed in *A Treatise on Probability* (Dow and Dow 1985; O'Donnell 1989; Bateman 1990; Littleboy 1990; Skidelsky 1992). In contrast, Shackle (1955, 1967, 1972), Winslow (1986) and Mini (1990) emphasize the subjectivism of economic behaviour: to them, Keynes presents the volatile characteristics of the economy emerging as a result of 'irrational forces, vicious tendencies, destructive fetishes and dangerous human proclivities'.

Some analyses reconcile these views, arguing that Keynes describes behaviour which is not strictly rational in a standard sense, but is nonetheless reasonable in a broader sense and is consistent with Herbert Simon's concepts of bounded and procedural rationality, explored in chapter 6 (e.g. Minsky 1975; Lawson 1981; Carabelli 1988; Littleboy 1990; Davidson 1991; Crotty 1992; Baddeley 1995; Howitt 1997; Runde 1997). For example, expectations and conventions are sensible and reasonable rather than strictly rational or irrational; they are not like customs/habits, they reflect rational, purpose-oriented behaviour under uncertainty, and they promote coherent behaviour (Littleboy 1990).

Keynes's fundamental psychological laws

Keynes was unusual amongst economists in that he constructed a model of the macroeconomy that focused on the impact of psychological forces in the macroeconomy. Keynes (1936, 1937) argued that economic and financial decision-making is driven by a series of 'fundamental psychological laws': the propensity to consume, attitudes to liquidity and expectations of returns from investment. Psychological forces are important when the world is uncertain: decision-making is fragile and because knowledge is very precarious, it is difficult to form reliable predictions of future events.

Expectations and the state of confidence

Expectations are central to Keynes's psychological analysis of the macroeconomy. He argues that entrepreneurs, when making decisions about the scale of their production, have not just one expectation about future production and profits, but a bundle of expectations held with varying degrees of probability and weight. When it comes to choices, however, the entrepreneur will act as if his/her behaviour is the outcome of one undoubting expectation held with certainty, and will utilize the expectation with the greatest weight (Keynes 1936, p. 24). Aside from some esoteric differences, Kahneman and Tversky's (1979) concept of weight (in the prospect theory weighting function) parallels the concept of weight in Keynes (1921, 1936). Keynes (1936) argues that rational judgments of weight underlie the convention of assuming that current events and recent results can be proxy for short-term expectations (Keynes 1936, p. 51).

Weight also determines the state of confidence – a global, diffuse force similar to Prechter and Parker's (2007) socionomic concept of social mood (explained in chapter 8). The state of confidence affects a number of macroeconomic phenomena. It plays a crucial role in determining investment indirectly because it affects profit expectations and demand for money. A weakening state of confidence is associated with lower weights and higher liquidity premiums. When the state of confidence is buoyant, judgments of weight are possible. When the state of confidence becomes more fragile, judgments of weight are more difficult. In the latter case, there will be no guide to rational action and nonrational forces will predominate. The state of confidence is not analysed in much detail in standard economic analyses, and Keynes argues that our understanding of it must be based on empirical observation rather than *a priori* theory.

It also links to Tversky and Kahneman's (1974) analysis of heuristics and biases, in particular the anchoring and adjustment heuristics. Keynes observes that recently realized results will be weighted heavily when expectations are formed because using more rigorous but complicated methods of forming forecasts of the future will be disproportionately costly. In this way, Keynes uses the concept of weight to explain the heuristics that determine business confidence: 'It is reasonable, therefore, to be guided to a considerable degree by the facts about which we feel somewhat confident, even though they may be less decisively relevant to the issue than other facts about which our knowledge is vague and scanty.' (Keynes 1936, p. 148)

Macroeconomic conventions

Conventional behaviour plays a key role in determining the state of long-term expectation, a force that has significant impacts on entrepreneurship and investment (Keynes 1936, pp. 152–53). According to Keynes, conventions may be rational, nonrational or irrational/psychological, depending on the nature of belief underlying them; for example, the convention of assuming that the existing situation will persist appears to combine rational and nonrational elements because it is based in knowledge: 'We are assuming, in effect, that the existing market valuation . . . is uniquely correct in relation to our existing knowledge of the facts which will influence the yield of an investment, and that it will only change in proportion to changes in this knowledge' (Keynes 1936, p. 152).

Keynes argues that the 'conventional valuation which is established as the outcome of the mass psychology of a large number of ignorant individuals is liable to change violently' (Keynes 1936, p. 154). Keynes's conventions have both a reasonable and a psychological element: they become self-fulfilling prophecies, and therefore to assume that they will continue becomes the most reasonable thing to believe, once the convention is established (Lawson 1995). Also, it is reasonable for an ignorant individual to rely on conventions because other economic actors may be acting on better information and 'we endeavour to fall back on the judgment of the rest of the world which is perhaps better informed' (Keynes 1936, p. 217). This links to the social learning and herding theories, as analysed in chapter 4. Conventions are maintained by psychological factors: people prefer stable routines; conventions lull anxiety created by uncertainty about the future (Earl 1983; Lawson 1995).

It is difficult to analyse conventions because they reflect the overlap between individual and aggregate behaviour and are associated with feedback effects: aggregate behaviour affects individual behaviour and *vice versa*. It may not be rational for one individual to believe, in isolation, that the current state of affairs can be projected into the future, but outcomes are determined by aggregate behaviour, and so a conventional belief held by many that the current situation is a sensible guide to the future does have a reasonable basis. What is individually rational and what is socially rational are different things, an insight also offered by Vernon L Smith in his analysis of the links between social rationality and individual irrationality in ecological rationality (see chapter 6).

Keynes also explained how conventions and behavioural biases affect money markets and attitudes towards money; for example, in the determination of interest rates: although the rate of interest is established by convention, dealers nonetheless perceive it to have an objective basis. The belief that the interest rate has its roots in objective grounds may lead to an inappropriate complex of interest rates prevailing due to these mistaken beliefs. This may lead to suboptimal levels of employment being maintained over periods of time as the conventional, relatively stable but high long-term rate of interest prevails. Some psychological analyses of money draw on Freudian psychodynamic themes in Keynes. For example, Winslow (1986) applies money-loving instincts and Freud's analysis of the anal personality, characterized by a triad of traits including miserliness, orderliness and cleanliness. In this way, Winslow blends ideas from Freud and Keynes to explain attitudes towards money.

Entrepreneurial animal spirits

According to Keynes, entrepreneurs will be guided by conventions in the same way as speculators are guided by them, but they will also be affected by broader socio-psychological forces, in particular animal spirits. The existence of animal spirits was postulated by Galen, an ancient Roman physician, who asserted that *spiritus animalis* had origins in the brain and mediated nerve function.

Linking Galen's animal spirits with economics, Keynes introduced animal spirits in his analysis of entrepreneurship: entrepreneurs cannot properly calculate the future benefits of investments because the future is not easily quantifiable. So entrepreneurs' animal spirits, which Keynes defines as a spontaneous urge to act, intervene even when there is no rational basis for action. He observes that most decisions:

> to do something positive, the full consequences of which will be drawn out over many days to come, can only be taken as a result of animal spirits – of spontaneous urge to action rather than inaction, and not as the outcome of a weighted average of quantitative benefits multiplied by quantitative probabilities. Enterprise only pretends to itself to be mainly actuated by the statements in its own prospectus, however candid and sincere. Only a little more than an expedition to the South Pole, is it based on an exact calculation of benefits to come.
>
> (Keynes 1936, pp. 161–62)

Keynes's analysis of animal spirits also emphasizes the role of emotions including hope and fear:

> Thus if the animal spirits are dimmed and the spontaneous optimism falters, leaving us to depend on nothing but a mathematical expectation, enterprise will fade and die; – though fears of loss may have a basis no more reasonable than hopes of profits had before.
>
> (1936, p. 162)

Entrepreneurs' reliance on animal spirits reflects uncertainty and limits on quantification. As Dow and Dow (2011) emphasize, Keynes did not describe animal spirits as an irrational phenomenon, and so the concept does not fit easily into economists' dichotomous categories of rational/irrational. For entrepreneurial investment decisions in particular, a large number of alternatives exist, and none is obviously more rational than the others. If it is not possible to rank alternatives, then entrepreneurs will be driven by motivations which are not rational in the sense of being evaluated in terms of consequences, but are instead determined by psychological forces:

> Generally speaking, in making a decision we have before us a large number of alternatives, none of which is demonstrably more 'rational' than the others, in the sense that we can arrange in order of merit the sum aggregate of the benefits obtainable from each. [Therefore] we fall back . . . on motives of another kind, which are not rational in the sense of being concerned with the evaluation of consequences but are decided by habit, instinct, preference, desire [and] will.
>
> (Keynes 1979, p. 294)

Agents are nonetheless doing the best that they can in the circumstances, and this conception of rational behaviour is consistent with Simon's (1979) concept of procedural rationality, in which agents' actions are the outcome of appropriate deliberation.

In terms of the concepts in *A Treatise on Probability*, if animal spirits are a desirable force, then they can be justified as a form of rational *action* even though they do not emerge from a rational belief, that is, a probability judgment. With uncertainty, knowledge will be vague. There may be no information available upon which entrepreneurs can base their expectations. Two courses of action are available: they can rely instead on nonrational forces to drive behaviour; or they can do nothing. Doing nothing delivers nothing. So it is often better to rely on animal spirits and spontaneous urges to act. Relying on animal spirits will not necessarily be an irrational *action* even though there is no basis for rational *belief*.

A behavioural analysis of macroeconomic interactions

In building macroeconomic models from microeconomic foundations, standard approaches are often grounded on dynamic stochastic general equilibrium (DSGE) models. These models are dynamic because they capture decisions over time, and they are stochastic because they incorporate a random element. Perhaps more importantly, they are founded on the rigorous microfoundations of general equilibrium theory in which firms and workers/households interact in supplying labour and producing goods/services. General equilibrium models rest on a range of assumptions about rational maximizing agents, perfect information, perfectly functioning markets and full employment, amongst other assumptions. One crucial behavioural assumption is the representative agent hypothesis: macroeconomic outcomes are understood in terms of interactions between homogeneous workers and firms – with individual differences and interactions generally relegated to stochastic error terms. This reflects a general characteristic of standard macroeconomic models. They often describe the behaviour of a very small number of representative individuals – multiplied.

Behavioural economics and DSGE models do not rest easily together. In addition, whilst the standard macroeconomic approach is prone to aggregation problems (the whole is not necessarily equal to the sum of its parts, even if the parts are the same on average), behavioural macroeconomics faces substantial additional challenges. It is inconsistent with the essence of a behavioural approach to use one representative agent to describe general behaviour. Individual differences, not only in risk aversion and time preference, but also in cognitive skills, personality traits and emotional predispositions, are central to behavioural economics. And even if representative agents can be described, it is not consistent with behavioural economics to assume that they act independently: they will interact with each other in response to social learning, social pressures and social preferences. These problems mean that behavioural macroeconomic theory will have to take a different approach.

Akerlof (2002) assessed progress towards the development of behavioural macroeconomic theory, arguing that the standard approaches did not convincingly address macroeconomic problems such as involuntary unemployment and under-saving. He assessed the progress of behavioural macroeconomics in terms of relaxing assumptions of perfect information (in the literature on asymmetric information); capturing involuntary unemployment in terms of social preferences such as fairness and reciprocity; using cognitive psychology to capture monetary policy-making; introducing prospect theory into the analysis of nominal wage resistance; incorporating time inconsistency into savings models using hyperbolic discounting function; and developing analyses of heuristics and biases to capture irrational exuberance in asset markets. Akerlof's assessment of behavioural macroeconomics, along with insights from Keynes, led to the development of Akerlof and Shiller's model of animal spirits in the macroeconomy, as described below.

Akerlof and Shiller's animal spirits

Akerlof and Shiller develop Keynes's analysis of the psychological forces in the macroeconomy to build a macroeconomic analysis based on the animal spirits of workers, savers, speculators and governments as well as entrepreneurs. In this, they extend Keynes's concept of animal spirits to macroeconomic actors in general in order to capture a wide range of macroeconomic phenomena, including financial crisis, depression and involuntary unemployment. They define animal spirits broadly as the psychological factors affecting human behaviour (Akerlof and Shiller 2009).

They define five animal spirits: confidence, fairness, corruption, money illusion and storytelling – the narratives that shape our sense of self and of others. Many of these nonrational forces are caught up with socio-psychological motivations and, whilst these are woolly concepts and therefore difficult to analyse, there is increasing evidence that they are relevant. Akerlof and Shiller argue that noneconomic motivations, irrationality and animal spirits are central to human decision-making. 'You pick the time. You pick the country. And you can be fairly well guaranteed that you will see at play in the macroeconomy the animal spirits that are the subject of this book' (Akerlof and Shiller 2009, p. 171).

Akerlof and Shiller's animal spirits will interact. If the state of confidence is strong and people are optimistic, then the macroeconomy will be vulnerable to waves of euphoria, optimism and over-confidence, precipitating herding and speculative bubbles; but when the state of confidence is weak and people are pessimistic, the macroeconomy will be prone to slumps and financial crises. These forces will spread via storytelling, word of mouth and false intuitions – for example, the false intuition that house prices can't fall – feeding herding and contagion, all perturbed by anything from dramatic news stories to sporting events. Asset prices will susceptible to feedback loops, with instability further magnified by leverage, with knock-on effects for the real economy. Herding and speculative bubbles will exacerbate instability, affecting wealth, investment and the availability of finance. In this way, Akerlof and Shiller's animal spirits determine market trends.

Overall, Akerlof and Shiller acknowledge that psychological and sociological analyses are often eschewed in standard macroeconomic analysis because they are arbitrary and difficult to quantify; nonetheless, they advocate a move away from economists' typical antipathy towards socio-psychological explanations. They emphasize the importance of history and stories, and of qualitative alongside quantitative analysis.

Macroeconomic actors

Following from Keynes and Akerlof and Shiller, the actors in the macroeconomy can be divided into four key sets of players: firms, households/workers, speculators and government. Each will be affected by the range of psychological/behavioural influences, with different aspects affecting them in different ways; moods and emotions have particular impacts, especially if they correlate with risk-taking. Effective decision-making will be constrained by cognitive biases and time inconsistency. Social influences have strong impacts in human decision-making, and people will tend to herd behind conventional wisdoms and actions.

Different groups will be affected in different ways. Entrepreneurs will be affected by fluctuations in mood and emotion, loosely categorized as animal spirits. They will be less susceptible to time inconsistency and herding because they will be more far-sighted than speculators and households. Speculators, as explained in chapter 11, will be strongly affected by emotions such as fear and greed; there will be differences between professionals and amateurs, with amateurs more susceptible to herding tendencies, time inconsistency and other forms of cognitive bias. Households will be particularly susceptible to cognitive bias and time inconsistency.

Individual differences such as age, education, income and socio-economic background will affect people's susceptibility to psychological constraints. Psychological factors and individual differences will partly explain the vulnerability of some households/individuals to financial fraud and exploitation. Households, speculators and entrepreneurs will interact and their psychologies will coalesce to affect the general state of confidence, generating self-fulfilling speculative episodes and financial fragility, especially when regulatory institutions are not designed to take account of these vulnerabilities.

In analysing the behaviour of these four groups of actors in more detail, it is possible to divide the behaviours according to some of the categories seen in standard macroeconomic texts: firms investing and producing; households consuming and saving; workers and firms searching for jobs and hiring employees; and governments making policy. The behaviour of these groups is analysed below.

Investment

Standard macroeconomic models are built on a representative agent hypothesis. For macroeconomic models of investment, the representative agent is the profit-maximizing firm. In early neoclassical versions of investment theory, the representative firm invests until the marginal productivity of capital is balanced by the user cost of capital, which captures the relative cost of capital inputs (Jorgenson 1963). In standard approaches, the firm is a black box: inputs go in, outputs come out, and what happens in between is not of interest. Standard models focus on the combinations and relative factor costs of capital and labour. Investment will also be determined by expectations of the future: in standard models, investment is the product of complex, forward-looking investment appraisal strategies. Whilst standard approaches allow subjectivity in entrepreneurs' expectations, it is assumed that these subjective judgments coincide, on average, with some objective probability distribution, ensuring that mistakes are not systematic. In Tobin's q models of investment, entrepreneurs can form rational expectations on the basis of stock market valuations. This requires an additional assumption that financial markets are efficient, with asset prices responding instantaneously to news and reflecting all currently available, relevant information about the profitability of firms. The entrepreneurs in standard approaches are characterized by substantive rationality, defined by Simon (1979) (as explained in chapter 6) as the achievement of objective goals given objective constraints. Standard approaches also imply organizational rationality: if a firm is monolithic then it can be treated as an individual, and so the organizational rationality of the firm coincides with the individual rationality of a monolithic entrepreneur (Simon 1972). In this way the firm in standard economic analyses is treated as a single, simple entity.

Overall, standard approaches focus on the use of complex mathematical techniques and algorithmic styles of decision-making, as opposed to the heuristic styles of decision-making seen in behavioural economics. Algorithmic approaches assume that investors, using the same information set, will form identical expectations centred about some objective probability distribution of outcomes. They will be forward looking in incorporating discount rates into their investment appraisal techniques. If these methods are used correctly, then the firm will be optimizing some objective function, given that constraints and investment will take place to the point at which the manager maximizes his/her profits by undertaking all investments with a net present value greater than or equal to zero. The discount rate used to derive the net present value will be equal to the real cost of borrowing, adjusted for risk. Algorithmic approaches are outlined in detail in conventional analyses of fixed asset investment activity, for example in Jorgenson's (1963) neoclassical model; in the q theories of Abel (1983) and others; and in real options theories of uncertainty and irreversibility in investment (Pindyck 1991; Dixit and Pindyck 1994). Despite some differences in analysis, these approaches can be understood as refinements of Jorgenson's basic model, with each refinement incorporating more thorough and complex approaches to the analysis of expectations and uncertainty into a basic model of substantively rational profit-maximizing firms (see Baddeley 2003 for a survey).

Behavioural theories of the firm

In the real world, entrepreneurs' decisions will be affected by a multiplicity of factors, and a crucial role is played by subjective factors such as business confidence and animal spirits. Keynes argues that profound uncertainty and fragile business confidence compromise the expectations-formation process, exacerbating volatility and pessimism in investor behaviour. Behavioural microeconomic analyses of real-world firms draw on themes from behavioural economics. Austrian analyses of entrepreneurship and investment draw on concepts similar to animal spirits: for example, Kirzner's (1973) analyses of entrepreneurship as the product of alertness directed by interest. Behavioural concepts such as attention bias are introduced into some theories of the firm. Entrepreneurial and empire-building activities may involve attempts to manage the attention of others, as with the setting of agendas at meetings and via the design of advertisements and shopping malls (Earl and Potts 2000; Earl 2005). Similarly, Hart and Moore's (1990, 2008) theory links with Kahneman and Tversky's (1979) prospect theory: for example, reference points are constructed around predetermined competitive contracts. Similarly, Fehr *et al.* (2011) incorporate prospect theory into a model of firm behaviour by focusing on long-term contracts: using a market experiment that separates responses to rigid versus flexible contracts and good versus bad states, they find empirical support for Hart and Moore's (1990, 2008) theory of the firm.

Entrepreneurs' heuristics

For macroeconomic theories of investment, the problem comes in unifying the approaches to capture the essence of investment behaviour. One difference is in the styles of decision-making. A key distinguishing characteristic of behavioural approaches relative to standard approaches is that behavioural approaches are more consistent with Simon's (1979) definition of procedural rationality (defined in chapter 6 as decision-making as the outcome of problem-solving, intuition and appropriate deliberation) than with substantive rationality. For entrepreneurs and investment, this implies that entrepreneurs will use heuristic methods rather than algorithmic methods in making their investment decisions (Baddeley 2006a).

In their behavioural theory of the firm, Cyert and March (1963) argue that the firm is not a monolithic structure as postulated by neoclassical theory, and instead is affected by conflicts between people within the firm generating satisficing, organizational slack and other inefficient behaviours. Similarly, Simon (1972) focuses on bounded rationality affected by constraints and limits to rationality. He also emphasizes the importance of other goals: entrepreneurs are not necessarily aiming to maximize. When complexity and uncertainty make global rationality impossible, firms will settle for what is satisfactory rather than what is best (Simon 1972). Behavioural biases emerge at one or more of the three key stages of the investment decision-making process: gathering information; predicting future events (for example, likely sales); and investment project appraisal. At each of these stages, businesses may make mistakes: information may be missing or misinterpreted; information may be processed inefficiently to give misleading predictions. If inappropriate appraisal techniques are used, then even accurate predictions may be misused (Simon 1979).

Procedurally rational entrepreneurs will use heuristics – simple common-sense rules of thumb based on experience – when deciding whether or not to invest in particular projects. In judging the value of investments, a procedurally rational entrepreneur will calculate how long it takes to pay off an investment project using payback period (PBP) calculations. And/or if they judge the value of a project in terms of its likely (undiscounted) cashflow relative to its cost, they will use the accounting rates of return (ARR) as an investment appraisal tool. PBPs and ARRs are based around simple assumptions about likely future events and do not require discounting methods (Baddeley 2006a). Entrepreneurs will also use gut feel and common sense, rather than complex mathematical techniques, in assessing investment plans. Different investors faced with the same information may form different expectations reflecting arbitrarily assigned margins of error. These errors will not cancel out, because entrepreneurs' judgments may be affected by herding and social learning. In a world of incomplete information, it will be procedurally rational to follow the crowd (Topol 1991), and/or to learn from past output signals about what other investors are doing (Acemoglu 1993). Herding and mimetic contagion will lead to nonrandom errors in expectations, generating systematic trends and path dependency in aggregate investment.

The use of algorithmic techniques is problematic because net present value calculations require judgments about discount rates. Making these judgments about the value of expenditure today over income tomorrow is likely to be difficult in a world constrained by endemic and immeasurable uncertainty about the future. Given these problems with algorithmic techniques, identifying simple and reliable proxies for net present value and/or internal rate of return is important. A procedurally rational investor may decide not to incur the costs involved in identifying a discount rate, either because they are ignorant that the value of money changes over time, or because they judge that current information is fallible and that the future is too uncertain for calculations based around discounting procedures to be of much use. The use of simple heuristics can be effective in an investment setting, and Baddeley (2006a) shows that, given some simplifying assumptions, heuristics such as the ARR and PBP approximate the results from algorithmic calculations including net present value and the internal rate of return. Judgments about complex and uncertain things such as discount rates may be unnecessary in some settings.

Risk and uncertainty in firm decision-making

Entrepreneurs' investment decisions will also be profoundly affected by immeasurable, Knightian uncertainty. This will prevent the application of clear and objective mathematical rules to guide their expectations of profit. Uncertainty creates a number of specific problems. First, information is incomplete and the data-generating processes dictating economic outcomes are often unknown; an investment decision is not like dealing a card from a pack of fifty-two cards, or buying a lottery ticket when you know that 1 million tickets are being sold. Secondly, investment decisions are often about nonrepeatable and unprecedented events, and this means that information about past outcomes (as might be captured by frequency data, for example) will be of little use. Thirdly, endogeneity means that economic realities are complex and mutable; expectations affect economic events that determine expectations (stock prices go up because people believe they will go up because stock prices are going up).

Future outcomes will be affected by current decisions based on expectations of the future formed today: intertemporal feedbacks between past, present and future will determine reality. Given these three sources of complexity, the objective basis for probability judgments may be missing or unknowable, and the third source of complexity will undermine, in the investment context, even the more subjectively based Bayesian probability concepts. Furthermore, cognitive limits on human information processing mean that individuals' subjective probability estimates are fallible (Tversky and Kahneman 1982; Baddeley *et al.* 2004).

Entrepreneurial decision-making: survey evidence

There have been a number of survey analyses of firms' real-world behaviour which provide some insight into whether firms and entrepreneurs are either procedurally rational or substantively rational. A lot of the survey evidence focuses on the use of investment appraisal techniques investigating the real-world use of complex algorithmic techniques versus simple heuristics such as PBP and ARR (Gordon 1955; Harcourt 1968; Sarnat and Levy 1969; Ramsey 1970; Dudley 1972; Gronchi 1986). Survey evidence reveals that heuristics such as the payback period technique and average rate of return are the techniques most commonly used, especially by small businesses (Neild 1964; Drury *et al.* 1992; Baddeley 1995, 2003, 2006a; Arnold and Hatzopoulos 1999, 2000).

Neild (1964) found that only 3 per cent of engineering firms used discounting algorithms. The majority (88 per cent) relied on heuristics such as payoff periods (67 per cent) or flat rates of return (21 per cent). Baddeley's (1995, 2006a) survey evidence shows that firms have a range of goals: maximizing sales or profits, industry leadership, growth; many mentioned the personal satisfaction of running a business, which chimes with the emphasis on animal spirits in behavioural macroeconomics. The entrepreneurs in this survey were more likely to rely on heuristics such as ARR and PBP (81 per cent of respondents). Not only were the firms not using the algorithmic techniques, but even if they were, they weren't necessarily using them properly: 45 per cent of the large firms using DCF methods did not realize the importance of a suitable discount rate, for example claiming that the question was 'not applicable'. Gut feel was identified as a key factor and was used by 28 per cent of large businesses, 50 per cent of medium-sized and 63 per cent of small businesses. Smaller firms may have been using gut feel as a substitute for mathematical algorithms as well as relying on general business skills and common sense. These findings suggest that psychological motivations are likely to have a significant impact on firms' decision-making.

In assessing the relative optimism or pessimism of enterpreneurs, businesses were also asked whether or not past investments had matched expectations. Business experience, instincts and gut feel are important when entrepreneurs are forming expectations and making final decisions about whether or not to invest in a project. In a face-to-face interview, one MD commented that

> it is difficult to assess the right approach – you would like to rely on mathematical calculation but don't believe that you can – although as a tool it's a great asset. But there will always be a gut feel, business experience element – as gut feel will tell you to base future expectations on historic information. The future is multifaceted, with many possible interactions and there can be no model to predict. Can you can come up with a model more predictable than people just pooling their gut feel reactions?
>
> (Baddeley 2006a, p.339)

Businesses were not always good at judging their performance, perhaps reflecting problems of over-confidence and under-confidence. Under-performance of investment projects was a function of firm size: 8 per cent of large firms, 14 per cent of medium-sized and 32 per cent of small firms under-performed relative to their expectations. In contrast, 10 per cent of large firms, 14 per cent of medium-sized firms and no small firms over-performed with their investments (Baddeley 1995, 2006a).

Consumption and saving

Akerlof and Shiller (2009) apply animal spirits to the puzzle of consumption and savings. Why do people accumulate credit card debt at high interest rates whilst simultaneously holding assets that earn low interest rates? People's decisions are affected by cues and frames. Akerlof and Shiller draw on experimental evidence from the application of the mental accounting models (explored in chapters 7 and 9) which analyse the limited fungibility of money: money will be perceived in different ways in different circumstances. Experiments show that people experiencing a windfall gain of $2400 will consume different proportions depending on the circumstances and context in which the windfall is received. If they receive a windfall as a sum to be spread over a series of monthly payments, then they will spend $1200. If it's a single lump sum, then they spend £785. If it is received as an inheritance, then they spend nothing. Rather than treating economic decisions together as one gigantic maximization problem, people assign different events to separate 'mental' accounts.

Saving is, by its nature, a forward-looking process and so people's attitudes towards the future, specifically their time preferences, have a crucial impact on their savings decisions.

As explored in chapter 9, behavioural economics postulates that people use hyperbolic or quasi-hyperbolic discounting functions in making judgments about the present value of future rewards. Angeletos *et al.* (2001) and Laibson *et al.* (2007) use behavioural discount functions to construct macroeconomic simulations, similar in empirical style to DSGE models including calibrated real business cycle models. Whilst these analyses suffer from similar limitations to standard calibrated models, for example in terms of objective, reliable methods for identifying the parameters used to calibrate the model, they do match real-world patterns of consumption and savings, and can help to explain why people accumulate credit card debt at high interest rates whilst simultaneously holding assets that earn low interest rates.

Another aspect of consumption and savings, which is addressed more effectively in behavioural macroeconomic models than in standard models, is consumer sentiment, which has been analysed in a number of ways, e.g. by George Katona (see Wärneryd 1982 for a review). In a macroeconomic context, consumer sentiment is significantly affected by noneconomic variables (Katona 1951; Earl 2005). Where consumer confidence is a function merely of conventional economic indicators, it can be modelled without any recourse to psychology, but aspects of 'the news' draw on emotions such as fear, anxiety and hope, and can make people nervous or euphoric, producing shifts in aggregate demand which are not generated directly by economic variables (Katona 1951). In this way, the psychological side of expectation formation operates as an 'intervening variable'.

This proposition is especially significant in affluent societies, particularly when there is widespread access to credit. When income and/or loans are available to spend on luxuries, macroeconomic forces will affect the timing of consumer durable purchases and adoption of new products (Smith 1975). When consumption is also affected by Veblen effects (conspicuous consumption of high-priced goods) interacting with demonstration effects (people observing others' consumption when deciding what to consume themselves), macroeconomic consumption has a different nature from microeconomic consumption, and so a macroeconomic analysis needs to do more than aggregate the consumption and savings decisions of one representative household.

Labour markets and unemployment

In standard economic models, labour markets are described in terms of interactions between profit-maximizing firms buying labour/selling goods and utility-maximizing households selling labour/buying goods. The explanatory power of these approaches is limited, though introducing asymmetric information into analyses does increase the external consistency of macroeconomic labour market models. Behavioural economists introduce a range of psychological phenomena into the analysis, focusing in particular on the role of social preferences including trust, reciprocity and fairness. Akerlof and Shiller (2009) apply their animal spirits to labour markets. Most markets trade goods which are inanimate and emotionless, but labour markets function differently.

Workers can adapt and change, with repercussions for work effort. Psychological and sociological factors play a key role. Workers want fair wages (Akerlof and Yellen 1990), and they resent their employers if their take-home wage falls, even if the fall in nominal wage is balanced by falling prices. Whilst this behaviour is attributed to money illusion in standard economics, Keynes (1936) explains it in terms of workers wanting to preserve their wages relative to other groups' wages (see also Shafir *et al.* 1997 for a survey of psychological explanations for money illusion). Similarly, workers reciprocate good treatment by trusting their employers. When wages fall, this sparks anger and resentment; workers' morale and sense of duty are offended. Work effort will decline and, even as wage costs fall, employers' profits will fall too because worker productivity is eroded.

Unemployment and efficiency wages

One standard explanation for unemployment is efficiency wages. Hiring workers involves a range of costs, including costs involved in the process of hiring, firing and training workers as well as other payroll costs. All this means that the cost of a worker is not just the wage they are paid. So a profit-maximizing firm, by raising wages, can increase profits by raising labour productivity and/or lowering other labour costs, and the efficient wage is the wage that minimizes unit labour costs, that is, total labour costs per unit of output. Efficiency wages involve paying workers a wage in excess of their marginal productivity, and this means that the standard labour demand/labour supply relationships will break down. Labour markets will not clear and involuntary unemployment emerges: workers are willing and able to work at the prevailing real wage but can't find a job.

Some efficiency wage models develop a standard approach by focusing on the impact of asymmetric information on hiring and search, and analysing the consequences in terms of involuntary unemployment. Firms pay workers a relatively high wage to prevent shirking by making other opportunities seem relatively less attractive, but paying workers a wage above their marginal productivity leads to excess labour supply and involuntary unemployment. It is this involuntary unemployment (rather than the high wage) which disciplines workers in reducing their propensity to shirk, because with high levels of involuntary unemployment workers will worry that they won't find a new job if they are fired for shirking (Shapiro and Stiglitz 1984). Other asymmetric information models focus on the role of high wages in overcoming problems of adverse selection; for example, higher-productivity workers will self-select into more highly paid jobs.

Behavioural models of efficiency wages move beyond asymmetric information analyses to focus on the deeper socio-psychological motivations underlying employer attitudes and worker effort. Akerlof (2002) identifies three psychological and sociological aspects to efficiency wages: reciprocity, fairness and social norms (analysed in more detail in chapter 5). Akerlof and Yellen (1990) develop some of the themes of fairness and inequity aversion in behavioural economics in a sociological model of the labour market, based on an effort–fair wage hypothesis: effort is proportional to the wage paid less subjective perceptions of the *fair* wage – which is determined by the average wage and reflects wages to high- and low-paid workers alike. If the wage paid is relatively low, effort and productivity will be disproportionately lower, and this explains why unemployment is higher for low-paid groups.

Reciprocity also plays a role in the labour market. Reciprocity is a feature of gift-exchange models developed from anthropology. Workers will reciprocate the 'gift' of a higher wage by working harder. Higher wages encourage effort and also loyalty, and with loyal staff a firm can reduce its labour turnover costs. Fehr *et al.* (1993) analyse gift-exchange games using experimental methods to show that players in experimental markets will offer prices above market-clearing levels. They interpret this as evidence in favour of fair wage theories of effort (Fehr *et al.* 1993).

Government policy-making

There has been a limited focus in behavioural economics on the psychology of policy-makers. Standard DSGE models have developed in response to the Lucas critique of government policy, which argues that discretionary fiscal and monetary policy is ineffective because it is undermined by rational expectations: rational agents anticipate discretionary policies and raise their inflationary expectations and wage demands in anticipation of higher inflation. Behavioural economics undermines this analysis because it is inconsistent with a rational expectations hypothesis. Given systematic behavioural biases, people's mistakes are unlikely to balance out on average, especially if people are susceptible to herding and social learning.

Kydland and Prescott (1977) and Barro and Gordon (1983) have developed the Lucas critique in focusing on the macroeconomic problem of dynamic inconsistency. Policies which are optimal in one period will generate endogenous changes in expectations, and a new optimal policy will emerge in the next period. The policy implication is that governments should not intervene. However, these approaches are based on assumptions not only of rational expectations and perfect information, but also of exponential discounting. Incorporating behavioural discount functions into macroeconomic models of policy-making may deliver different results and implications, particularly once political considerations are added into the mix. Political business cycles, and perhaps the Euro crisis and financial crisis too, are partly the product of politicians' present bias. Long-term strategies are undermined by short-term political contingencies and impulses, in much the same way that a smoker's plan to give up is undermined by a stressful domestic event. Policy-makers need pre-commitment devices, and perhaps central bank independence can be justified on the basis of behavioural insights about present bias as well as via more conventional justifications.

More broadly, Akerlof and Shiller (2009) argue that governments play an important role in complementing capitalism, and 'capitalism must live within certain rules' (p. 173). Given the overwhelming influence of animal spirits 'the government must set those rules' (p. 173). Our old financial system is a Humpty Dumpty – it's broken, cannot be fixed and must be replaced and, to moderate the current slump, Akerlof and Shiller advocate a two-target approach in which financial targets complement fiscal and monetary stimuli, for example via lending and capital injections, to ensure they are consistent with full employment.

Happiness

Happiness is a subjective feeling and therefore is affected by moods and emotions. It will also be affected by individual differences; for example, some evidence shows that the French claim to be unhappier than the Americans, even though, as objectively measured, their standard of living is greater. A wide range of socio-economic decisions will affect an individual's happiness, including marriage, divorce, criminality and addiction, amongst others. In *A Treatise on the Family* Becker (1991) applies rational choice principles to everyday decision-making, asserting that these reflect a rational, maximizing balancing of economic benefits and costs. For example, people marry and divorce when they perceive that the overall benefits from entering into or breaking the marriage contract outweigh the costs.

A lot of behavioural economics focuses on the ways in which these rational choice principles are violated in the real world. Anti-social and self-destructive behaviours may be the product of a complex range of motivations, including behaviours that are associated with irrational and/or ill-informed decision-making. Rather than balancing benefits and costs in a symmetrical and systematic way, people will prefer avoiding losses to making gains, and happiness will be affected by changing situations, not the *status quo*. In this way, hedonic psychology – the psychology of wellbeing – can be brought into the analysis of happiness. Anchoring effects will operate when people's decisions and choices reflect what they have experienced already: if they are happy with a given situation then they will anchor their expectations of future happiness to what they are currently experiencing. Framing effects will also bring the psychological context into people's reported perceptions of personal issues. When students are asked: 'Are you happy?' and 'When did you last have a date?', the students' answers were affected both by which question is asked first and by how things had gone the night before.

Utility and happiness

Kahneman and Tverksy's (1979) critique of expected utility theory (explored in chapter 7) does not focus specifically on problems with the basic concept of utility, though Loomes and Sugden's (1982) regret theory does start to unravel some of the limitations of a stark conception of utility. In later work, however, broader concepts of utility are addressed by Kahneman (2003, 2011). Utility is in essence about happiness, satisfaction, pleasure. Whilst standard approaches make utility seem quite an objective concept, it is inherently subjective – the subjectivity is acknowledged in a mathematical sense in expected utility theory, but in the process stripping out the emotional aspects of utility for reasons of tractability. Some areas of behavioural economics aim to develop a deeper understanding of utility and its complexities.

Standard conceptions of utility focus on one homogeneous quality, revealed through choice. Behavioural economists have a more nuanced view and distinguish between different sources of utility, including decision utility and experienced utility. Decision utility is about outcomes, and fits with a standard conception of utility. Experienced utility can be subdivided into instant utility, which is about current, real-time experiences; and remembered utility, which is retrospective and, because it focuses on current evaluations of past experiences, is susceptible to some of the biases and heuristics outlined in chapter 6, particularly biases emerging from the misapplication of the availability heuristic (Kahneman 1994; Kahneman et al. 1997). Kahneman et al. (1997) develop a normative theory of utility, focusing on the experienced utility from outcomes which are extended over time. They also allow a role for learning, noting that learning may bring together different types of utility. They also propose a neuroeconomic approach, postulating that remembered, chosen and experienced utility will each be associated with different neural areas. Conflicts will emerge because the different forms of utility may not coincide, for example, addicts anticipate utility and so choose to consume a drug, but then find that experienced utility is not so pleasurable, a conflict which was explored in more detail in chapter 10.

Kahneman and Tversky's research propelled a whole new approach to economics – hedonic psychology – the psychology of wellbeing. In one sense, hedonic psychology is a modern development of utilitarianism – a moral doctrine, associated with the English economist and philosopher Jeremy Bentham, asserting that actions should be assessed according to their impact on utility – on pleasure, satisfaction and happiness. Pareto focuses on a narrower concept, ophelimity – measuring just economic satisfaction to separate it from broader moral, political and religious aspects of utility. In hedonic psychology, people are making subjective judgments about their own happiness (for example, in the context of decisions such as to marry or divorce), and these judgments will not necessarily tie in with monetary measures. In marriage and divorce, for example, it is the change in circumstances that affects people's perceptions of their own happiness.

People will judge their own happiness against a benchmark of what they've experienced in the past. For married couples, their experience of marriage and divorce is determined by the recent past, so happiness peaks at the point of marriage but falls rapidly until, after (on average) two years of marriage, it stabilizes at a level equivalent to (and sometimes below) pre-marital happiness levels (Layard 2005). Stutzer and Frey (2006) develop these ideas, analysing marriage using German survey evidence: their analysis suggests that happy singles are more likely to select into marriage and unhappy people are likely to self-select into divorce. Different life events may not be separable in terms of their impacts on happiness; for example, Rowthorn (1999) notes that contagion effects may operate in marriage if attitudes and expectations influence the likelihood of divorce. DeNeve and Cooper (1998), in a meta-analysis of personality traits, found that personality traits, including the Big Five factors of extraversion and agreeableness, were significantly correlated with happiness, life satisfaction and positive affect, though the correlations with negative affect were less significant.

So, overall, happiness is about more than the balancing of monetary benefits and costs. There will be spillover effects, and socio-psychological factors will have an impact too. Layard (2005) analyses the paradoxes that underlie the pursuit of happiness, particularly issues of status, security and trust. Rising incomes in the advanced nations have coincided with increasing income disparities, declining job security and rising crime rates, all of which have compromised status, security and trust. Similarly, Frey (2008) focuses on the hedonic consequences of unemployment, emphasizing that employment offers more than an income. Subjective wellbeing is also compromised, and so unemployment involves not only the direct effects but also indirect impacts.

Happiness is a specific mood, but other moods will affect decision-making too. The recognition of differences between anticipated, experienced and remembered utility, as mentioned above, leaves a role for moods and emotions: for example, weather has an impact on mood, and through that on financial markets (see chapters 8 and 11; Hirshleifer and Shumway 2003; Kamstra *et al.* 2003). Happiness will affect other aspects of standard of living too. Wilson and Oswald (2005) find positive associations between marriage and health (both physical and psychological), identifying health gains from being married. Edlund (2005) focuses on the impact of marital decisions on labour mobility and migration, and hypothesizes that females will move to urban areas because they are attracted by the higher incomes of richer urban men. Gautier *et al.* (2005) assert that singles are more likely to pay higher property prices in cities because marriage markets are better in cities.

Wellbeing

What's the difference between wellbeing and happiness? General wellbeing is the macroeconomic manifestation of general happiness. Wellbeing is about standards of living – happiness plays a part in wellbeing, but so do other outcomes, for example access to healthcare, educational attainment, longevity, internet access, etc. General aspects of the quality of life are captured in measures such as the HDI and the Quality of Life Index (QLI). Wellbeing is a broader concept, and captures not only GDP/GNP and physical standards of living, but also the hedonic aspects. Wellbeing is a global concept reflecting incomes, physical standards of living, and happiness. There is increasing interest in measuring wellbeing, and behavioural economics offers some insights into how to capture the psychological, hedonic nature of happiness and to build this into a macroeconomic measure of aggregate wellbeing. Wellbeing has both intrinsic and instrumental value: instrumental because happiness promotes learning, productivity, creativity and health, which all have impacts on social welfare. But it also has an intrinsic value of its own, which partly links it with utilitarianism.

Analyses of wellbeing often focus on relationships, physiology and opportunities. Many aspects of everyday life affect our feelings of wellbeing: employment/unemployment, environment, commuting, social activities, environmental quality, illness and treatment, new technology. It is not always obvious what will be good for our wellbeing: *Facebook* may be good if it allows those who don't have other social opportunities to build online social networks, but if this is at the expense of real relationships, then the net impact is less clear. On the other hand, whilst the common conception may be that computer games are bad for wellbeing, studies of pro-social computer games have shown that these can enhance wellbeing, particularly as they link to social influence and the environment (Huppert and So 2011). Wellbeing is not just about mood. Mood and personality together play a role: for example, optimists are more likely to be happy and are also likely to have better life outcomes – as shown in a study of the longevity of nuns which found that optimistic nuns lived longer (Seligman 2003). Huppert and So (2011) argue that wellbeing concepts are complex. They focus on flourishing and 'functionings', which relate to Sen's capabilities. Functionings are enhanced by resilience, strong relationships and social networks, as well as feelings, moods and emotions. In conceptualizing wellbeing, it is important to focus not just on the hedonic aspects associated with individual physical pleasures, but also on more eudaemonic aspects associated with a full and active life.

Seaford outlines five wellbeing imperatives: connect, be active, take notice, keep learning and keep giving (Seaford *et al.* 2011). The relative importance of different drivers will vary across groups and areas, and behavioural concepts such as loss aversion will be relevant. For example, loss of income is hedonically disproportionately worse than a gain in income. Loss aversion, specifically aversion to losing time, might explain why people report that commuting substantially decreases their life satisfaction. Loss aversion also connects well with the intuition that job security is important, and negative correlations between wellbeing and unemployment have been identified. Part-time workers are also less happy than full-time workers. This was demonstrated in a case study on the Canadian Community Innovation Project, which explored the impact on perceptions of satisfaction in moving from income assistance (i.e. focus on money) to employment insurance (i.e. focus on jobs). Other factors that affect wellbeing include social capital. Wellbeing is also about social groups and networks: Baumeister and Leary (1995) discuss wellbeing as being about the need for connections. Personal resources such as sleep and physical activity also contribute to wellbeing.

Looking at it from the other direction, barriers to wellbeing include external barriers (for example time, money) and internal barriers (for example pessimism). There are also psychosocial barriers including habits, social norms, and feelings of powerlessness and exclusion. Overall wellbeing depends on social activity as well as economic activity.

Halpern (2005) discusses aspects of wellbeing in terms of conflicts between goals and outcomes: for example, being healthy and having a healthy lifestyle are not necessarily the same, and being healthy is more important to wellbeing than having a healthy lifestyle. This raises the question of the extent to which wellbeing drivers are under individual control. What externalities are created affecting the wellbeing of others? Driving a Porsche may generate negative externalities for others; relationships may generate positive externalities. There will also be unintended consequences: some institutions generate positive externalities even though that wasn't the original intention, for example, the 'school gate phenomenon' – the school gate is a place where families can meet other families and build connections, generating positive externalities, even though the school gate was not designed for this purpose.

Measuring wellbeing

One of the problems with a policy focus on wellbeing is its measurement. Even if goals are clear, we need effective and reliable measurement tools to assess whether or not these goals are being met. Maximizing growth in GDP/GNP implies a monetary measure of happiness and, whilst these have many limitations, they are relatively easy to calculate. Standard macroeconomic measurement also has problems because, whilst it appears that we have an objective unit of account in the form of money, if money has a value in itself then it cannot capture the value of other things. Nonetheless, it is probably even more difficult to construct a behavioural measure because there is no clear place to start in constructing an equivalent for broader measures of wellbeing. The main insights about wellbeing often start with the Easterlin paradox: cross-sectional analyses of reported happiness do not show that happiness increases with rising incomes (Easterlin 1974), and Kahneman (2011) notes that happiness flatlines beyond $75k.

One of the problems with wellbeing is how to capture and measure it effectively over time and across space. Subjective wellbeing is usually measured via surveys of life satisfaction. Some data also concentrate on outcomes in terms of 'illbeing' – mental health outcomes as a measure of the inverse of wellbeing – and this has some parallels with behavioural stocks of capital, for example, as seen in Becker, Grossman and Murphy's concept of addictive capital. Survey data can complicate cross-sectional comparisons of wellbeing. Value judgments can distort comparisons, especially if the focus is on simple rankings, because these do not take into account different expectations (for example, the fact that Denmark was recently ranked first in terms of wellbeing and France was much lower down may reflect different cultural expectations). Different speeds of adaptation to expectation will also affect survey measures of wellbeing, and simple rankings do not capture the spread and dispersion of outcomes. Separating relative versus absolute wellbeing is problematic without some basic unit of account, though, in the other direction, monetary measures of inequality do capture more about general wellbeing than a simple absolute measure of income.

Halpern (2009) explores some of the hidden sources of wellbeing. Spatial distributions of things that generate wellbeing have impacts too, complicating wellbeing measurement: a tree planted in a city has more positive impacts and externalities than a tree planted in the country because, even though either will contribute to environmental quality via carbon capture and storage, in a city a tree will increase wellbeing more because of its hedonic impacts. This phenomenon is difficult to capture, even using green GDP measures. It would also be useful to have ways of weighting wellbeing, for example, the wellbeing of children and young people is especially important to examine because they have more time ahead of them on average.

There are alternatives to happiness surveys, including surveys concentrating on particular aspects of wellbeing such as the Happy Planet Index, European Social Survey national accounts of wellbeing and ONS wellbeing data. Some survey analyses have identified interesting links between economic and financial events and broader evaluations of wellbeing. Deaton (2011) links financial crisis to wellbeing, and uses a range of self-reported wellbeing measures from Gallup polls to capture the impact, in the USA, of financial crisis and recession on people's emotions and their evaluation of their circumstances. Following the collapse of Lehman Brothers in 2008, Americans reported sharp declines in their evaluations of their circumstances accompanied by sharp increases in worry and stress, and declines in positive affect. The American population proved to be remarkably resilient however, and by the end of 2010 many of the survey measures had improved.

Some researchers have also measured happiness using semantic methods, for example by examining Twitter feeds. There are similar ways to measure confidence, for example counting Google searches for the gold price when people are feeling pessimistic about the financial situation. Another way to capture some aspects of happiness and wellbeing empirically is to use case studies of marriage and divorce, religion, etc.

Recent data collection initiatives have recognized limitations in wellbeing data and have adopted more complex approaches, for example in psychometric factor analysis – used in the European Social Survey. This incorporates three sets of factors: hedonic appraisal including feelings/emotions; positive functioning including competence/positive relationships; and positive attributes including resilience, optimism, self-esteem. The Office for National Statistics in the UK is developing new initiatives too, emphasizing multidimensional aspects and links with equality/sustainability, and in December 2011 released its first report (see also Matheson 2011). Four questions are incorporated into the integrated household survey focusing on householders' happiness, satisfaction, anxiety and worthiness (worthwhile things done), with rankings on a 0–10 scale. There are also plans to elaborate the data collection by including questions on opinion surveys. The problem with self-report surveys is that respondents might not be honest and/or may lack insight into their own circumstances. Nonetheless, measuring wellbeing does provide richer information about people's standards of living than the standard data focusing on employment/unemployment, inflation and growth.

Wellbeing and the environment

One aspect of wellbeing which is developing a pressing importance is the relationship between wellbeing and the environment. Environmental problems will have an impact on people's wellbeing, particularly if they create concerns amongst individuals. The European Commission (2002) conducted 7500 interviews for fifteen member states of the EU and found that 89 per cent of respondents were concerned about environmental pollution; 86 per cent about natural resources and waste generation; and 82 per cent about trends relating to nature and wildlife; 72 per cent were concerned about climate change; and 73 per cent believe that the environment influences the quality of life very much or quite a lot, relative to 64 per cent for economic and social factors. These attitudes are relatively robust over recent time with not much change since the global financial crisis and recession. The 2011 Eurobarometer Surveys on the environment and climate change found that 95 per cent of EU citizens feel that protecting the environment is personally important to them, and 76 per cent believe that environmental problems have a direct impact on their lives, though only 69 per cent believe that they should be personally responsible for using natural resources more effectively. For climate change, 68 per cent support environmental taxes, but just 53 per cent had taken some sort of action to combat climate change, and 66 per cent reduced and recycled waste. This survey evidence reveals some inconsistencies between people's beliefs about the significance of climate change and actions taken to combat climate change. In addition, some respondents seem not to realize that recycling is an activity that can help to combat climate change (European Commission 2011a).

Gowdy (2008) rejects the standard rational actor view that there is a trade-off between material consumption and environmental protection. Increasing per capita income does not increase wellbeing beyond a certain point, and drastic reductions in fossil fuel use will mean a reduction in production of consumer goods. But if welfare policy goals can shift from income to wellbeing more broadly defined then this will be a positive development. Similarly, in developing countries, reorienting policies towards living a full life rather than income creation would alleviate pressure on the environment.

Weber (2011) notes the importance of voluntary reductions in energy consumption, but most Western households fail to install energy-saving technologies even if they would save money in the long run by doing so. They also seem reluctant to make personal sacrifices in terms of lifestyle, and some argue that this is because they have not experienced the consequences of climate change. However, empirical evidence does not suggest that lack of experience reduces motivations to act. Actions to reduce energy use are not related to uncertainty about climate change existing, but have more to do with whether or not people think that their behaviour will be effective.

The desire to maintain the current quality of life will also lead to inertia, especially as conspicuous consumption can signal social status. The sacrifices that people are prepared to make will reflect their socio-economic conditions. A Pennsylvania survey analysed the role of wealth and environmental attitudes in environmental action, and found no significant association between personal economic conditions and environmental concerns, though people on lower incomes were less willing to incur monetary costs and richer people were less willing to sacrifice living standards and comforts (Pongiglione 2011). Other factors affecting positive environmental action include knowledge, an internal locus of control (taking personal responsibility), and perceived threats to personal health (Fransson and Gärling 1999).

To assess the impact of socio-economic status and environmental attitudes, Baddeley (2011) analysed survey responses from 2764 respondents to Northern Ireland's Continuous Household Survey 2009/10, using ordered probit techniques. The data suggest that apathy (low levels of reported concern about environmental issues) is associated with reduced environmental action. Environmental awareness (familiarity with common phrases about environmental conservation, etc.) correlates positively and significantly with the number of environmentally sustainable actions taken, though the survey data may be susceptible to self-reporting biases, given the positive normative connotations of positive environmental action. Larger household size also has a positive significant impact, perhaps because social pressure increases when environmental actions are observed and/or encouraged by others. Owner-occupiers also are more likely to engage in environmental action. Socio-economic status (as measured by whether or not a household depended on benefits), number of children, the age of housing, and whether or not householders were public rental tenants were insignificant, suggesting that poverty does not constrain environmental actions, and nor does the presence of children.

Leiserowitz (2006) notes that people claim to be very concerned about climate change, ranking it highly on lists of global threats; but when it comes closer to home and people are asked to judge more proximate threats, climate change is low on people's lists of priorities. Leiserowitz argues that people do not perceive climate change as a direct threat, and this links to the impact of vividness and emotions on behaviour: people do not have vivid, concrete, personally salient, affective images of climate change, and so environmental behaviour change is a low priority.

The evidence about the impact of first-hand (and devastating) experiences of environmental calamities is mixed. Spence *et al.* (2011) analysed UK survey data from 1822 individuals, and found that flood victims were more concerned about climate change and were more confident that their actions would have an effect. Other studies suggest that direct experience of the impacts of climate change may restrain action if it leads to cognitive suppression of frightening realities (Pongiglione 2011). Lorenzoni *et al.* (2007) observe that motivation depends on people believing that their actions will be effective, but a 2004 BBC poll shows that only about half of people think that behavioural changes will have an impact on climate change. This may link to feelings of powerlessness. Experience of detrimental consequences of climate change does not necessarily link to mitigation efforts and responses to questions about willingness to change behaviour to protect the environment. Whitmarsh (2008) reports survey evidence showing that the salience of risk does not predict behaviour: those who had experienced floods were no more likely to think that the problem could be solved. UK flood victims felt unable to control their situation during the floods, and so did not expect to be able to take effective action against climatic events in the future; there were no significant differences in the responses of UK flood victims and nonvictims in attitudes towards combating climate change (Whitmarsh 2008; Pongiglione 2011; Spence *et al.* 2011). Direct experience may in fact restrain action if cognitive dissonance/cognitive suppression take hold: fear and helplessness may be paralysing (McNamara and Grubb 2011; Pongiglione 2011).

Strauss (2008) analysed responses from a Swiss rural community: of ninety-five residents interviewed, most acknowledged that climate change was taking place, but they felt helpless and preferred to focus actions on things they felt able to control. Norgaard (2006) interviewed people in a Norwegian rural community and found that people recognized climatic changes and had high level of knowledge about the climate, but made no mitigation efforts, instead associating climate change with fear and helplessness. These feelings of helplessness may be exacerbated by a social organization of denial, because motivation is harder if people feel that they are acting alone and that there is no impetus to collective action.

Yates and Aronson (1983) emphasize salience and vividness, and argue that there is too much emphasis on initial costs; more vividness is needed in energy-saving advice. Similarly, Bazerman (2006) asserts that one problem is that environmental damage is not a vivid threat – it does not engage emotional, visceral responses and this encourages apathy. This could also link to salience and the availability heuristic: people form perceptions and decisions on the basis of recent experience, but if they have not experienced the consequences of environmental damage, they are less likely to worry about it (see also Sunstein 2006).

Neuroeconomic analyses of happiness

By definition, neuroeconomics is a microeconomic tool, and although 'hyperscanning' technology is being developed to enable the analysis of neural activations across groups of people, there is little that neuroeconomics can contribute when it comes to aggregate behaviour on a macroeconomic scale. There are, however, a number of studies exploring the neural correlates of wellbeing and happiness in individuals.

Lykken and Tellegen (1996) studied identical twins and found that genetic inheritance accounts for half of variance in happiness levels. Urry *et al.* (2004) used electroencephalograms to analyse the responses of eighty-four people to questions about mood and happiness. They found more activity in the left cortex associated with higher happiness levels. Davidson (2004) used fMRI techniques to establish that emotional stress leads to activations in the amygdala and the right prefrontal cortex, confirming some of the findings outlined in chapter 8 about the neural correlates of emotions. Davidson then constructed a bell curve of people in a resting state and found that the ratio of right and left prefrontal activations predicted a person's happiness

Habel *et al.* (2005) used fMRI techniques to analyse the responses of twenty-six healthy male subjects experiencing positive and negative emotional experiences. They found that, relative to a control task, sad and happy moods were associated with significant activations in the amygdala and hippocampus extending into the prefrontal cortex and anterior cingulate. Sadness was associated with stronger activations found in the ventrolateral prefrontal cortex, anterior cingulate cortex and temporal gyrus, whereas happiness was associated with stronger activations in the dorsolateral prefrontal cortex, the cingulate gyrus, the inferior temporal gyrus and the cerebellum. This suggests that the mood valence is affected by specific neural pathways.

Lutz *et al.* (2004) identified significant increases in gamma rhythms (neural oscillations associated with consciousness) during meditation, and also found significantly higher left prefrontal cortex activity in Himalayan monks when meditating. Davidson *et al.* (2003) also analysed the impact of meditation in exploring the relationships between wellbeing, affective style and mindfulness. Mindfulness involves being attentive to thoughts as a means of reducing stress. Davidson *et al.* analysed high-flying employees from a biotech firm who were enrolled in a two-month meditation course. The responses of this treatment group were compared with a control group. In the treatment group, after meditation the left prefrontal cortex was more active, perhaps because meditation had strengthened neural circuits in the left prefrontal cortex enabling more effective inhibition of amygdala activity, which is active in processing negative emotions. The effects endured and the experimenters could still see changes four months after the course had concluded.

Conclusions and policy implications

Behavioural macroeconomics is a young discipline and has yet to develop a coherent structure. As more insights are developed within microeconomic analyses of behaviour, these may be constructed convincingly into a theory of behavioural macroeconomics, but how to address problems of aggregation effectively remains a problem.

In terms of robust analytical approaches, it is unlikely that mathematical methods can be employed to give behavioural macroeconomic models with analytical solutions. The use of calibration, simulation and agent-based modelling could be extended to capture the complexities of macroeconomic interactions, but calibrating these models with appropriate parameter estimates remains a problem, and the subjectivity involved means that, even with these technically sophisticated methods there will be an element of *ad hoc*-ery.

One potential solution might be to build a model that separates out the various actors within the macroeconomy – identifying specific traits and constraints affecting that group and bringing the actors together using agent-based modelling. This approach could draw on some robust findings from the analysis of economic behaviour and psychology at a micro-scale. Different actors in the economy could be described differently, reflecting either their socio-economic context, their roles, and/or their basic traits and other individual differences. Another approach would be to treat the macroeconomy as an organism in itself and focus on the phenomena that emerge without trying to unravel the behavioural microfoundations. Either way, attention needs to shift towards moving the many useful behavioural insights from the microeconomy to the macroeconomy, and more work needs to be done to find ways of blending intuitive understandings of how macroeconomies operate with empirical and theoretical tools for guiding policy-making.

In standard analyses, rational agents have the potential to undermine systematic policy-making, and the implication is that policy-makers should stand back and focus on a hands-off, transparent approach. This style of thinking underlies the focus on inflation targeting and central bank independence that were popular before the 2007/08 financial crises and subsequent recessions. With the introduction of insights from behavioural economics into the mix, this policy stance must be adapted to allow that people are not necessarily rational and systematic in their decision-making, particularly when planning for the future. And as policy-makers extend their goals beyond monetary measures of welfare towards broader, qualitative goals including wellbeing and happiness, new behavioural approaches will be needed to define, measure and monitor these more diffuse and imprecise macroeconomic goals effectively. Managing the trade-off between realism and precision is a substantial challenge for behavioural macroeconomics, but if behavioural macroeconomics can produce approaches that are both compelling and tractable, then this will deliver clear benefits for macroeconomic policy.

Bibliography

Abdellaoui M, Baillon A, Placido L and Wakker P (2011) 'The rich domain of uncertainty: source functions and their experimental implementation', *American Economic Review*, 101(2), 695–723.

Abel AB (1983) 'Optimal investment under uncertainty', *American Economic Review*, 73(1), 228–33.

Abeler J, Falk A, Goette L and Huffman D (2011) 'Reference points and effort provision', *American Economic Review*, 101(2), 470–92.

Acemoglu D (1993) 'Learning about others' actions and the investment accelerator', *Economic Journal*, 103(417), 318–28.

Acquisti A (2004) 'Privacy in electronic commerce and the economics of immediate gratification', paper presented at Electronic Commerce Conference, May 2004. www.heinz.cmu.edu/~acquisti/papers/privacy-gratification.pdf

Acquisti A and Grossklags J (2006) 'What can behavioral economics teach us about privacy?', Keynote Paper presented at Emerging Trends in Information and Communication Security, International Conference (ETRICS) 2006; reprinted in Acquisti A, Gritzalis S, Lambrinoudakis C and di Vimercati S (eds) (2007) *Digital Privacy: Theory, Technologies and Practices*, Boca Raton, FL: Auerbach Publications, pp. 363–80.

Adler A (1979) *Superiority and Social Interest* (3rd edn), edited by Ansbacher HL and Ansbacher RR, New York: WW Norton.

Adler NE and Stewart J (2009) 'Reducing obesity: motivating action while not blaming the victim. explore connections between default options and obesity', *Milbank Quarterly*, 87(1), 49–70.

Adler SJ and Freedman AM (1990) 'Tobacco suit exposes ways cigarette firms keep the profits fat', *Wall Street Journal*, 5 March.

Adolphs R, Tranel D, Damasio H and Damasio AR (1995) 'Fear and the human amygdala', *Journal of Neuroscience*, 5(9), 5879–91.

Ainslie G (1974) 'Impulse control in pigeons', *Journal of the Experimental Analysis of Behavior*, 21(3), 485–89.

— (1991) 'Derivation of "rational" economic behavior from hyperbolic discount curves', *American Economic Review*, 81(2), 334–40.

Ainslie G and Haslam N (1992) 'Hyperbolic discounting', in Loewenstein G (ed.), *Choice Over Time*, Princeton, NJ: Russell Sage Foundation, pp. 57–92.

Ajzen I (1991) 'The theory of planned behavior', *Organizational Behavior and Human Decision Processes*, 50, 179–211.

Akerlof GA (2002) 'Behavioral macroeconomics and macroeconomic behavior', *American Economic Review*, 92(3), 411–33.

— (2005) *Explorations in Pragmatic Economics: Selected Papers of George A Akerlof and co-authors*, Oxford: Oxford University Press.

Akerlof GA and Dickens WT (1982) 'The economic consequences of cognitive dissonance', *American Economic Review*, 72(3), 307–19.

Akerlof GA and Kranton RE (2000) 'Economics and identity', *Quarterly Journal of Economics*, 15(3), 715–53.

— (2011) *Identity Economics – How our Identities Shape our Work, Wages and Well-being*, Princeton, NJ: Princeton University Press.

Akerlof G and Shiller R (2009) *Animal Spirits: How Human Psychology Drives the Economy and Why it Matters for Global Capitalism*, Princeton, NJ: Princeton University Press.

Akerlof G and Yellen JL (1990) 'The fair wage-effort hypothesis and unemployment', *Quarterly Journal of Economics*, 105(2), 255–83.

Alexander M and Christia F (2011) 'Context modularity of human altruism', *Science*, 334(6061), 1392–94.

Allais M (1953) 'Le comportement de l'homme rationnel devant le risque: critique des postulats et axiomes de l'Ecole Americaine', *Econometrica*, 21(4), 503–46.

Allcott H (2011) 'Social norms and energy conservation', *Journal of Public Economics*, 95(9/10), 1082–95.

Allcott H and Mullainathan S (2010) 'Behavior and energy policy', *Science*, 327, 1204–05.

Allport GW (1937) *Personality – A Psychological Interpretation*, New York: Holt, Reinhart & Winston.

— (1955) *Becoming – Basic Considerations for a Psychology of Personality*, New Haven, CT: Yale University Press.

— (1961) *Pattern and Growth in Personality*. Oxford: Holt, Reinhart & Winston.

Andersen S, Ertaç S, Gneezy U, Hoffman M and List JA (2011) 'Stakes matter in ultimatum games', *American Economic Review*, 101(7), 3427–39.

Anderson JL (1998) 'Embracing uncertainty: the interface of Bayesian statistics and cognitive psychology', *Conservation Ecology*, 2(1), www.consecol.org/vol2/iss1/art2

Anderson L and Holt C (1996) 'Classroom games: information cascades', *Journal of Economic Perspectives*, 10(4), 187–93.

— (1997) 'Information cascades in the laboratory', *American Economic Review*, 87(5), 847–62.

Anderson R and Moore T (2009) 'Information security: where computer science, economics and psychology meet', *Philosophical Transactions of the Royal Society Series A*, 367, 2717–27.

— (2008) 'Information security economics – and beyond', paper presented at Information Security Summit 2008, www.cl.cam.ac.uk/~rja14/Papers/econ_crypto.pdf.

Andreoni J (1990) 'Impure altruism and donations to public goods: a theory of warm glow giving', *Economic Journal*, 100, 464–77.

Angeletos G-M, Laibson D, Repetto A, Tobacman J and Weinberg S (2001) 'The hyperbolic consumption model: calibration, simulation and empirical evaluation', *Journal of Economic Perspectives*, 15(3), 47–68.

Anufriev M and Hommes CH (2007) *Evolution of Market Heuristics*, CeNDEF Working Papers 07–06, Amsterdam: Universiteit van Amsterdam, Center for Nonlinear Dynamics in Economics and Finance.

Apicella P, Ljungberg T, Scarnati E and Schultz W (1991) 'Responses to rewarding monkey dorsal and ventral striatum', *Experimental Brain Research*, 85, 491–500.

Ariely D (2008) *Predictably Irrational – The Hidden Forces that Shape Our Decisions*, New York: Harper Collins.

Ariely D, Loewenstein G and Prelec D (2003) 'Coherent arbitrariness: stable demand curves without stable preferences', *Quarterly Journal of Economics*, 118(1), 73–105.

Ariely DA, Bracha A and Meier S (2009a) 'Doing good or doing well? Image motivation and monetary incentives in behaving prosocially', *American Economic Review,* 99(1), 544–55.

Ariely D, Gneezy U, Loewenstein G and Mazar N (2009b) 'Large stakes and big mistakes', *Review of Economic Studies,* 76(2), 451–69.

Arkes HR and Bulmer C (1985) 'The psychology of sunk cost', *Organizational Behavior and Human Decision Processes*, 37(1), 93–110.

Arnold GC and Hatzopoulos PD (1999) '*Ex ante* investment appraisal methods and *ex post* financial performance assessment comparison and the calculation of the cost of capital in UK firms', Aston Business School Research Paper 9908, Birmingham: Aston Business School.

Asch SE (1955) 'Opinions and social pressure', *Scientific American*, 193(5), 31–35.

— (1956) *Studies of Independence and Conformity: A Minority of One Against a Unanimous Majority*, Psychological Monographs, 70 (Whole no. 416).

Asheim GB (2009) 'Strategic use of environmental information', *Environmental Resource Economics*, 46(2), 207–16.

Ashraf N, Karlan D and Yin W (2006) 'Tying Odysseus to the mast: evidence from a commitment savings product in the Philippines', *Quarterly Journal of Economics*, 121(2), 673–97.

Avenanti A, Bueti D, Galati G and Aglioti M (2005) 'Transcranial magnetic stimulation highlights the sensorimotor side of empathy for pain', *Nature Neuroscience*, 8, 955–60.

Avery C and Zemsky P (1998) 'Multi-dimensional uncertainty and herd behavior in financial markets', *American Economic Review*, 88, 724–48.

Axelrod R (1990) *The Evolution of Cooperation*, Harmondsworth: Penguin.

Backhouse RE and Bateman BW (2011) *Capitalist Revolutionary: John Maynard Keynes*, Cambridge, MA: Harvard University Press.

Baddeley AD (1997) *Human Memory: Theory and Practice* (revised edn), Hove, UK: Psychology Press.

— (2002) 'Is working memory still working?', *European Psychologist*, 7(2), 85–97.

Baddeley, H (2008) *Physics and the Human Body: Stories of Who Discovered What*, Milton Keynes: Authorhouse.

Baddeley M (1995) 'Rationality, expectations and investment', PhD thesis, University of Cambridge.

— (1999) 'Keynes on rationality, expectations and investment, 1999', in Sardoni C (ed.), *Keynes, Post Keynesianism and Political Economy: Essays in Honour of Geoff Harcourt*, Vol. 3, London: Routledge.

— (2002) 'Speculative bubbles', in Snowdon B and Vane H (eds), *Encyclopaedia of Macroeconomics*, Cheltenham: Edward Elgar.

— (2003) *Investment: Theories and Analysis*, Basingstoke: Palgrave Macmillan.

— (2004) 'Using e-cash in the new economy: an economic analysis of micropayments systems', *Journal of Electronic Commerce Research*, 5(4), 239–53, www.csulb.edu/web/journals/jecr/issues/20044/Paper3.pdf

— (2005) *Housing Bubbles, Herds and Frenzies: Evidence from British Housing Markets*, CCEPP Policy Brief PB02–05, Cambridge: Cambridge Centre for Economics and Public Policy, Department of Land Economy, University of Cambridge.

— (2006a) 'Behind the Black Box: a survey of real-world investment appraisal approaches', *Empirica*, 33(5), 329–50.

— (2006b) 'Bubbles or whirlpools? An empirical analysis of the impacts of speculation and financial uncertainty on investment', in Holt R and Pressman S (eds), *Empirical Post Keynesian Economics: Looking at the Real World*, New York: ME Sharpe.

— (2010) 'Herding, social influence and economic decision-making: socio-psychological and neuroscientific analyses', *Philosophical Transactions of the Royal Society Series B*, 365(1538), 281–90.

— (2011) *Energy, the Environment and Behaviour Change: Insights from Behavioural Economics*, Cambridge Working Papers in Economics No. 1162, Cambridge: Faculty of Economics, University of Cambridge.

Baddeley M and Fontana G (2006) 'Monetary policy in the information economy: old problems and new challenges, 2006', in Arestis P, Baddeley M and McCombie J (eds), *'New' Monetary Policy: Implications and Relevance*, Cheltenham: Edward Elgar.

Baddeley M and McCombie J (2004) 'An historical perspective on speculative bubbles and financial crisis: tulipmania and the South Sea Bubble', in Arestis P, Baddeley M and McCombie J (eds), *What Global Economic Crisis?* London: Palgrave Macmillan.

Baddeley M, Curtis A and Wood R (2004) 'An introduction to prior information derived from probabilistic judgments; elicitation of knowledge, cognitive bias and herding', in Curtis A and Wood R (eds), *Geological Prior Information: Informing Science and Engineering*, Special Publication No. 239, London: Geological Society, pp. 15–27.

Baddeley M, Christopoulos G, Pillas D, Schultz W and Tobler P (2007) *Herding and Social Pressure in Trading Tasks: A Behavioural Analysis*, Cambridge Working Papers in Economics No. 730, Cambridge: Faculty of Economics, University of Cambridge.

Baddeley M, Burke C, Tobler P and Schultz W (2010) *Impacts of Personality on Herding in Financial Decision-making*, Cambridge Working Papers in Economics No. 1006, Cambridge: Faculty of Economics No. 1225, University of Cambridge.

— (2012) *Herding in Financial Behavior: The Impact of Individual Differences*, Cambridge Working Papers in Economics, Cambridge: Faculty of Economics, University of Cambridge.

Baltagi, BH and Griffin JM (2001) 'The econometrics of rational addiction: the case of cigarettes', *Journal of Business and Economic Statistics*, 19(4), 449–54.

Bamberg S (2002) 'Effects of implementation intentions on the actual performance of new environmentally friendly behaviors – results of two field experiments', *Journal of Environmental Psychology*, 22(4), 399–411.

Bandura A, Ross D and Ross SA (1961) 'Transmission of aggression through imitation of aggressive models', *Journal of Abnormal and Social Psychology*, 63, 575–82.

Banerjee A (1992) 'A simple model of herd behavior', *Quarterly Journal of Economics*, 107(3), 797–817.

Barberis N and Thaler RH (2005) 'A survey of behavioral finance', in Thaler RH (ed.) *Advances in Behavioral Finance*, II, New York/Princeton, NJ: Russell Sage Foundation/Princeton University Press.

Barberis N, Shleifer A and Vishny RW (1998) 'A model of investor sentiment', reprinted in Thaler RH (2005) (ed.), *Advances in Behavioural Finance, II*, New York/Princeton, NJ: Russell Sage Foundation/Princeton University Press, pp. 423–49.

Bar-Hillel M (1973) 'On the subjective probability of compound events', *Organizational Behaviour and Human Performance*, 9, 396–406.

Bar-Hillel M and Falk R (1982) 'Some teasers concerning conditional probabilities', *Cognition*, 11(2), 109–22.

Barro RJ and Gordon DB (1983) 'A positive theory of monetary policy in a natural rate model', *Journal of Political Economy*, 91(4), 589–610.

Barsky RB, Juster TF, Kimball MS and Shapiro MC (1997) 'Preference parameters and behavioral heterogeneity: an experimental approach in the health and retirement study', *Quarterly Journal of Economics*, 112(2), 537–79.

Bateman BW (1990) 'The elusive logical relation: an essay on change and continuity in Keynes's thought', in Moggridge D (ed.), *Perspectives on the History of Economic Thought*, 4, Aldershot: Edward Elgar.

Bauer M, Cassar A, Chytilová J and Henrich J (2011) 'Warfare increases egalitarian and parochial motivations in children', paper presented to Sixth Annual CEDI Conference, Brunel University, Middlesex, 26 May 2011.

Baumeister RF and Leary MR (1995) 'The need to belong: desire for interpersonal attachments as fundamental human motivations', *Psychological Bulletin*, 117(3), 497–529.

Baumgartner T, Knoch D, Hotz P, Eisenegger C and Fehr E (2011) 'Dorsolateral and ventromedial prefrontal cortex orchestrate normative choice', *Nature Neuroscience*, 14, 1468–74.

Bazerman MH (2006) 'Climate change as a predictable surprise', *Climatic Change*, 77(1–2), 179–93.

Bechara A and Damasio AR (2005) 'The somatic marker hypothesis – a neural theory of economic decision', *Games and Economic Behavior*, 52(2005), 336–72.

Bechara A, Damasio H, Tranel D and Damasio AR (1997) 'Deciding advantageously before knowing the advantageous strategy', *Science*, 275, 1293–95.

Becker GS (1991) *A Treatise on the Family*, Cambridge, MA: Harvard University Press.

— (1965) 'A theory of the allocation of time', *Economic Journal*, 75(266), 493–517.

— (1993) 'The economic way of looking at behavior', *Journal of Political Economy*, 101(3), 385–409.

Becker GS and Murphy KM (1988) 'A theory of rational addiction', *Journal of Political Economy*, 96(4), 675–700.
— (2000) *Social Economics: Market Behaviour in a Social Environment*, Cambridge, MA: Harvard Business School.
— (2003) *Social Economics: Market Behaviour in a Social Environment*, Cambridge, MA: Belknap Press.
Becker GS, Grossman M and Murphy KM (1991) 'Rational addiction and the effect of price on consumption', *American Economic Review*, 81(2), 237–41.
— (1994) 'An empirical analysis of cigarette addiction', *American Economic Review*, 84(3), 396–418.
Becker LJ (1978) 'Joint effect of feedback and goal setting on performance: a field study of residential energy conservation', *Journal of Applied Psychology*, 63(4), 428–33.
Belot M and James J (2009) *Healthy School Meals and Educational Outcomes*, ISER Working Paper 2009–1, Colchester: Institute for Social and Economic Research, University of Essex.
Bénabou R and Tirole J (2003) 'Intrinsic and extrinsic motivation', *Review of Economic Studies*, 70(3), 489–520.
— (2006) 'Incentives and prosocial behavior', *American Economic Review*, 96(5), 1652–78.
Benartzi S and Thaler R (1995) 'Myopic loss aversion and the equity premium puzzle', *Quarterly Journal of Economics,* reprinted in Thaler RH (2005) *Advances in Behavioural Finance, II*, New York/Princeton, NJ: Russell Sage Foundation/Princeton University Press, pp. 202–23.
— (2001) 'Naïve diversification strategies in defined contribution savings plans', *American Economic Review*, 91, 79–98.
Berg JE, Dikhaut J and McCabe K (1995) 'Trust, reciprocity and social history', *Games and Economic Behavior*, 10(1), 122–42.
Bernardo A and Welch I (2001) *On the Evolution of Overconfidence and Entrepreneurs*, Cowles Foundation Discussion Paper No. 1307, New Haven, CT: Yale University.
Bernheim BD (1994) 'A theory of conformity', *Journal of Political Economy*, 102(5), 841–77.
— (2009) 'On the potential of neuroeconomics: a critical (but hopeful) appraisal', *American Economic Journal: Microeconomics*, 1(2), 1–41.
Bernheim BD and Rangel A (2004) 'Addiction and cue-triggered decision processes', *American Economic Review*, 94(5), 1558–90.
— (2007) 'Toward choice theoretic foundations for behavioural welfare economics', *American Economic Review*, 97, 464–70.
— (2009) 'Beyond revealed preference: choice-theoretic foundations for behavioral welfare economics', *Quarterly Journal of Economics*, 124(1), 51–104.
Bernheim BD, Skinner J and Weinberg S (2001) 'What accounts for the variation in retirement wealth among U.S. households?', *American Economic Review*, 91(4), 832–57.
Berns, G, Chappelow J, Zink C, Pagnoni G, Martin-Skurski M and Richards J (2005) 'Neurobiological correlates of social conformity and independence during mental rotation', *Biological Psychiatry*, 58, 245–53.
Bhatt M and Camerer C (2005) 'Self referential thinking and equilibrium as states of mind in games', *Games and Economic Behavior*, 52, 424–59.
Biddle M (2011) 'We can recycle plastic', www.ted.com/talks/lang/eng/mike_biddle.html, 17 October.
Bikhchandani S, Hirshleifer D and Welch I (1992) 'A theory of fads, fashions, custom and cultural change as informational cascades', *Journal of Political Economy*, 100(5), 992–1026.
— (1998) 'Learning from the behavior of others: conformity, fads and informational cascades', *Journal of Economic Perspectives*, 12(3), 151–70.
Binmore K (1999) 'Why experiment in economics?', *Economic Journal*, 109(453), F16–F24.
Binmore K and Shaked (2010a) 'Experimental economics: where next?' *Journal of Economic Behavior and Organisation*, 73, 87–100.
— (2010b) 'Experimental economics: where next? Rejoinder', *Journal of Economic Behavior and Organisation*, 73, 120–21.

BioRegional (nd) 'Helping to inform the Green Deal – green shoots from Pay As You Save', August, www.bioregional.com/news-views/publications/helping-to-inform-the-green-deal-green-shoots-from-pay-as-you-save/

Black JS, Stern PC and Elworth J (1985) 'Personal and contextual influences on household energy adaptations', *Journal of Applied Psychology*, 70(1), 3–21.

Blackmore S (1999) *The Meme Machine*, Oxford: Oxford University Press.

Blattman C and Miguel E (2010) 'Civil war', *Journal of Economic Literature*, 48(1), 3–57.

Bliss JP, Gilson RD and Deaton JE (1995) 'Human probability matching behaviour in response to alarms of varying reliability', *Ergonomics*, 38, 2300–12.

Bolton GE (1991) 'A comparative model of bargaining: theory and evidence', *American Economic Review*, 81(5), 1096–136.

Bolton GE and Ockenfels A (1998) 'Strategy and equity: an ERC-analysis of the Guth–van Damme game', *Journal of Mathematical Psychology*, 42(2), 215–26.

— (2000) 'ERC: a theory of equity, reciprocity and competition', *American Economic Review*, 90(1), 166–93.

Bonatti A and Hörner J (2011) 'Collaborating', *American Economic Review*, 101(2), 632–63.

Bond R and Smith P (1996) 'Culture and conformity: a meta-analysis of studies using Asch's (1952b, 1956) line judgment task', *Psychological Bulletin*, 119, 111–37.

de Bondt WFM and Thaler R (1985) 'Does the stock market overreact?' *Journal of Finance*, 40(3), 793–805.

Bonneau J and Preibusch S (2009) 'The privacy jungle: on the market for data protection in social networks', paper presented at Workshop on the Economics of Information Security 2009, www.cl.cam.ac.uk/~jcb82/doc/BP09-WEIS-privacy_jungle-print.pdf

Bord RJ, Fisher A and O'Connor RE (1998) 'Public perceptions of global warming: United States and international perspectives', *Climate Research*, 11, 75–84.

Borghans L, ter Weel B and Weinberg BA (2006) *People People: Social Capital and the Labour Market Outcomes of Underrepresented Groups*, NBER Working Paper 11985, Cambridge, MA: National Bureau of Economic Research.

Borghans L, Duckworth AL, Heckman JJ and Ter Weel B (2008) 'The economics and psychology of personality traits', *Journal of Human Resources*, 43(4), 972–1059.

Boylan R and El-Gamal M (1993) 'Fictitious play: a statistical study of multiple economic experiments', *Games and Economic Behavior*, 5, 205–22.

Bradford W and Harcourt GC (1997) 'Units and definitions', in Harcourt GC and Riach PA (eds), *A 'Second Edition' of The General Theory*, London: Routledge.

Braithwaite RB (1972) Editorial Foreword to Keynes JM (1921) *A Treatise on Probability*, London: Macmillan, pp. xv–xxii.

Breedlove SM, Rosenzweig MR and Watson NV (2007) *Biological Psychology: An Introduction to Behavioral, Cognitive and Clinical Neuroscience* (5th edn), Sunderland, MA: Sinauer Associates.

Breiter HC, Gollub RL, Weisskoff RM, Kennedy DN, Makris N, Berke JD, Goodman JM, Kantor HL, Gastfriend DR, Riorden JP, Matthew RT, Rosen BR and Hyman SE (1997) 'Acute effects of cocaine on human brain activity and emotion', *Neuron*, 19, 591–611.

Brocas I and Carrillo JD (2008) 'The brain as a hierarchical organization', *American Economic Review*, 98(4), 1312–46.

Brophy Haney A (2011) 'To disclose or not to disclose: what determines a firm's decision to voluntarily report carbon information?', paper presented at Electricity Policy Research Group Seminar, Cambridge, www.eprg.group.cam.ac.uk/wp-content/uploads/2010/10/110613-Haney.pdf

Brophy Haney A, Jones I and Pollitt M (2009) *UK Retailers and Climate Change: The Role of Partnership in Climate Strategies,* EPRG Working Paper No. 0925/Cambridge Working Papers in Economics No. 0950, Cambridge: Electricity Policy Research Group, Faculty of Economics, University of Cambridge.

Brophy Haney A, Jamasb T and Pollitt M (2009) *Smart Metering and Electricity Demand: Technology, Economics and International Experience*, EPRG Working Paper No. 0903, Cambridge: Electricity Policy Research Group, University of Cambridge.

Brown G and Hagen DA (2010) 'Behavioral economics and the environment', *Environmental Resource Economics*, 46(2), 139–46.

Brown GW (1951) 'Iterative solutions of games by fictitious play', in Koopmans TC (ed.), *Activity Analysis of Production and Allocation*, New York: Wiley.

Brunnermeier MK (2001) *Asset Pricing under Asymmetric Information: Bubbles, Crashes, Technical Analysis, and Herding*, Oxford: Oxford University Press.

Brutscher P-B (2011a) *Liquidity Constraints and High Electricity Use*, Cambridge Working Papers in Economics No. 1122/EPRG Working Paper No. 1106, Cambridge: Faculty of Economics/Electricity Policy Research Group, University of Cambridge.

— (2011b) *Payment Matters? An Exploratory Study into Pre-Payment Electricity Metering*, Cambridge Working Papers in Economics No. 1124/EPRG Working Paper No. 1108, Cambridge: Faculty of Economics/Electricity Policy Research Group, University of Cambridge.

Bryan G, Karlan D and Nelson S (2010) 'Commitment devices', *Annual Review of Economics*, 2, 671–98.

Burke C, Tobler P, Baddeley M and Schultz W (2010a) 'Neural mechanisms of observational learning', *Proceedings of the National Academy of Sciences*, 107(32), 14431–36.

Burke C, Baddeley M, Tobler P and Schultz W (2010b) 'Striatal BOLD response reflects the impact of herd information on financial decisions', *Frontiers – Human Neuroscience*, 4, 48, www.frontiersin.org/human_neuroscience/10.3389/fnhum.2010.00048/abstract

Camerer C (1997) 'Taxi drivers and beauty contests', *Engineering and Science*, 1, 10–19.

— (2003a) 'Strategising in the brain', *Science*, 300, 1673–75.

— (2003b) *Behavioral Game Theory: Experiments in Strategic Interaction*, Princeton, NJ: Princeton University Press.

— (2007) 'Neuroeconomics: using neuroscience to make economic predictions', *Economic Journal*, 117(519), C26–C42.

— (2008) 'The case for mindful economics', in Caplin A and Schotter A (eds), *The Foundations of Positive and Normative Economics: A Handbook*, New York: Oxford University Press, pp. 43–69.

Camerer C and Fehr E (2006) 'When does "economic man" dominate behaviour?', *Science*, 311, 47–52.

Camerer C and Ho T-H (1999) 'Experienced-weighted attraction learning in normal form games', *Econometrica*, 67(4), 827–74.

Camerer CF and Lovallo D (1999) 'Overconfidence and excess entry: an experimental approach', *American Economic Review*, 89(1), 306–18.

Camerer C and Weigelt K (1988) 'Experimental tests of a sequential equilibrium reputation model', *Econometrica*, 56(1), 1–36.

—— (1991) 'Information mirages in experimental asset markets', *Journal of Business*, 64(4), 463–493.

Camerer CF, Babcock L, Loewenstein G and Thaler RH (1997) 'Labour supply of New York City cab drivers: one day at a time', *Quarterly Journal of Economics,* 112(2), 407–41.

Camerer CF, Loewenstein G and Prelec D (2004a) 'Neuroeconomics: why economics needs brains', *Scandinavian Journal of Economics*, 106(3), 555–79.

Camerer CF, Loewenstein G and Rabin M (2004b) *Advances in Behavioral Economics*, Princeton, NJ: Princeton University Press/Russell Sage Foundation.

Camerer CF, Loewenstein G and Prelec D (2005) 'Neuroeconomics: how neuroscience can inform economics', *Journal of Economic Literature*, 43(1), 9–64.

Caplin A and Dean M (2007) 'The neuroeconomic theory of learning', *American Economic Review*, 97(2), 148–52.

— (2008a) 'Dopamine, reward prediction error and economics', *Quarterly Journal of Economics*, 23(2), 663–700.

— (2008b) 'Economic insights from "neuroeconomic" data', *American Economic Review*, 98(2), 169–74.

— (2009) 'Axiomatic neuroeconomics', in Glimcher PW, Fehr E, Camerer C, Rangel A and Poldrack RA (eds) (2008), *Neuroeconomics – Decision Making and the Brain*, San Diego, CA: Academic Press, pp. 21–31.

Carabelli A (1988) *On Keynes's Method*, London: Macmillan.

Carlsson F (2009) 'Design of state preference surveys: is there more to learn from behavioural economics?', *Environmental Resource Economics*, 46(2), 155–64.

Carnahan T and McFarland S (2007) 'Revisiting the Stanford Prison Experiment: could participant self-selection have led to the cruelty?', *Personality and Social Psychology Bulletin*, 33(5), 603–14.

Cartwright E (2011) *Behavioral Economics*, Abingdon, UK: Routledge.

Casti JL (2010) *Mood Matters: From Rising Skirt Lengths to the Collapse of World Powers*, New York: Springer.

Cattell RB (1971) *Abilities: Their Structure, Growth and Action*, New York: Houghton Mifflin.

Çelen B and Kariv S (2004) 'Observational learning under imperfect information', *Games and Economic Behavior*, 47(1), 72–86.

Centola D (2011) 'An experimental study of homophily in the adoption of health behaviour', *Science*, 334(6060), 1269–72.

Centorrino S, Djemaï E, Hopfensitz A, Milinski M and Seabright P (2011) *Smiling is a Costly Signal of Cooperation Opportunities: Experimental Evidence from a Trust Game*, CEPR Discussion Papers No. 8374, London: Centre for Economic Policy Research.

Cesarini D, Dawes CT, Johannesson M, Lichtenstein P and Wallace B (2009a) 'Genetic variation in preferences for giving and risk taking', *Quarterly Journal of Economics*, 124(2), 809–42.

Cesarini D, Lichtenstein P, Johannesson M and Wallace B (2009b) 'Heritability of overconfidence', *Journal of the European Economic Association*, 7(2–3), 617–27.

Cesarini D, Johannesson M, Lichtenstein P, Sandewall O and Wallace B (2010) 'Genetic variation in financial decision-making', *Journal of Finance*, 65(5), 1725–54.

Chaloupka, F (1991) 'Rational addictive behavior and cigarette smoking', *Journal of Political Economy*, 99(4), 722–42.

Chamley CP (2003) *Rational Herds – Economic Models of Social Learning*, Cambridge: Cambridge University Press.

Chen M, Lakshminarayanan V and Santos LR (2006) 'How basic are behavioral biases? Evidence from capuchin trading behavior', *Journal of Political Economy*, 14, 517–37.

Chen Y and Li SX (2009) 'Group identity and social preferences', *American Economic Review*, 99, 431–57.

Cheung Y-W and Friedman D (1997) 'Individual learning in normal form games: some laboratory results', *Games and Economic Behavior*, 19, 46–76.

Chirinko RS (1993) 'Business fixed investment spending: modelling strategies, empirical results and policy implications', *Journal of Economic Literature*, 31, 1875–1911.

Christopoulos GI, Tobler PN, Bossaerts P, Dolan RJ and Schultz W (2009) 'Neural correlates of value, risk and risk aversion contributing to decision making under risk', *Journal of Neuroscience*, 29(40), 12574–83.

Cialdini R (2007) *Influence: The Psychology of Persuasion*, New York: Harper Collins Business.

Clark D (2010) 'A social embedding of network security: trust, constraint, power and control', paper presented at Security and Human Behaviour Conference 2010, www.cl.cam.ac.uk/~rja14/shb08/clark-social-trust.pdf

Coates J (1990) 'Ordinary language economics – Keynes and Cambridge philosophers', PhD thesis, University of Cambridge.

— (1997) 'Keynes, vague concepts and fuzzy logic', in Harcourt GC and Riach PA (eds), *A 'Second Edition' of The General Theory*, London: Routledge.

Coates JM and Herbert J (2008) 'Endogenous steroids and financial risk taking on a London trading floor', *Proceedings of the National Academy of Sciences*, 105(16), 6167–72.

Coates JM, Gurnell M and Rustichini A (2009) 'Second-to-fourth digit ratio predicts success among high-frequency financial traders', *Proceedings of the National Academy of Sciences*, 106(2), 623–28.

Coates JM, Gurnell M and Sarnyai Z (2010) 'From molecule to market: steroid hormones and financial risk-taking', *Philosophical Transactions of the Royal Society Series B*, 365(1538), 331–43.

Cohen JD (2005) 'The vulcanization of the human brain: a neural perspective on interactions between cognition and emotion', *Journal of Economic Perspectives*, 19(4), 3–24.

Colander DC and Guthrie RS (1980) 'Great Expectations: what the Dickens do "rational expectations" mean?', *Journal of Post Keynesian Economics*, 32, 219–34.

Coleman J (1990) *Foundations of Social Theory*, Cambridge, MA: Harvard University Press.

Condie S and Ganguli JV (2011) 'Ambiguity and rational expectations equilibria', *Review of Economic Studies*, 78(3), 821–45.

Condie S, Ganguli JV and Illeditsch PK (2012) *Information Inertia*, School Science Research Network Working Paper 2084683. Available at SSRN: http://ssrn.com/abstract=2084683 or http://dx.doi.org/10.2139/ssrn.2084683

Conlisk J (1989) 'Three variants on the allais example', *American Economic Review*, 79(3), 392–407.

— (2011) 'Professor Zak's empirical studies on trust and oxytocin', *Journal of Economic Behavior and Organization*, 78(1–2), 160–66.

Conti G, Heckman J and Urzua S (2010) 'The education–health gradient', *American Economic Review*, 100(2), 234–38.

Cook PJ and Tauchen G (1982) 'The effect of liquor taxes on heavy drinking', *Bell Journal of Economics*, 13, 379–90.

Costa DL and Kahn ME (2010) *Energy Conservation 'Nudges' and Environmentalist Ideology: Evidence from a Randomized Residential Electricity Field Experiment*, NBER Working Paper 15939, Cambridge, MA: National Bureau of Economic Research.

Costa PT and McCrae RR (1992) 'Four ways five factors are basic', *Personality and Individual Differences*, 13, 653–65.

— (2005) *Personality in Adulthood – A Five-factor Theory Perspective*, New York: Guilford Press.

Cournot A (1838) 'Recherches sur les principes mathematizues de la theorie des richesses', Paris, France: L. Hachette; English translation by NT Bacon in *Economic Classics*, New York: Macmillan, 1897.

Crotty JR (1992) 'Neo-classical and Keynesian approaches to the theory of investment', *Journal of Post Keynesian Economics*, 144, 483–96.

Cunha F and Heckman JJ (2007) 'The technology of skill formation', *American Economic Review*, 97(2), 31–47.

Cunha F, Heckman JJ and Schennach SM (2010) 'Estimating the technology of cognitive and noncognitive skill formation', *Econometrica*, 78(3), 883–931.

Curtis A (2012) 'The science of subjectivity', *Geology*, 40(1), 95–96.

Cyert RM and March JG (1963) *A Behavioural Theory of the Firm*, Englewood Cliffs, NJ: Prentice Hall.

Damasio AR (1994/2006) *Descartes' Error: Emotion, Reason and the Human Brain*, London: Vintage (reissued in 2006).

Damasio AR, Everitt BJ and Bishop D (1996) 'The somatic marker hypothesis and the possible functions of the prefrontal cortex', *Philosophical Transactions of the Royal Society Series B*, 351 (1346), 1413–20.

Danchin E, Giraldeau L-A, Valone TJ and Wagner RH (2004) 'Public information: from nosy neighbours to cultural evolution', *Science*, 305, 487–91.

Darby S (2006) *The Effectiveness of Feedback on Energy Consumption*, London/Oxford: Defra/ Environmental Change Institute, University of Oxford.

Dasgupta P (2007) *Economics: A Very Short Introduction*, Oxford: Oxford University Press.

Davidson P (1991) 'Is probability theory relevant for uncertainty? a post-Keynesian perspective', *Journal of Economic Perspectives*, 5(1), 129–43.

— (1997) 'Are grains of sand in the wheels of international finance sufficient to do the job when boulders are often required?', *Economic Journal*, 107(442), 671–86.

— (2008) 'How to solve the U.S. housing problem and avoid a recession', Schwartz Center for Economic Policy Analysis Policy Note, New York: New School.

Davidson RJ (2004) 'Well-being and affective style: neural substrates and biobehavioural correlates', *Philosophical Transactions of the Royal Society Series B*, 359(1449), 1395–1411.

Davidson RJ, Kabat-Zinn J, Schumacher J et al. (2003) 'Alterations in brain and immune function produced by mindfulness meditation', *Psychosomatic Medicine*, 65(4), 564–70.

Davis JB (2006) 'Social identity strategies in recent economics', *Journal of Economic Methodology*, 13(3), 371–90.

— (2010) *Individuals and Identity in Economics*, Cambridge: Cambridge University Press.

Dawkins R (1976) *The Selfish Gene*, Oxford: Oxford University Press.

Deaton AS (2011) *The Financial Crisis and the Well-Being of Americans*, NBER Working Paper No. 17128, Cambridge, MA: National Bureau of Economic Research.

Deci E (1975) *Intrinsic Motivation*, New York: Plenum Press.

DellaVigna S and Malmendier U (2004) 'Contract design and self-control: theory and evidence', *Quarterly Journal of Economics*, 119(2), 353–402.

— (2006) 'Paying not to go to the gym', *American Economic Review*, 96(3), 694–719.

DeLong JB, Shleifer A, Summers L and Waldmann RJ (1991) 'The survival of noise traders in financial markets', *Journal of Business*, 64(1), 1–20.

DeNeve KM and Cooper H (1998) 'The happy personality: a metaanalysis of 137 personality traits and subjective well-being', *Psychological Bulletin*, 124, 197–229.

Dessi R and Rustichini A (2011) *Work for Image and Work for Pay*, Institut d'Économie Industrielle Working Paper, Toulouse: Université Toulouse, http://idei.fr/doc/wp/2011/dessi_rustichini_092011. pdf

Dickens WT and Flynn JR (2001) 'Heritability estimates versus large environmental effects: the IQ paradox resolved', *Psychological Review*, 108(2), 346–69.

Dietz T, Gardner GT, Gilligan J, Stern PC and Vandenbergh MP (2009) 'Household actions can provide a behavioral wedge to rapidly reduce U.S. carbon emissions', *Proceedings of the National Academy of Sciences*, 106(44), 18452.

Dixit AK and Pindyck RS (1994) *Investment under Uncertainty*, Princeton, NJ: Princeton University Press.

Dixit A and Skeath S (2004) *Games of Strategy* (2nd edn), New York: WW Norton.

Dohmen T and Falk A (2011) 'Performance pay and multidimensional sorting: productivity, preferences and gender', *American Economic Review*, 101(2), 556–90.

Dohmen T, Falk A, Huffman D and Sunde U (2007) *Are Risk Aversion and Impatience Related to Cognitive Ability?*, IZA Discussion Paper No. 2735, Bonn: Institute for Study of Labour.

— (2008) 'Representative trust and reciprocity: prevalence and determinants', *Economic Inquiry*, 46(1), 84–90.

Dolan, P, Hallsworth M, Halpern D, King D and Vlaev I (2010) *Mindspace – Influencing Behaviour through Public Policy*, London: Cabinet Office/Institute for Government.

Dow A and Dow S (1985) 'Animal spirits and rationality', in Lawson T and Pesaran H (eds), *Keynes' Economics – Methodological Issues*, Beckenham, UK: Croom Helm.

— (2011) 'Animal spirits revisited', *Capitalism and Society*, 6(2), article 1.

Drury C, Braund S, Osborne P and Tayles M (1992) *A Survey of Management Account Practices in UK Manufacturing Companies*, Research Report 32, London: Chartered Association of Certified Accountants.

Dudley CL (1972) 'A note on reinvestment assumptions in choosing between net present value and internal rate of return', *Journal of Finance*, 27(4), 907–15.

Duflo E, Kremer M and Robinson J (2011) 'Nudging farmers to use fertilizer: theory and experimental evidence from Kenya', *American Economic Review*, 101(6), 2350–90.

Dwyer, GP, Williams AW, Battalio RC and Mason TL (1993) 'Test of rational expectations in a stark setting', *Economic Journal*, 101, 1452–59.

Earl PE (1983) *The Economic Imagination: Towards a Behavioural Analysis of Choice*, New York: Sharpe.

— (2005) 'Economics and psychology in the twenty-first century', *Cambridge Journal of Economics*, 29(6), 909–26.

Earl PE and Potts J (2000) 'Latent demand and the browsing shopper', *Managerial and Decision Economics*, 21 (3–4), 111–12.

Easterlin RA (1974) 'Does economic growth improve the human lot?', in David PA and Reder MW (eds), *Nations and Households in Economic Growth: Essays in Honor of Moses Abramovitz*, New York: Academic Press.

The Economist (2011a) 'The Rorschach test: a few blots on the copybook', *The Economist*, 12 November, 89.

— (2011b) 'Following the footprints', *The Economist Technology Quarterly*, 4 June.

Edlund L (2005) 'Sex and the city', *Scandinavian Journal of Economics*, 107(1), 25–44.

Eisner R (1997) 'The marginal efficiency of capital and investment', in Harcourt GC and Riach PA (eds), *A 'Second Edition' of The General Theory*, London: Routledge.

Ellsberg D (1961) 'Risk, ambiguity and the Savage axioms', *Quarterly Journal of Economics*, 75(4), 643–69.

Elster J (1996) 'Rationality and the emotions', *Economic Journal*, 106(438), 136–97.

— (1998) 'Emotions and economic theory', *Journal of Economic Literature*, 36(1), 47–74.

Energy Saving Trust (2011) *Savings and Statistics Media Factsheet 2011–12*, www.energysavingtrust.org.uk/Publications2/Corporate/Research-and-insights/Savings-and-statistics-media-fact sheet-2011-2012

EPRI (2009) *Assessment of Achievable Potential from Energy Efficiency and Demand Response Programs, January 2009*, Palo Alto, CA: Electric Power Research Institute.

Erber R, Wang M and Poe J (2004) 'Mood regulation and decision making: is irrational exuberance really a problem?', in Brocas I and Carrillo JD (eds), *The Psychology of Economic Decisions*, Vol. II, Oxford: Oxford University Press, pp. 197–210.

Erev I and Roth A (1998) 'Predicting how people play games: reinforcement learning in experimental games with unique, mixed-strategy equilibria', *American Economic Review*, 88(4), 848–81.

European Commission (2002) *Flash Eurobarometer Survey 2002*, Europa archive, http://ec.europa.eu/environment/archives/barometer/flash_02.htm

— (2011a) *Special Eurobarometer 365: Attitudes of European Citizens Towards the Environment*, http://ec.europa.eu/environment/pdf/ebs_365_en.pdf

— (2011b) *Special Eurobarometer 372: Climate Change*, http://ec.europa.eu/public_opinion/archives/ebs/ebs_372_en.pdf

Eysenck H (1967) *The Biological Basis of Personality*, Springfield, IL: Thomas.

— (1975) *The Inequality of Man*, London: Maurice Temple Smith.

— (1991) 'Dimensions of personality: 16, 5 or 3? Criteria for a taxonomic paradigm', *Personality and Individual Differences*, 12, 773–90.

Eysenck H and Eysenck S (1975) *Manual of the Eysenck Personality Questionnaire*, London: Hodder & Stoughton.

— (1976) *Psychoticism as a Dimension of Personality*. London: Hodder & Stoughton.

Eysenck S and Eysenck H (1978) 'Impulsiveness and venturesomeness: their position in a dimensional system of personality description', *Psychological Reports*, 43(3), 1247–55.

Eysenck S, Eysenck H and Barrett P (1985) 'A revised version of the psychoticism scale', *Personality and Individual Differences*, 6(1), 21–29.

Falk A and Fischbacher U (2006) 'A theory of reciprocity', *Games and Economic Behavior*, 54, 293–315.

Fama EF (1965) 'The behavior of stock-market prices', *Journal of Business*, 38(1), 34–105.

Farrell P and Fuchs VR (1982) 'Schooling and health: the cigarette connection', *Journal of Health Economics*, 1, 217–30.

Faruqui A and Sergici S (2010) 'Household response to dynamic pricing of electricity – a survey of 15 experiments', *Journal of Regulatory Economics*, 38, 193–225.

Faruqui A, Sergici S and Sharif A (2010) 'The impact of informational feedback on energy consumption – a survey of the experimental evidence', *Energy*, 35(4), 1598–1608.

Fehr E and Gächter S (2000) 'Cooperation and punishment in public goods experiments', *American Economic Review*, 90(4), 980–94.

Fehr E and Gintis H (2007) 'Human motivation and social cooperation: experimental and analytic foundations', *Annual Review of Sociology*, 33, 43–64.

Fehr E and Rangel A (2011) 'Neuroeconomic foundations of economic choice – recent advances', *Journal of Economic Perspectives*, 25(4), 3–30.

Fehr E and Schmidt KM (1999) 'Theory of fairness, competition and cooperation', *Quarterly Journal of Economics*, 114(3), 817–68.

— (2010) 'On inequity aversion: a reply to Binmore and Shaked', *Journal of Economic Behavior and Organisation*, 73, 101–8.

Fehr E and Tyran J-R (2005) 'Individual irrationality and aggregate outcomes', *Journal of Economic Perspectives*, 19(4), 43–66.

Fehr EG, Kirchsteiger G and Riedl A (1993) 'Does fairness prevent market clearing? An experimental investigation', *Quarterly Journal of Economics*, 108(2), 437–59.

Fehr E, Fischbacher U and Kosfeld M (2005) 'Neuroeconomic foundations of trust and social preferences: initial evidence', *American Economic Review*, 95(2), 346–51.

Fehr E, Hart O and Zehnder C (2011) 'Contracts as reference points – experimental evidence', *American Economic Review*, 101(2), 493–525.

Feinberg RM (1977) 'Risk aversion, risk and the duration of unemployment', *Review of Economics and Statistics*, 59(3), 264–71.

Fellner, W (1961) 'Distortion of subjective probabilities as a reaction to uncertainty', *Quarterly Journal of Economics*, 75, 670–94.

Festinger L (1957) *A Theory of Cognitive Dissonance*, Stanford, CA: Stanford University Press.

Finucane M, Alhakami A, Slovic P and Johnson S (2000) 'The affect heuristic in judgements of risk and benefits', *Journal of Behavioural Decision-Making*, 3(1), 1–7.

Fisher I (1930) *The Rate of Interest*, New York: Macmillan.

Fishman A and Gneezy U (2011) *A Field Study of Social Learning*, Working Paper 2011–21, Ramat Gan, Israel: Department of Economics, Bar-Ilan University, www.biu.ac.il/soc/ec/wp/2011–21.pdf

Forbes W (2009) *Behavioural Finance*, Chichester, UK: Wiley.

Fowler JF and Christakis NA (2010) 'Cooperative behavior cascades in human social networks', *Proceedings of the National Academy of Sciences, USA*, 107(12), 5334–38.

Fox CR and Poldrack RA (2009) 'Prospect theory and the brain', in Glimcher PW, Camerer CF, Fehr E and Poldrack RA (eds), *Neuroeconomics: Decision-making and the Brain*, London: Academic Press/Elsevier.

Frank L (2011) *The Neurotourist – Postcards from the Edge of Brain Science*, Oxford: One World.

Fransson N and Gärling T (1999) 'Environmental concern: conceptual definitions, measurement methods and research findings', *Journal of Environmental Psychology*, 19, 369–82.

Frederick S (2005) 'Cognitive reflection and decision-making', *Journal of Economic Perspectives*, 19(4), 25–42.

Frederick S, Loewenstein G and O'Donoghue T (2002) 'Time discounting: a critical review', *Journal of Economic Literature*, 40(2), 351–401.

French K and Poterba J (1991) 'Investor diversification and international equity markets', *American Economic Review*, 81, 222–26.

Freud S (1899) *The interpretation of dreams* (1899), in *The Complete Psychological Works of Sigmund Freud*, London: Hogarth Press.

— (1921) *Beyond the pleasure principle*, in *The Complete Psychological Works of Sigmund Freud*, London: Hogarth Press.

— (1940) *An outline of psychoanalysis*, in *The Complete Psychological Works of Sigmund Freud*, London: Hogarth Press.

— (1949) *The Ego and the Id*, in *The Complete Psychological Works of Sigmund Freud*, London: Hogarth Press.

Frey BS (1997) 'A constitution of knaves crowds out civic virtues', *Economic Journal*, 107, 1043–53.

— (ed.) (2008) *Happiness – A Revolution in Economics*, Cambridge, MA: MIT Press.

Frey BS and Jegen R (2001) 'How intrinsic motivation is crowded out and in', *Journal of Economic Surveys*, 15(5), 589–611.

Frey BS and Oberholtzer-Gee F (1997) 'The cost of price incentives: an empirical analysis of motivation crowding out', *American Economic Review*, 87, 746–55.

Friedman M (1953) 'The methodology of positive economics', in *Essays in Positive Economics*, Chicago: University of Chicago Press, pp. 3–43.

Frith CD and Singer T (2008) 'The role of social cognition in decision making', *Philosophical Transactions of the Royal Society Series B*, 363(1511), 3875–86.

Frith U and Frith C (2003) 'Development and neurophysiology of mentalizing', *Philosophical Transactions of the Royal Society Series B*, 358(1431), 459–73.

Fung A and O'Rourke D (2000) 'Reinventing environmental regulation from the grassroots up: explaining and expanding the success of the toxics release inventory', *Environmental Management*, 25(2), 115–27.

Gabaix X and Laibson D (2000) 'A boundedly rational decision algorithm', *American Economic Review*, 90(2), 433–38.

Galton F (1886) 'Regression towards mediocrity in hereditary stature', *Journal of the Anthropological Institute of Great Britain and Ireland*, 15, 246–63.

Gautier PA, Svarer M and Teulings CN (2005) *Marriage and the City*, IZA Discussion Papers 1491, Institute for the Study of Labor (IZA).

Genesove D and Mayer C (2001) 'Loss aversion and seller behavior: evidence from the housing market', *Quarterly Journal of Economics*, 116, 1233–60.

Gerrard B (1994) 'Beyond rational expectations: a constructive interpretation of Keynes's analysis of behaviour under uncertainty', *Economic Journal*, 104, 327–37.

Gigerenzer G (2004) 'On fear of terrorist attack, dread risk, September 11 and fatal traffic accidents', *Psychological Science*, 15(4), 286–87.

— (2007) *Gut Feelings: The Intelligence of the Unconscious*, London: Penguin.

Gigerenzer G and Goldstein DG (1996) 'Reasoning the fast and frugal way: models of bounded rationality', *Psychological Review*, 103, 650–69.

Gigerenzer G, Todd PM and ABC Research Group (1999) *Simple Heuristics That Make Us Smart (Evolution and Cognition)*, New York: Oxford University Press.

Glimcher PW (2003) *Decisions, Uncertainty and the Brain – The Science of Neuroeconomics*, Cambridge, MA: MIT Press/Bradford Books.

— (2011) *Foundations of Neuroeconomic Analysis*, New York: Oxford University Press.

Glimcher P and Rustichini A (2004) 'Neuroeconomics – the consilience of brain and decision', *Science*, 306, 447–52.

Glimcher PW, Dorris MC and Bayer HM (2005) 'Physiological utility theory and the neuroeconomics of choice', *Games and Economic Behavior*, 52, 213–56.

Glimcher PW, Kable J and Louie K (2007) 'Neuroeconomic studies of impulsivity: no or just as soon as possible', *American Economic Review*, 97(2), 142–47.

Glimcher PW, Camerer CF, Fehr E and Poldrack RA (eds) (2009) *Neuroeconomics – Decision Making and the Brain*, London: Academic Press, Elsevier/Society for Neuroeconomics.

Gneezy U and Potters J (1997) 'An experiment on risk taking and evaluation periods', *Quarterly Journal of Economics*, 112(2), 631–45.

Gneezy U and Rustichini A (2000a) 'A fine is a price', *Journal of Legal Studies*, 29(1), 1–17.

— (2000b) 'Pay enough or don't pay at all', *Quarterly Journal of Economics*, 115(3), 791–810.

— (2004) 'Gender and competition at a young age', *American Economic Review*, 94(2), 377–81.

Goeree JK and Holt CA (2001) 'Ten little treasures of game theory and ten intuitive contradictions', *American Economic Review*, 91(5), 1402–22.

Goetzman WN and Peles N (1997) 'Cognitive dissonance and mutual fund investors', *Journal of Financial Research*, 20(2),145–58.

Goldstein N, Cialdini R and Griskevicius V (2008) 'A room with a viewpoint: using norm-based appeals to motivate conservation behaviors in a hotel setting', *Journal of Consumer Research*, 35, 472–82.

Gonzalez C, Dana J, Koshino H and Just M (2005) 'The framing effect and risky decisions: examining cognitive functions with fMRI', *Journal of Economic Psychology*, 26, 1–20.

Gordon MJ (1955) 'The payoff period and the rate of profit', *Journal of Business*, 28(4), 253–60.

Gould P (1970) 'Is statistix inferens the geographical name for a wild goose?', *Economic Geography*, 46, 438–48.

Gourville JT (1998) 'Pennies-a-day: the effect of temporal reframing on transaction evaluation', *Journal of Consumer Research*, 24(4), 395–408.

— (2003) 'The effects of monetary magnitude and level of aggregation on the temporal framing of price', *Marketing Letters*, 14(2), 125–35.

Gourville JT and Soman D (1998) 'Payment depreciation: the behavioural effects of temporally separating payments from consumption', *Journal of Consumer Research*, 25(2), 160–74.

Gowdy JM (2008) 'Behavioural economics and climate change policy', *Journal of Economic Behavior and Organisation*, 68, 632–44.

Goyal S (2009) *Connections: An Introduction to the Economics of Networks*, Princeton, NJ: Princeton University Press.

Granade HC, Creyts J, Derkach A, Farese P, Nyquist S and Ostrowski K (2009) *Unlocking Energy Efficiency in the US Economy*, McKinsey and Company.

Green L and Myerson J (2004) 'A discounting framework for choice with delayed and probabilistic rewards', *Psychological Bulletin*, 130(5), 769–92.

Grigorenko EL and Sternberg RJ (1995) 'Thinking styles', in Saklofske DH and Zeidner M (eds), *Perspectives on Individual Differences: International Handbook of Personality and Intelligence*, New York: Plenum Press, pp. 205–29.

Gronchi S (1986) 'On investment criteria based on the internal rate of return', *Oxford Economic Papers*, New Series, 38(1), 174–80.

Grønhøj A and Thøgersen J (2012) 'Action speaks louder than words: the effect of personal attitutes and family norms on adolescents' pro-environmental behavior', *Journal of Economic Psychology*, 33(1), 292–302.

Grubb M, Brophy Haney A and Wilde J (2009) 'Plugging the gap in energy efficiency policies: the emergence of the UK "carbon reduction commitment"', *European Review of Energy Markets*, 3(2), 33–62.

Gruber J and Köszegi B (2001) 'Is addiction "rational"? Theory and evidence', *Quarterly Journal of Economics*, 116(4), 1261–1303.

Gul F and Pesendorfer W (2001) 'Temptation and self control', *Econometrica*, 69(6), 1403–35.

— (2008) 'The case for mindless economics', in Caplin A and Schotter A (eds), *The Foundations of Positive and Normative Economics: A Handbook*, New York: Oxford University Press, pp. 3–39.

Güth W, Schmittberger R and Schwarze B (1982) 'An experimental analysis of ultimatum bargaining', *Journal of Economic Behavior and Organisation*, 3, 367–88.

Habel U, Klein M, Kellermann T, Shah NJ and Schneider F (2005) 'Same or different? Neural correlates of happy and sad mood in healthy males', *NeuroImage*, 26(1), 206–14.

Haines MP and Spear SF (1996) 'Changing the perception of the norm: a strategy to decrease binge drinking among college students', *Journal of American College Health*, 45, 134–40.

Halpern D (2005) *Social Capital*, Cambridge: Polity Press.

— (2009) *The Hidden Wealth of Nations*, Cambridge: Polity Press.

Hampton A, Bossaerts P and O'Doherty J (2008) 'Neural correlates of mentalizing-related computations during strategic interactions in humans', *Proceedings of the National Academy of Sciences*, 105(18), 6741–46.

Haney C, Banks WC and Zimbardo PG (1973) 'Study of prisoners and guards in a simulated prison', *Naval Research Reviews*, 9, 1–17.

Hansen WB and Graham JW (1991) 'Preventing alcohol, marijuana and cigarette use among adolescents: peer pressure resistance training versus establishing conservative norms', *Preventive Medicine*, 20, 414–30.

Harcourt GC (1968) 'Investment decision criteria, investment incentives and the choice of technique', *Economic Journal*, 78(309), 77–95.

Hardin G (1968) 'The tragedy of the commons', *Science*, 162(3859), 1243–48.

Hargreaves T, Nye M and Burgess J (2010) 'Making energy visible: a qualitative field study of how householders interact with feedback from smart energy monitors', *Energy Policy*, 38, 6111–19.

Harlow JM (1868) 'Recovery from the passage of an iron bar through the head', *Publications of the Massachusetts Medical Society*, 2: 327–47. Republished in Macmillan MB (2002) *An Odd Kind of Fame: Stories of Phineas Gage*, Cambridge, MA: MIT Press.

Harper DGC (1982) 'Competitive foraging in mallards: "ideal free" ducks', *Animal Behaviour*, 30, 575–84.

Harris C and Laibson D (2001) 'Dynamic choices of hyperbolic consumers', *Econometrica*, 69(4), 935–57.

Harrison GW, Lau MI and Williams MB (2002) 'Estimating individual discount rates in Denmark: a field experiment', *American Economic Review*, 92(5), 1606–17.

Harrison R (1997) 'Jeremy Bentham', in Eatwell J, Milgate M and Newman P (eds), *The New Palgrave Dictionary of Economics*, London: Macmillan.

Hart O and Moore J (1990) 'Property rights and the nature of the firm', *Journal of Political Economy*, 98(6), 1119–58.

— (2008) 'Contracts as reference points', *Quarterly Journal of Economics*, 123(1), 1–48.

Hartman RS, Doane MJ and Woo CK (1991) 'Consumer rationality and the status quo', *Quarterly Journal of Economics*, 106(1), 141–62.

Hassett KA and Metcalf GE (1995) 'Energy tax credits and residential conservation investment: evidence from panel data', *Journal of Public Economics*, 57(2), 201–17.

— (1996) 'Can irreversibility explain the slow diffusion of energy saving technologies?', *Energy Policy*, 24(1), 7–8.

Hathaway SR and McKinley JC (1943) *MMPI Manual*, New York: Psychological Corporation.

Hayek FA (1952) *The Sensory Order: An Inquiry into the Foundations of Theoretical Psychology*. London: Routledge.

Haynes MR (2011) 'Dissociating the valence-dependent neural and genetic contributions to decision making under risk', PhD thesis, Physiology, Development and Neuroscience, University of Cambridge UK.

Heckman J (2001) 'Accounting for heterogeneity, diversity and general equilibrium in evaluating social programmes', *Economic Journal*, 111(475), F654–99.

Heckman J, Moon SH, Pinto R, Savelyev P and Yavitz A (2010a) 'The rate of return to the HighScope Perry Preschool Program', *Journal of Public Economics*, 94(1–2), 114–28.

— (2010b) 'Analyzing social experiments as implemented: a reexamination of the evidence from the HighScope Perry Preschool Program', *Quantitative Economics*, 1(1), 1–46.

Heider F (1958) *The Psychology of Interpersonal Relations*, New York: Wiley.

Henrich J, Boyd R, Bowles S, Camerer C, Fehr E, Gintis H and McElreath R (2001) 'In search of *homo economicus*: behavioral experiments in 15 small-scale societies', *American Economic Review*, 91(2), 73–78.

Henrich J, Boyd R, Bowles S, Camerer C, Fehr E and Gintis H (eds) (2004) *Foundations of Human Sociality – Economics Experiments and Ethnographic Evidence from Fifteen Small-scale Societies*, Oxford: Oxford University Press.

Hepburn C, Duncan S and Papachristodoulou A (2010) 'Behavioral economics, hyperbolic discounting and environmental policy', *Environmental Resource Economics*, 46(2), 189–206.

Herrmann E, Call J, Hernàndez-Lloreda MV, Hare B and Tomasello M (2007) 'Humans have evolved specialised skills of social cognition: the cultural intelligence hypothesis', *Science* 317, 1360–66.

Hikosaka O, Sakamoto M and Usui S (1989) 'Functional properties of monkey caudate neurons. III. Activities related to expectation of target and reward', *Journal of Neurophysiology*, 61, 814–32.

Hirschman AO (1965) 'Obstacles to development: a classification and a quasi-vanishing act', *Economic Development and Cultural Change*, 13(4), 385–93.

Hirshleifer D and Shumway T (2003) 'Good day sunshine: stock returns and the weather', *Journal of Finance*, 58(3), 1009–32.

Ho T-H, Camerer C and Weigelt K (1998) 'Iterated dominance and iterated best response in experimental "p-beauty contest" games', *American Economic Review*, 88(4), 947–69.

Hodgson GM (1985) 'Persuasion, expectations and the limits to Keynes', in Lawson T and Pesaran H (eds), *Keynes' Economics – Methodological Issues*, Beckenham, UK: Croom Helm.

Hong H and Stein J (1999) 'A unified theory of underreaction, momentum trading and overreaction in asset markets', *Journal of Finance*, 54, 2143–84.

Hope BT, Nagarkar D, Leonard S and Wise RA (2007) 'Long-term upregulation of protein kinase A and adenylate cyclase levels in human smokers', *Journal of Neuroscience*, 27(8), 1964–72.

Houser D, Bechara A, Keane M, McCabe K and Smith V (2005) 'Identifying individual differences: an algorithm with application to Phineas Gage', *Games and Economic Behavior*, 52, 373–85.

Howitt P (1997) 'Expectations and uncertainty in contempary Keynesian models', in Harcourt GC and Riach PA (eds), *A 'Second Edition' of The General Theory*, London: Routledge.

Huang GT (2005) *The Economics of Brains*, Technology Review, Cambridge, MA: MIT Press, www.technologyreview.com/biomedicine/14439/

Hume D (1739) *A Treatise of Human Nature*, Oxford: Oxford University Press.

Huppert FA and So TTC (2011) *Flourishing across Europe: Application of a New Conceptual Framework for Defining Well-being*, Social Indicators Research, www.springerlink.com/content/4858x2122m1n1211/fulltext.pdf (DOI: 10.1007/s11205-011-9966-7).

Iacoboni M (2005) 'Neural mechanisms of imitation', *Current Opinion in Neurobiology*, 15, 632–37.

IEA (2007) *Mind the Gap – Quantifying Principal Agent Problems in Energy Efficiency*, Paris: OECD/International Energy Agency.

— (2011) *Key World Energy Statistics*, Paris: OECD/International Energy Agency.

Ifcher J and Zarghamee H (2011) 'Happiness and time preference: the effect of positive affect in a random-assignment experiment', *American Economic Review*, 101(7), 3109–29.

Isoni A, Loomes G and Sugden R (2011) 'The willingness to pay – willingness to accept gap, the "endowment effect," subject misconceptions and experimental procedures for eliciting valuations: Comment', *American Economic Review*, 101(2), 991–1011.

Iyengar S and Lepper M (2000) 'When choice is demotivating', *Journal of Personality and Social Psychology*, 79(6), 995–1006.

Jaffe A and Stavins R (1994) 'The energy efficiency gap, what does it mean?', *Energy Policy*, 22(10), 804–10.

Jensen K, Call J and Tomasello M (2007) 'Chimpanzees are rational maximizers in an ultimatum game', *Science*, 318, 107–9.

Jin GZ and Leslie P (2003) 'The effect of information on product quality: evidence from restaurant hygiene grade cards', *Quarterly Journal of Economics*, 118, 409–51.

Johansson-Stenman O and Konow J (2010) 'Fair air: distributive justice and environmental economics', *Environmental Resource Economics* 46(2), 147–66.

Jorgenson DW (1963) 'Capital theory and investment behaviour', *American Economic Review*, 53, 247–59.

Jung CG (1923) *Psychological Types*, New York: Harcourt Brace.

— (1991) *The Archetypes and the Collective Unconscious* (2nd edn), Abingdon, UK: Routledge.

Kahneman D (1994) 'New challenges to the rationality assumption', *Journal of Institutional and Theoretical Economics*, 150, 18–36.

— (2003) 'Maps of bounded rationality: psychology for behavioral economics', *American Economic Review*, 93(5), 1449–75.

— (2011) *Thinking, Fast and Slow*, London: Allen Lane.

Kahneman D and Tversky A (1973) 'On the psychology of prediction', *Psychological Review*, 80, 237–51; reprinted in Kahneman D, Slovic P and Tversky A (eds) (1982) *Judgement under Uncertainty: Heuristics and Biases*, Cambridge: Cambridge University Press, pp. 48–68.

— (1974) 'Subjective probability: a judgement of representativeness', *Cognitive Psychology*, 3, 430–54.

— (1979) 'Prospect theory – an analysis of decision under risk', *Econometrica*, 47(2), 263–92.

— (1982) 'Subjective probability: a judgement of representativeness', in Kahneman D, Slovic P and Tversky A (eds) *Judgement under Uncertainty: Heuristics and Biases*, Cambridge: Cambridge University Press, pp. 32–47.

— (1984) 'Choices, values and frames', *American Psychologist*, 39(4), 341–50.

— (1986) 'Rational choice and the framing of decisions', *Journal of Business*, 59(4), 5251–78.

— (1991) 'Loss aversion in riskless choice: a reference-dependent model', *Quarterly Journal of Economics*, 106(4), 1039–61.

— (eds) (2000) *Choices, Values and Frames*, Cambridge: Cambridge University Press/Russell Sage Foundation.

Kahneman D, Knetsch JL and Thaler RH (1986) 'Fairness as a constraint on profit seeking: entitlements in the market', *American Economic Review*, 76(4), 728–41.

— (1990) 'Experimental tests of the endowment effect and Coase theorem', *Journal of Political Economy*, 98, 1325–48.

— (1991) 'Anomalies: the endowment effect, loss aversion and status quo bias', *Journal of Economic Perspectives*, 5(1), 193–206.

Kahneman D, Slovic P and Tversky A (1982) (eds) *Judgement under Uncertainty: Heuristics and Biases*, Cambridge: Cambridge University Press.

Kahneman D, Wakker PP and Sarin R (1997) 'Back to Bentham? Explorations of experienced utility', *Quarterly Journal of Economics*, 112(2), 375–406.

Kaiser F and Fuhrer U (2003) 'Ecological behavior's dependency on different forms of knowledge', *Applied Psychology: An International Review*, 52(4), 598–613.

Kamstra MJ, Kramer LA and Levi MD (2003) 'Winter blues: a SAD stock market cycle', *American Economic Review* 93(1), 324–43.

Kaplan H, Hill K, Lancaster J and Hurtado AM (2000) 'A theory of human life history evolution: diet, intelligence and longevity', *Evolutionary Anthropology*, 9, 156–85.

Karau SJ and Williams KD (1993) 'Social loafing: a meta-analytic review and theoretical integration', *Journal of Personality and Social Psychology*, 65(4), 681–706.

Katona GA (1951) *Psychological Analysis of Economic Behaviour*, New York: McGraw-Hill.

— (1975) *Psychological Economics*, New York: Elsevier.

Katz ML and Shapiro C (1994) 'Systems competition and network effects', *Journal of Economic Perspectives*, 8(2), 93–115.

Kelly GA (1955) *The Psychology of Personal Constructs*, New York: Norton.

Kempton W and Montgomery L (1982) 'Folk quantification of energy', *Energy* 7(10), 817–27.

Kempton W, Feuermann D and McGarity A (1992) '"I always turn it on super": user decisions about when and how to operate room air conditioners', *Energy and Building*, 18, 177–200.

Keynes JM (1921) *A Treatise on Probability*, London: Macmillan/Royal Economic Society.

— (1930) *A Treatise on Money*, London: Macmillan.

— (1936) *The General Theory of Employment, Interest and Money*, London: Macmillan/Royal Economic Society.

— (1937) 'The general theory of employment', *Quarterly Journal of Economics*, 51, 209–23.

— (1979) *The General Theory and After: A Supplement, Collected Writings of John Maynard Keynes*, Vol. 29, London: Macmillan/Royal Economic Society.

Kindleberger CP and Aliber RZ (2005) *Manias, Panics and Crashes: A History of Financial Crises* (5th edn), London: Palgrave Macmillan.

King-Casas B, Tomlin D, Anen C, Camerer CF, Quartz SR and Read Montague P (2005) 'Getting to know you: reputation and trust in a two-person economic exchange', *Science*, 308(5718), 78–83.

Kirby KN (1997) 'Bidding on the future: evidence against normative discounting of delayed rewards', *Journal of Experimental Psychology: General*, 126(1), 54–70.

Kirman A (1993) 'Ants, rationality and recruitment', *Quarterly Journal of Economics*, 108(1), 137–56.

Kirman A and Teschl M (2004) 'On the emergence of economic identity', *Revue de Philosophique Economique*, 9(1), 59–86.

Kirzner I (1973) *Perception, Opportunity and Profit: Studies in the Theory of Entrepreneurship*, Chicago: Chicago University Press.

Klucharev V, Hytönen K, Rijpkema M, Smidts A and Fernández G (2009) 'Reinforcement learning signal predicts social conformity', *Neuron*, 61(1), 140–51.

Klucharev V, Munneke MAM, Smidts A and Fernández G (2011) 'Downregulation of the posterior medial frontal cortex prevents social conformity', *Journal of Neuroscience*, 31(33), 11934–40.

Knetsch JL (1989) 'The endowment effect and evidence of nonreversible indifference curves', *American Economic Review*, 79, 1277–84.

Knetsch JL (2010) 'Values of gains and losses: reference states and choice of measure', *Environmental and Resource Economics*, 46(2), 179–88.

Knight F (1921) *Risk, Uncertainty and Profit*, New York: Houghton Mifflin.

Knutson B and Bossaerts P (2007) 'Neural antecedents of financial decisions', *Journal of Neuroscience*, 27(31), 8174–77.

Knutson B, Rick S and Wimmer GE (2007) 'Neural predictors of purchases', *Neuron*, 53, 147–56.

Koepp MJ, Gunn RN, Lawrence AD, Cunningham VJ, Dagher A, Jones T, Brooks DJ, Bench CJ and Grasby PM (1998) 'Evidence for striatal dopamine release during a video game', *Nature*, 393, 266–68.

Koppl R (2002) *Big Players and the Economic Theory of Expectations*, Basingstoke, UK: Palgrave.

Kosfeld M, Heinrichs M, Zak PJ, Fischbacher U and Fehr E (2005) 'Oxytocin increases trust in humans', *Nature*, 435, 673–76.

Kregel JA (1976) 'Economic methodology in the face of uncertainty: the modeling methods of the Keynesians and Post Keynesians', *Economic Journal*, 86, 209–25.

Kuhnen C and Knutson B (2005) 'The neural basis of financial risk taking', *Neuron*, 47(5),763–70.

Kyburg HE (1997). 'Expertise and context in uncertain inference', in Feltovich PJ, Ford KM and Hoffman RR (eds), *Expertise in Context: Human and Machine*, Cambridge, MA: MIT Press, pp. 499–514.

Kydland FE and Prescott EC (1977) 'Rules rather than discretion: the inconsistency of optimal plans', *Journal of Political Economy*, 85(3), 473–91.

Laibson D (1997) 'Golden eggs and hyperbolic discounting', *Quarterly Journal of Economics*, 112, 443–78.

— (2001) 'A cue-theory of consumption', *Quarterly Journal of Economics*, 116(1), 81–119.

Laibson D, Repetto A and Tobacman J (2007) *Estimating Discount Functions with Consumption Choices over the Lifecycle*, NBER Working Paper 13314, Cambridge, MA: National Bureau of Economic Research.

Lakshminaryanan V, Chen MK and Santos LR (2008) 'Endowment effect in capuchin monkeys', *Philosophical Transactions of the Royal Society B*, 363, 3837–44.

Lawson T (1981) 'Keynesian model building and the rational expectations critique', *Cambridge Journal of Economics*, 5(4), 311–26.

— (1995) 'Expectations and economics', in Dow S and Hillard J (eds), *Keynes, Uncertainty and Knowledge*, Cheltenham: Edward Elgar, pp. 77–106.

Layard RL (2005) *Happiness: Lessons from a New Science*, London: Allen Lane/Penguin.

Le Bon G (1896) *The Crowd: A Study of the Popular Mind*, London: Unwin, http://socserv.socsci. mcmaster.ca/~econ/ugcm/3ll3/lebon/Crowds.pdf

Le Doux JE (1996) *The Emotional Brain*, New York: Simon & Schuster.

Lee L, Amir O and Ariely D (2009) 'In search of homo economicus: cognitive noise and the role of emotion in preference consistency', *Journal of Consumer Research*, 36(2), 173–87.

van der Leij MJ (2011) 'Experimenting with buddies', *Science*, 334(6060), 1220–21.

Leiserowitz A (2006) 'Climate change risk perception and policy preferences: the role of affect, imagery and values', *Climatic Change*, 77, 45–72.

Leiserowitz A, Maibach E, Roser-Renouf C, Smith N and Dawson E (2012) 'Climategate, public opinion, and the loss of trust', *American Behavioral Scientist*, in press.

Lewit EM and Coate D (1982) 'The potential for using excise taxes to reduce smoking', *Journal of Health Economics*, 1, 121–45.

Lewit EM and Grossman M (1981) 'The effects of government regulation on teenage smoking', *Journal of Law and Economics*, 24, 545–69.

Liebman J and Zeckhauser R (2008) *Simple Humans, Complex Insurance, Subtle Subsidies*, NBER Working Paper 14330, Cambridge, MA: National Bureau of Economic Research.

List JA (2003) 'Does market experience eliminate market anomalies?', *Quarterly Journal of Economics*, 118(1), 41–71.

Littleboy B (1990) *On Interpreting Keynes: A Study in Reconciliation*, London: Routledge.

Lo AW (2001) 'Bubble, rubble, finance in trouble?', edited luncheon Address delivered 1 June at the Third Annual Institute of Psychology and Markets Conference.

Lo AW and Repin DV (2002) 'The psychophysiology of real-time financial risk processing', *Journal of Cognitive Neuroscience*, 14(3), 323–39.

Lo A, Repin DV and Steenbarger BN (2005) 'Fear and greed in financial markets: a clinical study of day traders', *American Economic Review*, 95(2), 352–59.

Locke EA and Latham G (2002) 'Building a practically useful theory of goal setting and task motivation', *American Psychologist*, 57(9), 705–17.

— (2006) 'New directions in goal-setting theory', *Current Directions in Psychological Science*, 15(5), 265–68.

Loewenstein GF (1996) 'Out of control: visceral influences on decision making', *Organizational Behavior and Human Decision Processes*, 65(3), 272–92; reprinted in Camerer CF, Lowewenstein G and Rabin M (2004) *Advances in Behavioral Economics*, Princeton, NJ: Princeton University Press/Russell Sage Foundation.

— (2000) 'Emotions in economic theory and economic behaviour', *American Economic Review* 90(2), 426–32.

Loewenstein GF and O'Donoghue T (2004) *Animal Spirits: Affective and Deliberative Processes in Economic Behaviour*, CAE Working Paper 04-14, New York: Center for Analytic Economics, Cornell University.

Loewenstein GF and Prelec D (1992) 'Anomalies in intertemporal choice: evidence and an interpretation', *Quarterly Journal of Economics*, 3(4), 573–97.

Loewenstein GF and Ubel P (2010) 'Economics behaving badly', *New York Times*, 14 July, www.nytimes.com/2010/07/15/opinion/15loewenstein.html

Loewenstein GF, Thompson L and Bazerman MH (1989) 'Social utility and decision making in interpersonal contexts', *Journal of Personality and Social Psychology*, 57, 426–41.

Loewenstein GF, Weber EU, Hsee CK and Welch N (2001, 2007) 'Risk as feelings', *Psychological Bulletin*, 127(3), 267–86; reprinted in Loewenstein GF (ed.) (2007) *Exotic Preferences: Behavioral Economics and Human Motivation*, Oxford: Oxford University Press, pp. 567–611.

Lohrenz T, McCabe K, Camerer CF and Montague PR (2007) 'Neural signature of fictive learning signals in a sequential investment task', *Proceedings of the National Academy of Sciences*, 104(22), 9493–98.

Loomes G and Sugden R (1982) 'Regret theory: an alternative theory of choice under uncertainty', *Economic Journal*, 92(368), 805–24.

Lorenzoni I, Nicholson-Cole S and Whitmark L (2007) 'Barriers perceived to engaging with climate change among the UK pulic and their policy implications', *Global Environmental Change*, 17, 445–59.

Lutz A, Greischar LL, Rawlings NB, Ricard M and Davidson RJ (2004) 'Long-term mediators self-induce amplitude gamma synchrony during mental practice', *Proceedings of the National Academy of Sciences*, 101, 16, 369–73.

Lykken D and Tellegen A (1996) 'Happiness is a stochastic phenomenon', *Psychological Science*, 7(3), 186–89.

Lynch A (1996) *Thought Contagion: How Belief Spreads through Society*, New York: Basic Books.

— (2003) 'An introduction to the evolutionary epidemiology of ideas', *Biological Physicist*, 3, 7–14.

Madrian B and Shea D (2001) 'The power of suggestion: inertia in 401(k) participation and savings behavior', *Quarterly Journal of Economics*, 116(4), 1149–87.

Malmendier U and Lee YH (2011) 'The bidder's curse', *American Economic Review*, 101(2), 749–87.

Manski CF (1993) 'Identification of endogenous social effects: the reflection problem', *Review of Economic Studies*, 60, 531–42.

— (2000) 'Economic analysis of social interactions', *Journal of Economic Perspectives*, 14(3), 115–36.

Markowitz H (1952) 'Portfolio selection', *Journal of Finance*, 7(1), 77–91.

Martin-Soelch C, Missimer J, Leenders KL and Schultz W (2003) 'Neural activity related to the processing of increasing monetary reward in smokers and non-smokers', *European Journal of Neuroscience*, 18, 680–88.

de Martino B, Kumaran D, Seymour B and Dolan RJ (2006) 'Frames, biases and rational decision-making in the human brain', *Science*, 313, 684–87.

Matheson J (2011) *Measuring what Matters: National Statistician's Reflections on the National Debate on Measuring National Well-being*, London: Office for National Statistics.

McCabe K, Houser D, Ryan L, Smith V and Trouard T (2001) 'A functional imaging study of cooperation in two-person reciprocal exchange', *Proceedings of the National Academy of Sciences*, 98(20), 11832–35.

McClure SM, Laibson DI, Loewenstein G and Cohen JD (2004) 'Separate neural systems value immediate and delayed rewards', *Science*, 306, 503–7.

McCrae RR and Costa PT (1987) 'Validation of the five-factor model of personality across instruments and observers', *Journal of Personality and Social Psychology*, 52, 81–90.

— (1989) 'The structure of interpersonal traits: Wiggins's circumplex and the five-factor model', *Journal of Personality and Social Psychology*, 56, 586–95.

McNamara S and Grubb M (2011) *The Psychological Underpinnings of the Consumer Role in Energy Demand and Carbon Abatement*, Cambridge Working Papers in Economics No. 1126/EPRG Working Paper No. 1110, Cambridge: Electricity Policy Research Group/Faculty of Economics, University of Cambridge.

McQuade TJ (2006) 'Science and market as adaptive classifying systems', *Advances in Austrian Economics*, 9, 51–86.

Meeks JG (1991) 'Keynes on the rationality of decision procedures under uncertainty: the investment decision', in Meeks JG (ed.), *Thoughtful Economic Man*, Cambridge: Cambridge University Press.

Mehra R and Prescott E (1985) 'The equity premium: a puzzle', *Journal of Monetary Economics*, 15, 145–61.

Metcalfe J and Mischel W (1999) 'A hot/cool-system analysis of delay of gratification: dynamics of willpower', *Psychological Review*, 106(1), 3–19.

Meyer G, Viglione D, Mihura J, Erard R, Erdberg P and Miguel F (2011) *Rorschach Performance Assessment System*, www.r-pas.org

Milgram S (1963) 'Behavioral study of obedience', *Journal of Abnormal and Social Psychology*, 67, 371–78.

— (1967) 'The small world problem', *Psychology Today*, 1(1), 60–67.

Mini P (1990) *Keynes, Bloomsbury and the General Theory*, London: Macmillan.

Minsky HP (1975) *John Maynard Keynes*, New York: Columbia University Press.

— (1978) *The Financial Instability Hypothesis: A Restatement*, Thames Papers in Political Economy, North East London Polytechnic, reprinted in Arestis P and Skouras T (eds) (1985) *Post Keynesian Economic Theory*, Armonk, NY: ME Sharpe.

— (1986) *Stabilizing an Unstable Economy*, New Haven, CT: Yale University Press.

— (1997) 'Negative expertise', in Feltovich PJ, Ford KM and Hoffman RR (eds), *Expertise in Context: Human and Machine*, Cambridge, MA: MIT Press and American Association for Artificial Intelligence, pp. 515–21.

Mischel W and Ebbesen EB (1970) 'Attention in delay of gratification', *Journal of Personality and Social Psychology*, 16, 329–37.

Mischel W and Shoda Y (1995) 'A cognitive–affective theory system of personality: reconceptualizing situations, dispositions, dynamics and invariance in personality structure', *Psychological Review*, 102, 246–68.

Mischel W, Ebbesen EB and Zeiss AR (1972) 'Cognitive and attentional mechanisms in delay of gratification', *Journal of Personality and Social Psychology*, 21(2), 204–18.

Mischel W, Shoda Y and Rodriguez ML (1989) 'Delay of gratification in children', *Science*, 244(4907), 933–38.

Mobilia P (1990) 'An economic analysis of addictive behavior: the case of gambling', PhD thesis, City University of New York (cited in Becker *et al.* 1991).

Moore T, Clayton R and Anderson R (2009) 'The economics of online crime', *Journal of Economic Perspectives*, 23(3), 3–20.

Mulcahy NJ and Call J (2006), 'Apes save tools for future use', *Science*, 312(5776), 1038–40.

Mullainathan S (2002) 'A memory based model of bounded rationality', *Quarterly Journal of Economics*, 117(3), 735–74.

Mullainathan S and Thaler RH (2000) *Behavioral Economics* (September 2000), Working Paper No. 00-27, Cambridge, MA: Department of Economics, Massachusetts Institute of Technology.

Muth JF (1961) 'Rational expectations and the theory of price movements', *Econometrica*, 29(3), 315–35.

Myers IB (1981) *Gifts Differing: Understanding Personality Type*, Mountain View, CA: Davies Black.

Nagel R (1995) 'Unraveling in guessing games: an experimental study', *American Economic Review*, 85(5), 1313–26.

Nalebuff B (1987) 'Puzzles: choose a curtain, duel-ity, two point conversions and more', *Journal of Economic Perspectives*, 1(2), 157–63.

Naqvi NH, Rudrauf D, Damasio H and Bechara A (2007) 'Damage to the insula disrupts addiction to cigarette smoking', *Science*, 315, 531–34.

Neild RR (1964) *Replacement Policy*, National Institute Economic Review, London: National Institute of Economics.

von Neumann J and Morgenstern O (1944) *Theory of Games and Economic Behavior*, Princeton, NJ: Princeton University Press.

Nolan JM, Schultz PW, Cialdini RB, Goldstein NJ and Griskevicius V (2008) 'Normative social influence is underdetected', *Personality and Social Psychology Bulletin*, 34, 913–23.

Norgaard KM (2006) 'People want to protect themselves a little bit: emotions, denial and social movement non-participation', *Sociological Inquiry*, 76, 372–96.

Norgaard KM (2009) *Cognitive and Behavioural Challenges in Responding to Climate Change*, Policy Research Working Paper 4940, Washington, DC: World Development Report Team, World Bank.

Nye M and Burgess J (2008) *Promoting Durable Change in Household Waste and Energy Use Behaviour*, London: Department for Environment, Food and Rural Affairs.

Nye M and Hargreaves T (2010) 'Exploring the social dynamics of pro-environmental behaviour change: a comparative study of intervention processes at home and work', *Journal of Industrial Ecology*, 14(1), 137–49.

Odean T (1998) 'Are investors reluctant to realize their losses?', *Journal of Finance*, 53, 1775–98.

O'Donnell RM (1989) *Keynes: Philosophy, Economics and Politics: The Philosophical Foundations of Keynes's Thought and Their Influence on his Economics and Politics*, London: Macmillan.

O'Donoghue T and Rabin M (1999) 'Doing it now or later', *American Economic Review*, 89(1), 103–24.

O'Donoghue T and Rabin M (2001) 'Choice and procrastination', *Quarterly Journal of Economics*, 116(1), 121–60.

Ofgem (2011) *What Can Behavioural Economics Say about GB Energy Consumers?*, London: Office of Gas and Electricity Markets.

Olekalns N and Bardsley P (1996) 'Rational addiction to caffeine: an analysis of coffee consumption', *Journal of Political Economy*, 104(5), 1100–104.

Orphanides A and Zervos D (1995) 'Rational addiction with learning and regret', *Journal of Political Economy*, 103(4), 739–58.

Osborne M, Gintis H and Bowles S (2001) 'The determinants of earnings: a behavioral approach', *Journal of Economic Literature*, 39(4), 1137–76.

O'Shea M (2005) *The Brain – A Very Short Introduction*, New York: Oxford University Press.

Palfrey J and Zittrain J (2011) 'Better data for a better internet', *Science*, 334(6060), 1210–11.

Pallack MS, Cook DA and Sullivan JJ (1980) 'Commitment and energy conservation', *Applied Social Psychology Annual*, 1, 235–53.

Parkin DM, Boyd L and Walker LC (2011) 'The fraction of cancer attributable to lifestyle and environmental factors in the UK in 2010', *British Journal of Cancer*, 105, S77–S81.

Parkinson S and Baddeley M (2011) *An Economic Analysis of Group Decisions by Juries*, Cambridge Working Papers in Economics No. 1128, Cambridge: Faculty of Economics, University of Cambridge.

Pasinetti LL (1997) 'The marginal efficiency of investment', in Harcourt GC and Riach PA (eds) *A 'Second Edition' of The General Theory*, London: Routledge.

Pattanayak SK, Yang J-C, Dickinson KL, Poulos C, Patil SR, Mallick RK, Blitstein JL and Praharaj P (2009) 'Shame or subsidy revisited: social mobilization for sanitation in Orissa, India', *Bulletin of the World Health Organisation*, 87, 580–87.

Pavlov I (1927) *Conditioned Reflexes – An Investigation of the Physiological Activity of the Cerebral Cortex*, translated and edited by Anrep GV, Mineola, NY: Dover Publications.

Pervin LA (1984) *Personality: Theory and Research*, 4th edn, New York: John Wiley.

Phelps ES and Pollak RA (1968) 'On second-best national savings and game-equilibrium growth', *Review of Economic Studies*, 35, 185–99.

Pillas D (2006) 'Studies in economic herding behaviour', MPhil thesis, University of Cambridge.

Pindyck, RS (1991) 'Irreversibility, uncertainty and investment', *Journal of Economic Literature*, 29, 1110–48.

Plott CR and Zeiler K (2005) 'The willingness to pay – willingess to accept gap, the "endowment effect," subject misconceptions and experimental procedures for eliciting valuations', *American Economic Review*, 95(3), 530–35.

— (2007) 'Exchange asymmetries incorrectly interpreted as evidence of endowment effect theory and prospect theory?', *American Economic Review*, 97(4), 1449–66.

— (2011) 'The willingness to pay – willingess to accept gap, the "endowment effect," subject misconceptions and experimental procedures for eliciting valuations: Reply', *American Economic Review*, 101(2), 1012–28.

Pollak RA (1970) 'Habit formation and dynamic demand functions', *Journal of Political Economy*, 78, 748–63.

— (1976) 'Habit formation and long-run utility functions', *Journal of Economic Theory*, 13, 272–97.

Polson D and Curtis A (2010) 'Dynamics of uncertainty in geological interpretation', *Journal of the Geological Society*, 167, 5–10.

Pongiglione F (2011) *Climate Change and Individual Decision Making: An Examination of Knowledge, Risk Perception, Self-Interest and their Interplay*, FEEM Working Paper, Milan: Fondazione Eni Enrico Mattei.

Porter D and Smith V (1995) 'Futures contracting and dividend uncertainty in experimental asset markets', *Journal of Business*, 68(4), 509–47.

Porter D and Smith VL (2008) 'Thar she blows: can bubbles be rekindled with experienced subjects?' *American Economic Review*, 98(3), 924–37.

Post T, van den Assem MJ, Baltussen G and Thaler RH (2008) 'Deal or no deal? Decision making under risk in a large-payoff game show', *American Economic Review*, 98(1), 38–71.

Prechter RR (2003) *Socionomics: The Science of History and Social Prediction*, Gainesville, FL: New Classics Library.

Prechter RR and Parker WD (2007) 'The financial/economic dichotomy in social behavioral dynamics: the socionomic perspective', *Journal of Behavioural Finance*, 8(2), 84–108.

Prelec D and Loewenstein G (1998) 'The red and the black: mental accounting of savings and debt', *Marketing Science*, 17(1), 4–28.

Prinz JJ (2005) 'Imitation and moral development', in Hurley S and Chater N (eds), *Perspectives On Imitation – From Neuroscience to Social Science, Vol. 2: Imitation, Human Development and Culture*, Cambridge, MA: MIT Press, pp. 267–82.

Putnam RD (2001) *Bowling Alone: The Collapse and Revival of American Community*, New York: Simon & Schuster.

de Quervain DJ-F, Fischbacher U, Treyer V, Schellhammer M, Schnyder U, Buck A and Fehr E (2004) 'The neural basis of altruistic punishment', *Science*, 305, 1254–58.

Rabin M (1993) 'Incorporating fairness into game theory and economics', *American Economic Review*, 83, 1281–1302.

Raby CR, Alexis DM, Dickinson A and Clayton NS (2007) 'Planning for the future by western scrub-jays', *Nature*, 445(7130), 919–21.

Ramsey F (1931) *The Foundations of Mathematics and Other Logical Essays*, edited by Braithwaite RB, London: Kegan Paul, Trench, Trubner and Co.

Ramsey JB (1970) 'The marginal efficiency of capital, the internal rate of return and net present value: an analysis of investment criteria', *Journal of Political Economy*, 78(5), 1017–27.

Randa DG, Arbesman S and Christakis NA (2011) 'Dynamic social networks promote cooperation in experiments with humans', *Proceedings of the National Academy of Sciences*, 108(48), 19193–98.

Ratiu P, Talos IF, Haker, S, Lieberman and Everett P (2004) 'The tale of Phineas Gage, digitally remastered', *Journal of Neurotrauma*, 21(5), 637–43.

Read D (2001) 'Is time-discounting hyperbolic or subadditive?' *Journal of Risk and Uncertainty*, 23(1), 5–32.

Read D, Loewenstein G and Rabin M (1999) 'Choice bracketing', *Journal of Risk and Uncertainty*, 19, 171–97.

Reutskaja E, Nagel R, Camerer CF and Rangel A (2011) 'Search dynamics in consumer choice under time pressure: an eye tracking study', *American Economic Review*, 101(2), 900–926.

Reynolds T W, Bostrom A, Read D and Granger Morgan M (2010) 'Now what do people know about global climate change? Surveys of educated laypeople', *Risk Analysis*, 30(10), 1520–38.

Rick S and Loewenstein G (2008) 'Intangibility in intertemporal choice', *Philosophical Transactions of the Royal Society B*, 363(1511), 3813–24.

Rilling JK, Gutman DA, Zeh TR, Pagnoni G, Berns GS and Kilts CD (2002) 'A neural basis for social cooperation', *Neuron*, 35, 495–405.

Rizzello S (2004) 'Knowledge as a path-dependence process', *Journal of Bioeconomics*, 6, 255–74.

Rizzolatti G and Craighero L (2004) 'The mirror neuron system', *Annual Reviews of Neuroscience*, 27, 169–92.

Rizzolatti G, Craighero L and Fadiga L (2002) 'The mirror system in humans', in Stamenov MI and Gallese V (eds) *Mirror Neurons and the Evolution of Brain and Language*, Advances In Consciousness Research No. 42, Amsterdam: John Benjamins, pp. 37–59.

Robson AJ (2001) 'Biological basis of economic behaviour', *Journal of Economic Literature*, 39(8), 11–33.

Romer PM (2000) 'Thinking and feeling', *American Economic Review*, 90(2), 439–43.

van Rooj M and Van Orden G (2011) 'It's about space, it's about time, neuroeconomics and the brain sublime', *Journal of Economic Perspectives*, 25(4), 31–56.

Rosser B and Rosser M (2006) 'Institutional evolution of environmental management under global economic growth', *Journal of Economic Issues*, 45, 421–29.

Roth AE, Prasnikar V, Masahiro O-F and Zamir S (1991) 'Bargaining and market behavior in Jerusalem, Ljubljana, Pittsburgh and Tokyo: an experimental study', *American Economic Review*, 81, 1068–95.

Rotter JB, Chance JE and Phares EJ (1972) *Applications of a Social Learning Theory of Personality*, Oxford: Holt, Rinehart & Winston.

Rowson J (2011) *Socialising with the Brain: Beyond Nudge and Neuromania*, London: Royal Society for the Encouragement of Arts, Manufactures and Commerce (RSA).

Rowthorn RE (1999) 'Marriage and trust: some lessons from economics', *Cambridge Journal of Economics*, 23, 661–91.

Runde J (1997) 'Keynesian methodology', in Harcourt GC and Riach PA (eds), *A 'Second Edition' of The General Theory*, London: Routledge.

Rustichini A (2005a) 'Emotion and reason in making decisions', *Science*, 310(5754), 1624–25.

— (2005b) 'Neuroeconomics: present and future', *Games and Economic Behavior*, 52, 201–12.

— (2009) 'Is there a method of neuroeconomics?', *American Economic Journal: Microeconomics*, 1(2), 48–59.

Saklofske DH and Zeidner M (1995) *Perspectives on Individual Differences: International Handbook of Personality and Intelligence*, New York: Plenum Press.

Sally D and Hill EL (2006) 'The development of interpersonal strategy: Autism, theory-of-mind, cooperation and fairness', *Journal of Economic Psychology*, 27(1), 73–97.

Salmon T (2001) 'An evaluation of econometric models of adaptive learning', *Econometrica*, 69(6), 1597–1628.

Samuelson PA (1937) 'A note on measurement of utility', *Review of Economic Studies*, 4(2), 155–61.

— (1977) 'St. Petersburg paradoxes: defanged, dissected and historically described', *Journal of Economic Literature*, 15(1), 24–55.

Samuelson W and Zeckhauser R (1988) 'Status quo bias in decision making', *Journal of Risk and Uncertainty*, 1(1), 7–59.

Sanfey AG (2007) 'Social decision-making: insights from game theory and neuroscience', *Science* 318, 598–602.

Sanfey AG, Rilling JK, Aronson JA, Nystrom LE and Cohen JD (2003) 'The neural basis of economic decision-making in the ultimatum game', *Science*, 300, 1755–58.

Sanfey AG, Loewenstein G, McClure S and Cohen J (2006) 'Neuroeconomics: cross-currents in research on decision-making', *Trends in Cognitive Science*, 10(3), 108–15.

Santos LR and Chen MK (2009) 'The evolution of rational and irrational economic behavior: evidence and insight from a non-human primate species', in Glimcher PW, Camerer CF, Fehr E and Poldrack RA (eds), *Neuroeconomics: Decision-making and the Brain*, London: Academic Press/Elsevier.

Sarnat M and Levy H (1969) 'The relationship of rules of thumb to the internal rate of return: a restatement and generalisation', *Journal of Finance*, 24(3), 479–90.

Sauer R (2011) 'Does it pay for women to volunteer?', presentation to Empirical Microeconomics Seminar, Faculty of Economics, University of Cambridge, www.sv.uio.no/econ/forskning/aktuelt/arrangementer/torsdagseminaret/2010/papers/sauer.pdf

Savage LJ (1954) *The Foundations of Statistics*, New York: Wiley.

Scharfstein DS and Stein JC (1990) 'Herd behaviour and investment', *American Economic Review* 80(3), 465–79.

Schneider W and Shiffrin RM (1977) 'Controlled and automatic human information processing', *Psychological Review* 84, 1–66.

Schultz PW (1999) 'Changing behaviour with normative feedback interventions: a field experiment on curbside recycling', *Basic and Applied Social Psychology*, 21, 25–36.

Schultz PW, Nolan JM, Cialdini RB, Goldstein NJ and Griskevicius V (2007) 'The constructive, destructive and reconstructive power of social norms', *Psychological Science*, 18(5), 429–34.

Schultz W (2002) 'Getting formal with dopamine and reward', *Neuron*, 36, 241–63.

— (2006) 'Behavioral theories and the neurophysiology of reward', *Annual Review of Psychology*, 57, 87–115.

— (2008) 'Midbrain dopamine neurons: a retina of the reward system?', in Glimcher PW, Fehr E, Camerer C, Rangel A and Poldrack RA (eds), *Neuroeconomics: Decision-making and the Brain*, San Diego, CA: Academic Press, pp. 323–29.

Schultz W, Dayan P and Montague PR (1997) 'A neural substrate of prediction and reward', *Science*, 275(5306), 1593–99.

Schultz W, Preuschoff K, Camerer C, Hsu M, Fiorillo CD and Tobler PN (2008) 'Explicit neural signals reflecting reward uncertainty', *Philosophical Transations of the Royal Society B*, 363(1511), 3801–11.

Schumacher EF (1993) *Small is Beautiful: A Study of Economics as if People Mattered*, Ilford: Abacus.

Schwarz N (2000) 'Emotion, cognition, and decision making', *Cognition and Emotion*, 14(4), 433–40.

Seabright P (2004) *Company of Strangers – A Natural History of Economic Life*, Princeton, NJ: Princeton University Press.

Seaford C, Jacobs M, Swinson J, Oliff-Cooper J and Taylor M (2011) *The Practical Politics of Well-being*, London: New Economics Foundation, www.neweconomics.org/sites/neweconomics.org/files/The_Practical_Politics_of_Wellbeing.pdf.

Seligman MEP (2003) *Authentic Happiness: Using the New Positive Psychology to Realize Your Potential for Lasting Fulfillment*, London: Nicholas Brealey.

Sen A (1977) 'Rational fools: a critique of the behavioural foundations of economic theory', *Philosophy and Public Affairs*, 6, 317–44.

— (1991) 'Beneconfusion', in Meeks JGT (ed.), *Thoughtful Economic Man: Essays on Rationality, Moral Rules and Benevolence*, Cambridge: Cambridge University Press.

— (1999) *Reason Before Identity*, New Delhi: Oxford University Press.

— (2004) 'Capabilities, lists, and public reason: continuing the conversation', *Feminist Economics*, 10(3), 77–80.

Shackle GLS (1955) *Uncertainty in Economics and Other Reflections*, Cambridge: Cambridge University Press.

— (1967) *The Years of High Theory: Invention and Tradition in Economic Thought 1926–1939*, Cambridge: Cambridge University Press.

— (1972) *Epistemics and Economics: A Critique of Economic Doctrines*, Piscataway, NJ: Transaction Publishers.

Shafir E, Diamond P and Tversky A (1997) 'Money illusion', *Quarterly Journal of Economics*, 112(2), 341–74.

Shapiro C and Stiglitz J (1984) 'Equilibrium unemployment as a worker discipline device', *American Economic Review*, 74(3), 433–44.

Shapiro C and Varian HR (1998) *Information Rules: A Strategic Guide to the Network Economy*, Cambridge, MA: Harvard Business School Press.

Sharot T, Riccardi AM, Raio CM and Phelps EA (2007) 'Neural mechanisms mediating optimism bias', *Nature*, 450(7166), 102–5.

Shefrin H (2002) *Beyond Greed and Fear: Understanding Behavioral Finance and the Psychology of Investing*, Oxford: Oxford University Press.

Shefrin H and Statman M (1985) 'The disposition to sell winners too easily and ride losers too long: theory and evidence', *Journal of Finance*, 40, 777–90.

Shibasaki H (2008) 'Human brain mapping: hemodynamic response and electrophysiology', *Clinical Neurophysiology*, 119(4), 731–43.

Shiller RJ (1995) 'Conversation, information and herd behavior', *American Economic Review*, 85(2), 181–85.

— (2000) *Irrational Exuberance*, Princeton, NJ: Princeton University Press.

— (2003) 'From efficient markets theory to behavioral finance', *Journal of Economic Perspectives*, 17(1), 83–104.

Shiv B, Loewenstein G, Bechara A, Damasio H and Damasio AR (2005) 'Investment behaviour and the negative side of emotion', *Psychological Science* 16(6), 435–39.

Shleifer A (2000) *Inefficient Markets – An Introduction to Behavioral Finance*, Oxford: Clarendon Press.

Shogren JF and Hayes DJ (1997) 'Resolving differences in willingness to pay and willingness to accept: Reply', *American Economic Review*, 87(1), 241–44.

Shogren JF and Taylor LO (2008) 'On behavioural-environmental economics', *Review of Environmental Economics and Policy*, 2(1), 26–44.

Shogren JF, Shin S, Hayes D and Kliebenstein J (1994) 'Resolving differences in willingness to pay and willingness to accept', *American Economic Review*, 84: 255–70.

Shogren JF, Parkhurst GM and Banerjee P (2010) 'Two cheers and a qualm for behavioral environmental economics', *Environmental and Resource Economics*, 46(2), 235–47.

Simon HA (1955) 'A behavioural model of rational choice', *Quarterly Journal of Economics*, 69, 99–118.

— (1967) 'Motivational and emotional controls of cognition', *Psychological Review*, 74, 29–39.

— (1972) 'Theories of bounded rationality', in McGuire CB and Radner R (eds), *Decision and Organisation*, Amsterdam: North Holland, pp. 161–76.

— (1979) 'From substantive to procedural rationality', in Hahn FH and Hollis M (eds), *Philosophy and Economic Theory*, Oxford: Oxford University Press, pp. 65–86.

— (1990) 'A mechanism for social selection and successful altruism', *Science*, 250, 1665–68.

Singer T and Fehr E (2005) 'The neuroeconomics of mind reading and empathy', *American Economic Review*, 95(2), 340–45.

Singer T, Seymour B, O'Doherty J, Kaube H, Dolan R and Frith C (2004) 'Empathy for pain involves the affective but not sensory components of pain', *Science*, 3030(5661), 1157–62.

Skidelsky R (1992) *John Maynard Keynes – The Economist as Saviour 1920–1937*, London: Macmillan.

Skinner BG (1974) *About Behaviorism*, New York: Vintage.

Skinner DC (1999) *Introduction to Decision Analysis* (2nd edn), Gainesville, FL: Probabilistic Publishing.

Slovic P (2010) *The Feeling of Risk: New Perspectives on Risk Perception*, London: Earthscan.

Slovic P, Finucane M, Peters E and MacGregor DG (2004), 'Risk as analysis and risk as feelings: some thoughts about affect, reason, risk and rationality', *Risk Analysis*, 24(2), 311–22.

Small DA and Loewenstein G (2003) 'Helping the victim or helping a victim: altruism and identifiability', *Journal of Risk and Uncertainty*, 26(1), 5–16.

— (2005) 'The devil you know: the effects of identifiability on punishment', *Journal of Behavioral Decision Making*, 18, 311–18.

Small DA, Loewenstein G and Slovic P (2007) 'Sympathy and callousness: the impact of deliberative thought on donations to identifiable and statistical victims', *Organizational Behavior and Human Decision Processes*, 102, 143–53.

Smith A (1759) *The Theory of Moral Sentiments*, Oxford: Clarendon Press.

Smith K and Dickhaut J (2005) 'Economics and emotions: institutions matter', *Games and Economic Behavior*, 52, 316–35.

Smith TG and Tasnádi A (2007) 'A theory of natural addiction', *Games and Economics Behavior*, 59, 316–44.

Smith VL (1975) 'The primitive hunter culture, Pleistocene extinction, and the rise of agriculture', *Journal of Political Economy*, 83(4), 727–55.

— (1994) 'Economics in the laboratory', *Journal of Economic Perspectives*, 8(1), 113–31.

— (1998) 'Two faces of Adam Smith', *Southern Economic Journal*, 65(1), 1–19.

— (2003a) 'Constructivist and ecological rationality in economics', *American Economic Review*, 93(3), 465–508.

— (2003b) 'Interview: Vernon Smith', *Region Focus*, Spring, 32–35, Richmond: Federal Reserve Bank of Richmond. www.richmondfed.org/publications/research/region_focus/2003/spring/pdf/interview.pdf

Sobel J (2009) 'Neuroeconomics: a comment on Bernheim', *American Economic Journal: Microeconomics*, 1(2), 60–67.

Sornette D (2003) *Why Stock Markets Crash: Critical Events in Complex Financial Systems*, Princeton, NJ: Princeton University Press.

Soros G (1987) *The Alchemy of Finance*, New York: Simon & Schuster.

de Sousa R (1987) *The Rationality of Emotion*, Cambridge, MA: MIT Press.

Spence A, Poortinga W, Butler C and Pidgeon NF (2011) 'Perceptions of climate change and willingness to save energy related to flood experience', *Nature Climate Change*, 1(1), 46–49.

Steel P (2012) *The Procrastination Equation*, Harlow: Pearson Education.

Steele GR (2002) 'Hayek's sensory order', *Theory & Psychology*, 12(3), 387–409.

Stein EA, Pankiewicz J, Harsch HH, Cho JK, Fuller SA, Hoffmann RG, Hawkins M, Rao SM, Bandettini PA and Bloom AS (1998) 'Nicotine-induced limbic cortical activation in the human brain: a functional MRI study', *American Journal of Psychiatry*, 155, 1009–15.

Stern PC (1992) 'What psychology knows about energy conservation', *American Psychologist*, 47(10), 1224–32.

— (2000) 'Toward a coherent theory of environmentally significant behavior', *Journal of Social Issues*, 56(3), 407–24.

Stern PC, Aronson E, Darley JM, Hill DH, Hirst E, Kempton W and Wilbanks TJ (2006) 'The effectiveness of incentives for residential energy conservation', *Evaluation Review*, 10(2), 147–76.

Stern PC, Kietz T, Gardner GT, Gilligan J and Vandenbergh MP (2010) 'Energy efficiency merits more than a nudge', *Science*, 328, 308–9.

Stigler GG (1945) 'The cost of subsistence', *Journal of Farm Economics*, 27(2), 303–14.

Stiglitz J (2006) 'A new agenda for global warming', *Economists Voice*, July. www.bepress.com/ev

Strauss S (2008) 'Global models, local risks: responding to climate change in the Swiss Alps', in Crate S and Nuttall M (eds), *Anthropology and Climate Change: From Encounters to Actions*, Walnut Creek, CA: Left Coast Press.

Strotz RH (1955) 'Myopia and inconsistency in dynamic utility maximization', *Review of Economic Studies*, 23, 165–80.

Stutzer A and Frey BS (2006) 'Does marriage make people happy, or do happy people get married?', *Journal of Socio-Economics*, 35, 326–47.

Sugden R (2005) 'Imitation and rationality', in Hurley S and Chater N (eds), *Perspectives on Imitation – From Neuroscience to Social Science, Vol. 2: Imitation, Human Development and Culture*, Cambridge, MA: MIT Press, pp. 301–16.

Sunstein C (2006) 'The availability heuristic, intuitive cost–benefit analysis and climate change', *Climatic Change*, 77, 195–210.

Surowiecki J (2004) *The Wisdom of Crowds: Why the Many are Smarter than the Few*, London: Abacus.

Tajfel H (1970) 'Experiments in intergroup discrimination', *Scientific American*, 223(5), 96–102.

Tajfel H and Turner JC (1979) 'An integrative theory of intergroup conflict', in Austin WG and Worchel S (eds), *The Social Psychology of Intergroup Relations*, Monterey, CA: Brooks-Cole.

Thaler RH (1980) 'Toward a positive theory of consumer choice', *Journal of Economic Behavior and Organization*, 1, 39–60.

— (1981) 'Some empirical evidence on dynamic inconsistency', *Economic Letters*, 8, 201–07.

— (1985) 'Mental accounting and consumer choice', *Marketing Science*, 4(3), 199–214.

— (1990) 'Saving, fungibility, and mental accounts', *Journal of Economic Perspectives*, American Economic Association, 4(1), 193–205.

— (1991) 'Some empirical evidence on dynamic inconsistency', in Thaler RH (ed.), *Quasi Rational Economics*, New York: Russell Sage Foundation, pp. 127–36.

— (1997) 'Irving Fisher: modern behavioral economist', *American Economic Review*, 87(2), 439–41.

— (1999) 'Mental accounting matters', *Journal of Behavioral Decision Making*, 12, 183–206.

— (2000a) 'From *Homo economicus* to *Homo sapiens*', *Journal of Economic Perspectives*, 14(1), 133–141.

— (2000b) *Quasi Rational Economics*, New York: Russell Sage Foundation.

— (2005) *Advances in Behavioural Finance*, II, New York/Princeton, NJ: Russell Sage Foundation/Princeton University Press.

Thaler RH and Benartzi S (2004), 'Save More Tomorrow(TM): using behavioral economics to increase employee saving', *Journal of Political Economy*, 112, 164–87.

Thaler RH and Shefrin HM (1981) 'An economic theory of self-control', *Journal of Political Economy*, 89(2), 392–406.

Thaler RH and Sunstein C (2008) *Nudge – Improving Decisions about Health, Wealth and Happiness*, New Haven, CT: Yale University Press.

Thaler RH, Tversky A, Kahneman D and Schwartz A (1997) 'The effect of myopia and loss aversion on risk taking: an experimental test', *Quarterly Journal of Economics*, 112(2), 647–61.

Thombs DL, Wolcott BJ and Farkash LG (1997) 'Social context, perceived norms and drinking behavior in young people', *Journal of Substance Abuse*, 9, 257–67.

Thorndike EL (1911) *Animal Intelligence*, New York: Macmillan.

Titmuss RM (1970) *The Gift Relationship*, London: Allen Unwin.

Tobin J (1969) 'A general equilibrium approach to monetary theory', *Journal of Money, Credit and Banking*, 11, 15–29.

— (1974) 'The new economics one decade older', in *Eliot Janeway Lectures on Historical Economics in Honour of Joseph Schumpeter 1972*, Princeton, NJ: Princeton University Press.

— (1978) 'A proposal for international monetary reform', *Eastern Economic Journal*, 4(3/4), 153–59.

Todd PM and Gigerenzer G (2000) 'Précis of simple heuristics that make us smart', *Behavioral and Brain Science*, 23, 727–80.

Topol R (1991) 'Bubbles and volatility of stock prices: effect of mimetic contagion', *Economic Journal*, 101(407),786–800.

Townsend JL (1987) 'Cigarette tax, economic welfare and social class patterns of smoking', *Applied Economics*, 19, 355–65.

Trope Y and Fishbach A (2000) 'Counteractive self-control in overcoming temptation', *Journal of Personality and Social Psychology*, 79(4), 493–506.

Tuckett D (2009) 'Addressing the psychology of financial markets', *Economics – The Open Access, Open-Assessment E-Journal*, 3, 2009-40, http://dx.doi.org/10.5018/economics-ejournal. ja.2009-40

— (2011) *Minding the Markets: An Emotional Finance View of Financial Instability*, Basingstoke: Palgrave Macmillan.

Tupes EC and Christal RE (1961) *Recurrent Personality Factors Based on Trait Ratings*, Technical Report ASD-TR-61-97, Lackland Air Force Base, TX: Personnel Laboratory, Air Force Systems Command.

Tversky A and Kahneman D (1972) 'Subjective probability: a judgment of representativeness', *Cognitive Psychology*, 3, 430–54.

— (1974) 'Judgement under uncertainty: heuristics and biases', *Science*, 185, 1124–31.

— (1981) 'The framing of decisions and the psychology of choice', *Science*, 211(4481), 453–58.

— (1982) 'Judgements of and by representativeness', in Kahneman D, Slovic P and Tversky A (eds) *Judgement under Uncertainty: Heuristics and Biases*, Cambridge: Cambridge University Press, pp. 84–98.

— (1983) 'Extensional versus intuitive reasoning: the conjunction fallacy in probability judgment', *Psychological Review*, 90(4), 293–315.

— (1986) 'Rational choice and the framing of decisions', *Journal of Business*, 59(4), 5251–78.

— (1992) 'Advances in prospect theory: cumulative representation of uncertainty', *Journal of Risk and Uncertainty*, 5(4), 297–323.

Urry HL, Nitschke JB, Dolski I, Jackson DC, Dalton KM, Mueller CJ, Rosenkranz MA, Ryff CD, Singer BH and Davidson RJ (2004) 'Making a life worth living: neural correlates of well-being', *Psychological Science*, 15(6), 367–72.

Urry HL, van Reekum CM, Johnstone T, Kalin NH, Thurow ME, Schaefer HS, Jackson CA, Frye CJ, Greischar LL, Alexander AL and Davidson RJ (2006) 'Amygdala and ventromedial prefrontal cortex are inversely coupled during regulation of negative affect and predict the diurnal pattern of cortisol secretion among older adults', *Journal of Neuroscience* 26(16), 4415–25.

US National Research Council (2010) *Advancing the Science of Climate Change*, Washington, DC: National Academies Press.

Varian HR (2003) *Intermediate Microeconomics: A Modern Approach* (6th edn), London: Norton.

Viscuis WK, Magat WA and Huber J (1987) 'An investigation of the rationality of consumer valuations of multiple health risks', *Rand Journal of Economics*, 18, 465–79.

Von Gaudecker H-M, van Soest A and Wengström E (2011) 'Heterogeneity in risky choice behavior in a broad population', *American Economic Review*, 101(2), 664–94.

Warner JT and Pleeter S (2001) 'The personal discount rate: evidence from military downsizing programs', *American Economic Review*, 91(1), 33–53.

Wärneryd, KE (1982) 'The life and work of George Katona', *Journal of Economic Psychology*, 2, 1–31.

Watson JB and Rayner R (1920) 'Conditioned emotional reactions', *Journal of Experimental Psychology*, 3(1), 1–14.

Watts DJ (2003) *Small Worlds – The Dynamics of Networks between Order and Randomness*, Princeton, NJ: Princeton University Press.

Watts DJ and Strogatz SH (1998) 'Collective dynamics of "small-world" networks', *Nature*, 393(6684), 409–10.

Weber EU (2011) 'Psychology: climate change hits home', *Nature Climate Change*, 1, 25–26.

Weisberg M and Muldoon R (2009) 'Epistemic landscapes and the division of cognitive labour', *Philosophy of Science*, 76(2), 225–52.

Weitzman M (2009) 'On modelling and interpreting the economics of catastrophic climate change', *Review of Economics and Statistics*, 91, 1–19.

Wertenbroch K (1998) 'Consumption self-control by rationing purchase quantities of virtue and vice', *Marketing Science*, 17(4), 317–337.

Whitmarsh L (2008) 'Are flood victims more concerned about climate change than other people? The role of direct experience in risk perception and behavioural response', *Journal of Risk Research*, 11, 351–74.

Wilkinson N (2008) *An Introduction to Behavioral Economics*, Basingstoke: Palgrave Macmillan.

Wilson CM and Oswald AJ (2005) *How Does Marriage Affect Physical and Psychological Health? A Survey of the Longitudinal Evidence*, IZA Discussion Papers 1619, Institute for the Study of Labor (IZA).

Wilson TD and Schooler JW (1991) 'Thinking too much: introspection can reduce the quality of preferences and decisions', *Journal of Personality and Social Psychology*, 60(2), 181–92.

Windmann S, Kirsch P, Mier D, Stark R, Walter B, Onur G and Vaitl D (2006) 'On framing effects in decision making: linking lateral versus medial orbitofrontal cortex activation to choice outcome processing', *Journal of Cognitive Neuroscience*, 18(7), 1198–211.

Winslow EG (1986) 'Keynes and Freud: psychoanalysis and Keynes's account of the "animal spirits" of capitalism', *Social Research*, 534, 549–78.

Yaari ME (1977) 'Consistent utilization of an exhaustible resource, or how to eat an appetite-arousing cake', Working Paper, Jerusalem: Hebrew University, Center for Research in Mathematical Economics and Game Theory.

Yates SM and Aronson E (1983) 'A social psychological perspective on energy conservation in residential buildings', *American Psychologist*, 38(4), 435–44.

Yoshida W and Ishii S (2006) 'Resolution of uncertainty in prefrontal cortex', *Neuron* 50(5), 781–89.

YouGov (2011) *Feeling the Chill*, http://today.yougov.co.uk/consumer/feeling-chill, 11 October.

Zajonc RB (1984) 'On the primacy of affect', *American Psychologist*, 39(2), 119–23.

Zak PJ, Borja K, Matzner WT and Kurzban R (2005) 'The neuroeconomics of distrust: sex differences in behavior and physiology', *American Economic Review*, 95(2), 360–63.

Zimbardo PG (2007) *The Lucifer Effect – How Good People Turn Evil*, London: Rider/Random House.

Index